# Lovesick Ellie



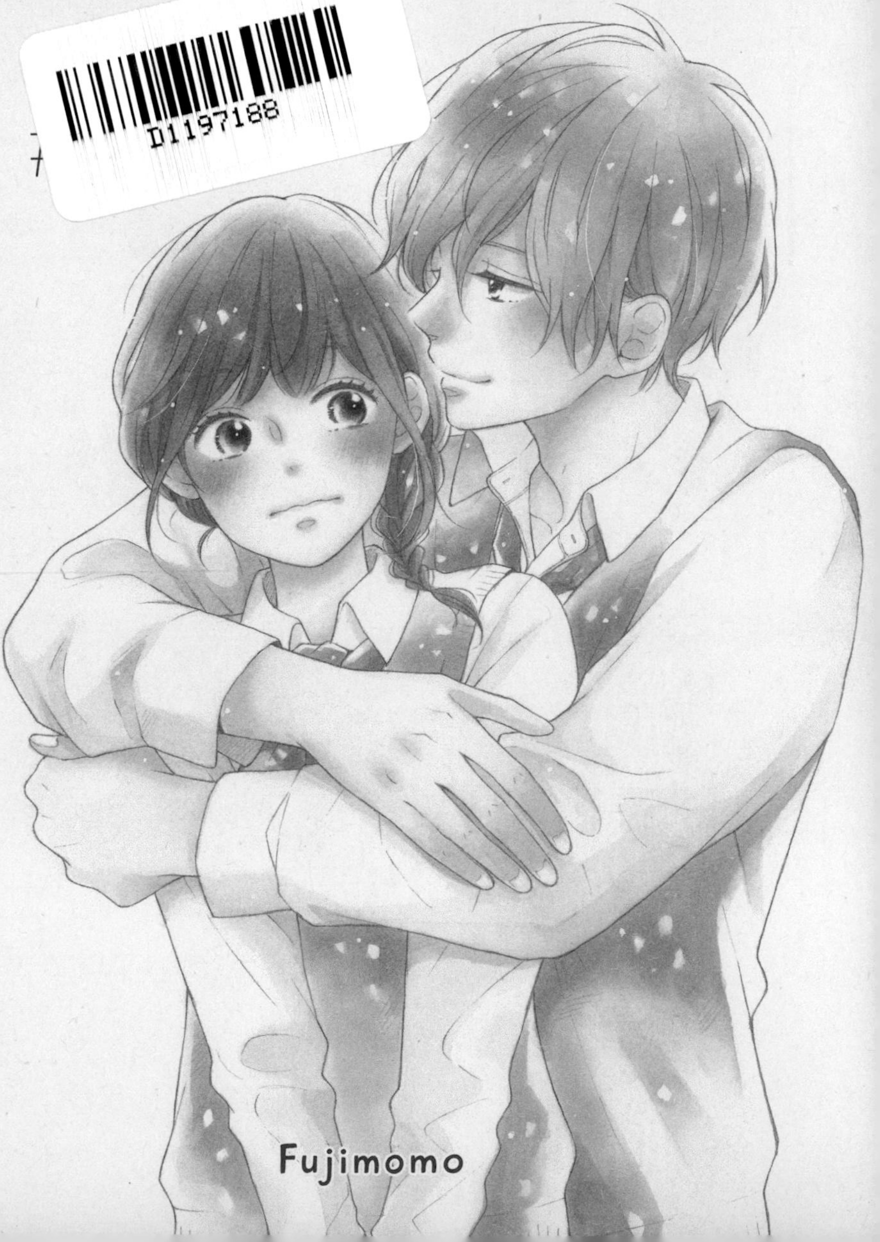

Fujimomo

*Lovesick Ellie*
contents

# characters

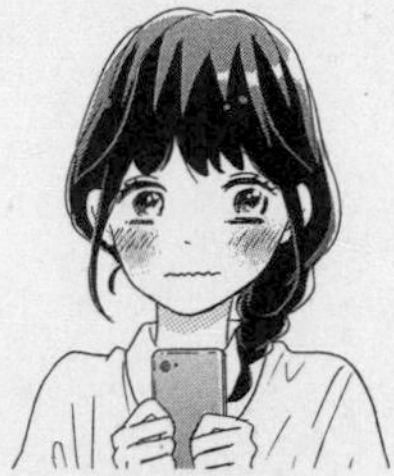

**ERIKO ICHIMURA**
**Ellie**
A plain high school girl. Spends her days tweeting Omie-kun-centric fantasies.

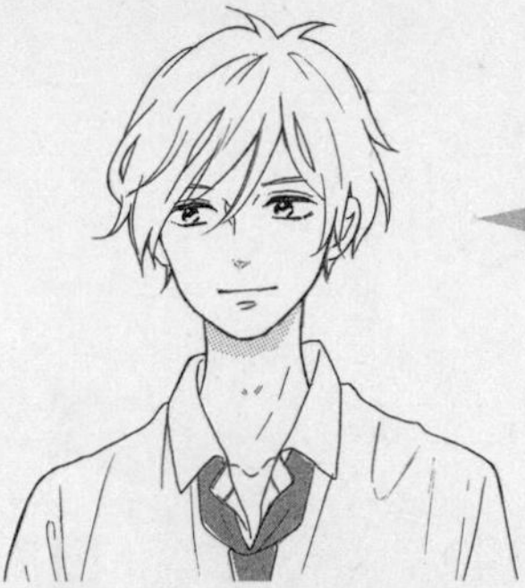

**AKIRA OHMI**
**Omie-kun**
Everyone's favorite popular boy on the outside. Irritable and childish on the inside.

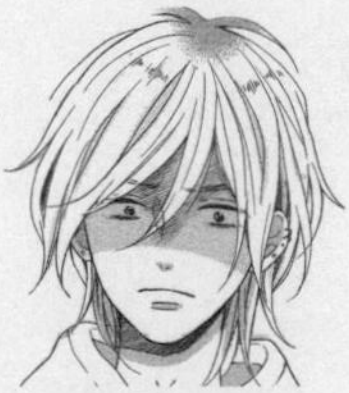

**REO TAKAGI**
Sara-chan's childhood friend. Looks like a delinquent.

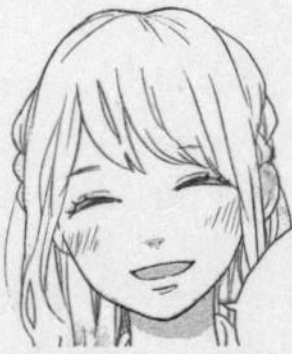

**SARA-CHAN**
Ellie's first friend.

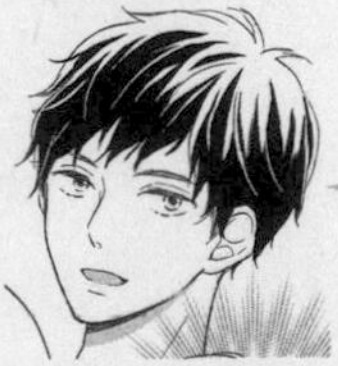

**SHIOTA-SENSEI**
Ellie's homeroom teacher and Omie-kun's uncle.

# story

Plain Ellie and handsome Omie-kun: a match made in...Twitter? Even as he is strung along by Ellie's Perv Power, Omie-kun finds himself increasingly drawn to her. Their feelings culminate in mutual attraction, but Omie-kun adopts a cold attitude in order to protect her... In spite of their misunderstandings, the two reconcile and confirm each other's feelings after Sports Day, turning Ellie's love into a great flood!

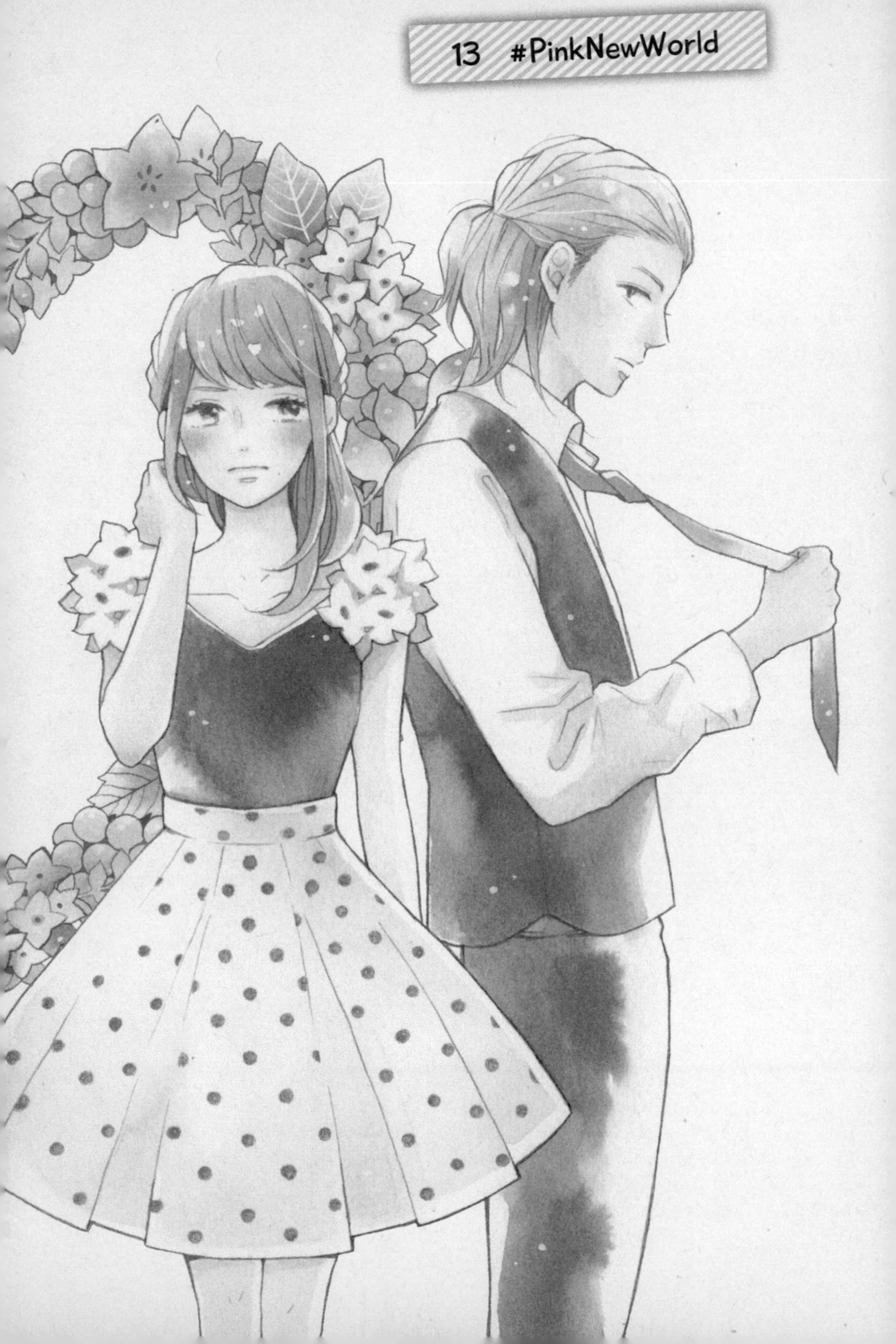
13 #PinkNewWorld

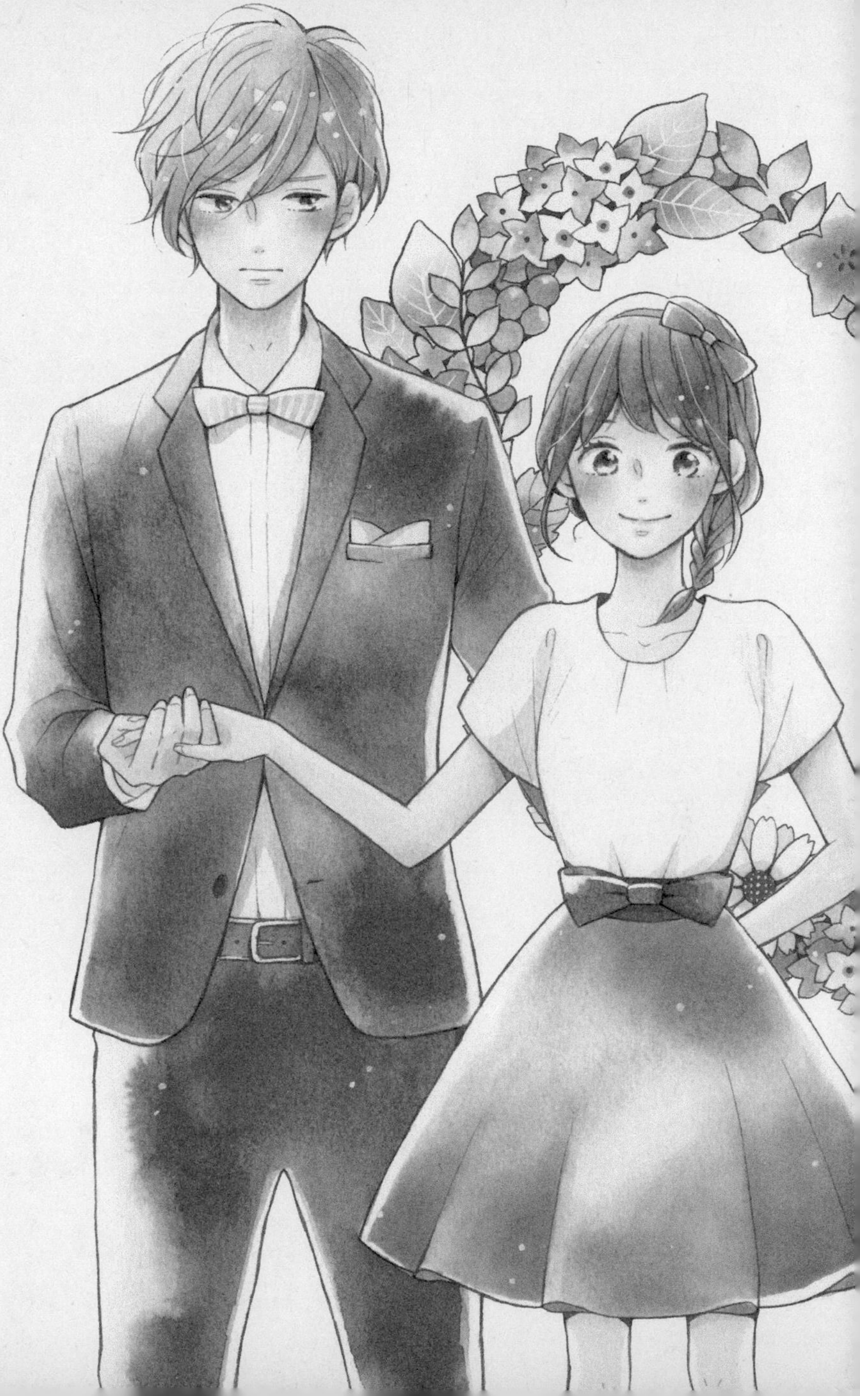

Lovesick
Ellie

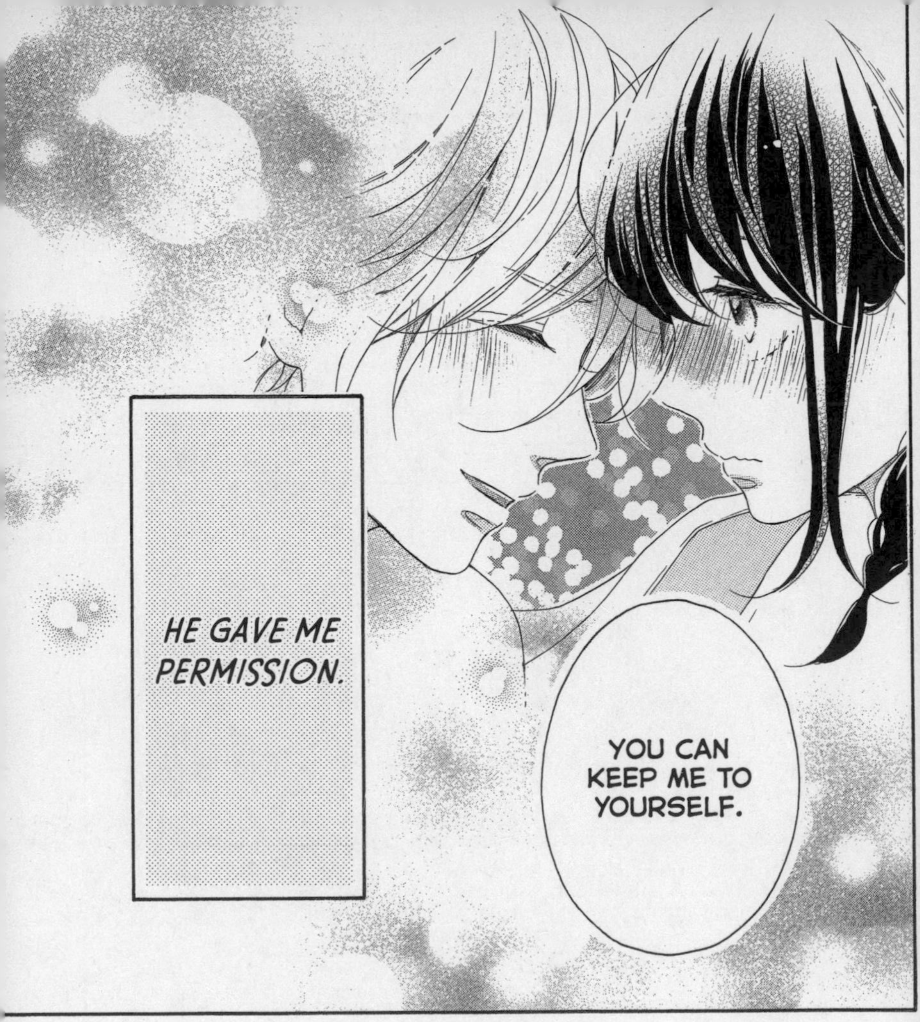
YOU CAN KEEP ME TO YOURSELF.
HE GAVE ME PERMISSION.

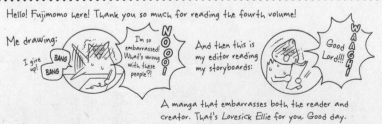

Hello! Fujimomo here! Thank you so much for reading the fourth volume!

Me drawing:

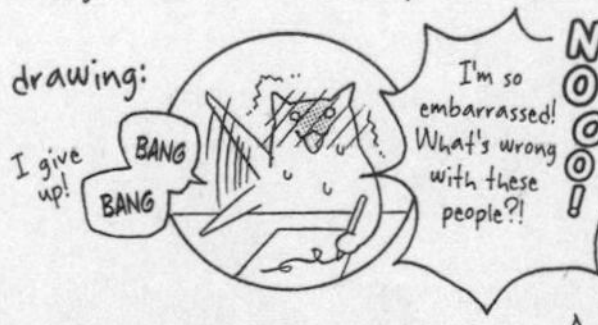
NOOOO!
I'm so embarrassed! What's wrong with these people?!
BANG
BANG
I give up!

And then this is my editor reading my storyboards:

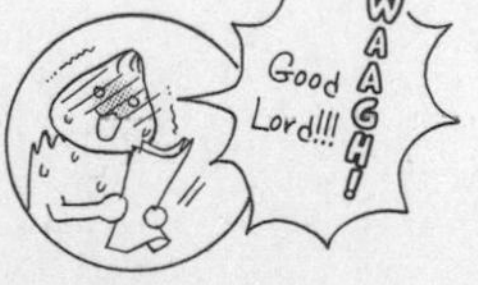
WAAGH!
Good Lord!!!

A manga that embarrasses both the reader and creator. That's *Lovesick Ellie* for you. Good day.

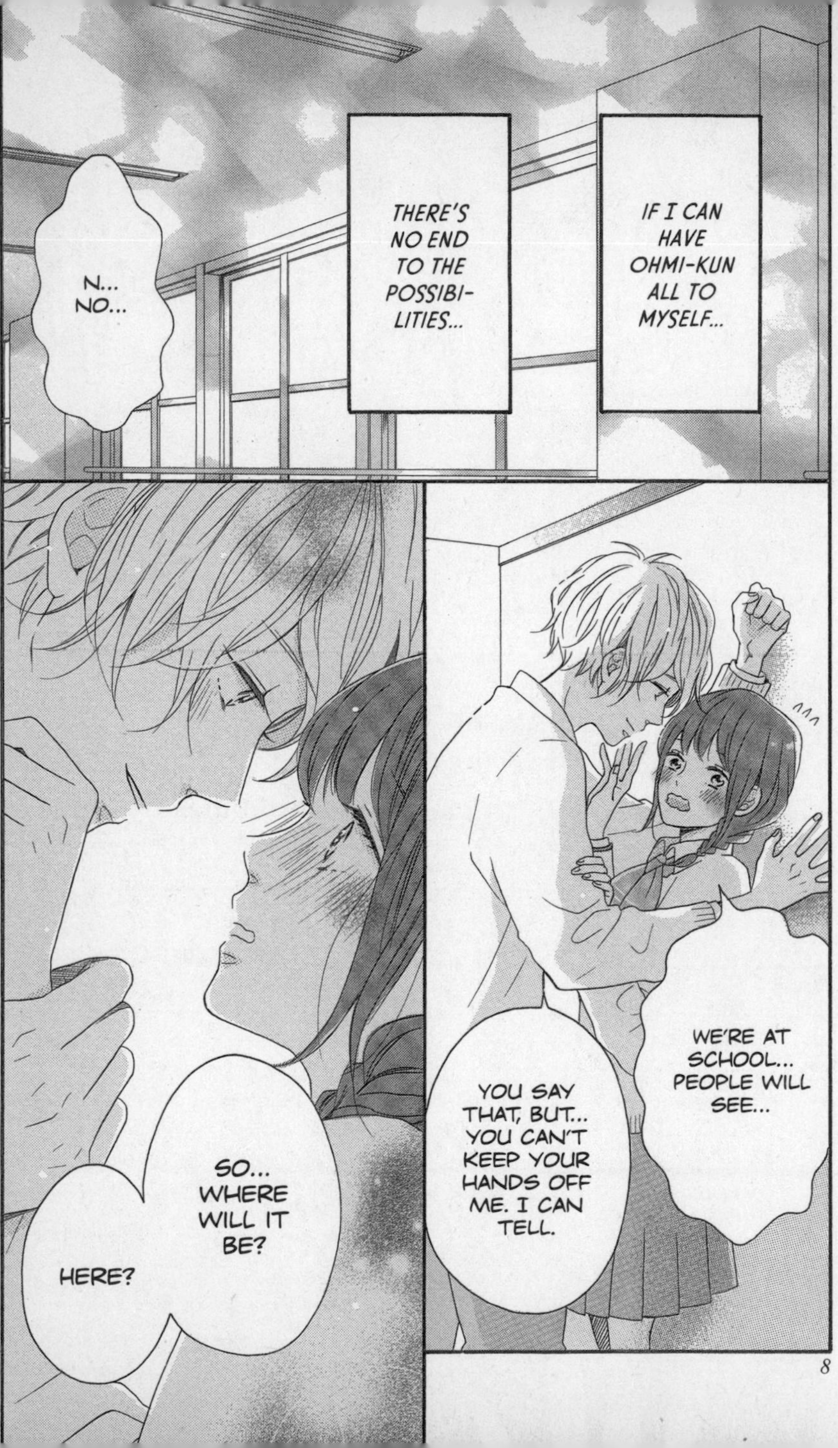
IF I CAN HAVE OHMI-KUN ALL TO MYSELF...
THERE'S NO END TO THE POSSIBILITIES...
N... NO...
WE'RE AT SCHOOL... PEOPLE WILL SEE...
YOU SAY THAT, BUT... YOU CAN'T KEEP YOUR HANDS OFF ME. I CAN TELL.
SO... WHERE WILL IT BE?
HERE?

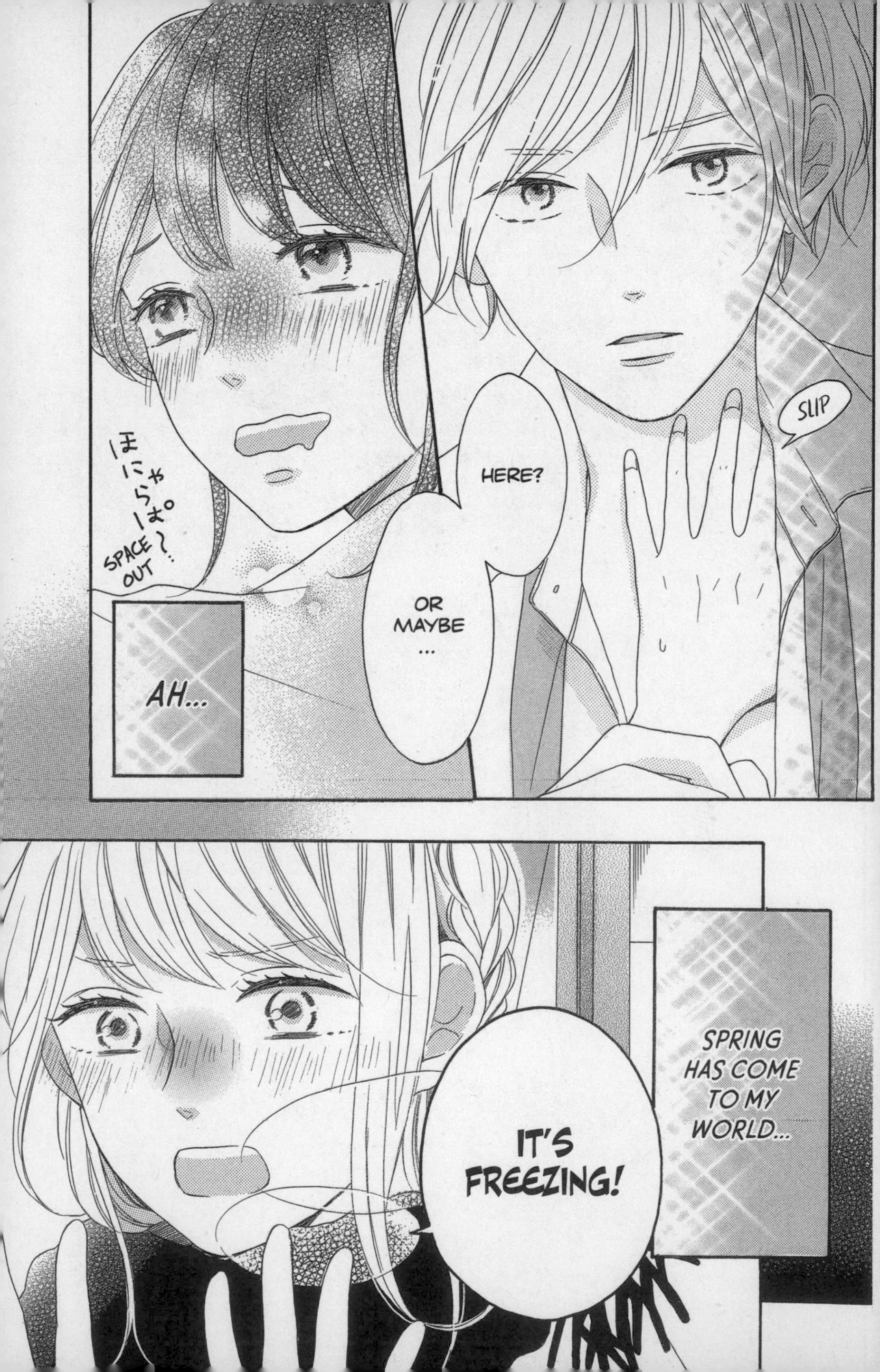
SLIP
HERE?
OR MAYBE ...
ほにゃらぱ～…
SPACE OUT
AH...
SPRING HAS COME TO MY WORLD...
IT'S FREEZING!

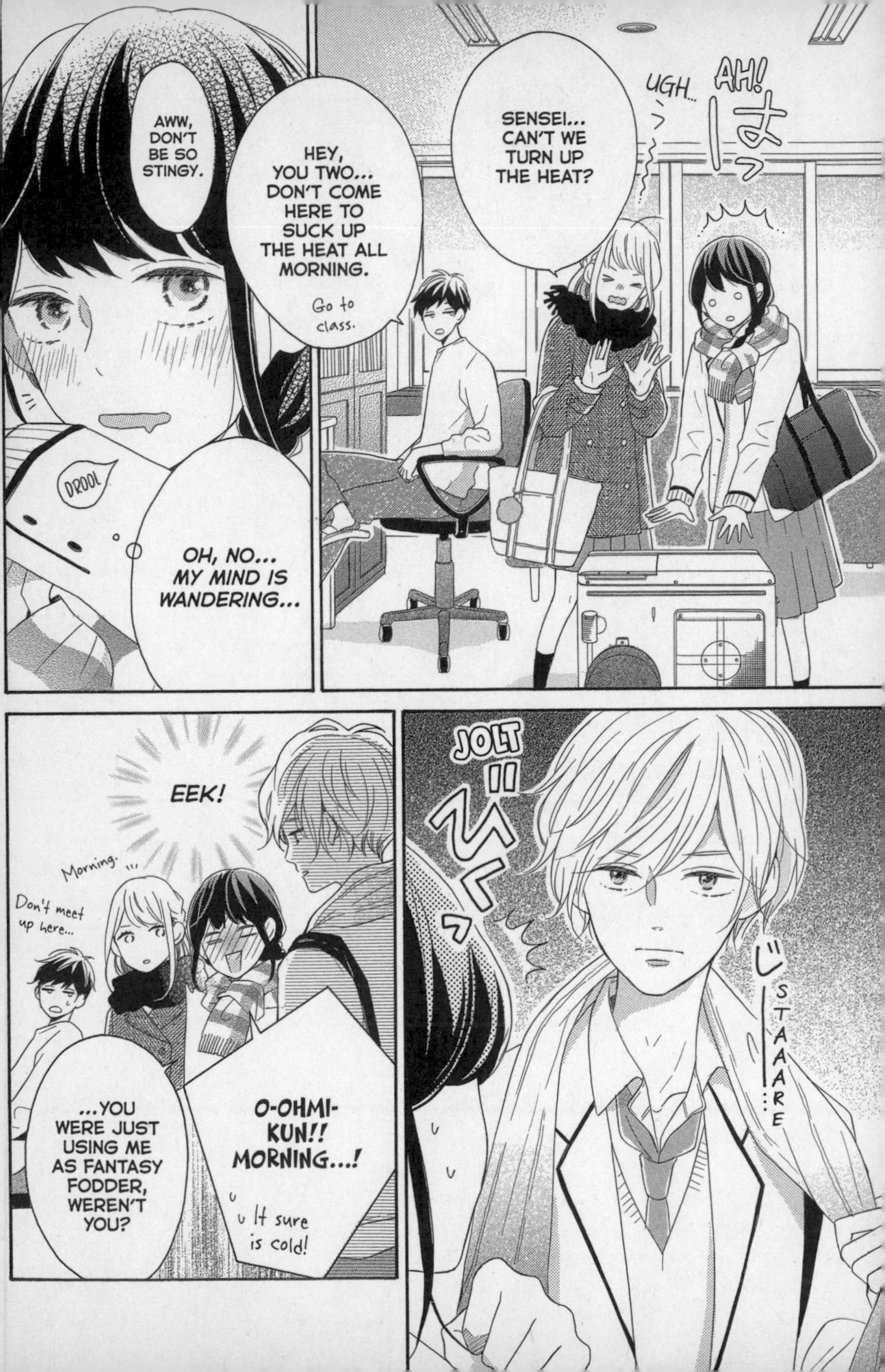
UGH...
AH!
はっ
SENSEI... CAN'T WE TURN UP THE HEAT?
HEY, YOU TWO... DON'T COME HERE TO SUCK UP THE HEAT ALL MORNING.
Go to class.
AWW, DON'T BE SO STINGY.
DROOL
OH, NO... MY MIND IS WANDERING...
JOLT
STAAARE...
EEK!
Morning.
Don't meet up here...
O-OHMI-KUN!! MORNING...!
It sure is cold!
...YOU WERE JUST USING ME AS FANTASY FODDER, WEREN'T YOU?

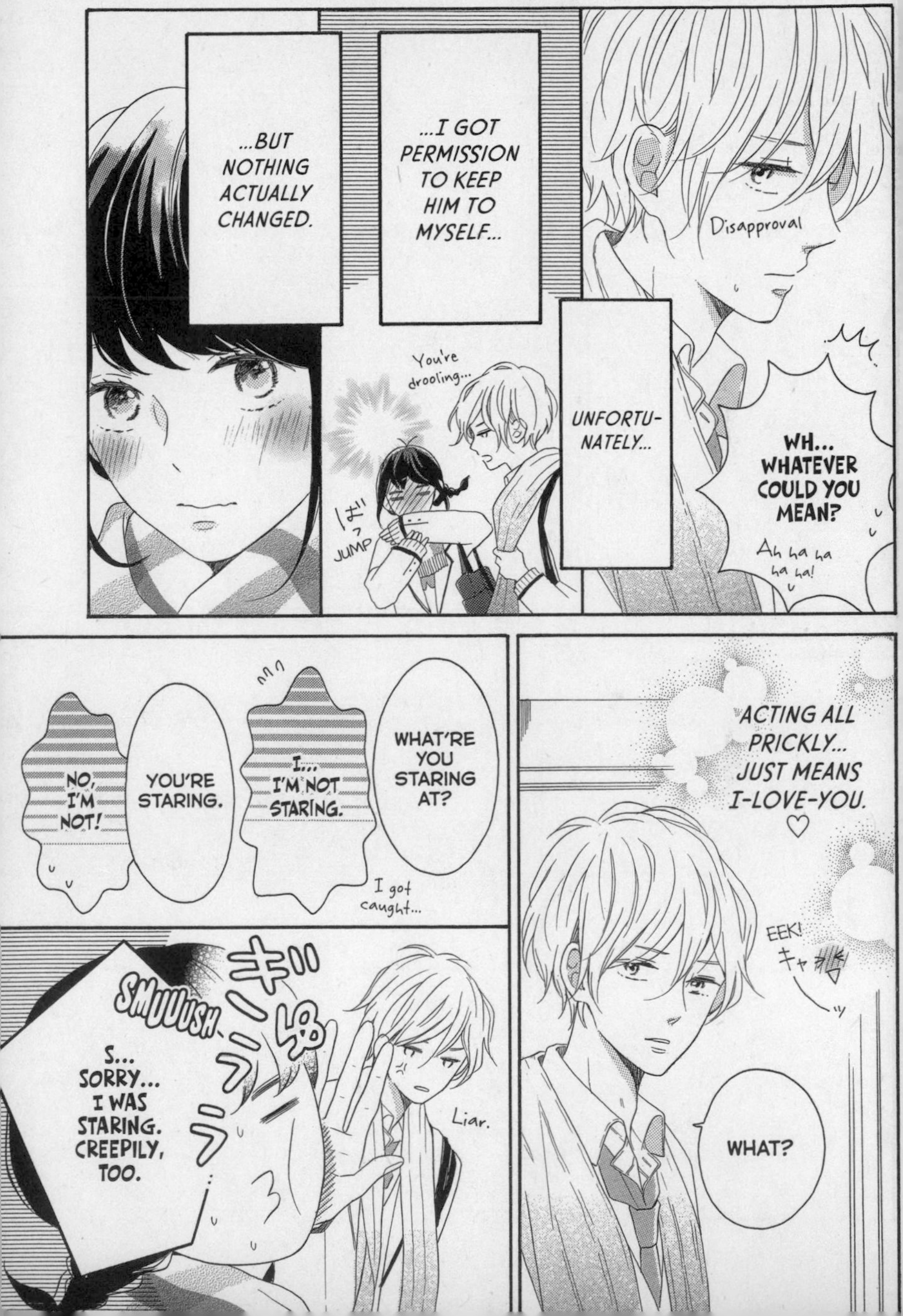
Disapproval
WH... WHATEVER COULD YOU MEAN?
Ah ha ha ha ha!
...I GOT PERMISSION TO KEEP HIM TO MYSELF...
You're drooling...
ばっ
JUMP
UNFORTU-NATELY...
...BUT NOTHING ACTUALLY CHANGED.
ACTING ALL PRICKLY... JUST MEANS I-LOVE-YOU. ♡
EEK!
キャッ
WHAT?
WHAT'RE YOU STARING AT?
I got caught...
I... I'M NOT STARING.
YOU'RE STARING.
NO, I'M NOT!
ぎゅうう
SMUUUSH
Liar.
S... SORRY... I WAS STARING. CREEPILY, TOO.

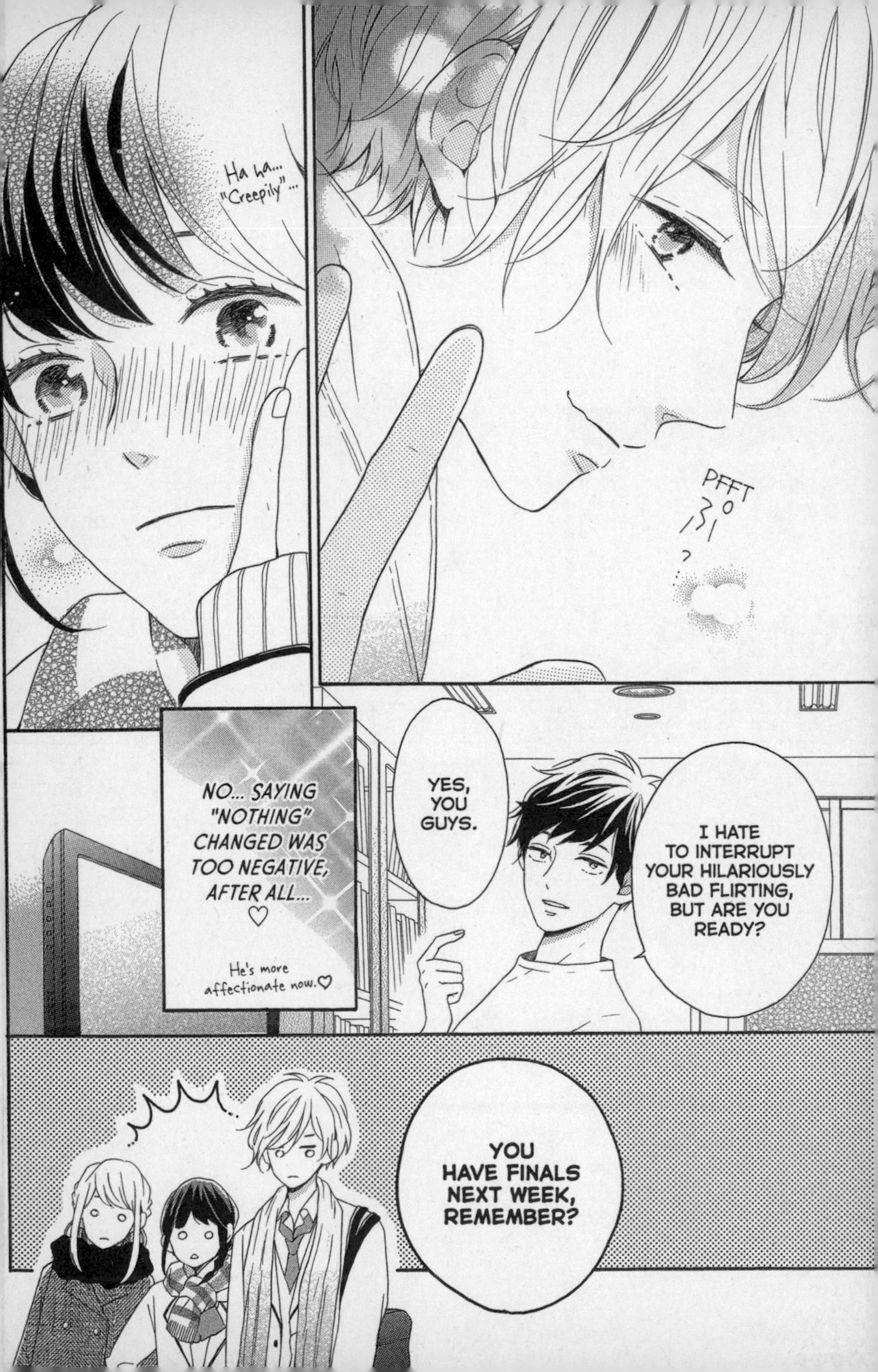
PFFT
Ha ha... "Creepily"...
I HATE TO INTERRUPT YOUR HILARIOUSLY BAD FLIRTING, BUT ARE YOU READY?
YES, YOU GUYS.
NO... SAYING "NOTHING" CHANGED WAS TOO NEGATIVE, AFTER ALL... ♡
He's more affectionate now.♡
YOU HAVE FINALS NEXT WEEK, REMEMBER?

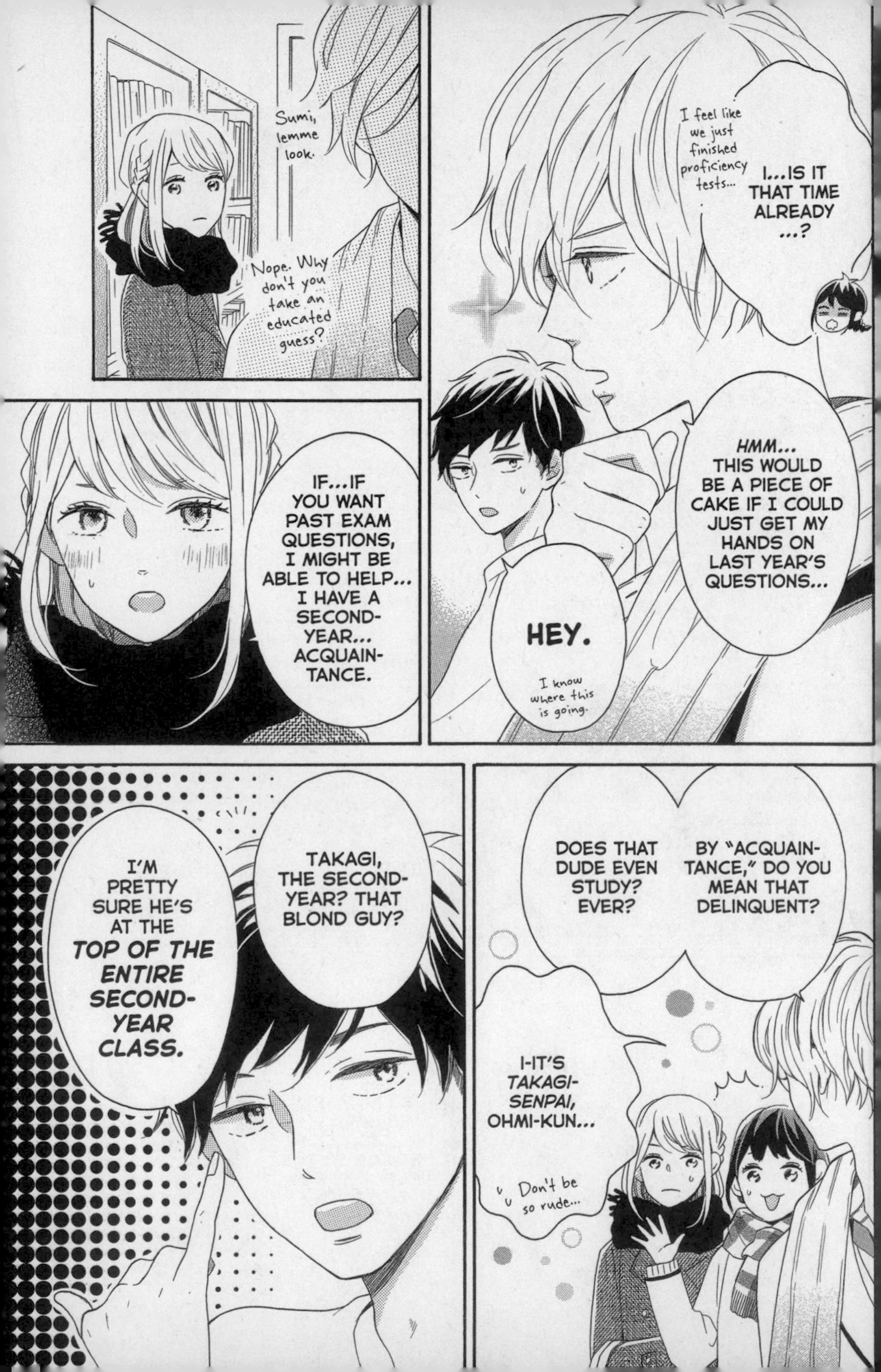

I...IS IT THAT TIME ALREADY ...?
I feel like we just finished proficiency tests...
*HMM...* THIS WOULD BE A PIECE OF CAKE IF I COULD JUST GET MY HANDS ON LAST YEAR'S QUESTIONS...
HEY.
I know where this is going.
Sumi, lemme look.
Nope. Why don't you take an educated guess?
IF...IF YOU WANT PAST EXAM QUESTIONS, I MIGHT BE ABLE TO HELP... I HAVE A SECOND-YEAR... ACQUAINTANCE.
BY "ACQUAINTANCE," DO YOU MEAN THAT DELINQUENT?
DOES THAT DUDE EVEN STUDY? EVER?
I-IT'S *TAKAGI-SENPAI*, OHMI-KUN...
Don't be so rude...
TAKAGI, THE SECOND-YEAR? THAT BLOND GUY?
I'M PRETTY SURE HE'S AT THE *TOP OF THE ENTIRE SECOND-YEAR CLASS.*

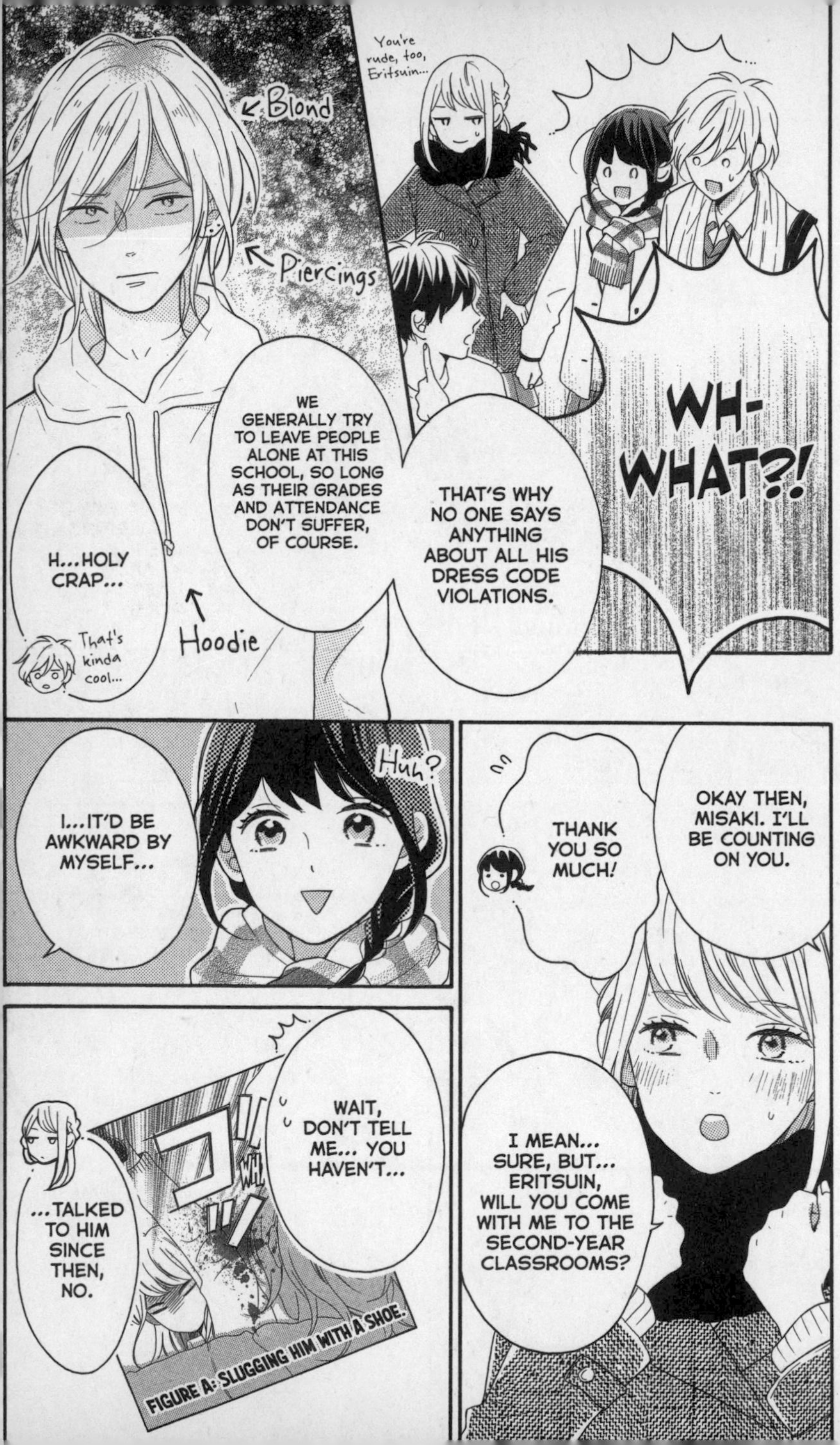
...
WH-WHAT?!
You're rude, too, Eritsuin...
WE GENERALLY TRY TO LEAVE PEOPLE ALONE AT THIS SCHOOL, SO LONG AS THEIR GRADES AND ATTENDANCE DON'T SUFFER, OF COURSE.
THAT'S WHY NO ONE SAYS ANYTHING ABOUT ALL HIS DRESS CODE VIOLATIONS.
← Blond
← Piercings
← Hoodie
H...HOLY CRAP...
That's kinda cool...
OKAY THEN, MISAKI. I'LL BE COUNTING ON YOU.
THANK YOU SO MUCH!
I MEAN... SURE, BUT... ERITSUIN, WILL YOU COME WITH ME TO THE SECOND-YEAR CLASSROOMS?
Huh?
I...IT'D BE AWKWARD BY MYSELF...
WAIT, DON'T TELL ME... YOU HAVEN'T...
...TALKED TO HIM SINCE THEN, NO.
FIGURE A: SLUGGING HIM WITH A SHOE.

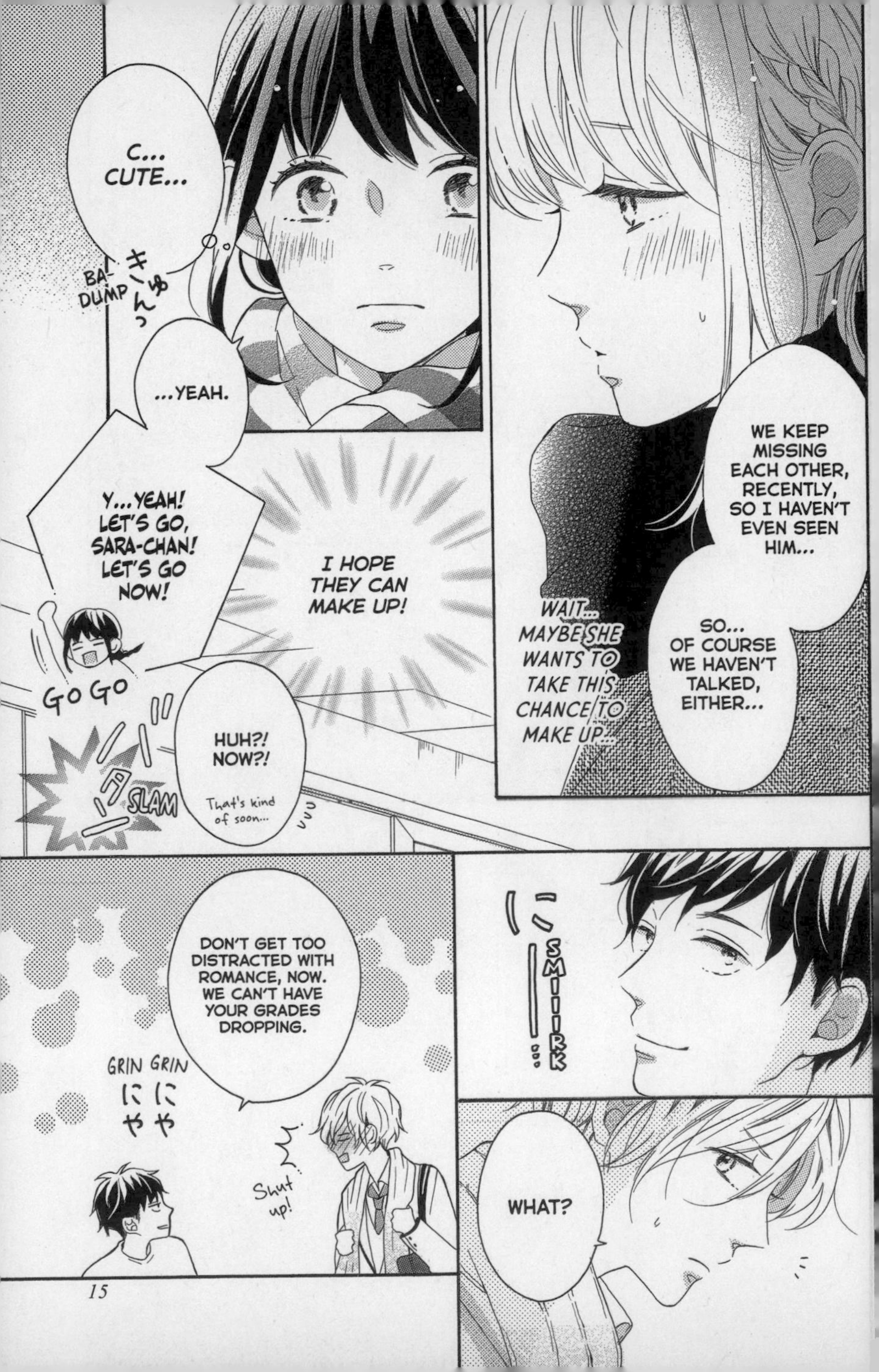
WE KEEP MISSING EACH OTHER, RECENTLY, SO I HAVEN'T EVEN SEEN HIM...
SO... OF COURSE WE HAVEN'T TALKED, EITHER...
WAIT... MAYBE SHE WANTS TO TAKE THIS CHANCE TO MAKE UP...
C... CUTE...
きゅんっ
BA-DUMP
...YEAH.
I HOPE THEY CAN MAKE UP!
Y...YEAH! LET'S GO, SARA-CHAN! LET'S GO NOW!
GO GO
HUH?! NOW?!
That's kind of soon...
SLAM
SMIIIRK
WHAT?
DON'T GET TOO DISTRACTED WITH ROMANCE, NOW. WE CAN'T HAVE YOUR GRADES DROPPING.
GRIN GRIN
にやにや
Shut up!

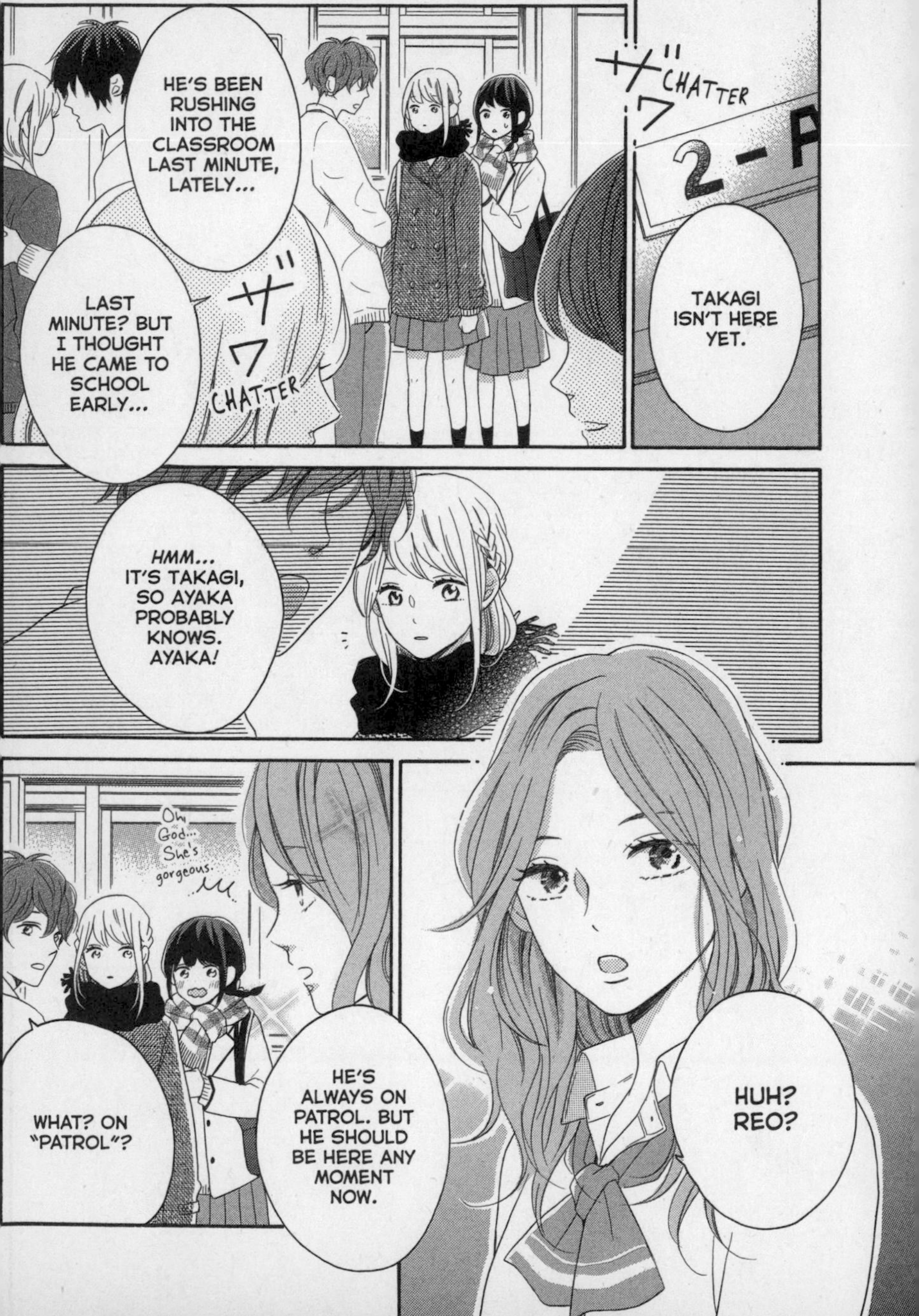
CHATTER
TAKAGI ISN'T HERE YET.
HE'S BEEN RUSHING INTO THE CLASSROOM LAST MINUTE, LATELY...
CHATTER
LAST MINUTE? BUT I THOUGHT HE CAME TO SCHOOL EARLY...
HMM... IT'S TAKAGI, SO AYAKA PROBABLY KNOWS. AYAKA!
HUH? REO?
HE'S ALWAYS ON PATROL. BUT HE SHOULD BE HERE ANY MOMENT NOW.
Oh God... She's gorgeous.
WHAT? ON "PATROL"?

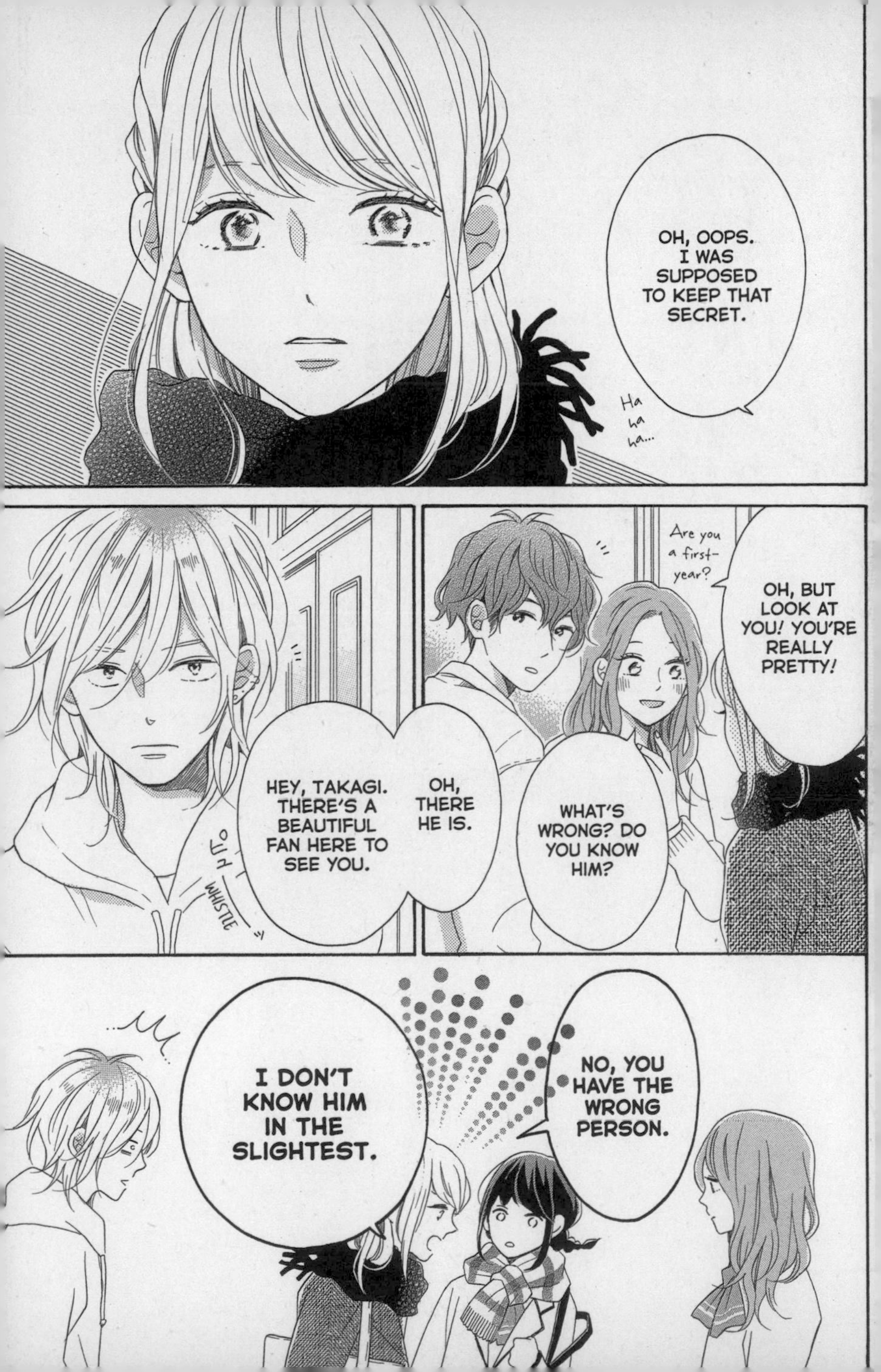
OH, OOPS. I WAS SUPPOSED TO KEEP THAT SECRET.
Ha ha ha...
OH, BUT LOOK AT YOU! YOU'RE REALLY PRETTY!
Are you a first-year?
WHAT'S WRONG? DO YOU KNOW HIM?
OH, THERE HE IS.
HEY, TAKAGI. THERE'S A BEAUTIFUL FAN HERE TO SEE YOU.
WHISTLE
NO, YOU HAVE THE WRONG PERSON.
I DON'T KNOW HIM IN THE SLIGHTEST.

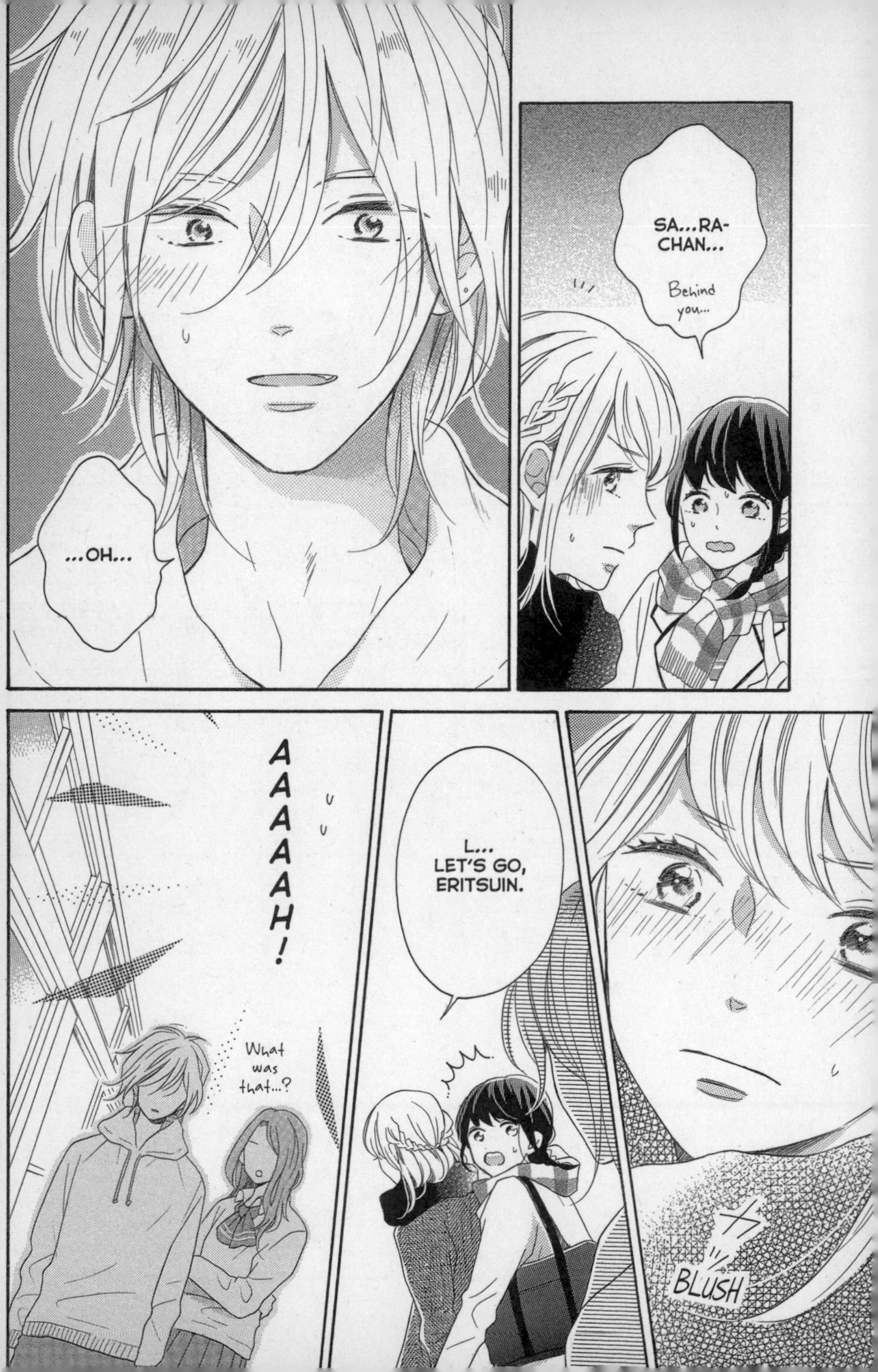
SA...RA-CHAN...
Behind you...
...OH...
BLUSH
L... LET'S GO, ERITSUIN.
AAAAAAH!
What was that...?

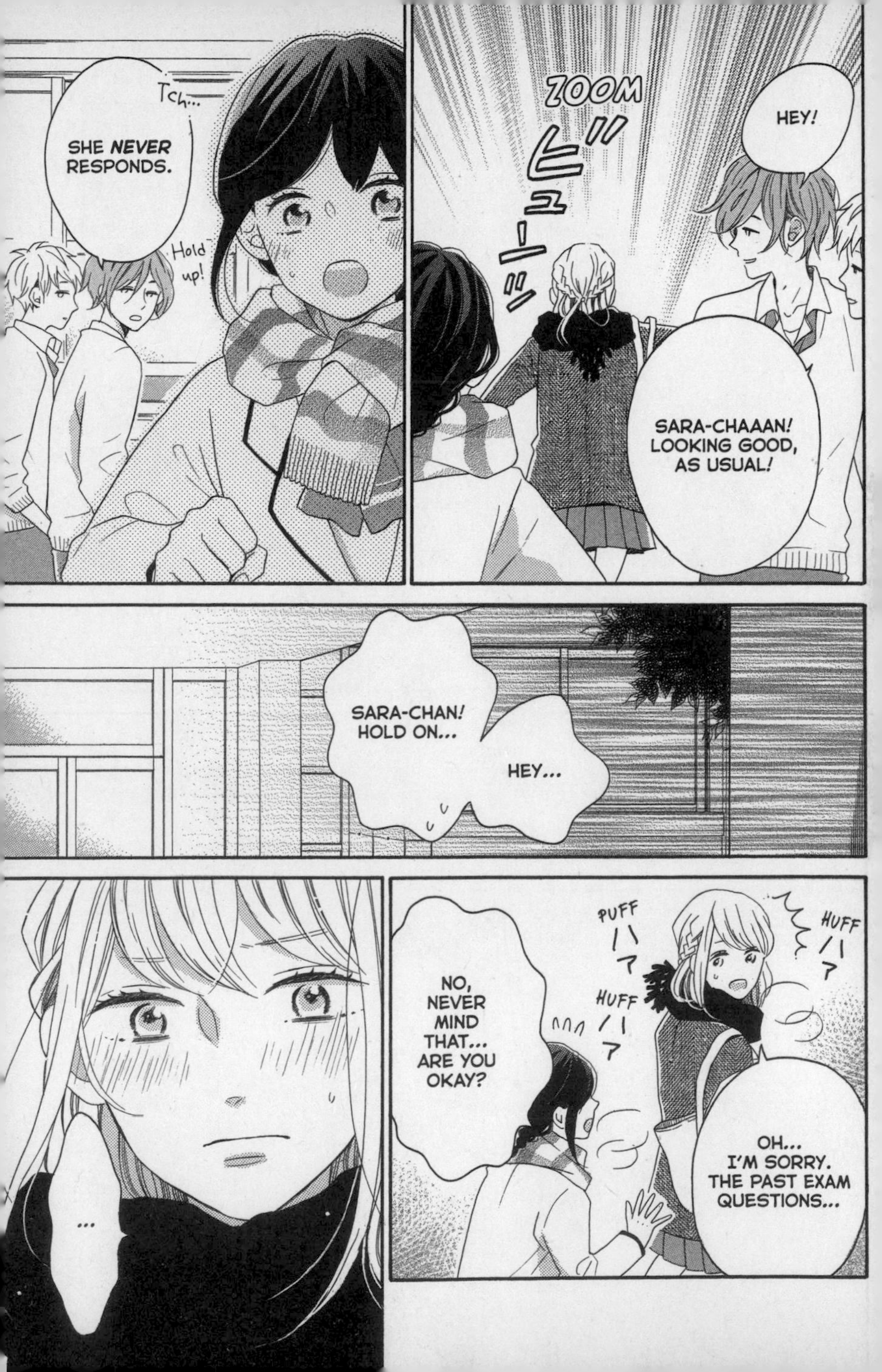
HEY!
ZOOM
SARA-CHAAAN! LOOKING GOOD, AS USUAL!
Tch...
SHE NEVER RESPONDS.
Hold up!
SARA-CHAN! HOLD ON...
HEY...
HUFF
PUFF
HUFF
OH... I'M SORRY. THE PAST EXAM QUESTIONS...
NO, NEVER MIND THAT... ARE YOU OKAY?
...

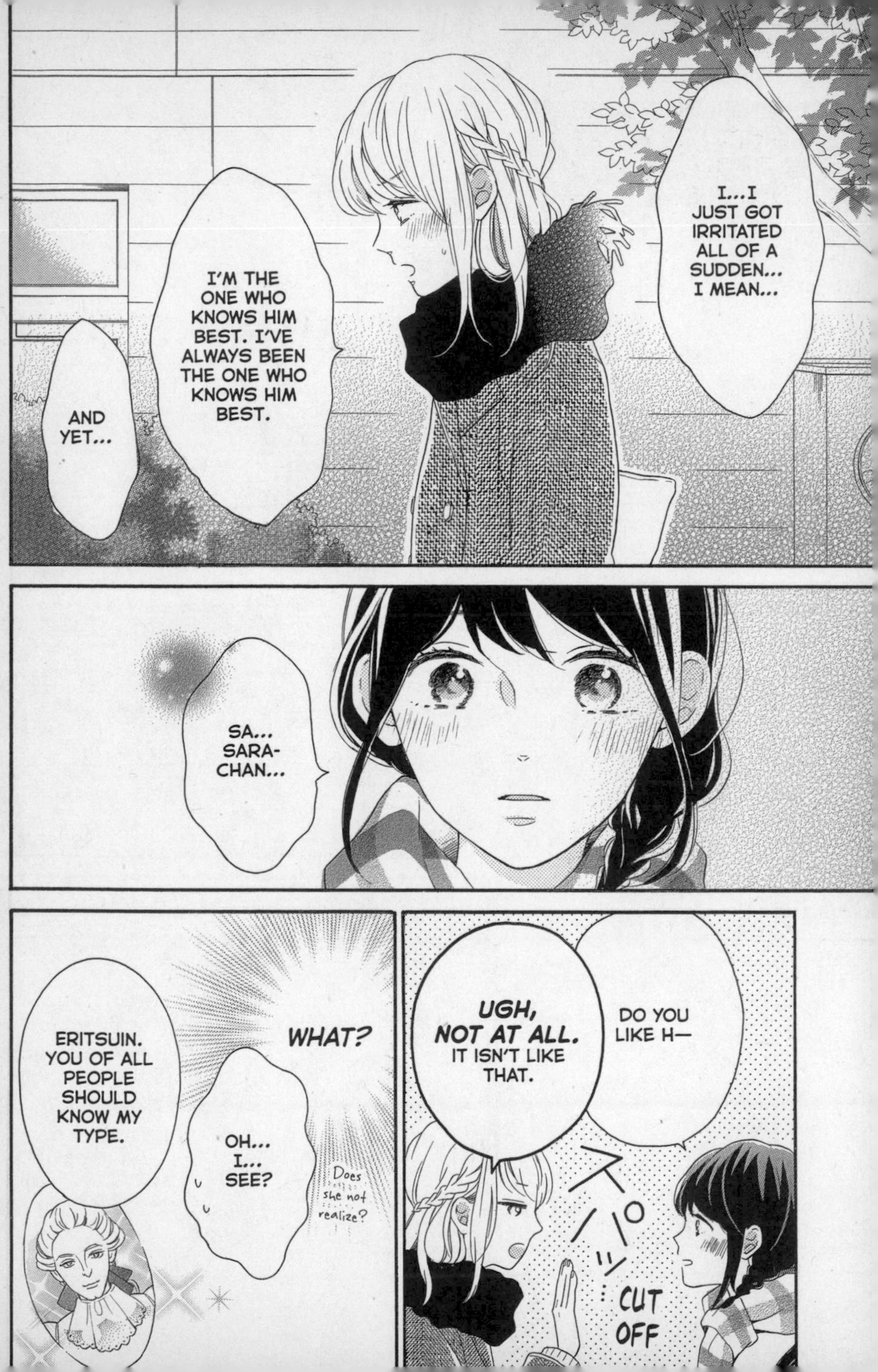
I...I JUST GOT IRRITATED ALL OF A SUDDEN... I MEAN...
I'M THE ONE WHO KNOWS HIM BEST. I'VE ALWAYS BEEN THE ONE WHO KNOWS HIM BEST.
AND YET...
SA... SARA-CHAN...
DO YOU LIKE H—
UGH, NOT AT ALL. IT ISN'T LIKE THAT.
CUT OFF
WHAT?
ERITSUIN. YOU OF ALL PEOPLE SHOULD KNOW MY TYPE.
OH... I... SEE?
Does she not realize?

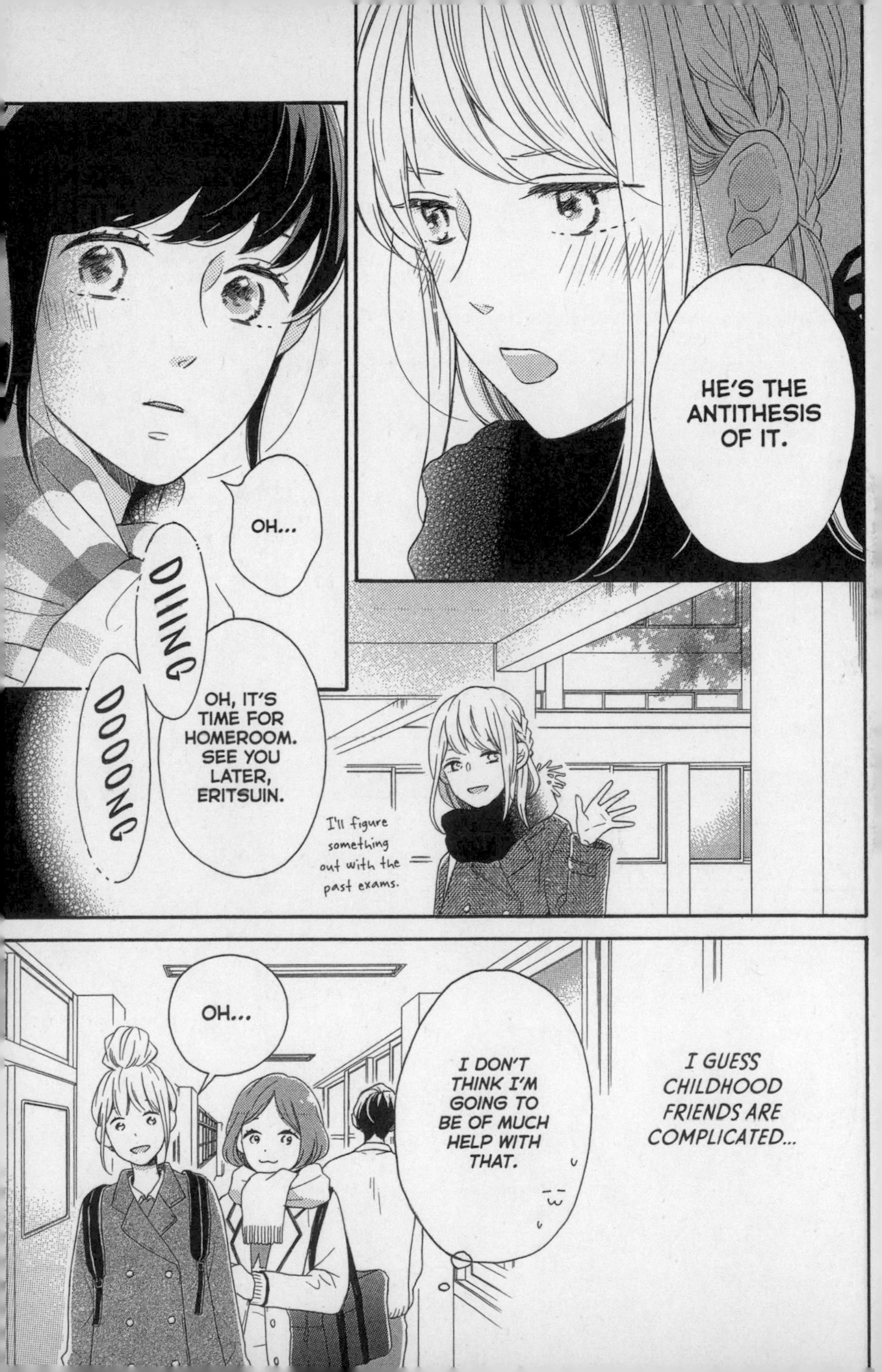
HE'S THE ANTITHESIS OF IT.
OH...
DIIING DOOOONG
OH, IT'S TIME FOR HOMEROOM. SEE YOU LATER, ERITSUIN.
I'll figure something out with the past exams.
I GUESS CHILDHOOD FRIENDS ARE COMPLICATED...
I DON'T THINK I'M GOING TO BE OF MUCH HELP WITH THAT.
OH...

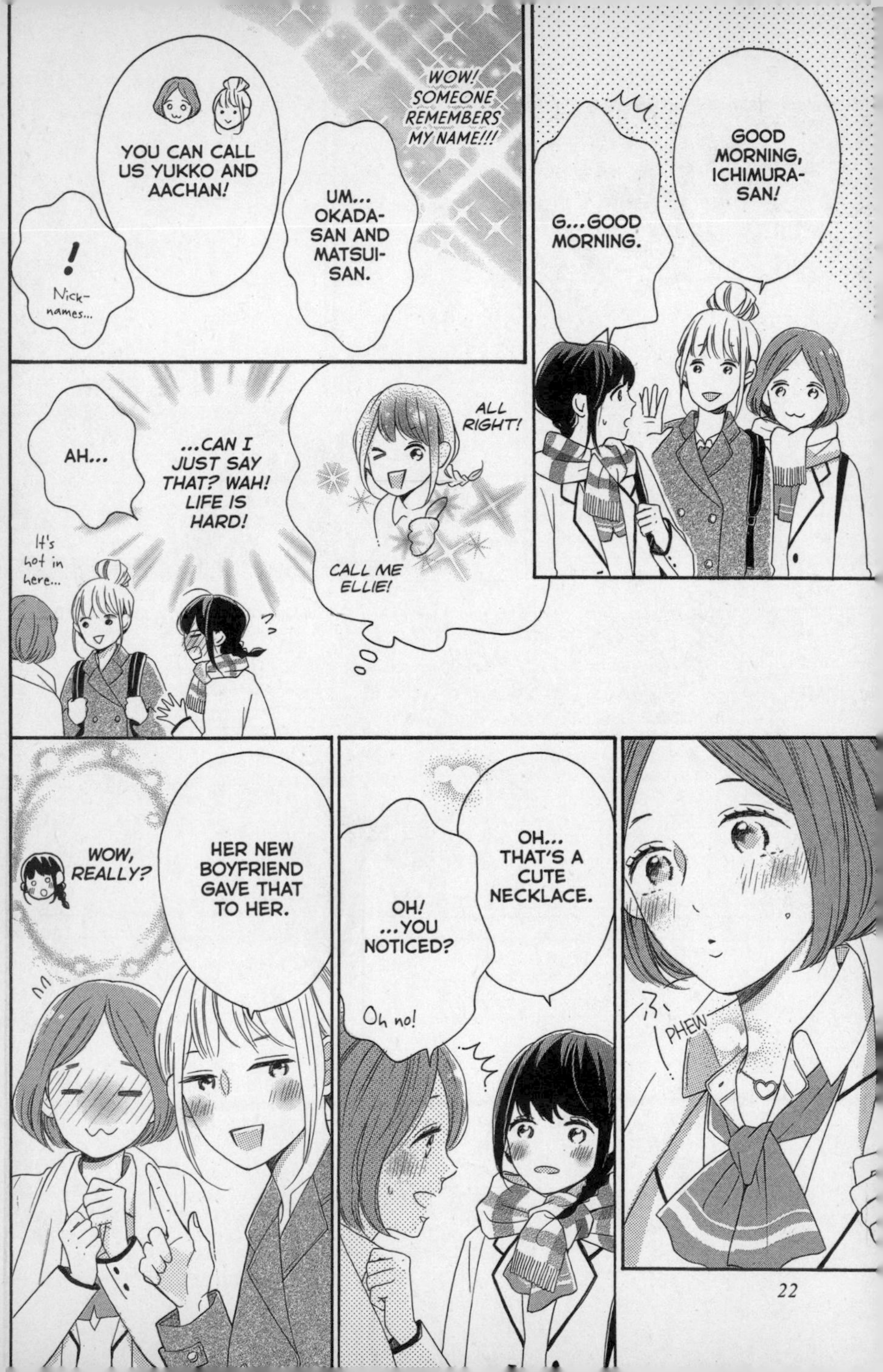
GOOD MORNING, ICHIMURA-SAN!
G...GOOD MORNING.
WOW! SOMEONE REMEMBERS MY NAME!!!
UM... OKADA-SAN AND MATSUI-SAN.
YOU CAN CALL US YUKKO AND AACHAN!
!
Nick-names...
ALL RIGHT!
CALL ME ELLIE!
...CAN I JUST SAY THAT? WAH! LIFE IS HARD!
AH...
It's hot in here...
PHEW
OH... THAT'S A CUTE NECKLACE.
OH! ...YOU NOTICED?
Oh no!
HER NEW BOYFRIEND GAVE THAT TO HER.
WOW, REALLY?

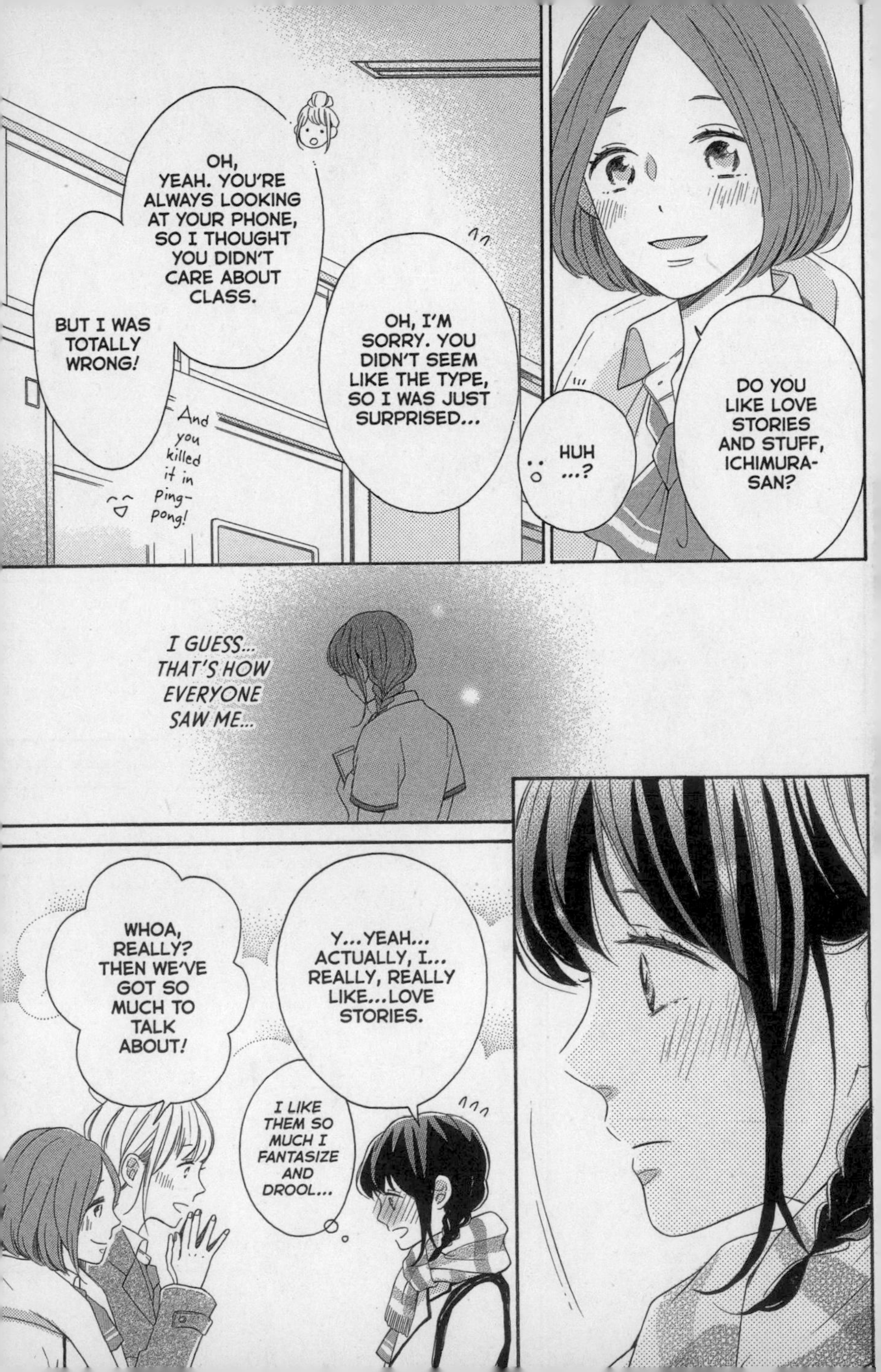
DO YOU LIKE LOVE STORIES AND STUFF, ICHIMURA-SAN?
HUH ...?
OH, I'M SORRY. YOU DIDN'T SEEM LIKE THE TYPE, SO I WAS JUST SURPRISED...
OH, YEAH. YOU'RE ALWAYS LOOKING AT YOUR PHONE, SO I THOUGHT YOU DIDN'T CARE ABOUT CLASS.
BUT I WAS TOTALLY WRONG!
And you killed it in ping-pong!
I GUESS... THAT'S HOW EVERYONE SAW ME...
Y...YEAH... ACTUALLY, I... REALLY, REALLY LIKE...LOVE STORIES.
I LIKE THEM SO MUCH I FANTASIZE AND DROOL...
WHOA, REALLY? THEN WE'VE GOT SO MUCH TO TALK ABOUT!

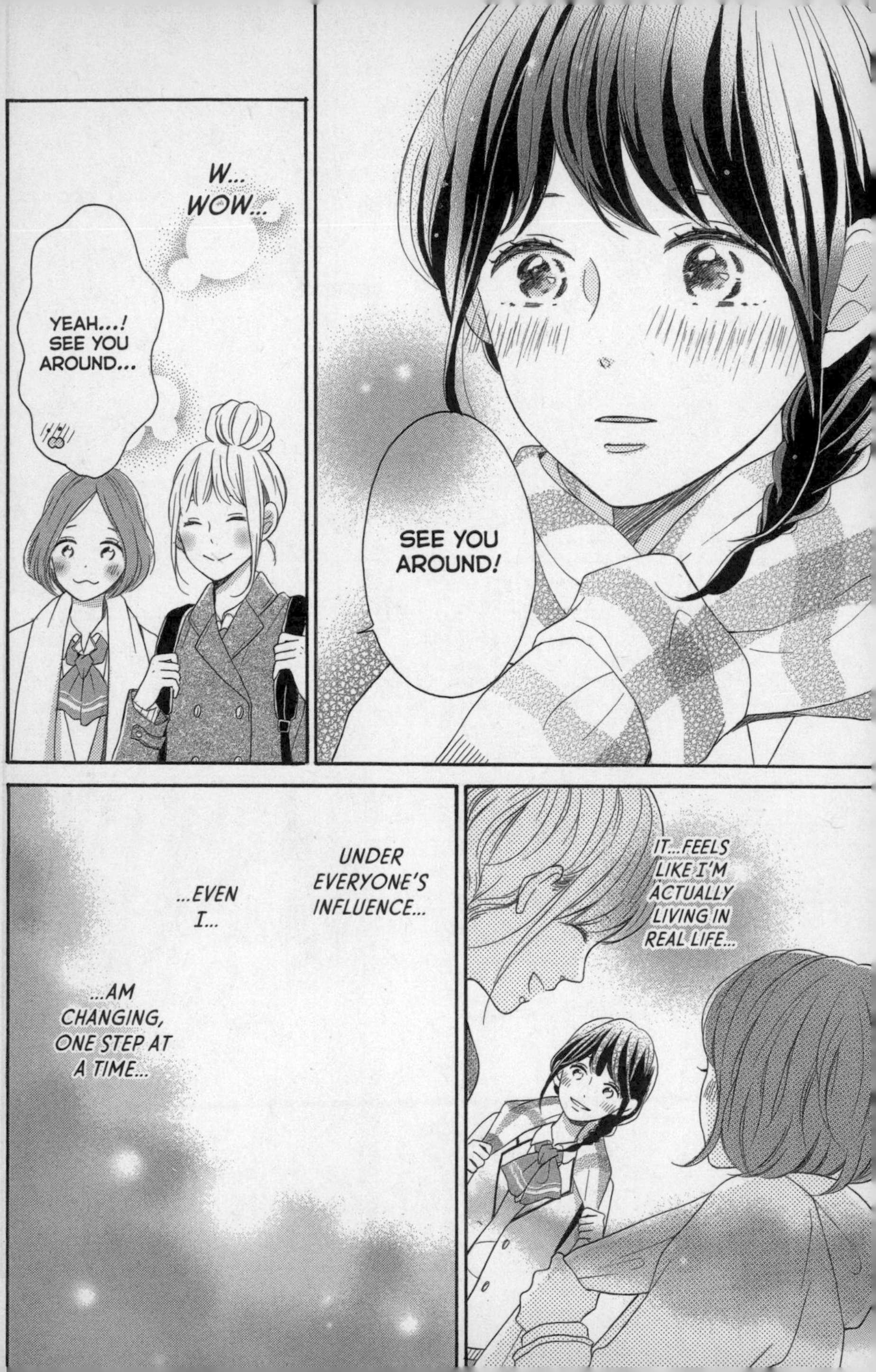
SEE YOU AROUND!
W... WOW...
YEAH...! SEE YOU AROUND...
IT...FEELS LIKE I'M ACTUALLY LIVING IN REAL LIFE...
UNDER EVERYONE'S INFLUENCE...
...EVEN I...
...AM CHANGING, ONE STEP AT A TIME...

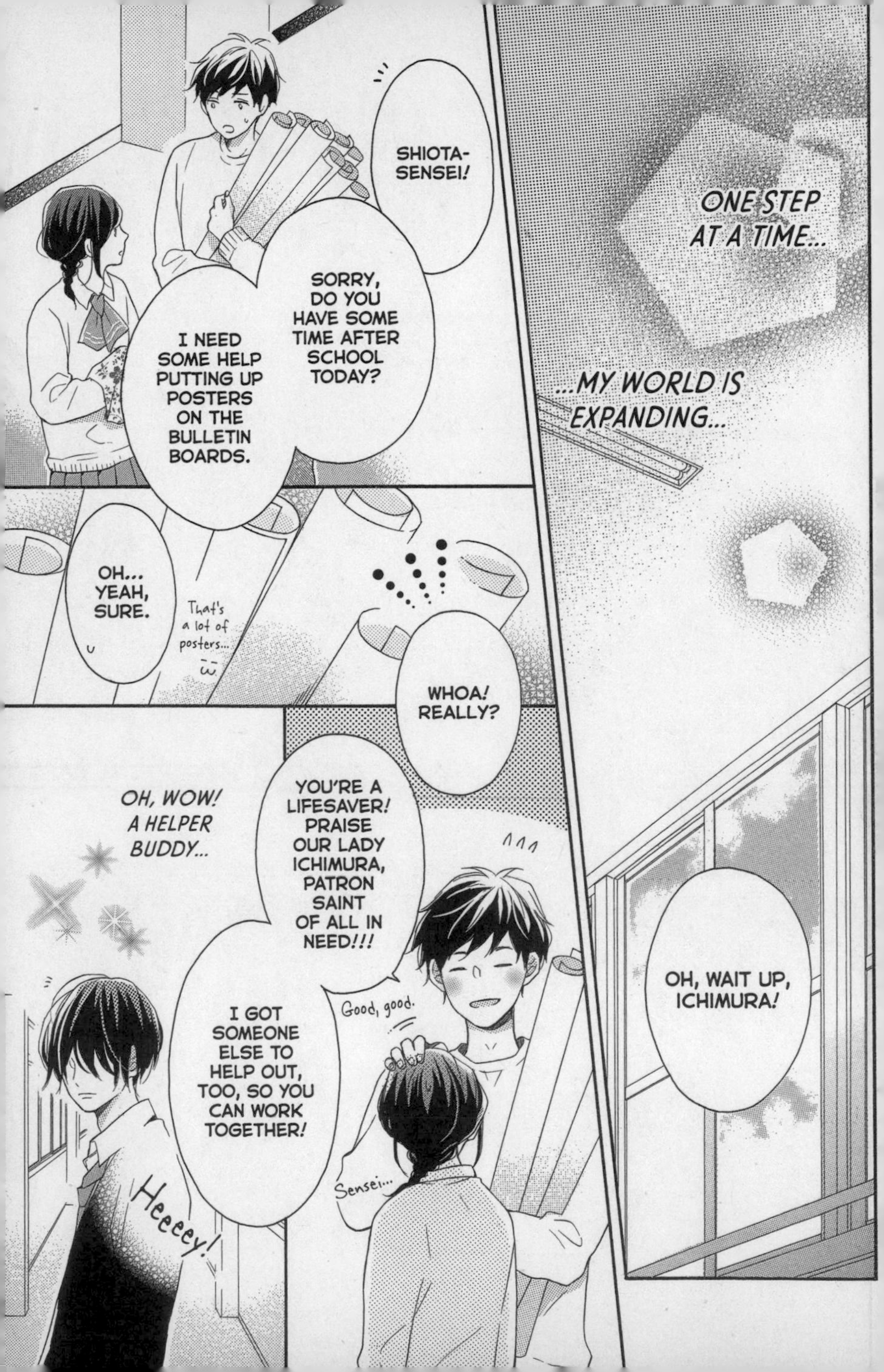
ONE STEP AT A TIME...
...MY WORLD IS EXPANDING...
OH, WAIT UP, ICHIMURA!
SHIOTA-SENSEI!
SORRY, DO YOU HAVE SOME TIME AFTER SCHOOL TODAY?
I NEED SOME HELP PUTTING UP POSTERS ON THE BULLETIN BOARDS.
OH... YEAH, SURE.
That's a lot of posters...
WHOA! REALLY?
YOU'RE A LIFESAVER! PRAISE OUR LADY ICHIMURA, PATRON SAINT OF ALL IN NEED!!!
I GOT SOMEONE ELSE TO HELP OUT, TOO, SO YOU CAN WORK TOGETHER!
Good, good.
Sensei...
OH, WOW! A HELPER BUDDY...
Heeeey!

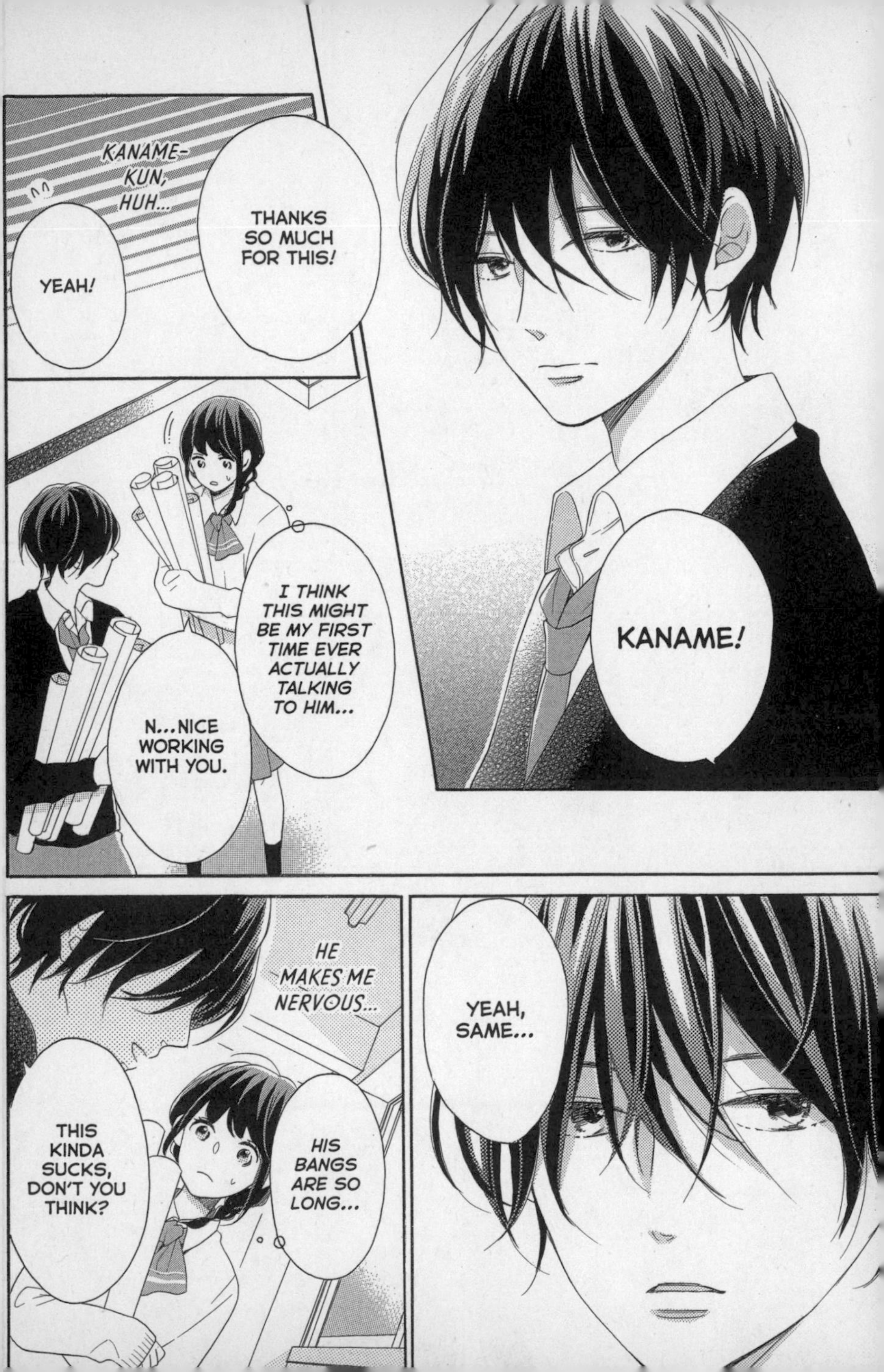
KANAME!
THANKS SO MUCH FOR THIS!
KANAME-KUN, HUH...
YEAH!
I THINK THIS MIGHT BE MY FIRST TIME EVER ACTUALLY TALKING TO HIM...
N...NICE WORKING WITH YOU.
YEAH, SAME...
HE MAKES ME NERVOUS...
HIS BANGS ARE SO LONG...
THIS KINDA SUCKS, DON'T YOU THINK?

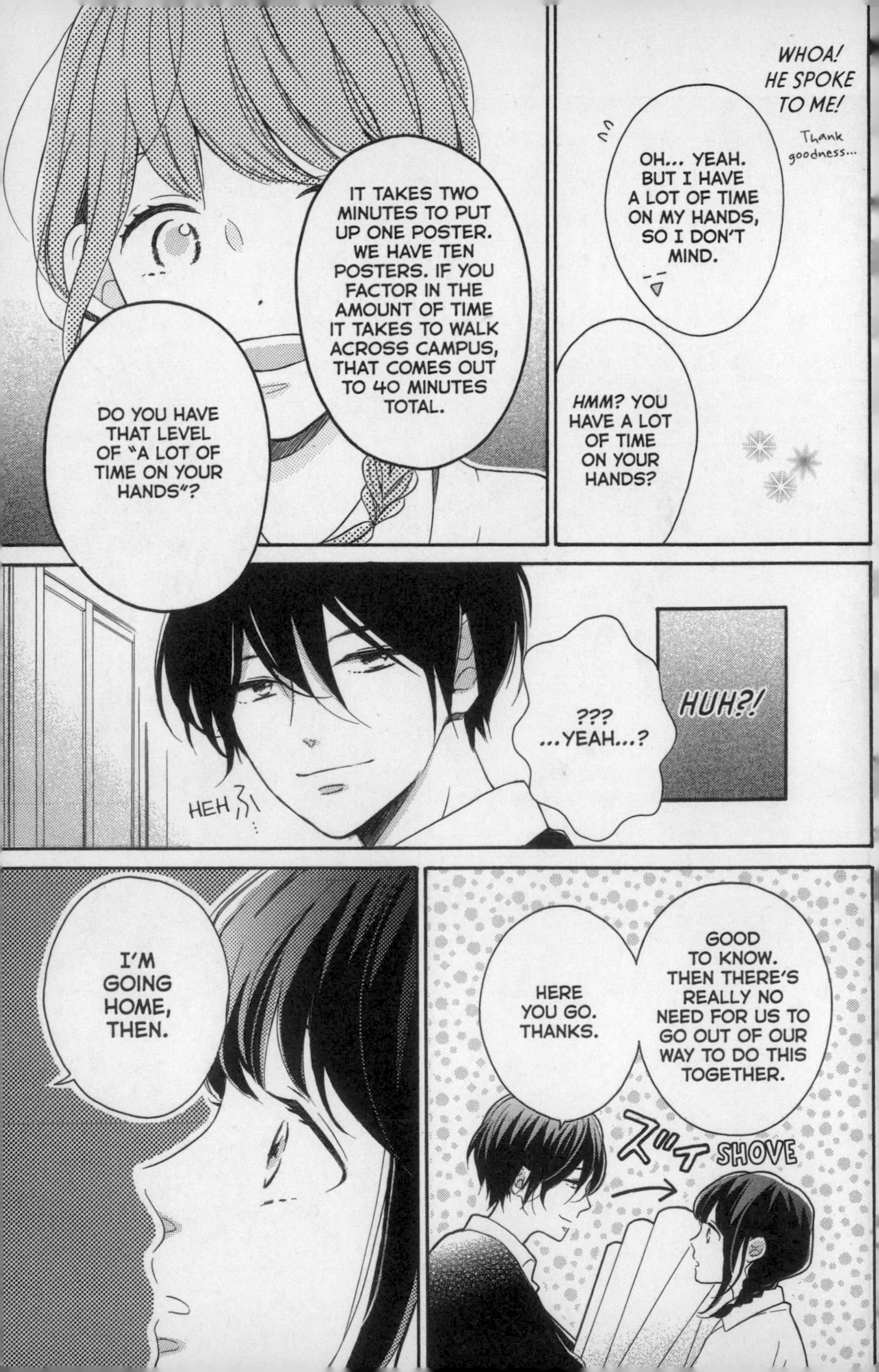
WHOA! HE SPOKE TO ME!
Thank goodness...
OH... YEAH. BUT I HAVE A LOT OF TIME ON MY HANDS, SO I DON'T MIND.
*HMM?* YOU HAVE A LOT OF TIME ON YOUR HANDS?
IT TAKES TWO MINUTES TO PUT UP ONE POSTER. WE HAVE TEN POSTERS. IF YOU FACTOR IN THE AMOUNT OF TIME IT TAKES TO WALK ACROSS CAMPUS, THAT COMES OUT TO 40 MINUTES TOTAL.
DO YOU HAVE THAT LEVEL OF "A LOT OF TIME ON YOUR HANDS"?
HUH?!
??? ...YEAH...?
HEH
GOOD TO KNOW. THEN THERE'S REALLY NO NEED FOR US TO GO OUT OF OUR WAY TO DO THIS TOGETHER.
HERE YOU GO. THANKS.
SHOVE
I'M GOING HOME, THEN.

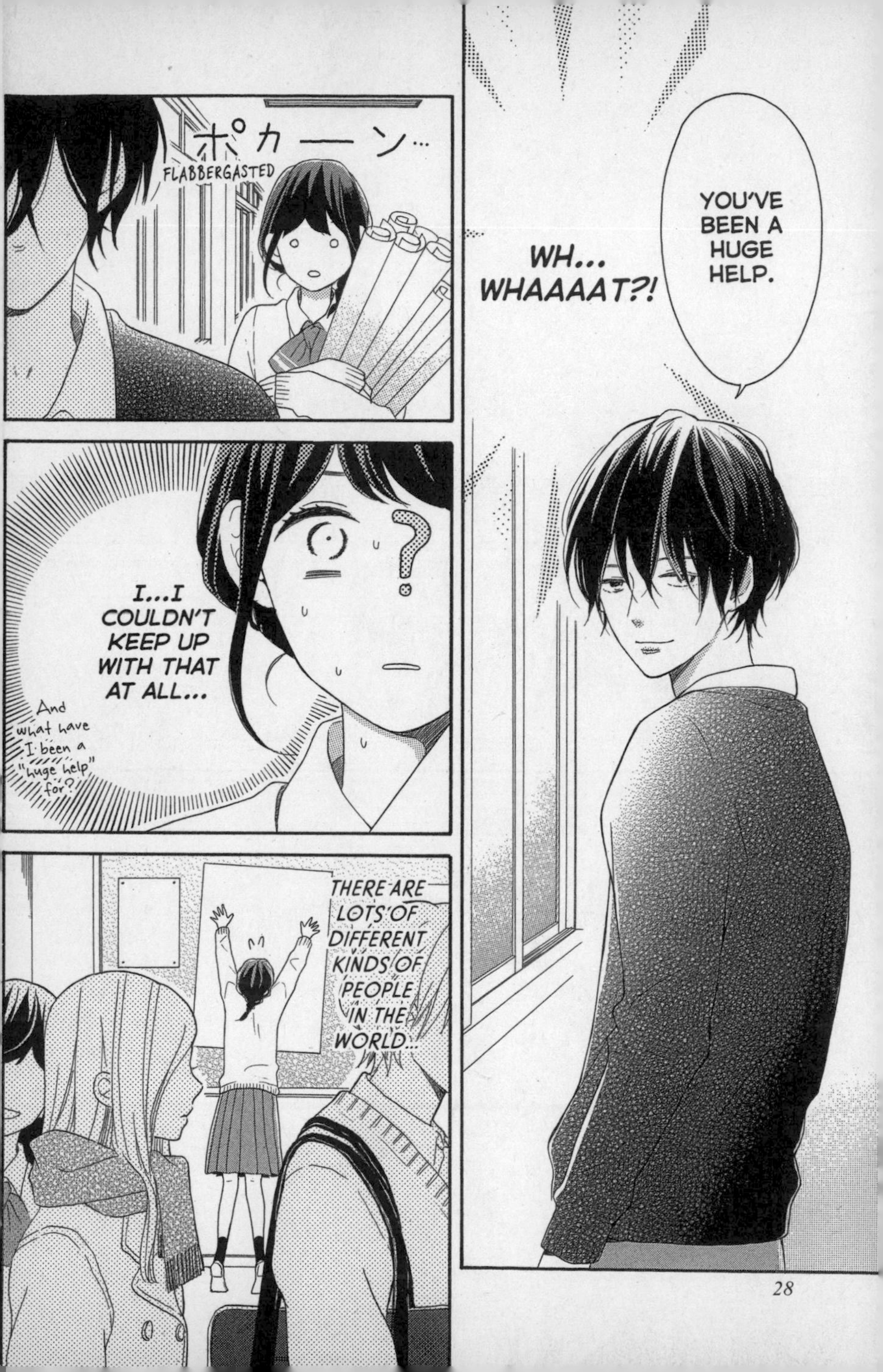
YOU'VE BEEN A HUGE HELP.
WH... WHAAAAT?!
ポカーン…
FLABBERGASTED
I...I COULDN'T KEEP UP WITH THAT AT ALL...
And what have I been a "huge help" for?
THERE ARE LOTS OF DIFFERENT KINDS OF PEOPLE IN THE WORLD...

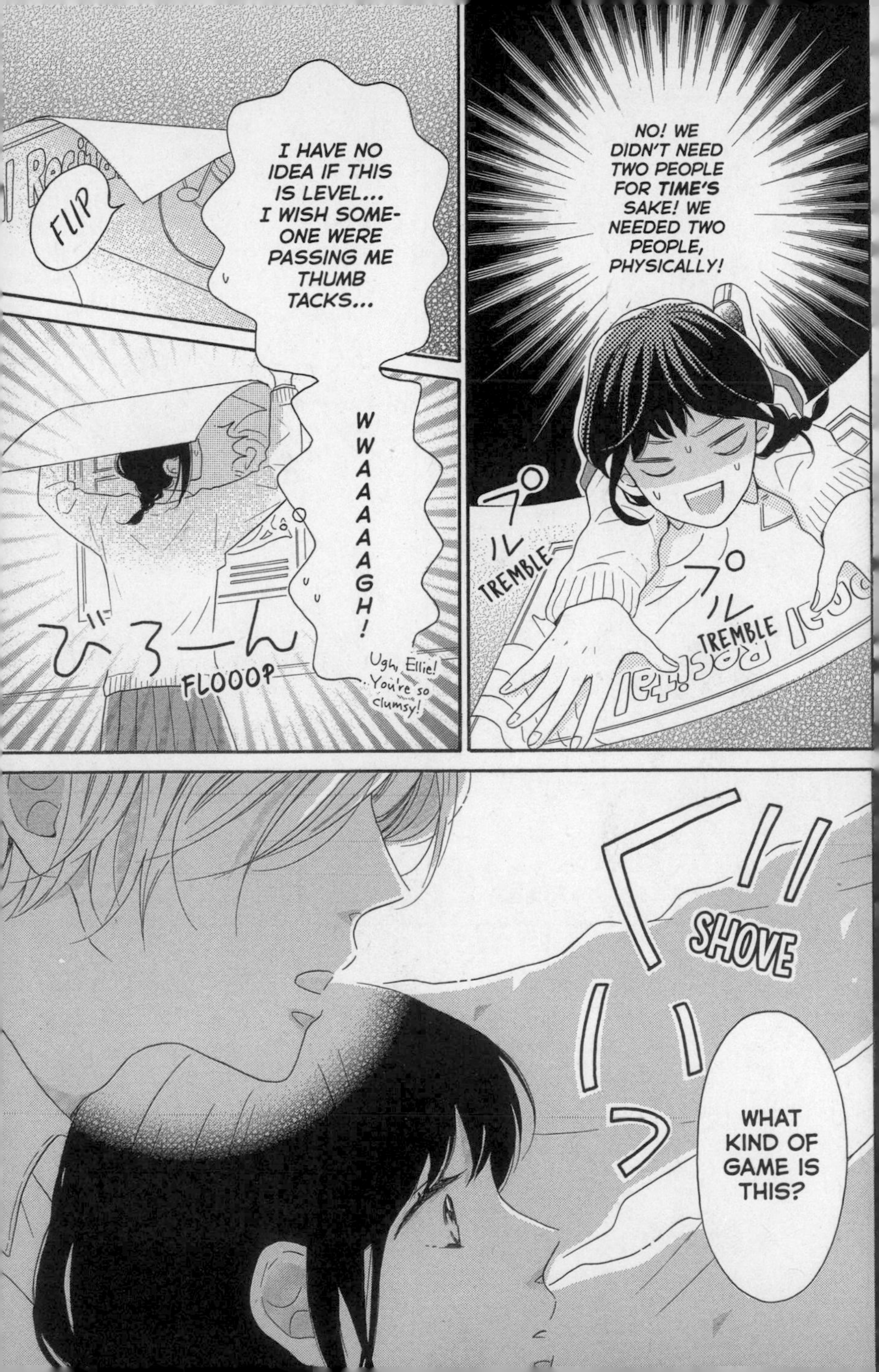
NO! WE DIDN'T NEED TWO PEOPLE FOR TIME'S SAKE! WE NEEDED TWO PEOPLE, PHYSICALLY!
プル
TREMBLE
プル
TREMBLE
I HAVE NO IDEA IF THIS IS LEVEL... I WISH SOME-ONE WERE PASSING ME THUMB TACKS...
FLIP
WWAAAAAAAAGH!
びろーん
FLOOOP
Ugh, Ellie! You're so clumsy!
SHOVE
WHAT KIND OF GAME IS THIS?

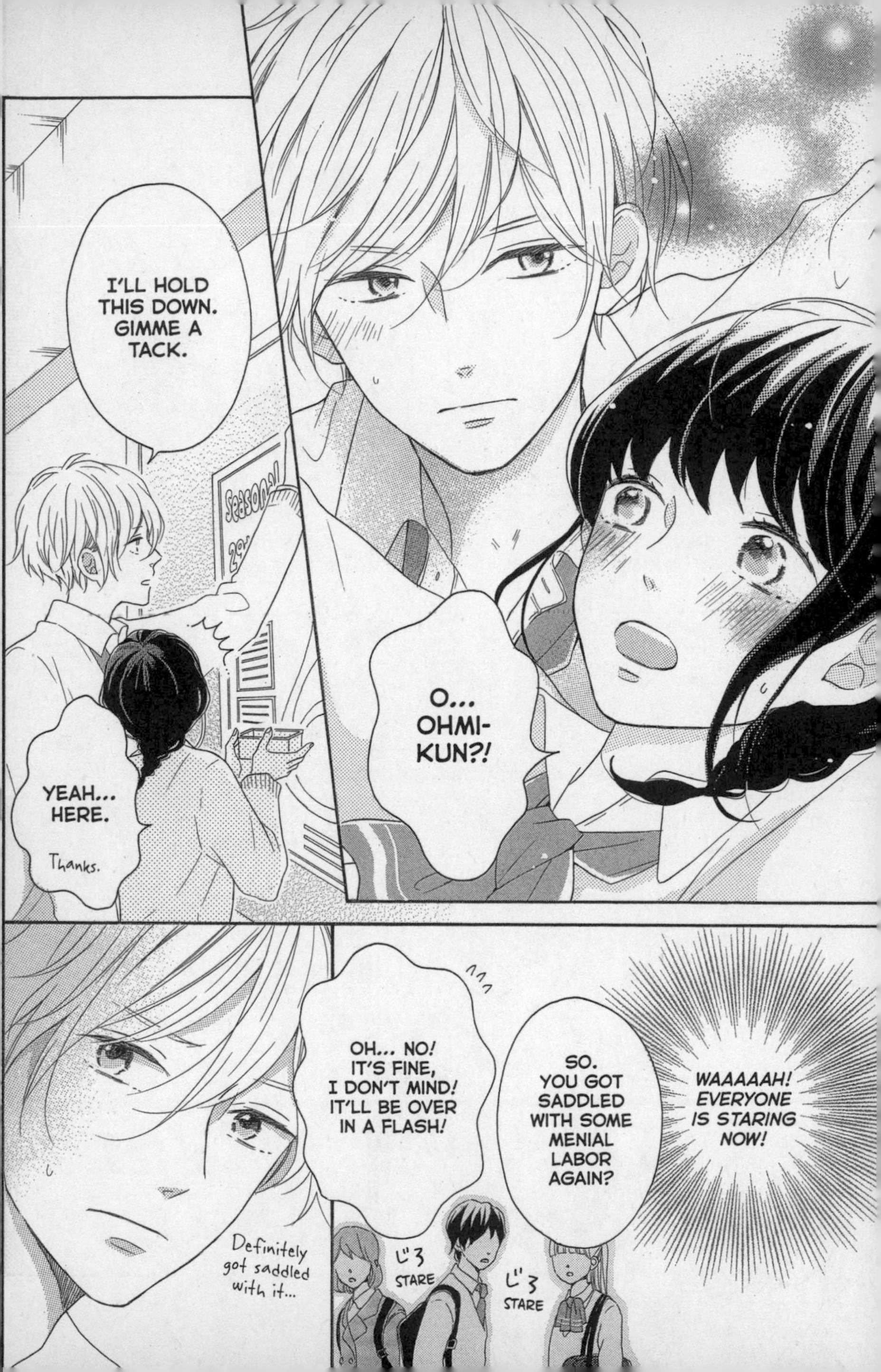
O... OHMI-KUN?!
I'LL HOLD THIS DOWN. GIMME A TACK.
Seasonal
YEAH... HERE.
Thanks.
WAAAAAH! EVERYONE IS STARING NOW!
SO. YOU GOT SADDLED WITH SOME MENIAL LABOR AGAIN?
OH... NO! IT'S FINE, I DON'T MIND! IT'LL BE OVER IN A FLASH!
じろ STARE
じろ STARE
Definitely got saddled with it...

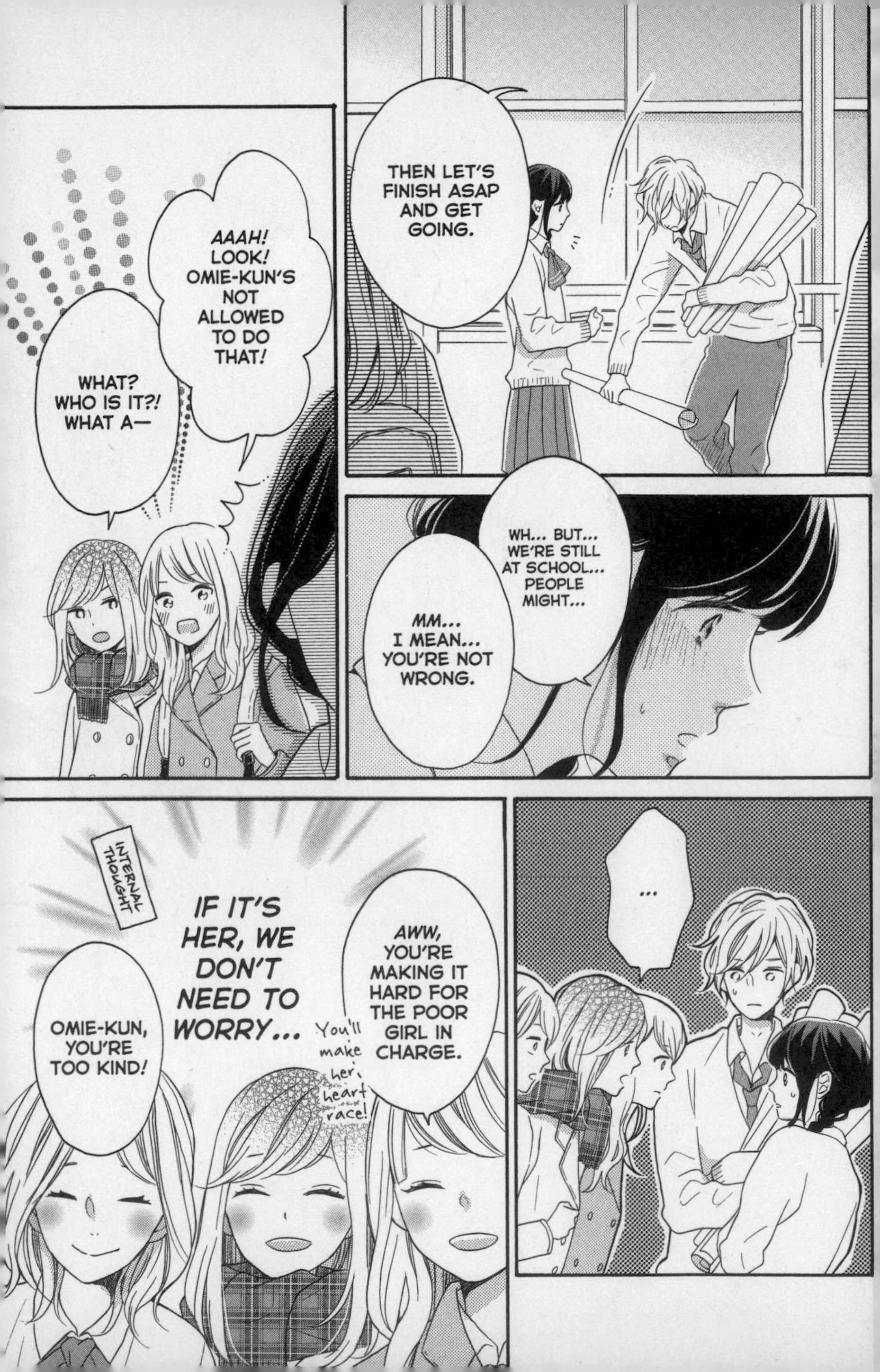
THEN LET'S FINISH ASAP AND GET GOING.
WH... BUT... WE'RE STILL AT SCHOOL... PEOPLE MIGHT...
MM... I MEAN... YOU'RE NOT WRONG.
AAAH! LOOK! OMIE-KUN'S NOT ALLOWED TO DO THAT!
WHAT? WHO IS IT?! WHAT A—
...
AWW, YOU'RE MAKING IT HARD FOR THE POOR GIRL IN CHARGE.
You'll make her heart race!
IF IT'S HER, WE DON'T NEED TO WORRY...
INTERNAL THOUGHT
OMIE-KUN, YOU'RE TOO KIND!

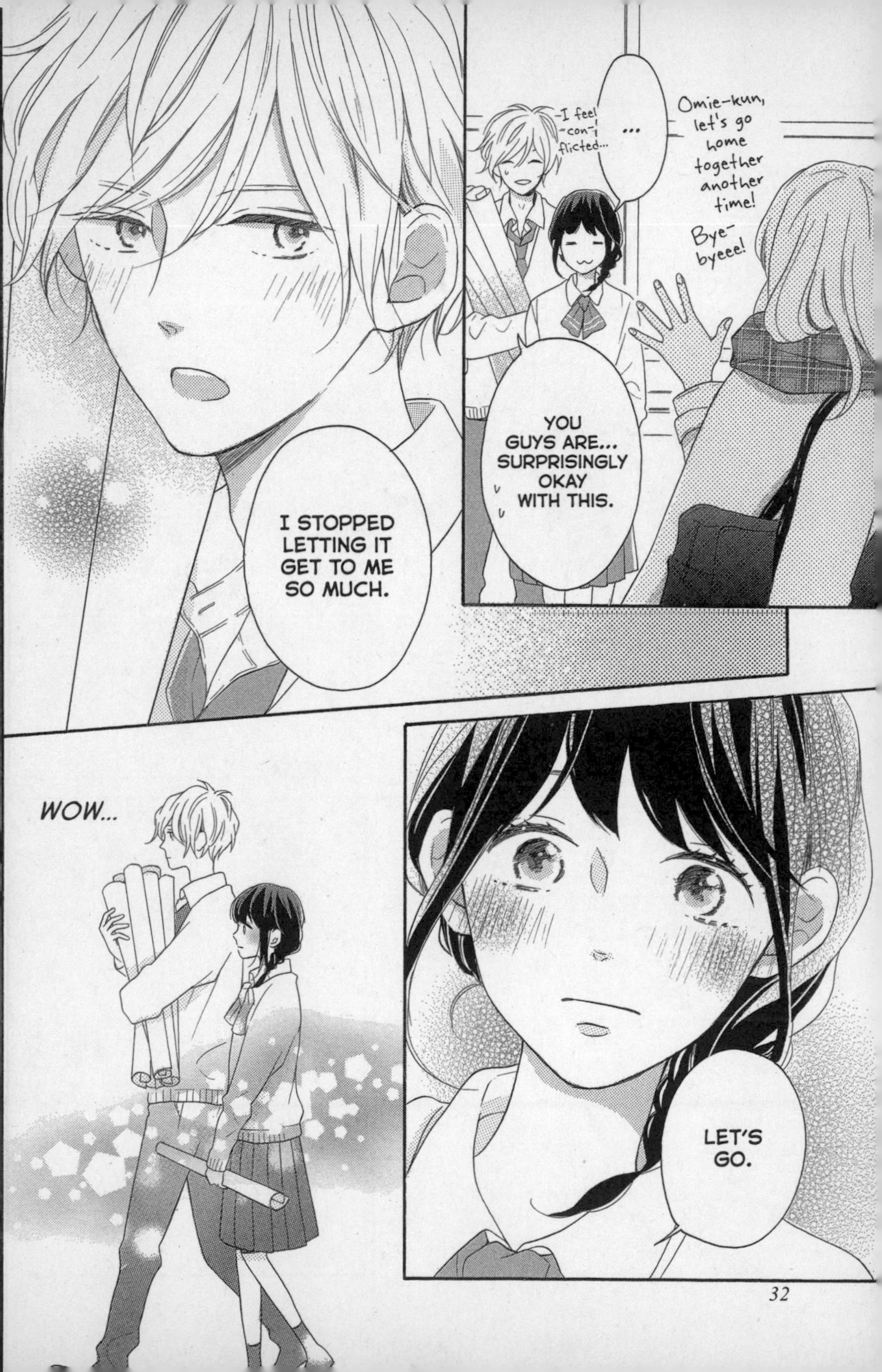
Omie-kun, let's go home together another time!
Bye-byeee!
...
I feel con-flicted...
YOU GUYS ARE... SURPRISINGLY OKAY WITH THIS.
I STOPPED LETTING IT GET TO ME SO MUCH.
LET'S GO.
WOW...

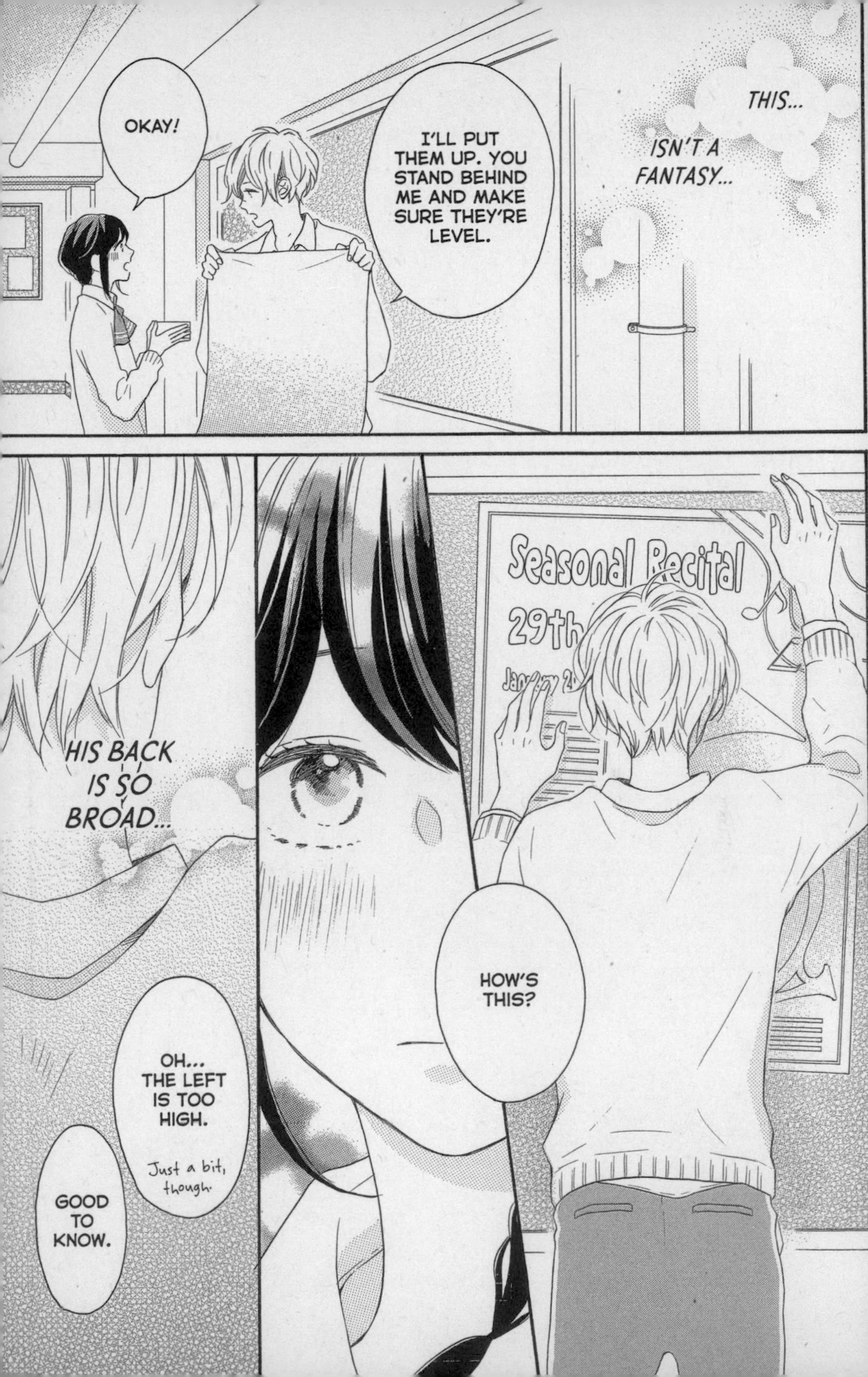
THIS...
ISN'T A FANTASY...
I'LL PUT THEM UP. YOU STAND BEHIND ME AND MAKE SURE THEY'RE LEVEL.
OKAY!
Seasonal Recital
29th
HOW'S THIS?
HIS BACK IS SO BROAD...
OH... THE LEFT IS TOO HIGH.
Just a bit, though.
GOOD TO KNOW.

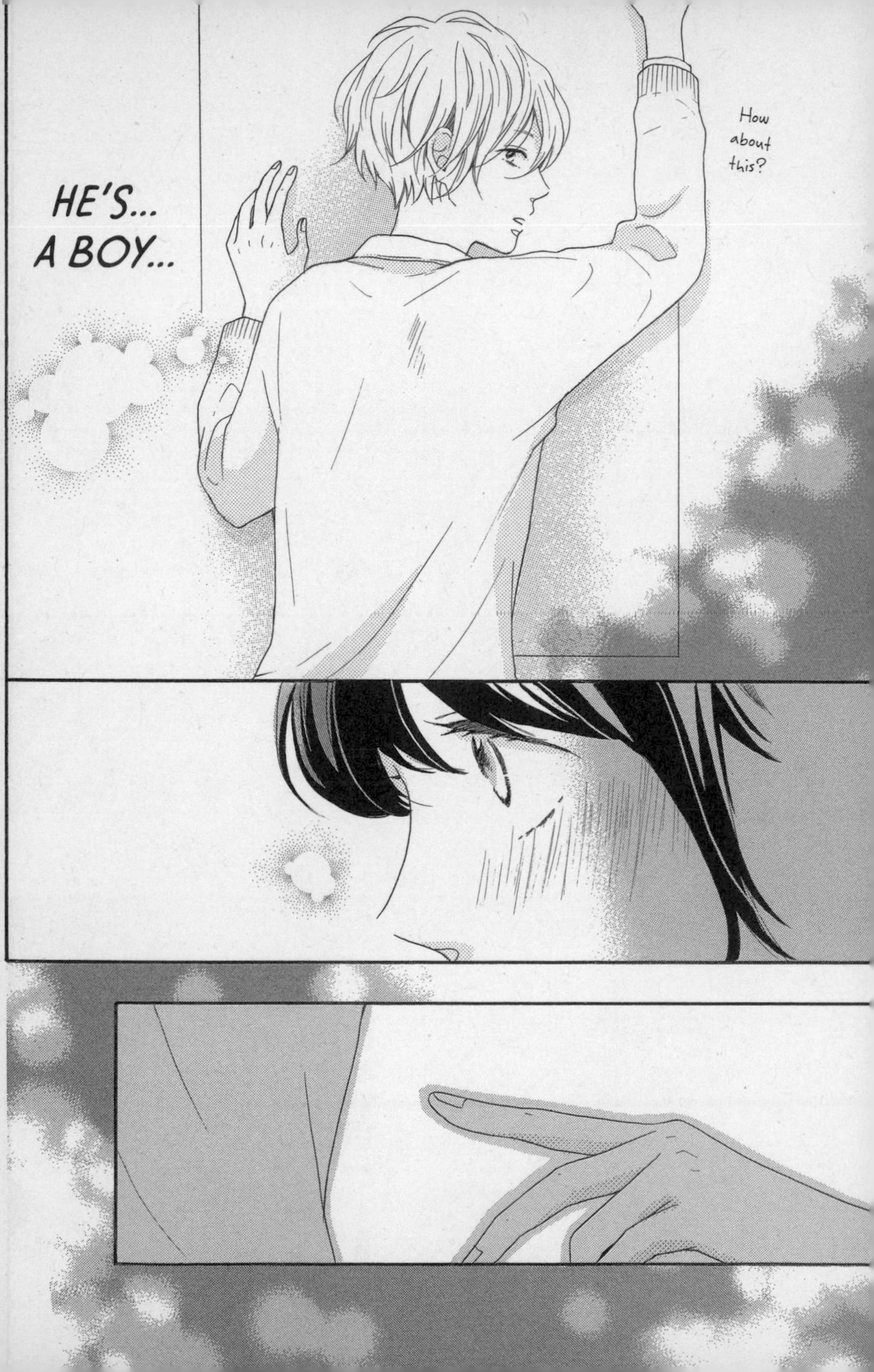
How about this?
HE'S... A BOY...

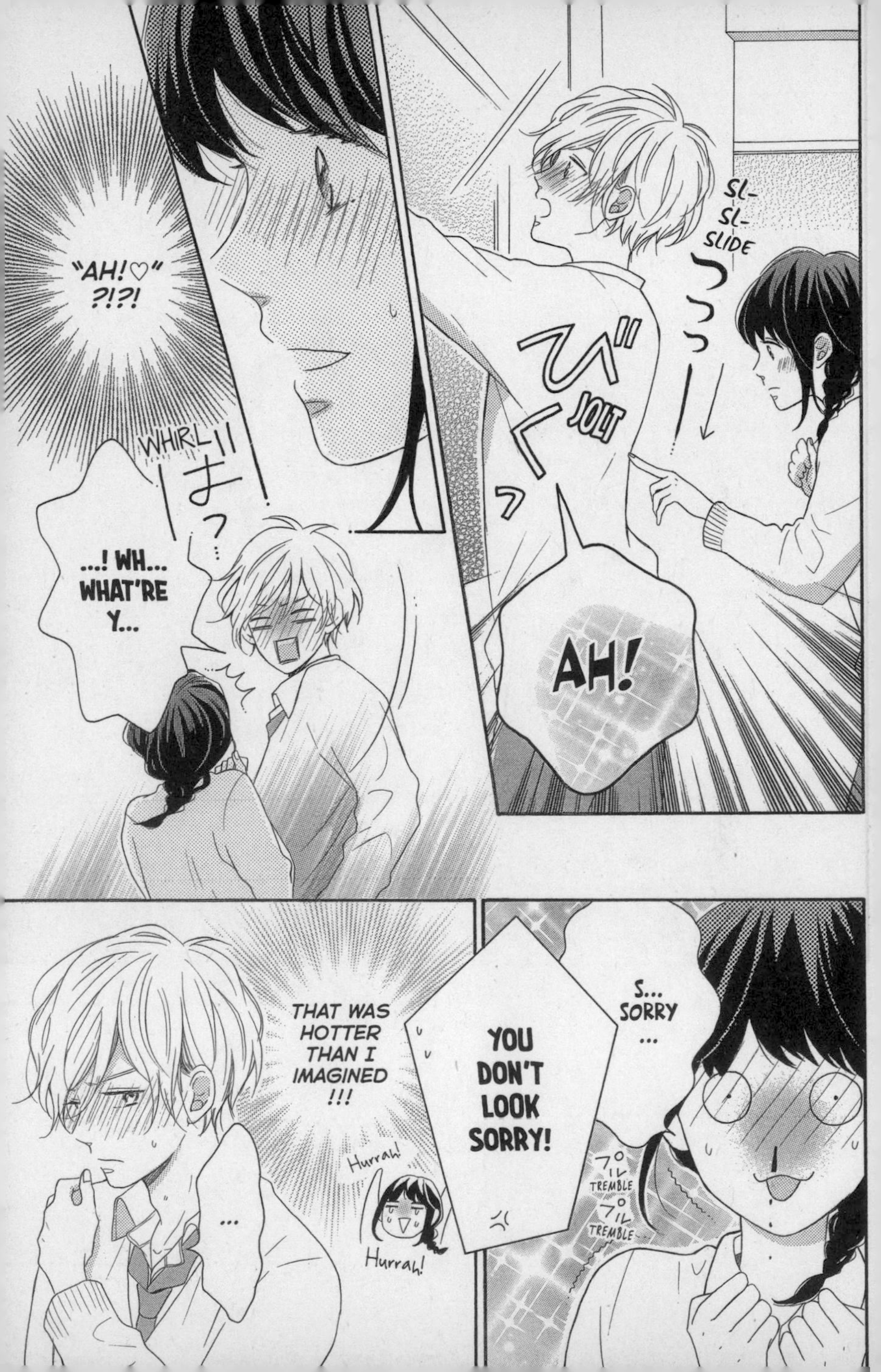
SL-SL-SLIDE
JOLT
AH!
"AH!♡" ?!?!
WHIRL
...! WH... WHAT'RE Y...
S... SORRY ...
YOU DON'T LOOK SORRY!
TREMBLE TREMBLE
THAT WAS HOTTER THAN I IMAGINED !!!
Hurrah! Hurrah!
...

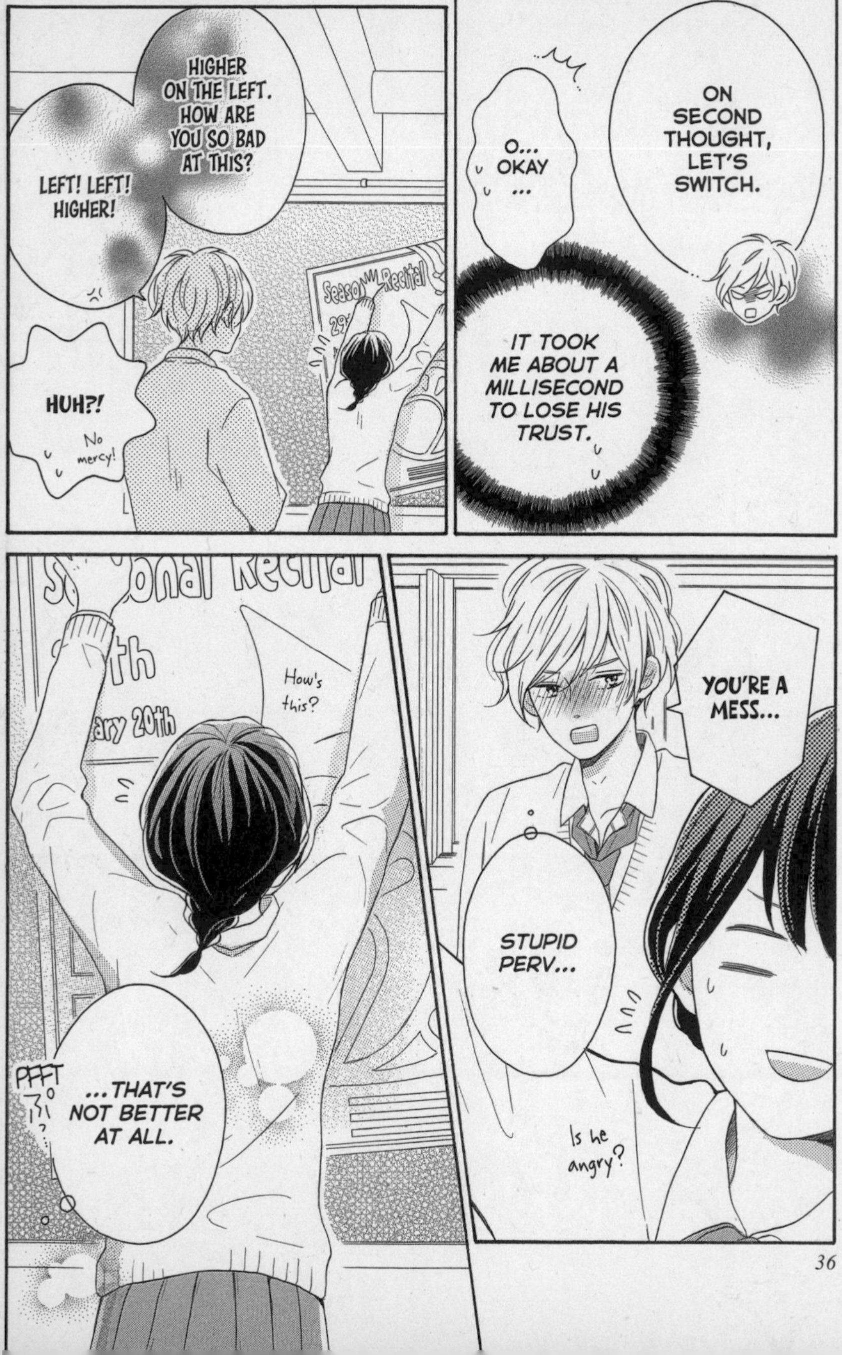
ON SECOND THOUGHT, LET'S SWITCH.
O... OKAY ...
IT TOOK ME ABOUT A MILLISECOND TO LOSE HIS TRUST.
HIGHER ON THE LEFT. HOW ARE YOU SO BAD AT THIS?
LEFT! LEFT! HIGHER!
Season Recital
HUH?!
No mercy!
YOU'RE A MESS...
STUPID PERV...
Is he angry?
How's this?
PFFT
...THAT'S NOT BETTER AT ALL.

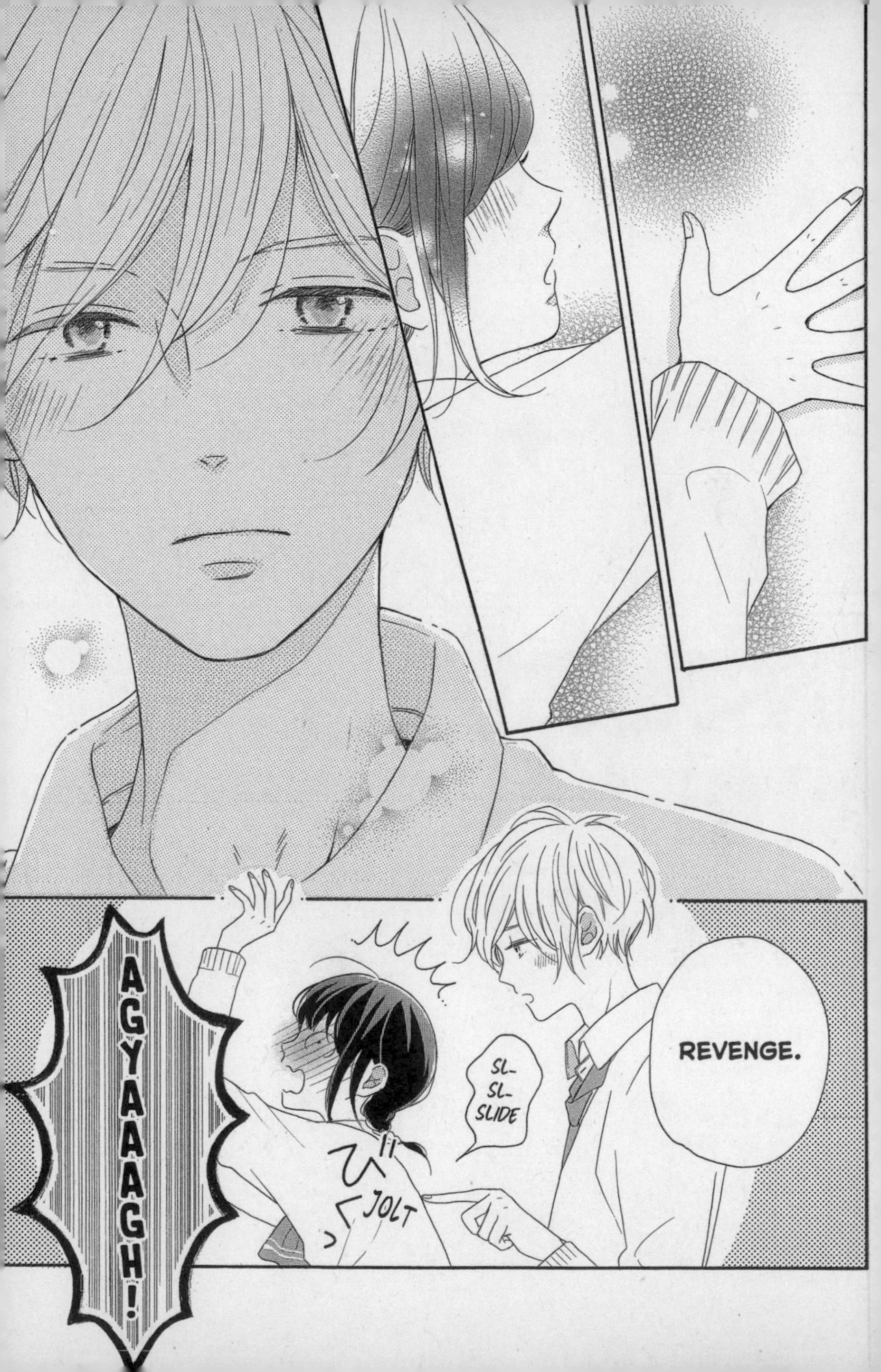
REVENGE.
SL-
SL-
SLIDE
JOLT
AGYAAAAGH!

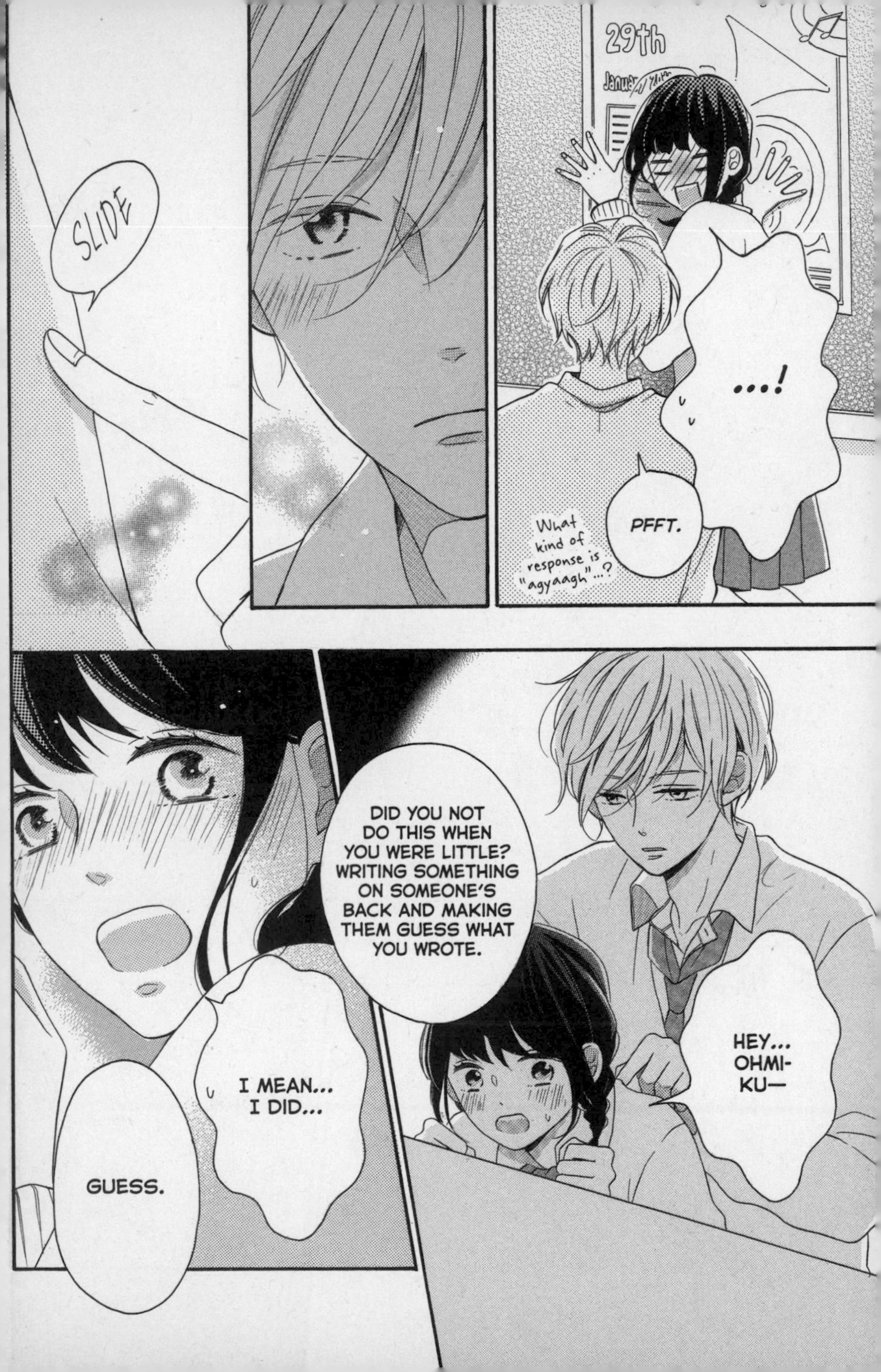
29th
...!
PFFT.
What kind of response is "agyaagh"...?
SLIDE
HEY... OHMI-KU—
DID YOU NOT DO THIS WHEN YOU WERE LITTLE? WRITING SOMETHING ON SOMEONE'S BACK AND MAKING THEM GUESS WHAT YOU WROTE.
I MEAN... I DID...
GUESS.

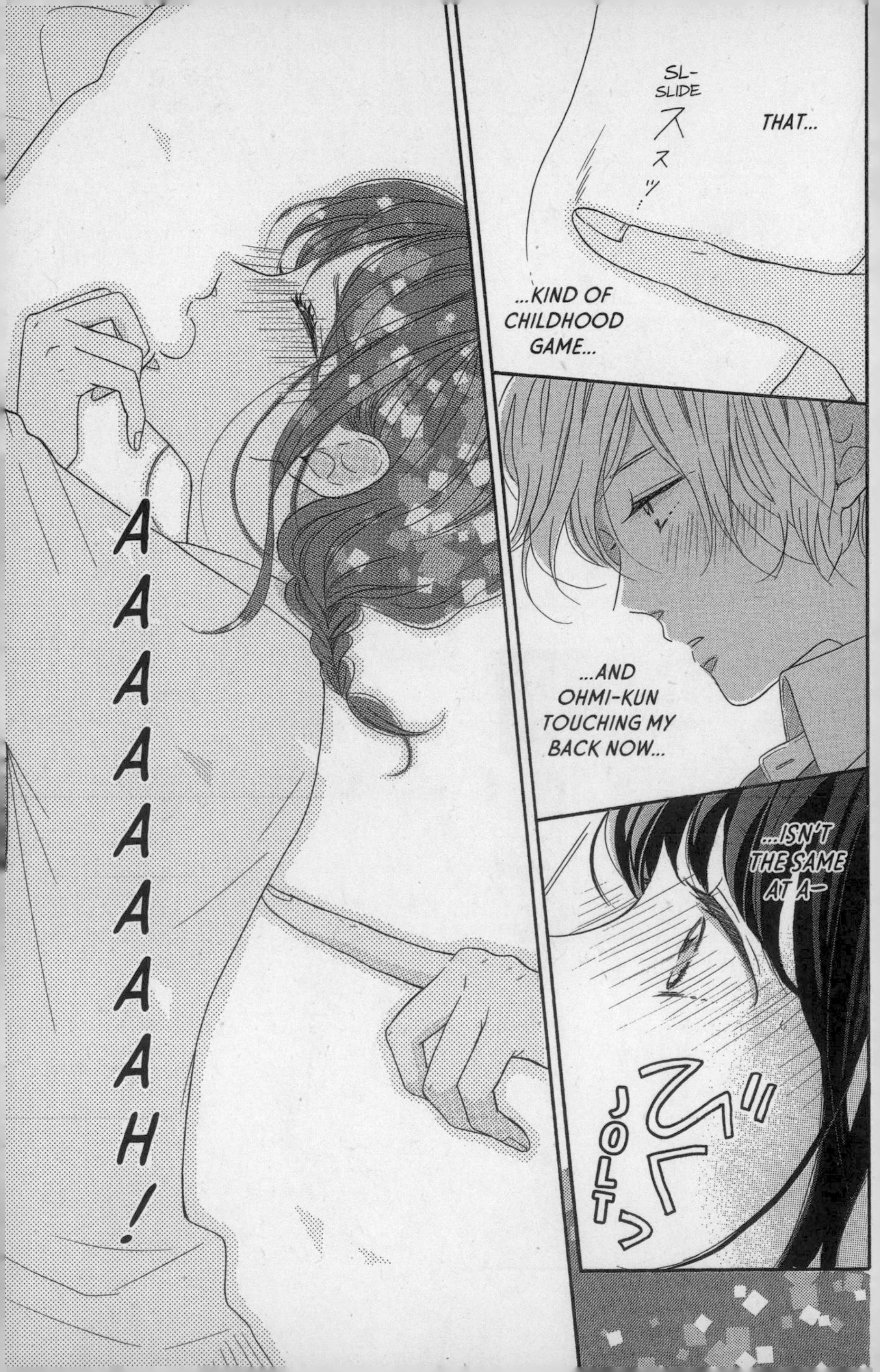
SL-
SLIDE
ススッ…
THAT...
...KIND OF CHILDHOOD GAME...
...AND OHMI-KUN TOUCHING MY BACK NOW...
...ISN'T THE SAME AT A-
JOLT
AAAAAAAAH!

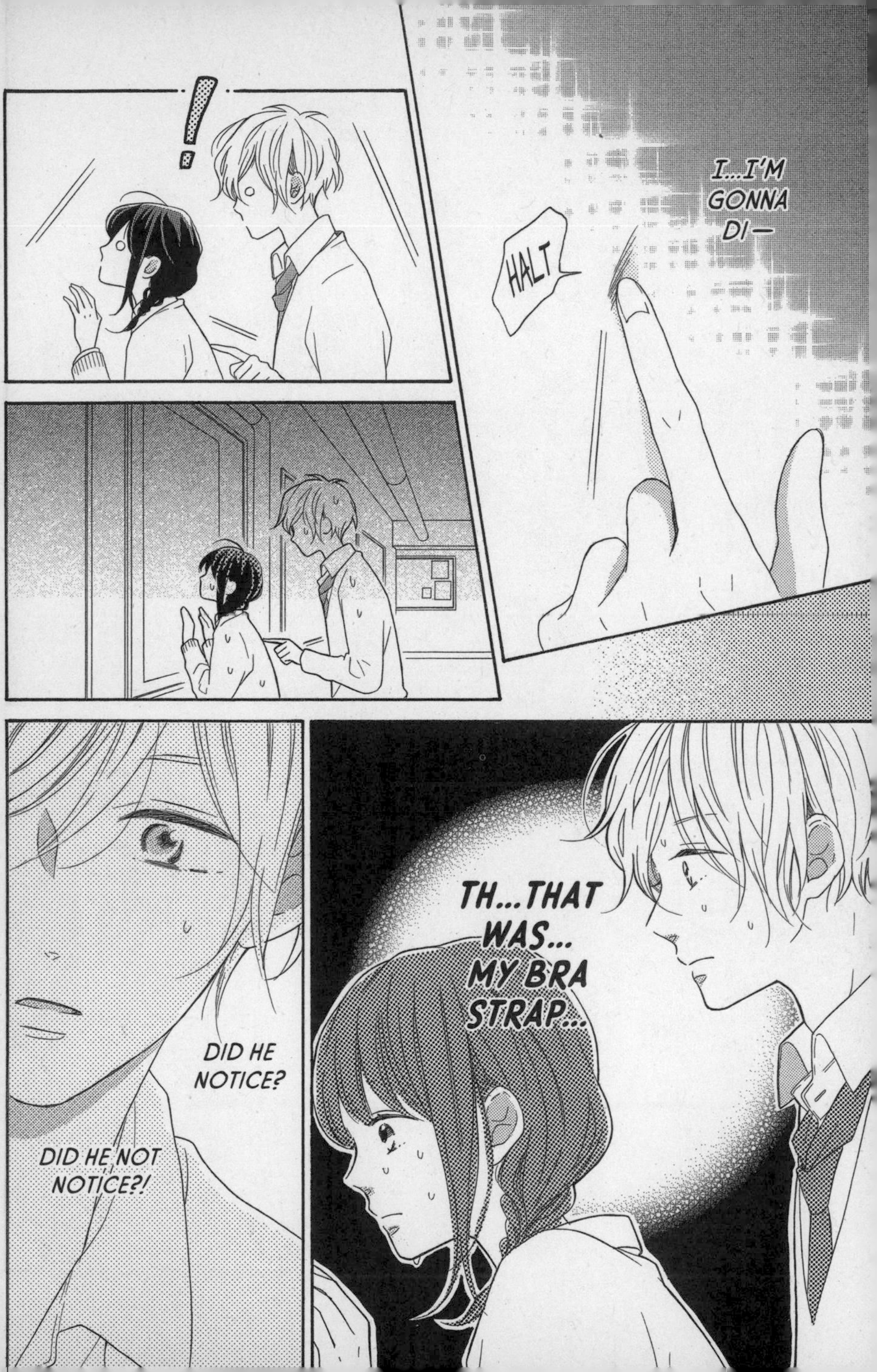
I...I'M GONNA DI—
HALT
!
TH...THAT WAS... MY BRA STRAP...
DID HE NOTICE?
DID HE NOT NOTICE?!

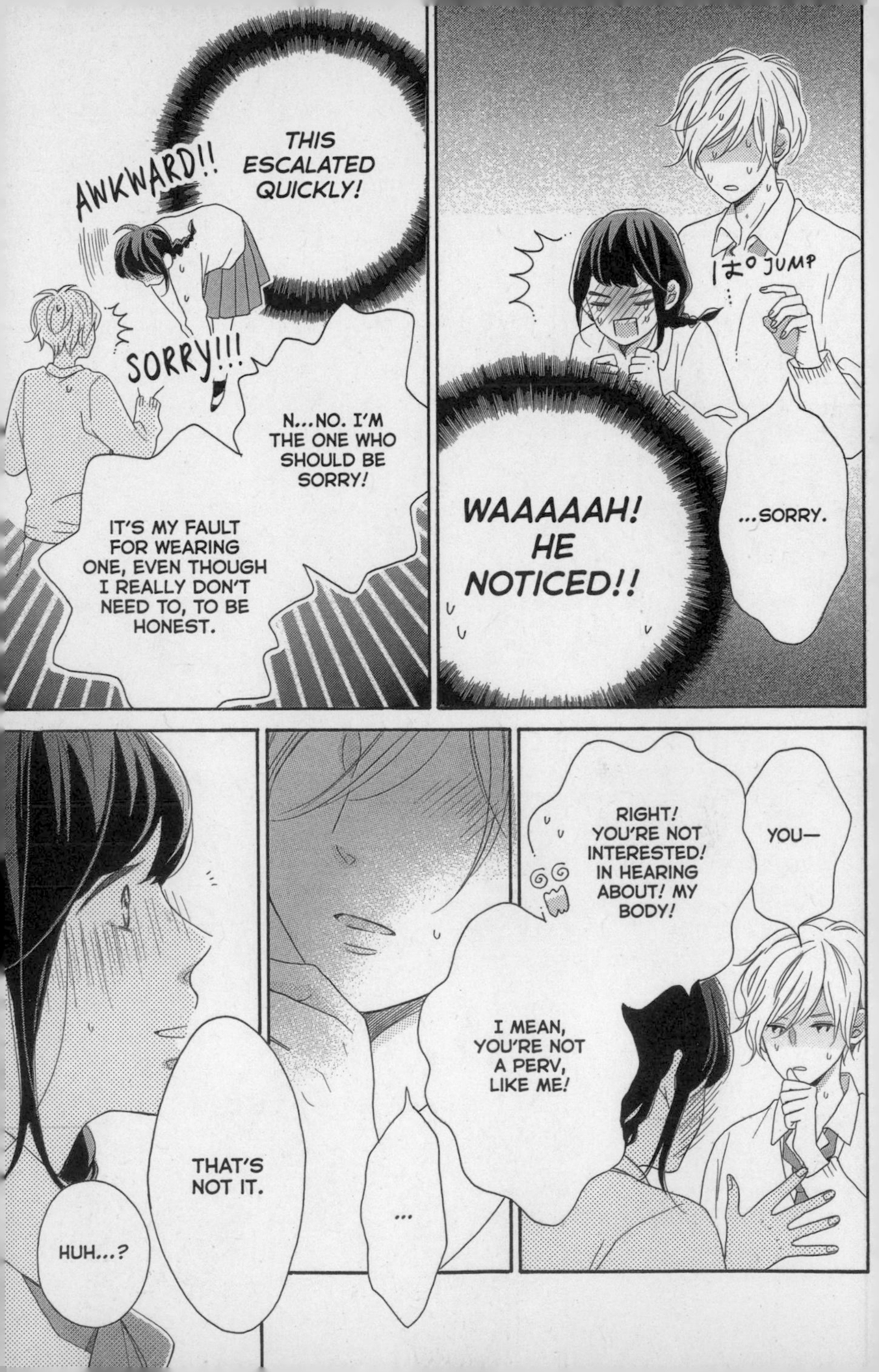

は° JUMP
...SORRY.
WAAAAAH! HE NOTICED!!
THIS ESCALATED QUICKLY!
AWKWARD!!
SORRY!!!
N...NO. I'M THE ONE WHO SHOULD BE SORRY!
IT'S MY FAULT FOR WEARING ONE, EVEN THOUGH I REALLY DON'T NEED TO, TO BE HONEST.
YOU—
RIGHT! YOU'RE NOT INTERESTED! IN HEARING ABOUT! MY BODY!
I MEAN, YOU'RE NOT A PERV, LIKE ME!
...
THAT'S NOT IT.
HUH...?

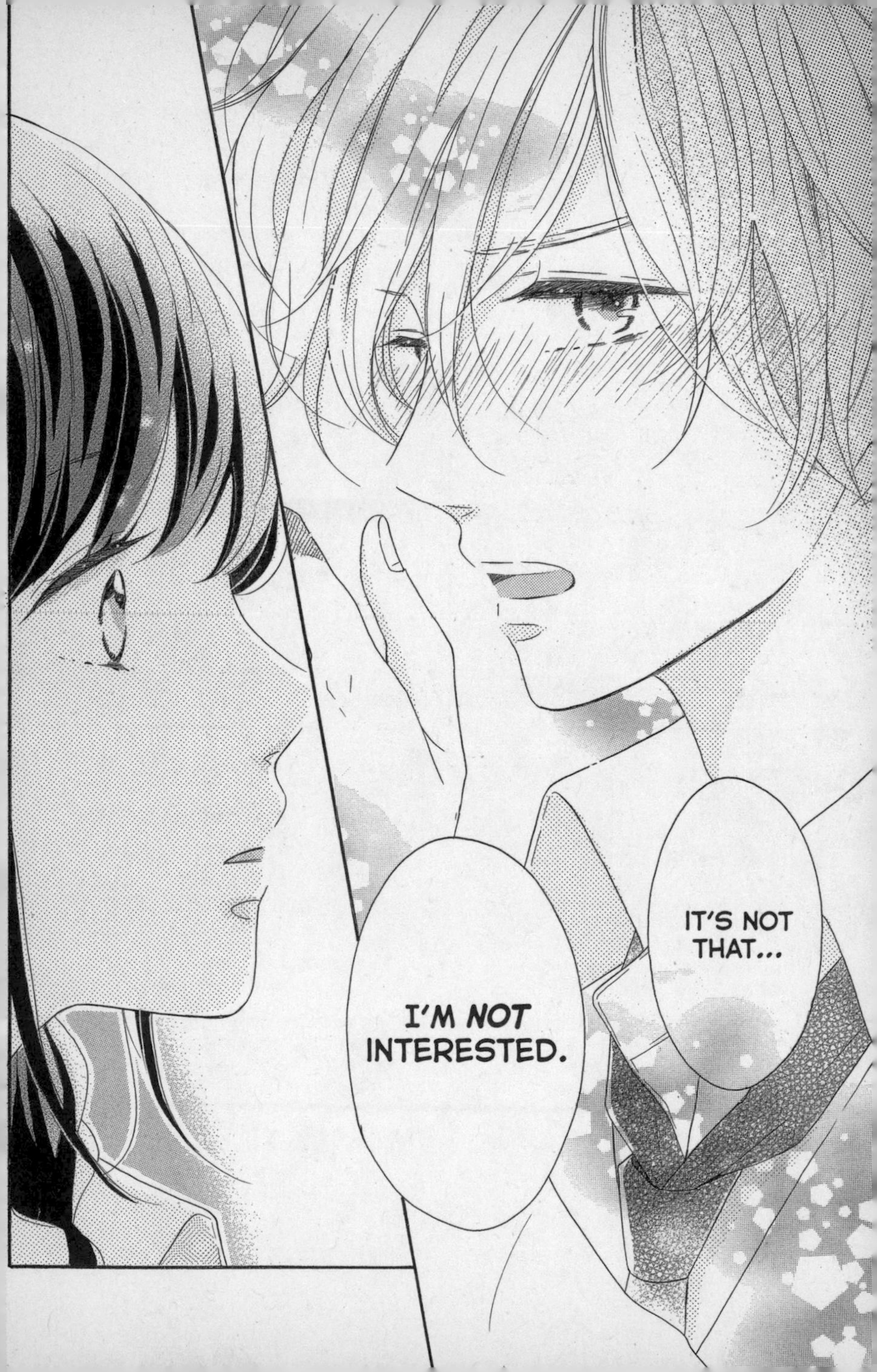
IT'S NOT THAT...
I'M *NOT* INTERESTED.

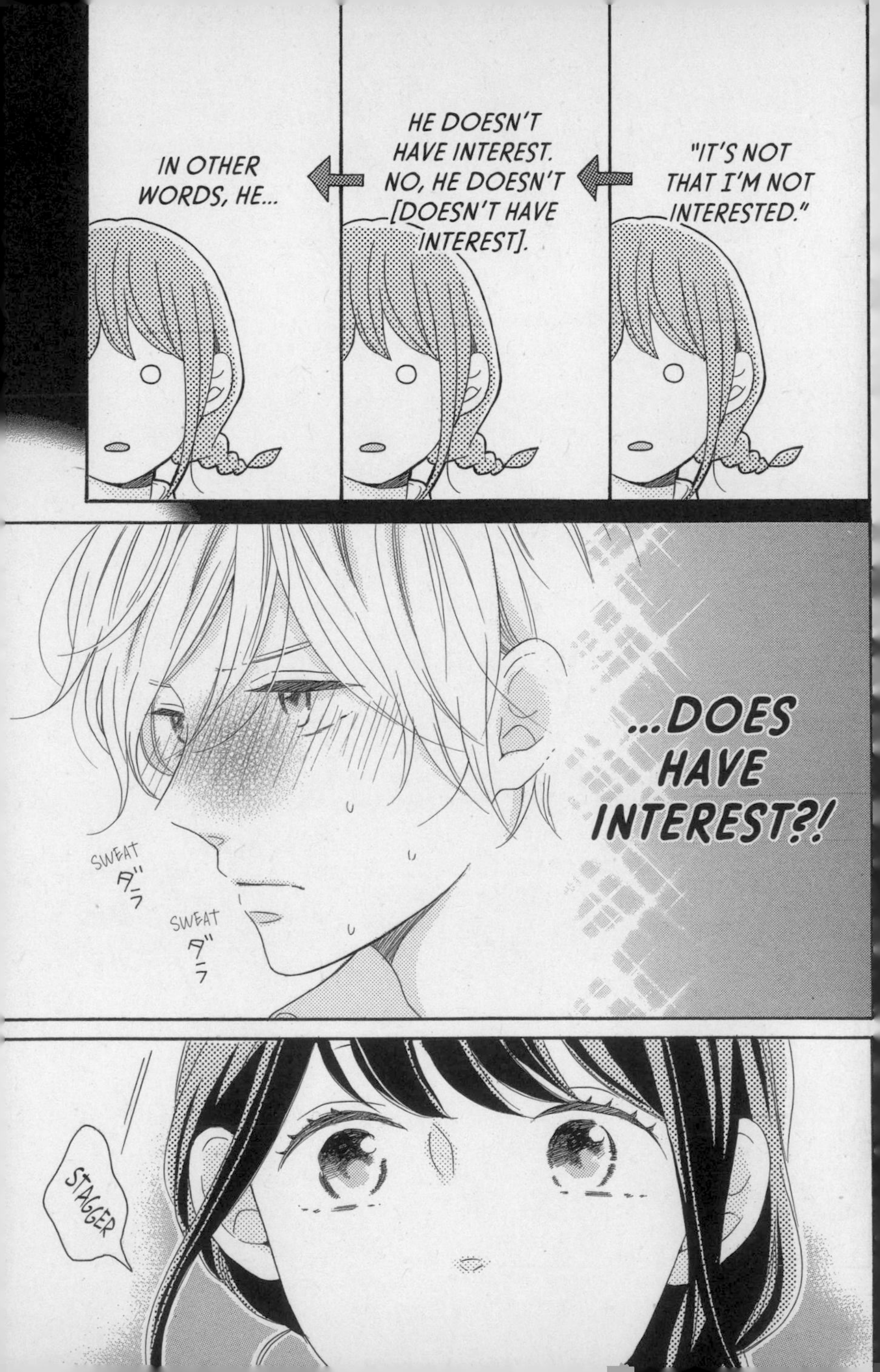
"IT'S NOT THAT I'M NOT INTERESTED."
HE DOESN'T HAVE INTEREST. NO, HE DOESN'T [DOESN'T HAVE INTEREST].
IN OTHER WORDS, HE...
...DOES HAVE INTEREST?!
SWEAT ダラ
SWEAT ダラ
STAGGER

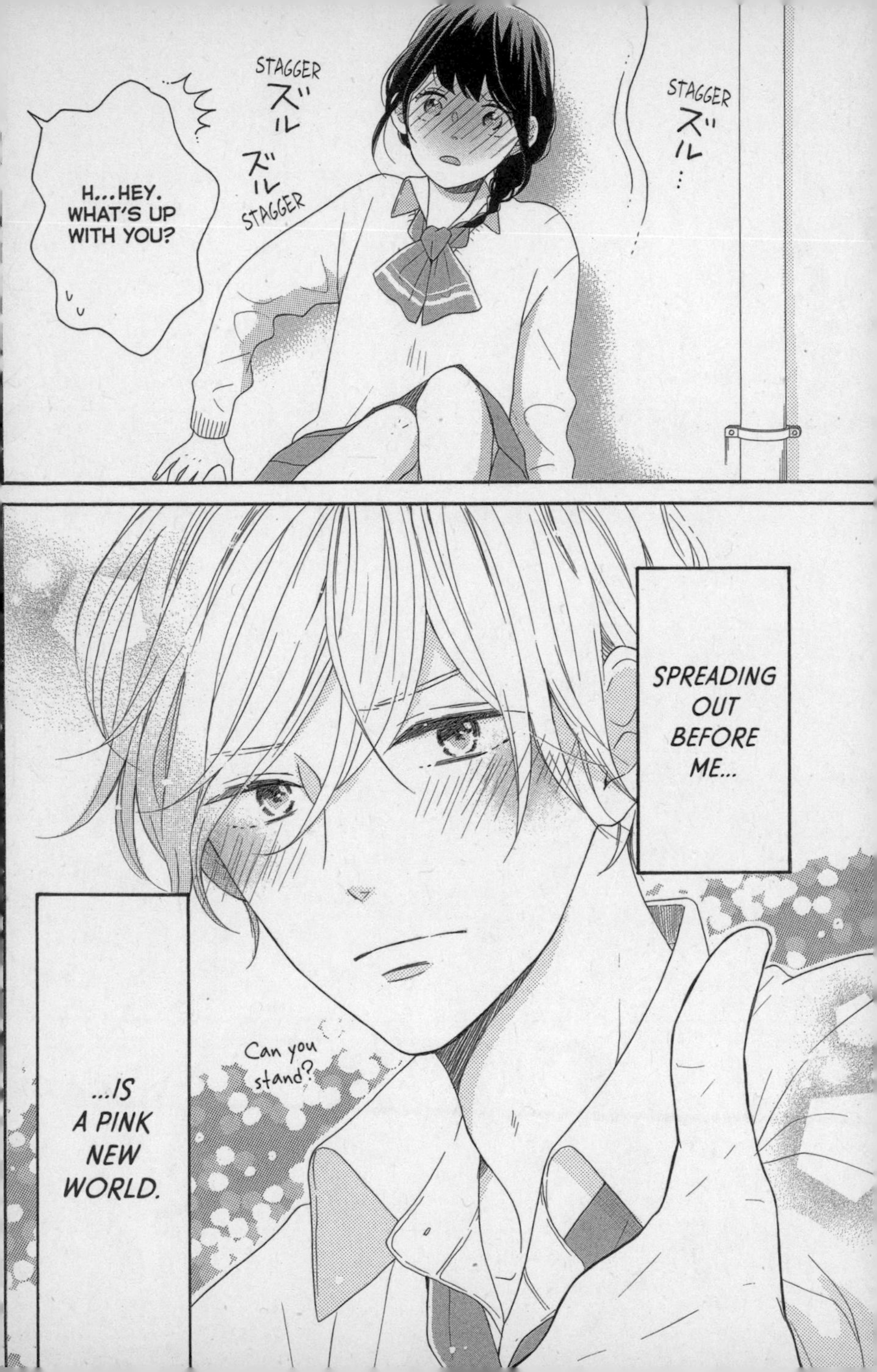
STAGGER
ズル…
STAGGER
ズル
ズル
STAGGER
H...HEY. WHAT'S UP WITH YOU?
SPREADING OUT BEFORE ME...
Can you stand?
...IS A PINK NEW WORLD.

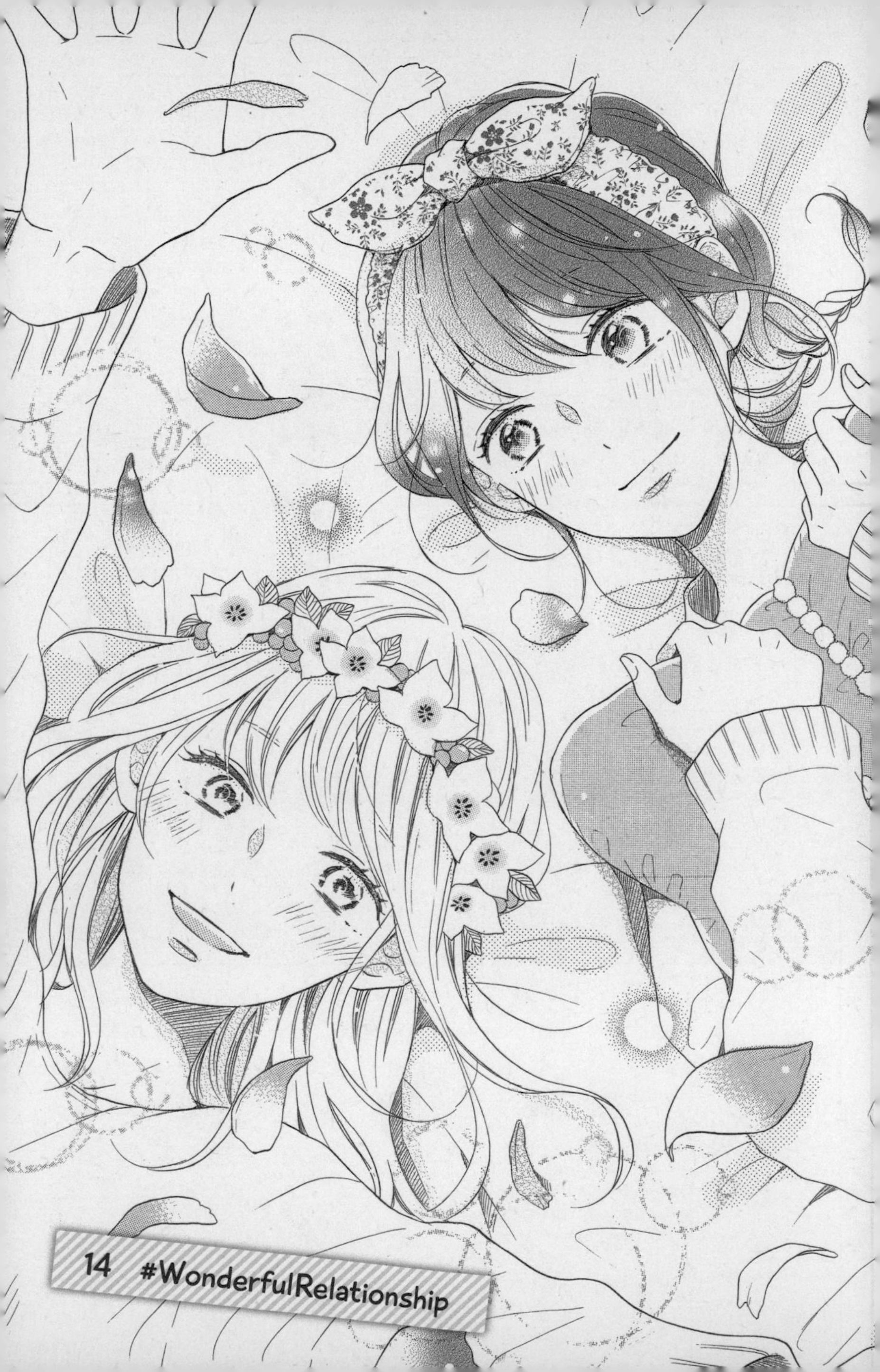
14 #WonderfulRelationship

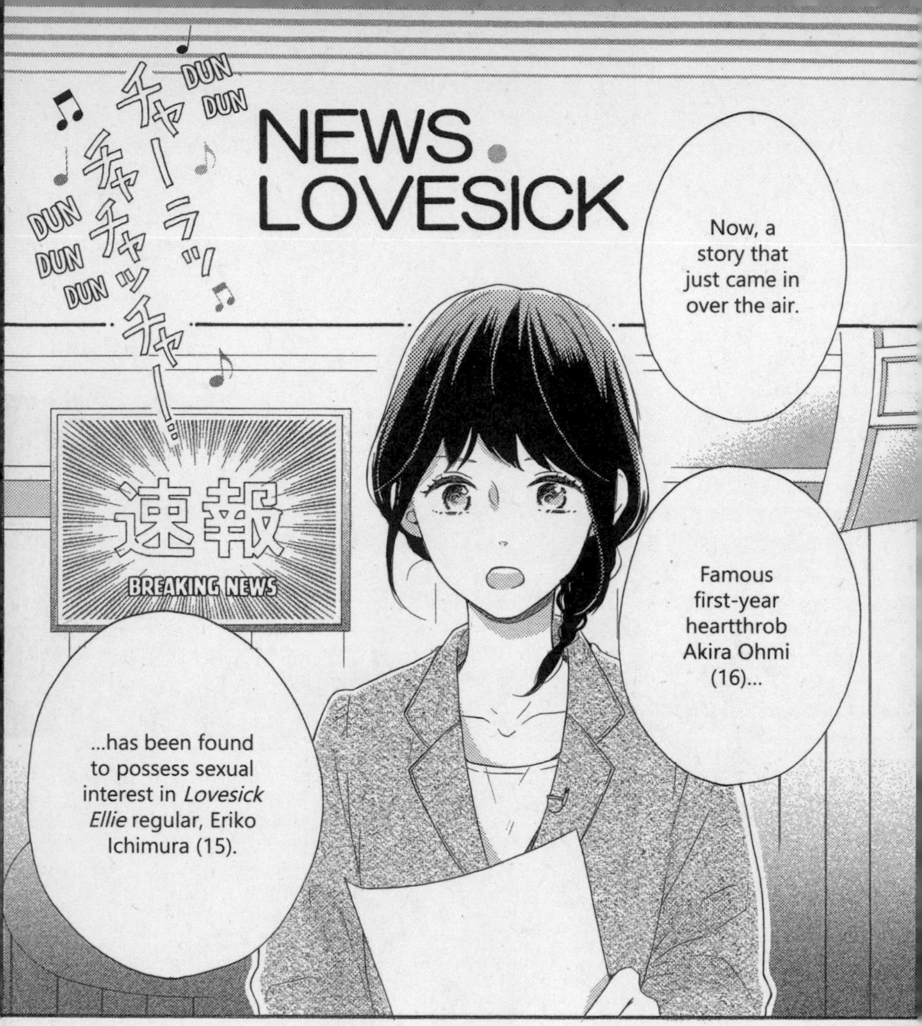
NEWS LOVESICK
チャーラッチャッチャー!
DUN DUN
DUN DUN DUN
速報
BREAKING NEWS
Now, a story that just came in over the air.
Famous first-year heartthrob Akira Ohmi (16)...
...has been found to possess sexual interest in *Lovesick Ellie* regular, Eriko Ichimura (15).

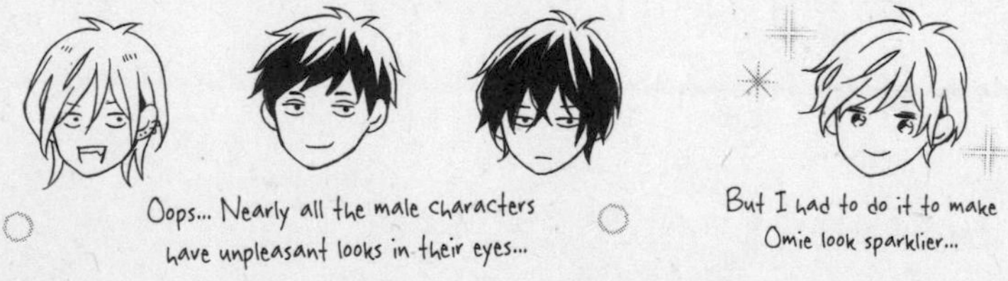
Oops... Nearly all the male characters have unpleasant looks in their eyes...
But I had to do it to make Omie look sparklier...

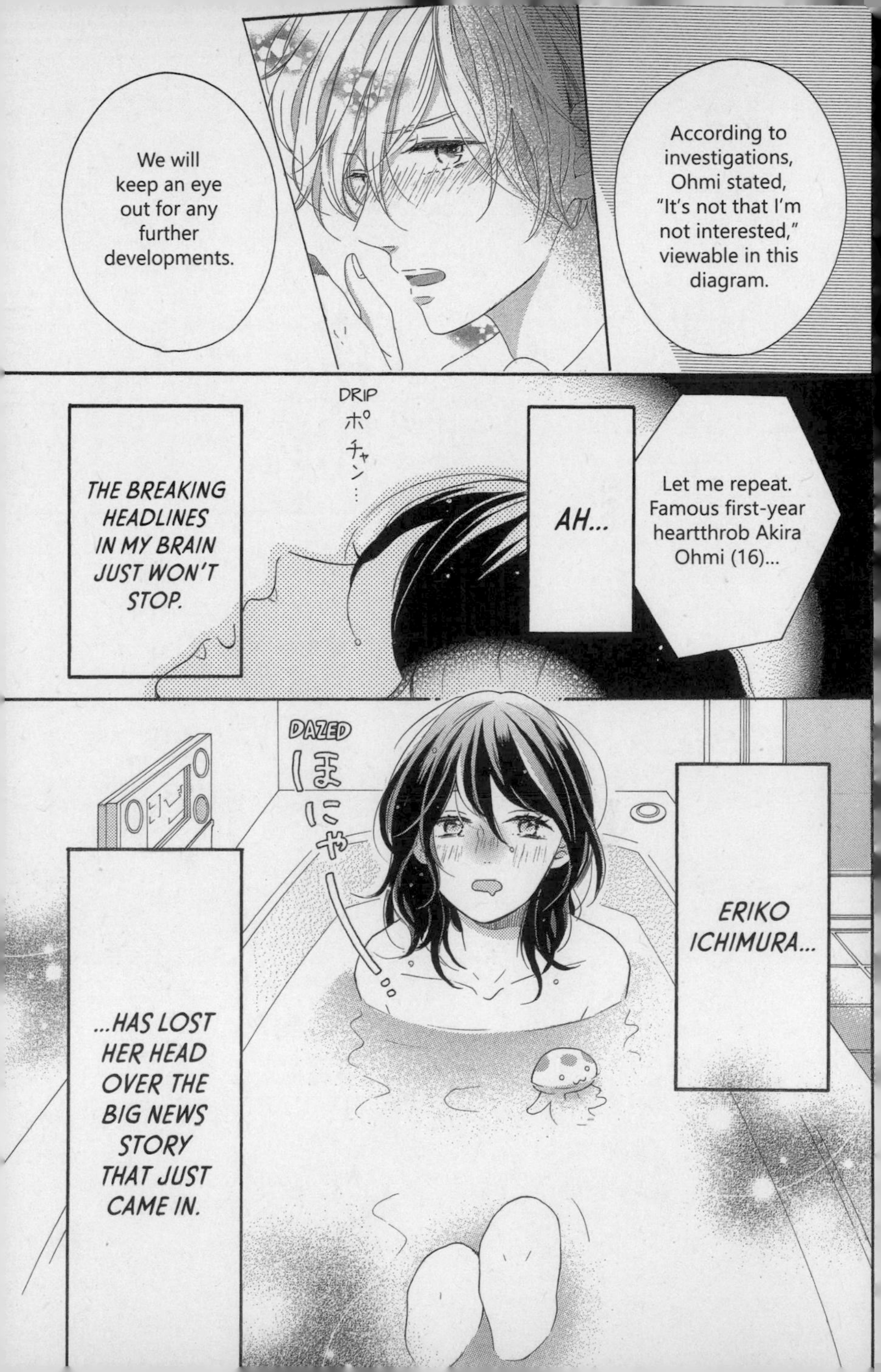
According to investigations, Ohmi stated, “It’s not that I’m not interested,” viewable in this diagram.
We will keep an eye out for any further developments.
Let me repeat. Famous first-year heartthrob Akira Ohmi (16)...
AH...
DRIP
ポチャン…
THE BREAKING HEADLINES IN MY BRAIN JUST WON’T STOP.
ERIKO ICHIMURA...
DAZED
ほにゃー
...HAS LOST HER HEAD OVER THE BIG NEWS STORY THAT JUST CAME IN.

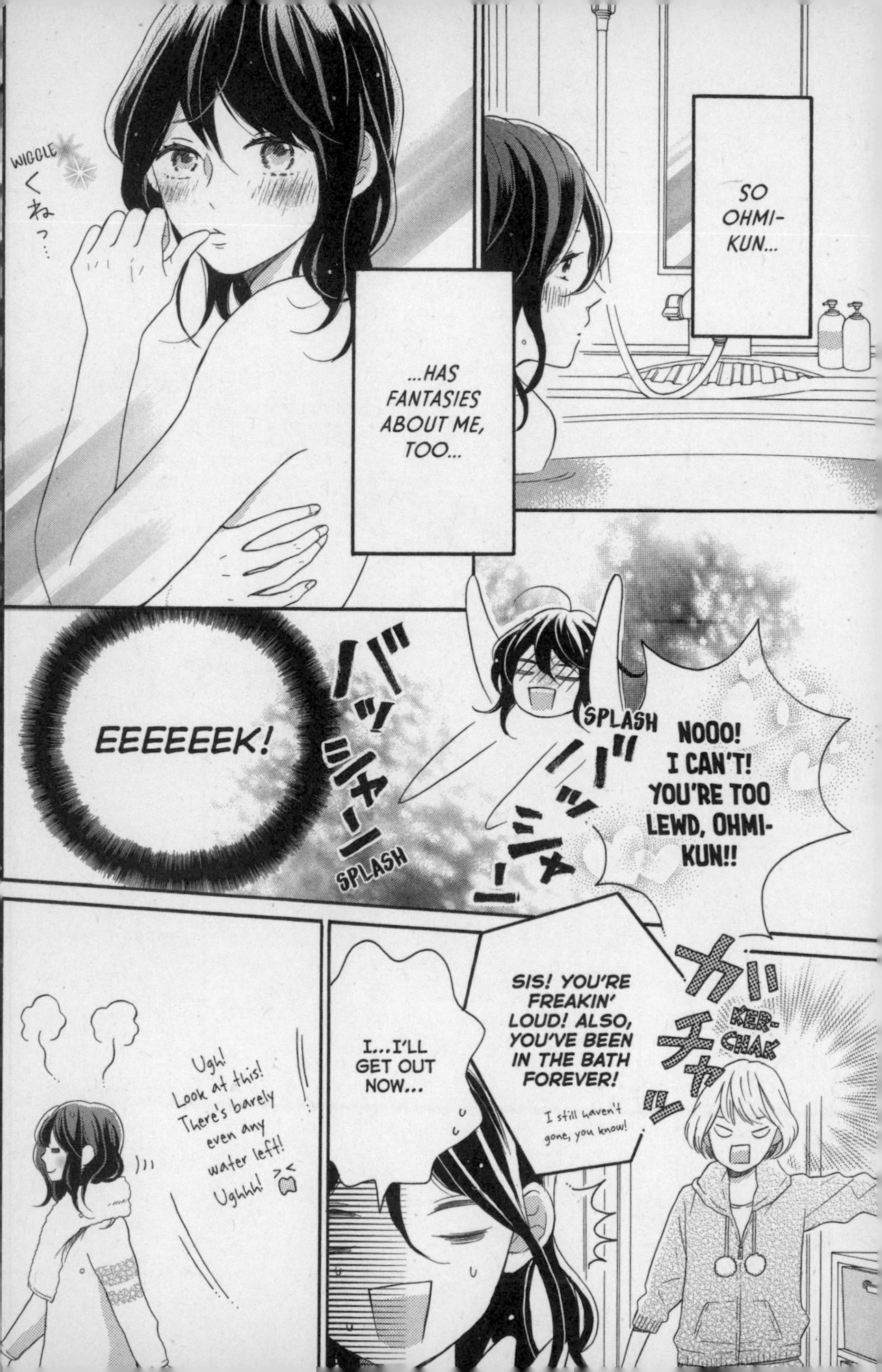
SO OHMI-KUN...
...HAS FANTASIES ABOUT ME, TOO...
WIGGLE
くねっ…
NOOO! I CAN'T! YOU'RE TOO LEWD, OHMI-KUN!!
SPLASH
バッシャーン
EEEEEEK!
バッシャーン
SPLASH
ガチャッ
KER-CHAK
SIS! YOU'RE FREAKIN' LOUD! ALSO, YOU'VE BEEN IN THE BATH FOREVER!
I still haven't gone, you know!
I...I'LL GET OUT NOW...
Ugh! Look at this! There's barely even any water left! Ughhh!

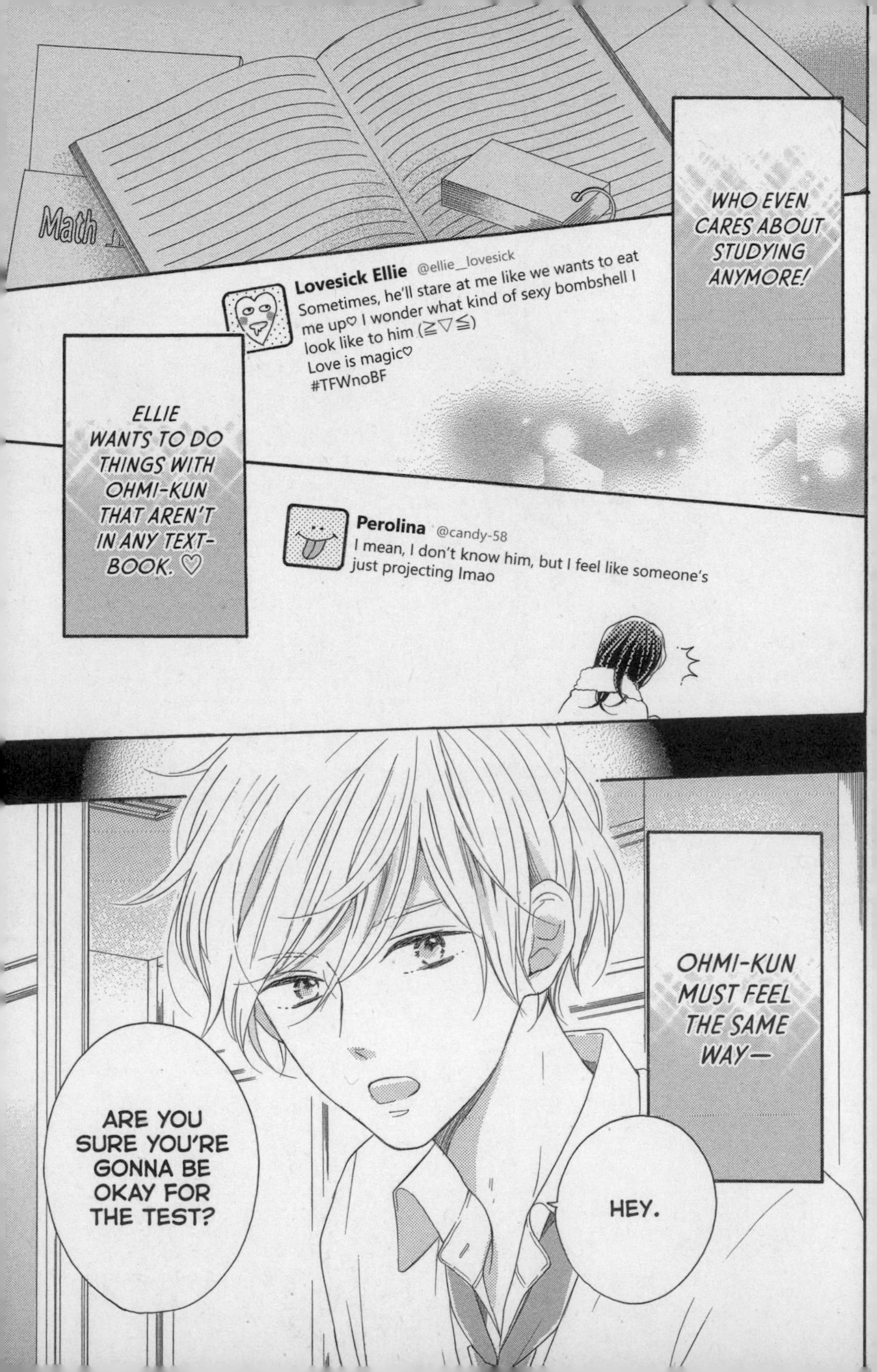
WHO EVEN CARES ABOUT STUDYING ANYMORE!
Math
Lovesick Ellie @ellie__lovesick
Sometimes, he'll stare at me like we wants to eat me up♡ I wonder what kind of sexy bombshell I look like to him (≧▽≦)
Love is magic♡
#TFWnoBF
ELLIE WANTS TO DO THINGS WITH OHMI-KUN THAT AREN'T IN ANY TEXT-BOOK. ♡
Perolina @candy-58
I mean, I don't know him, but I feel like someone's just projecting lmao
OHMI-KUN MUST FEEL THE SAME WAY—
HEY.
ARE YOU SURE YOU'RE GONNA BE OKAY FOR THE TEST?

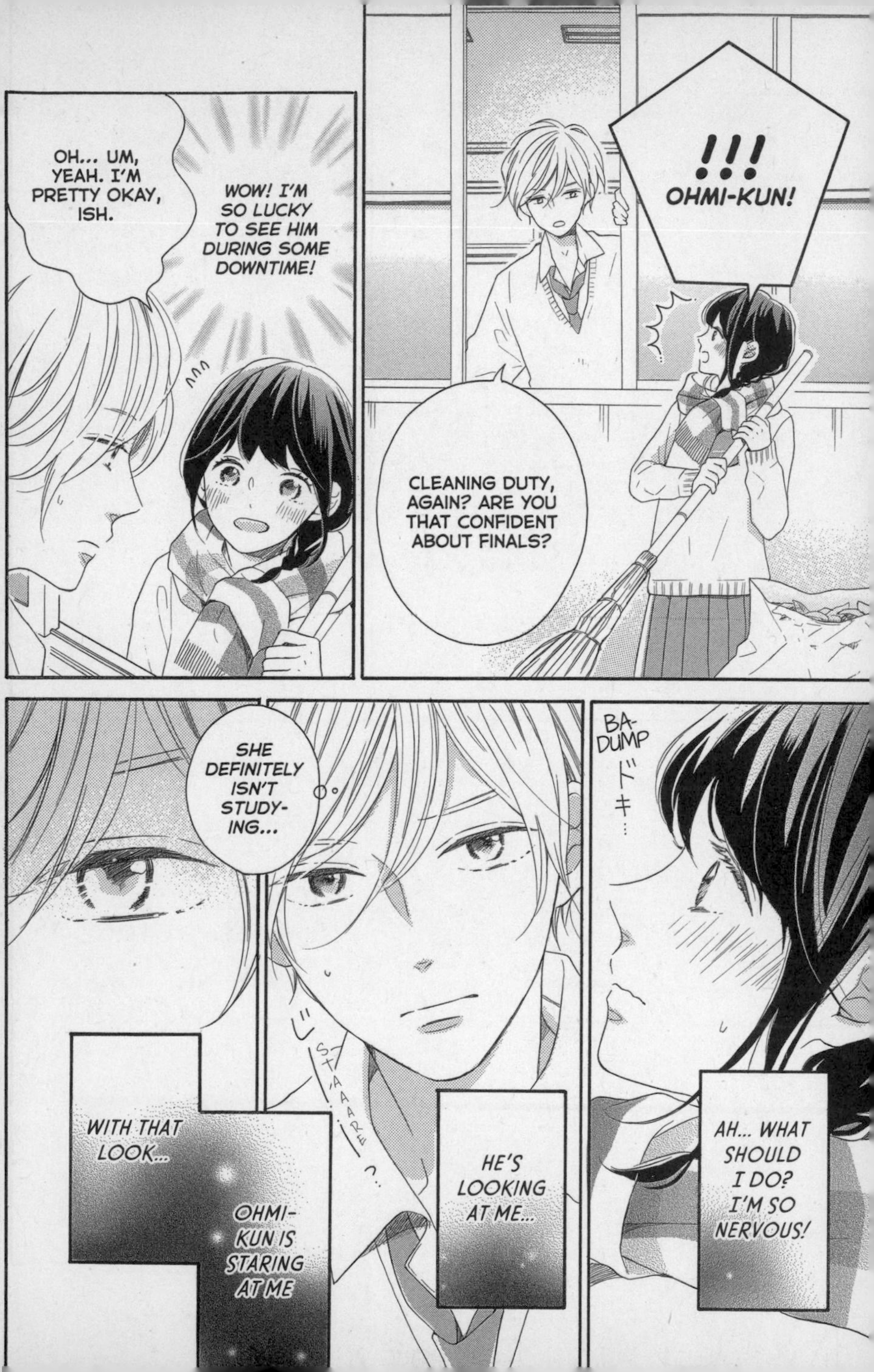
!!!
OHMI-KUN!
CLEANING DUTY, AGAIN? ARE YOU THAT CONFIDENT ABOUT FINALS?
WOW! I'M SO LUCKY TO SEE HIM DURING SOME DOWNTIME!
OH... UM, YEAH. I'M PRETTY OKAY, ISH.
BA-DUMP
ドキ…
AH... WHAT SHOULD I DO? I'M SO NERVOUS!
SHE DEFINITELY ISN'T STUDYING...
じ
STAAARE
HE'S LOOKING AT ME...
WITH THAT LOOK...
OHMI-KUN IS STARING AT ME

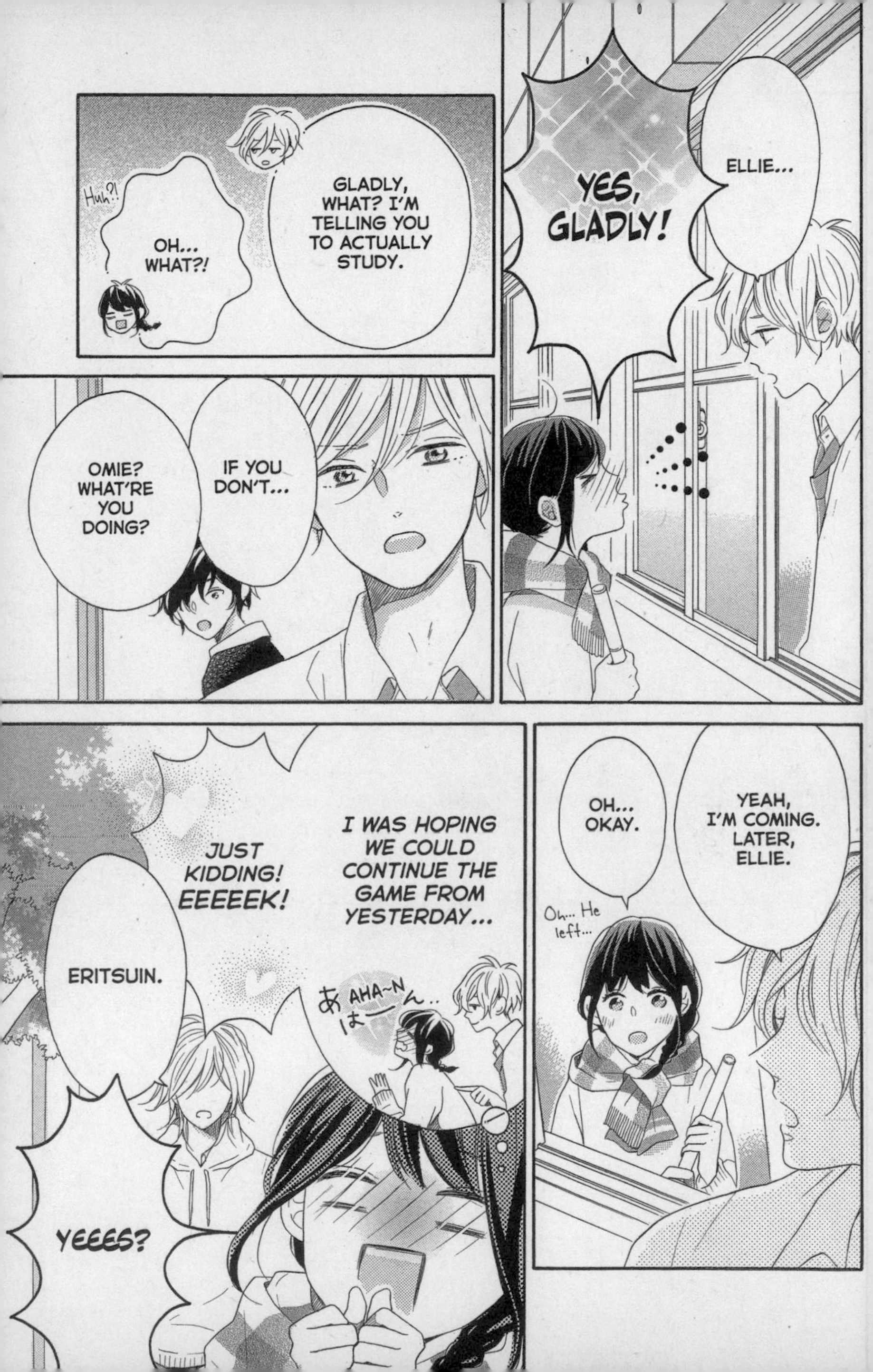
ELLIE...
YES, GLADLY!
GLADLY, WHAT? I'M TELLING YOU TO ACTUALLY STUDY.
Huh?!
OH... WHAT?!
IF YOU DON'T...
OMIE? WHAT'RE YOU DOING?
YEAH, I'M COMING. LATER, ELLIE.
OH... OKAY.
Oh... He left...
I WAS HOPING WE COULD CONTINUE THE GAME FROM YESTERDAY...
JUST KIDDING! EEEEEK!
AHA~N
あはーん..
ERITSUIN.
YEEES?

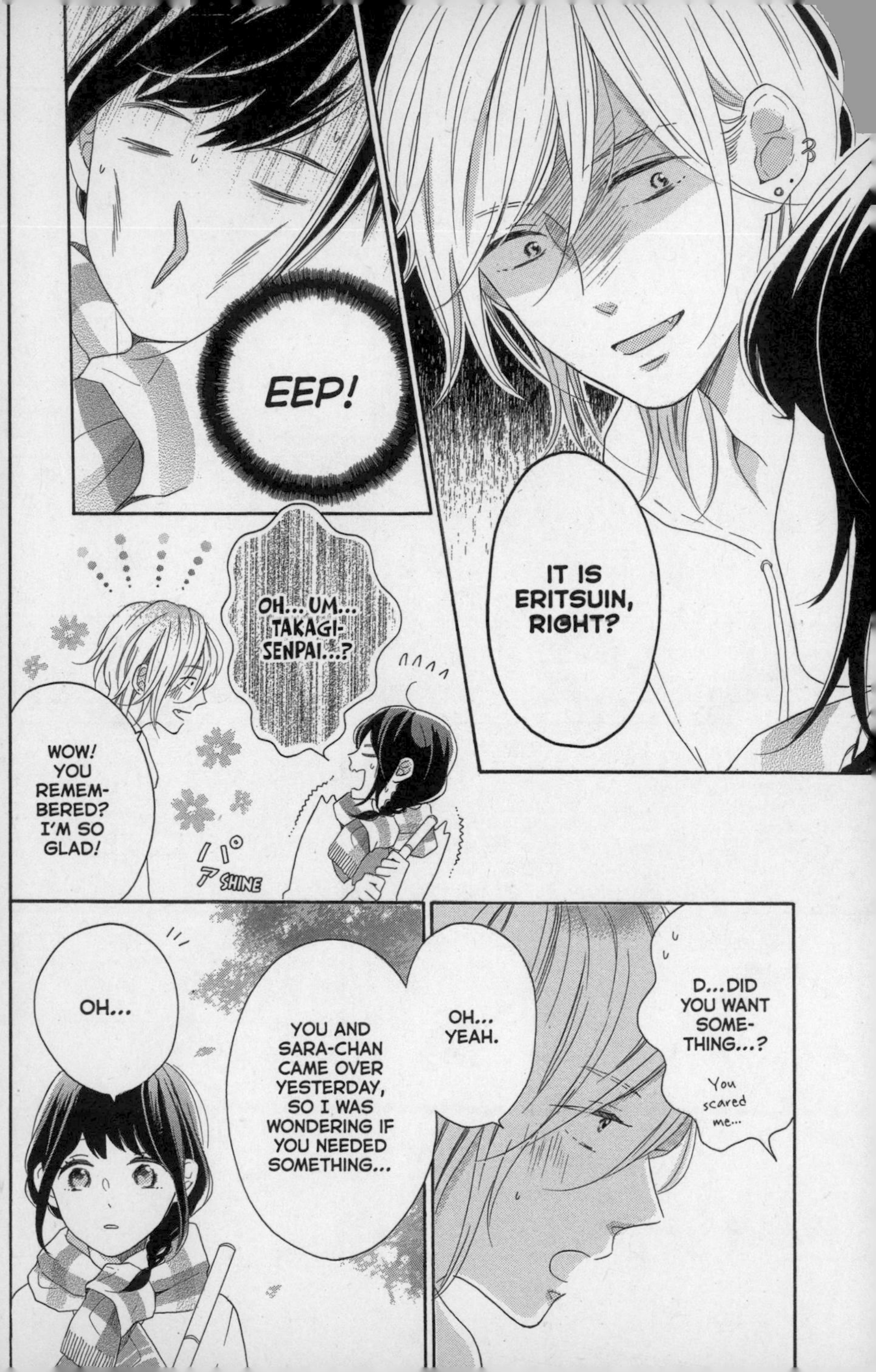
IT IS ERITSUIN, RIGHT?
EEP!
OH... UM... TAKAGI-SENPAI...?
WOW! YOU REMEMBERED? I'M SO GLAD!
SHINE
D...DID YOU WANT SOMETHING...?
You scared me...
OH... YEAH.
YOU AND SARA-CHAN CAME OVER YESTERDAY, SO I WAS WONDERING IF YOU NEEDED SOMETHING...
OH...

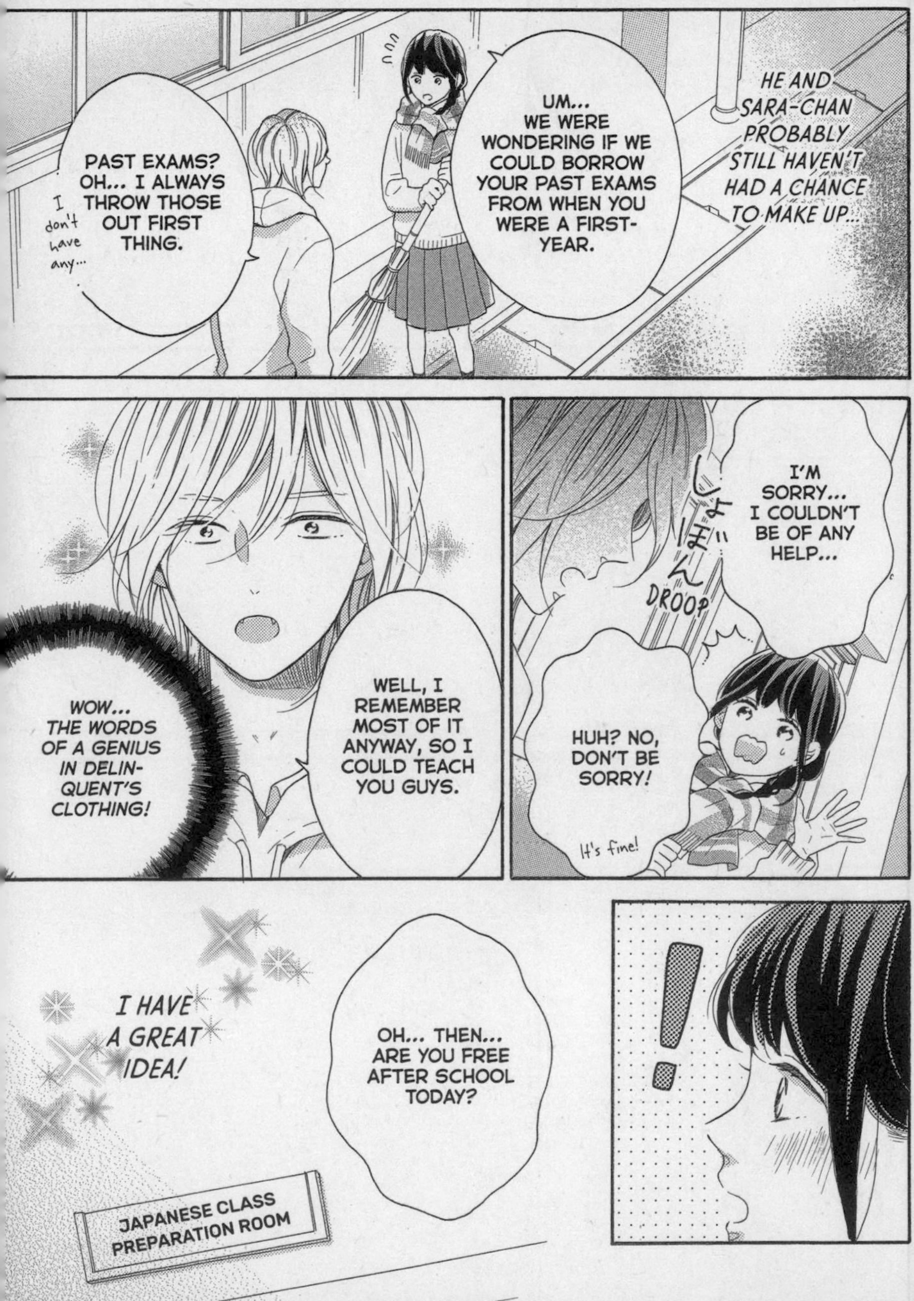
HE AND SARA-CHAN PROBABLY STILL HAVEN'T HAD A CHANCE TO MAKE UP...
UM... WE WERE WONDERING IF WE COULD BORROW YOUR PAST EXAMS FROM WHEN YOU WERE A FIRST-YEAR.
PAST EXAMS? OH... I ALWAYS THROW THOSE OUT FIRST THING.
I don't have any...
I'M SORRY... I COULDN'T BE OF ANY HELP...
しょぼーん
DROOP
HUH? NO, DON'T BE SORRY!
It's fine!
WELL, I REMEMBER MOST OF IT ANYWAY, SO I COULD TEACH YOU GUYS.
WOW... THE WORDS OF A GENIUS IN DELIN-QUENT'S CLOTHING!
!
OH... THEN... ARE YOU FREE AFTER SCHOOL TODAY?
I HAVE A GREAT IDEA!
JAPANESE CLASS PREPARATION ROOM

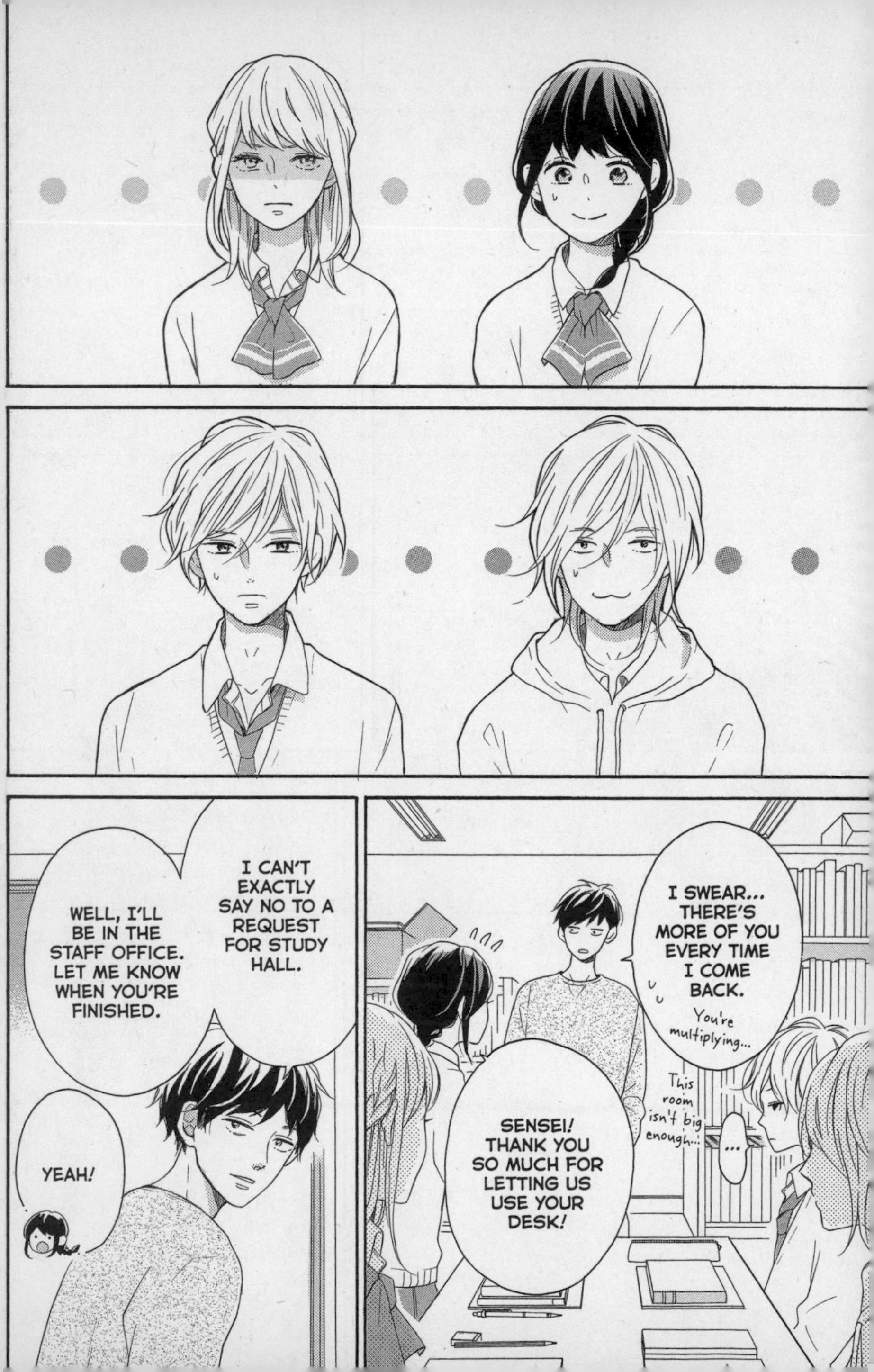
I SWEAR... THERE'S MORE OF YOU EVERY TIME I COME BACK.
You're multiplying...
This room isn't big enough...
...
SENSEI! THANK YOU SO MUCH FOR LETTING US USE YOUR DESK!
I CAN'T EXACTLY SAY NO TO A REQUEST FOR STUDY HALL.
WELL, I'LL BE IN THE STAFF OFFICE. LET ME KNOW WHEN YOU'RE FINISHED.
YEAH!

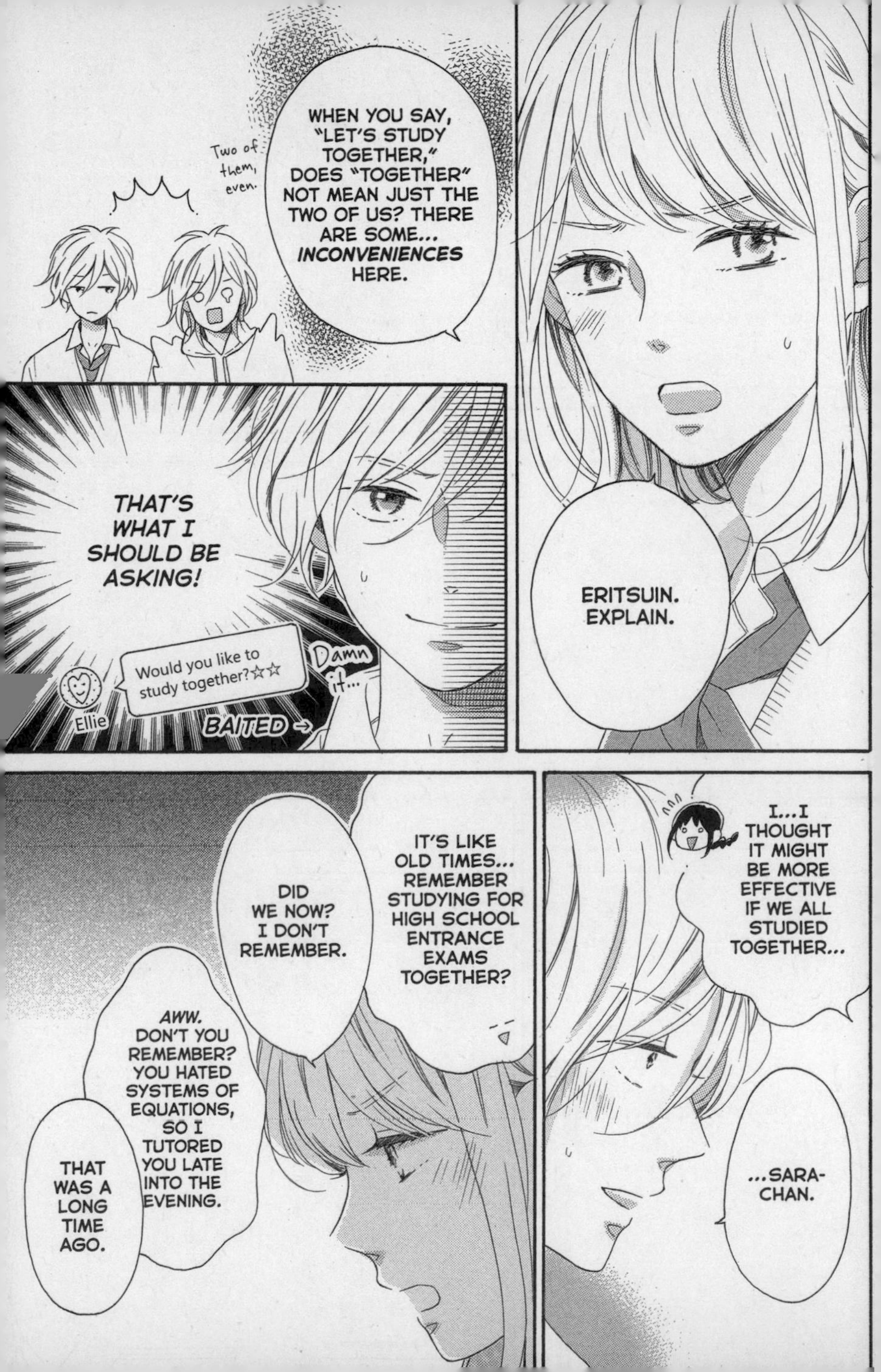
ERITSUIN. EXPLAIN.
WHEN YOU SAY, "LET'S STUDY TOGETHER," DOES "TOGETHER" NOT MEAN JUST THE TWO OF US? THERE ARE SOME... *INCONVENIENCES* HERE.
Two of them, even.
*THAT'S WHAT I SHOULD BE ASKING!*
Damn it...
Would you like to study together?☆☆
Ellie
BAITED →
I...I THOUGHT IT MIGHT BE MORE EFFECTIVE IF WE ALL STUDIED TOGETHER...
...SARA-CHAN.
IT'S LIKE OLD TIMES... REMEMBER STUDYING FOR HIGH SCHOOL ENTRANCE EXAMS TOGETHER?
DID WE NOW? I DON'T REMEMBER.
*AWW.* DON'T YOU REMEMBER? YOU HATED SYSTEMS OF EQUATIONS, SO I TUTORED YOU LATE INTO THE EVENING.
THAT WAS A LONG TIME AGO.

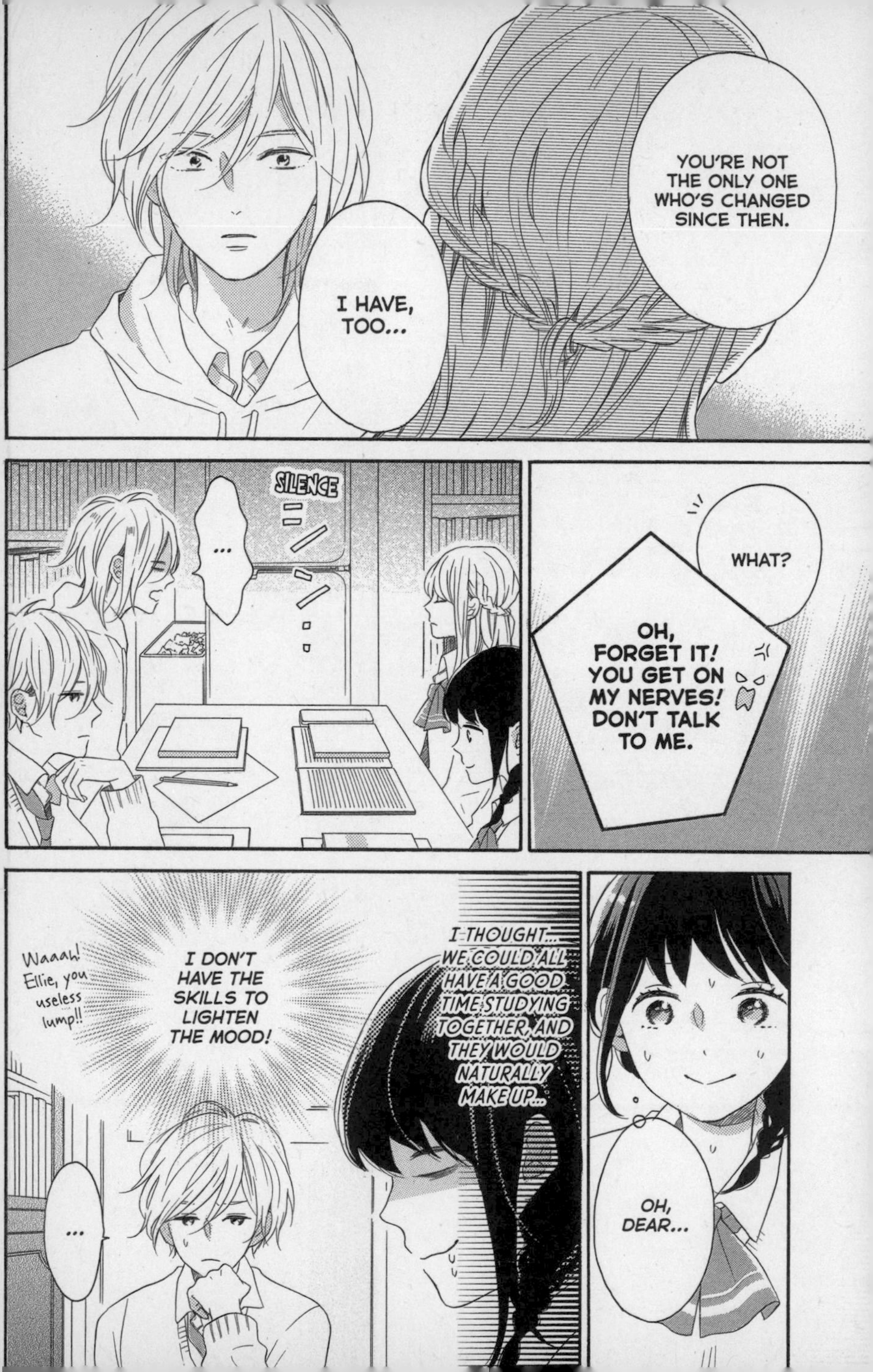
YOU'RE NOT THE ONLY ONE WHO'S CHANGED SINCE THEN.
I HAVE, TOO...
WHAT?
OH, FORGET IT! YOU GET ON MY NERVES! DON'T TALK TO ME.
SILENCE
...
OH, DEAR...
I THOUGHT... WE COULD ALL HAVE A GOOD TIME STUDYING TOGETHER, AND THEY WOULD NATURALLY MAKE UP...
I DON'T HAVE THE SKILLS TO LIGHTEN THE MOOD!
Waaah! Ellie, you useless lump!!
...

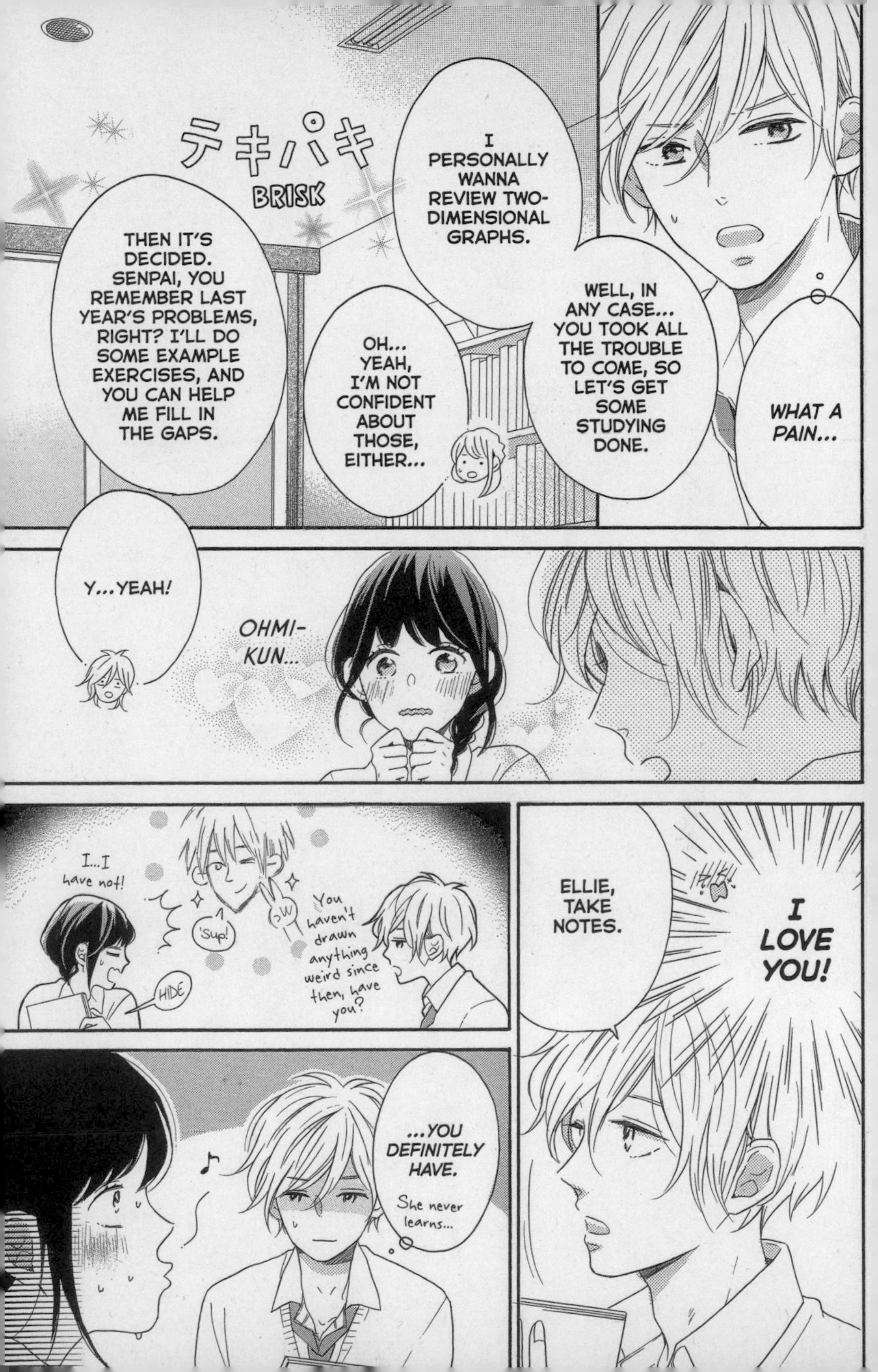
WHAT A PAIN...
WELL, IN ANY CASE... YOU TOOK ALL THE TROUBLE TO COME, SO LET'S GET SOME STUDYING DONE.
I PERSONALLY WANNA REVIEW TWO-DIMENSIONAL GRAPHS.
OH... YEAH, I'M NOT CONFIDENT ABOUT THOSE, EITHER...
テキパキ
BRISK
THEN IT'S DECIDED. SENPAI, YOU REMEMBER LAST YEAR'S PROBLEMS, RIGHT? I'LL DO SOME EXAMPLE EXERCISES, AND YOU CAN HELP ME FILL IN THE GAPS.
OHMI-KUN...
Y...YEAH!
ELLIE, TAKE NOTES.
I LOVE YOU!
You haven't drawn anything weird since then, have you?
'Sup!
I...I have not!
HIDE
...YOU DEFINITELY HAVE.
She never learns...

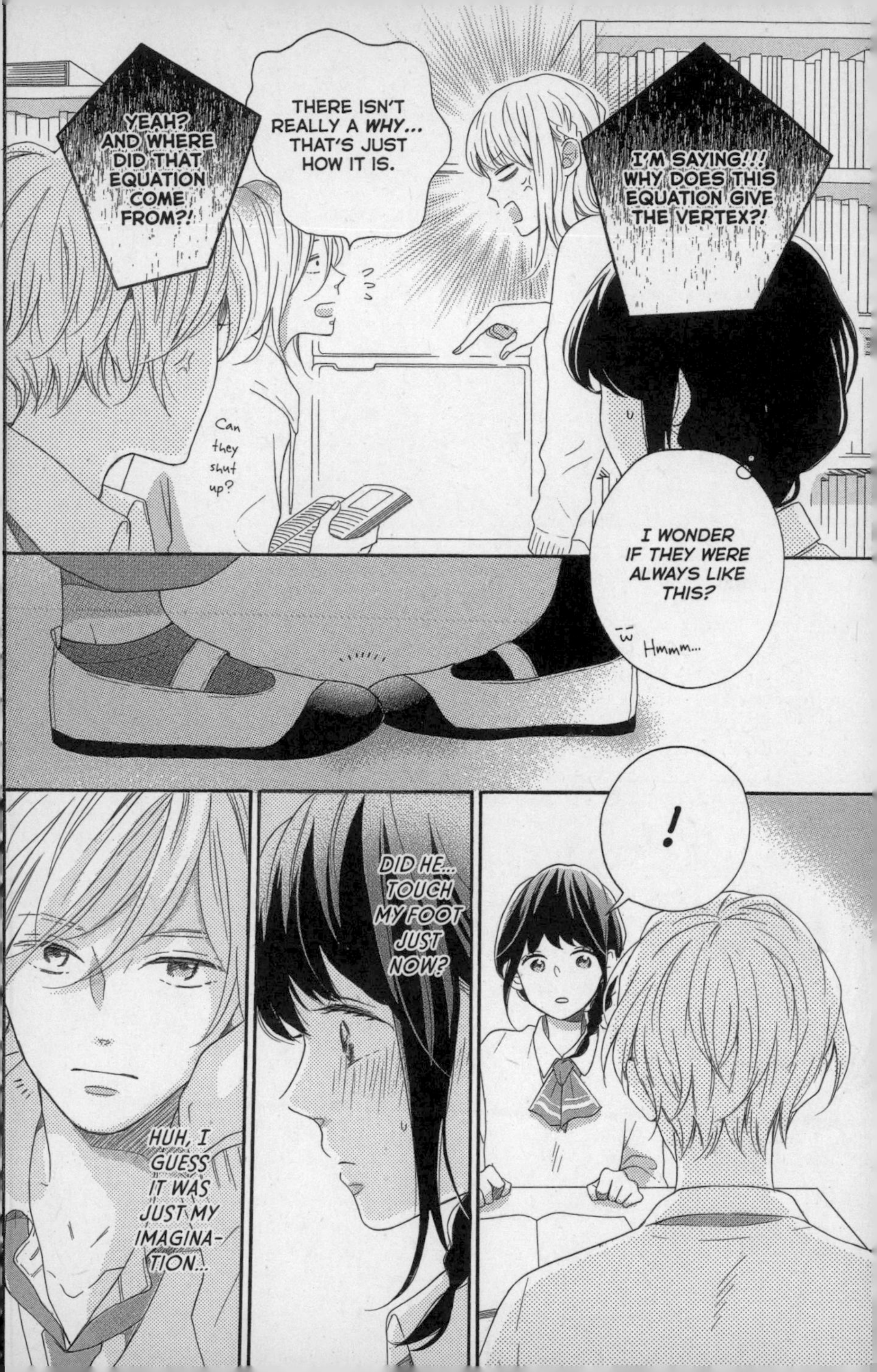
I'M SAYING!!! WHY DOES THIS EQUATION GIVE THE VERTEX?!
THERE ISN'T REALLY A *WHY*... THAT'S JUST HOW IT IS.
YEAH? AND WHERE DID THAT EQUATION COME FROM?!
Can they shut up?
I WONDER IF THEY WERE ALWAYS LIKE THIS?
Hmmm...
!
DID HE... TOUCH MY FOOT JUST NOW?
HUH, I GUESS IT WAS JUST MY IMAGINATION...

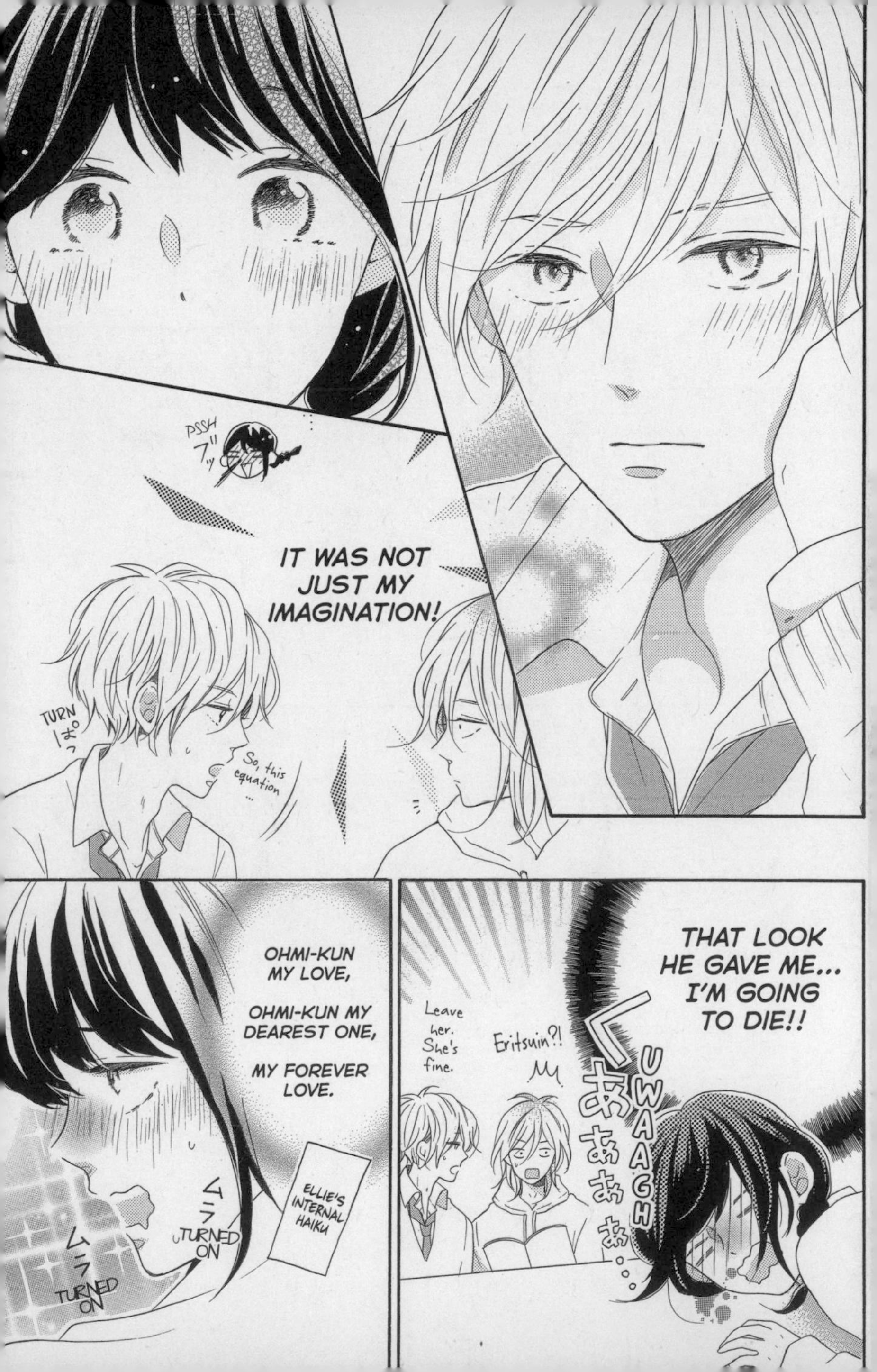

PSSH
IT WAS NOT JUST MY IMAGINATION!
TURN
So, this equation ...
THAT LOOK HE GAVE ME... I'M GOING TO DIE!!
UWAAGH
Eritsuin?!
Leave her. She's fine.
OHMI-KUN MY LOVE,
OHMI-KUN MY DEAREST ONE,
MY FOREVER LOVE.
ELLIE'S INTERNAL HAIKU
TURNED ON
TURNED ON

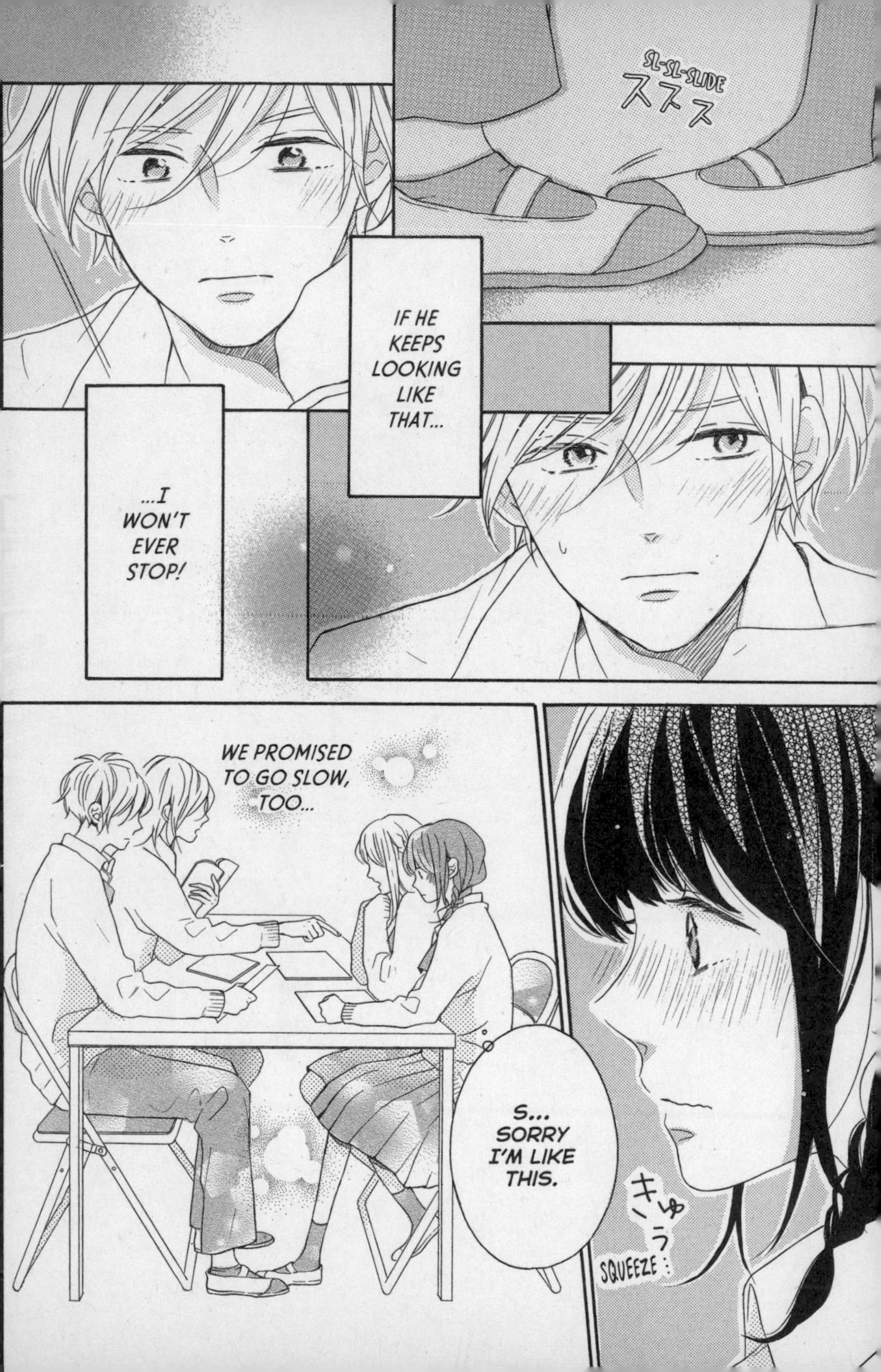
SL-SL-SLIDE
ススス
IF HE KEEPS LOOKING LIKE THAT...
...I WON'T EVER STOP!
S... SORRY I'M LIKE THIS.
きゅう
SQUEEZE
WE PROMISED TO GO SLOW, TOO...

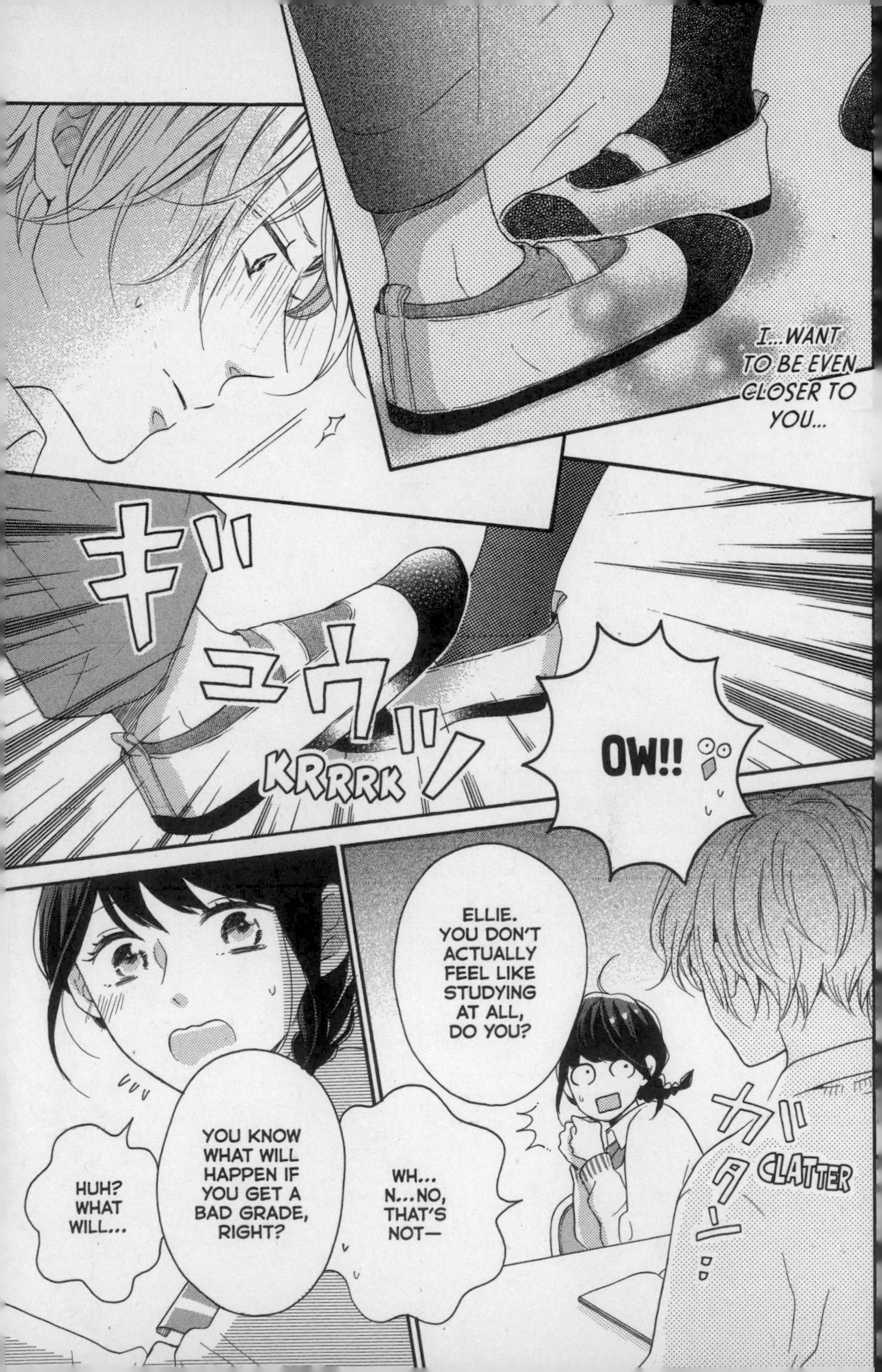
I...WANT TO BE EVEN CLOSER TO YOU...
OW!!
KRRRK
ELLIE. YOU DON'T ACTUALLY FEEL LIKE STUDYING AT ALL, DO YOU?
CLATTER
WH... N...NO, THAT'S NOT—
YOU KNOW WHAT WILL HAPPEN IF YOU GET A BAD GRADE, RIGHT?
HUH? WHAT WILL...

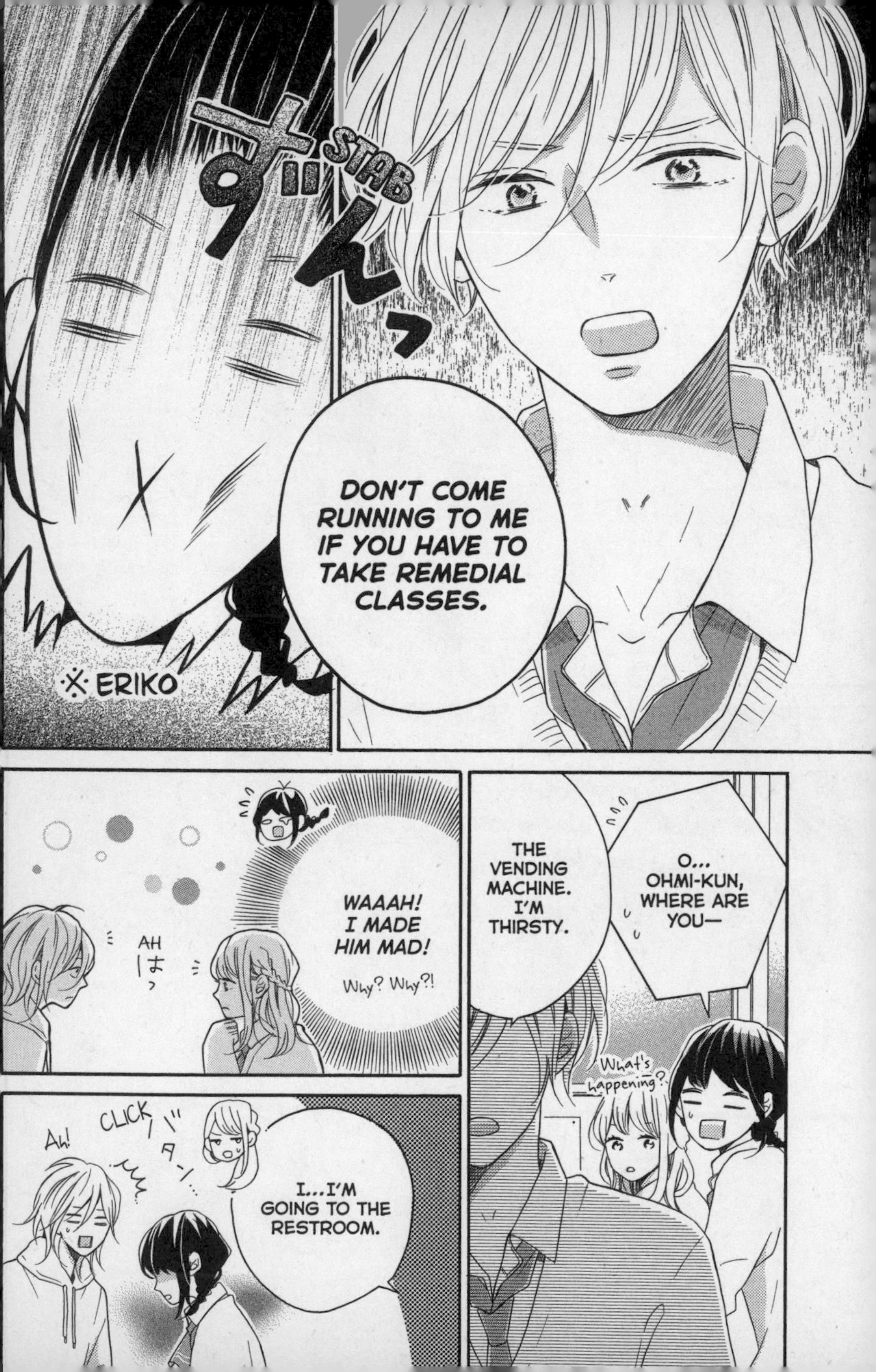
DON'T COME RUNNING TO ME IF YOU HAVE TO TAKE REMEDIAL CLASSES.
STAB
※ERIKO
O... OHMI-KUN, WHERE ARE YOU—
THE VENDING MACHINE. I'M THIRSTY.
What's happening?
AH はっ
WAAAH! I MADE HIM MAD!
Why? Why?!
CLICK
Ah!
I...I'M GOING TO THE RESTROOM.

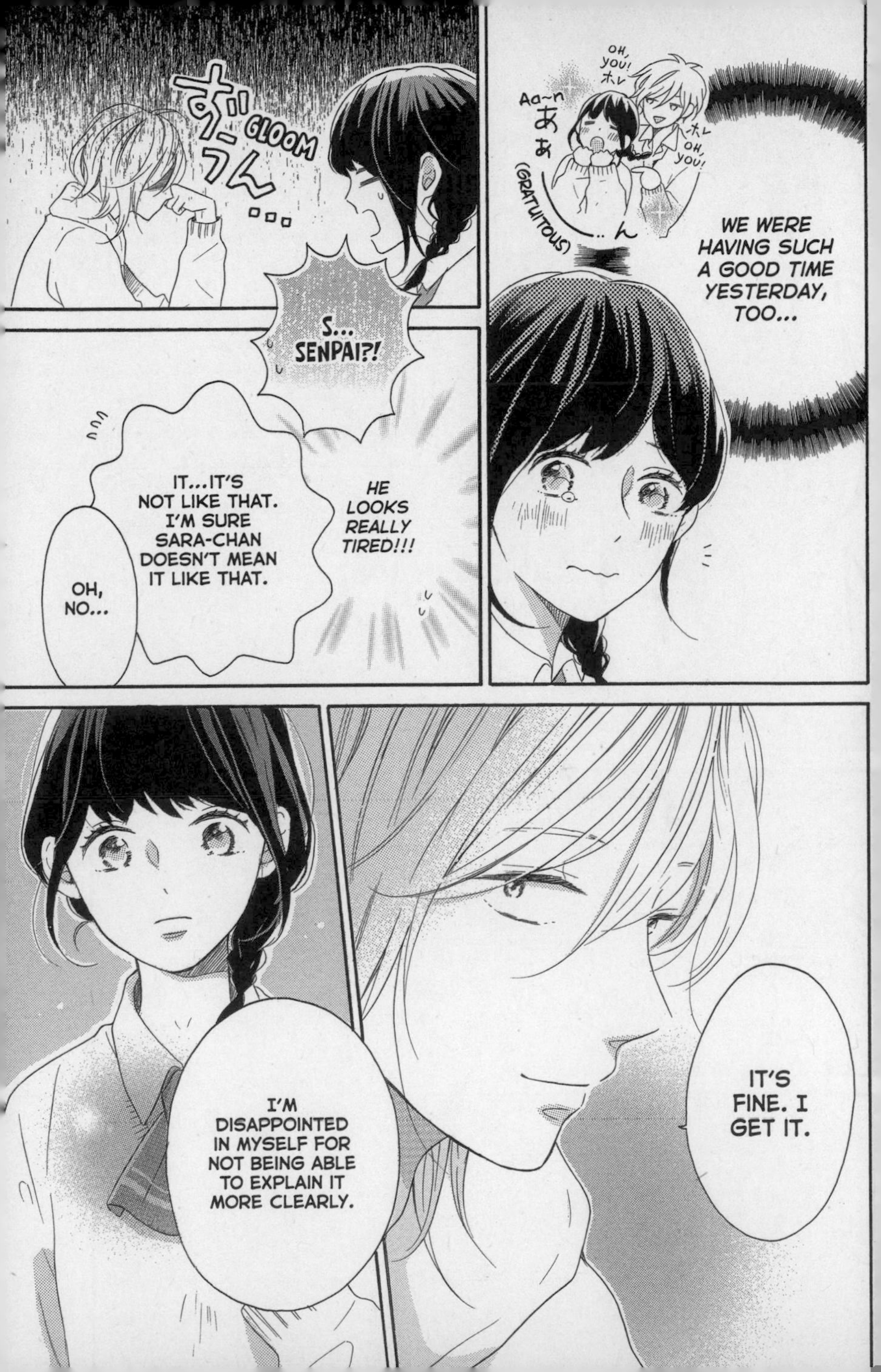
OH, YOU! ホレ
ホレ OH, YOU!
Aa~n あぁ
(GRATUITOUS)
...ん
WE WERE HAVING SUCH A GOOD TIME YESTERDAY, TOO...
すぅーうん GLOOM
S... SENPAI?!
HE LOOKS REALLY TIRED!!!
IT...IT'S NOT LIKE THAT. I'M SURE SARA-CHAN DOESN'T MEAN IT LIKE THAT.
OH, NO...
IT'S FINE. I GET IT.
I'M DISAPPOINTED IN MYSELF FOR NOT BEING ABLE TO EXPLAIN IT MORE CLEARLY.

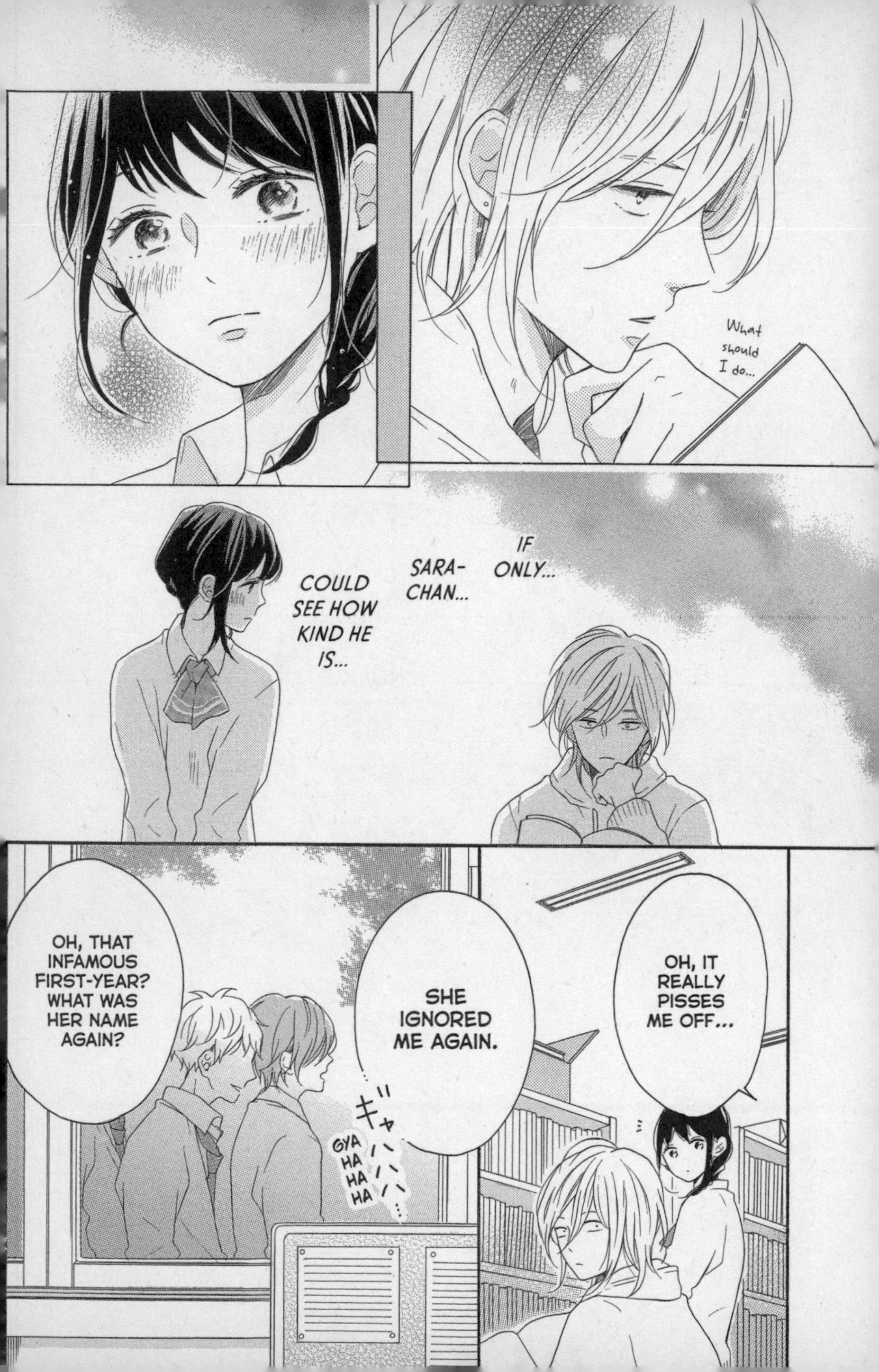
What should I do...
IF ONLY...
SARA-CHAN...
COULD SEE HOW KIND HE IS...
OH, IT REALLY PISSES ME OFF...
SHE IGNORED ME AGAIN.
OH, THAT INFAMOUS FIRST-YEAR? WHAT WAS HER NAME AGAIN?
ギャハハハ
GYA HA HA HA

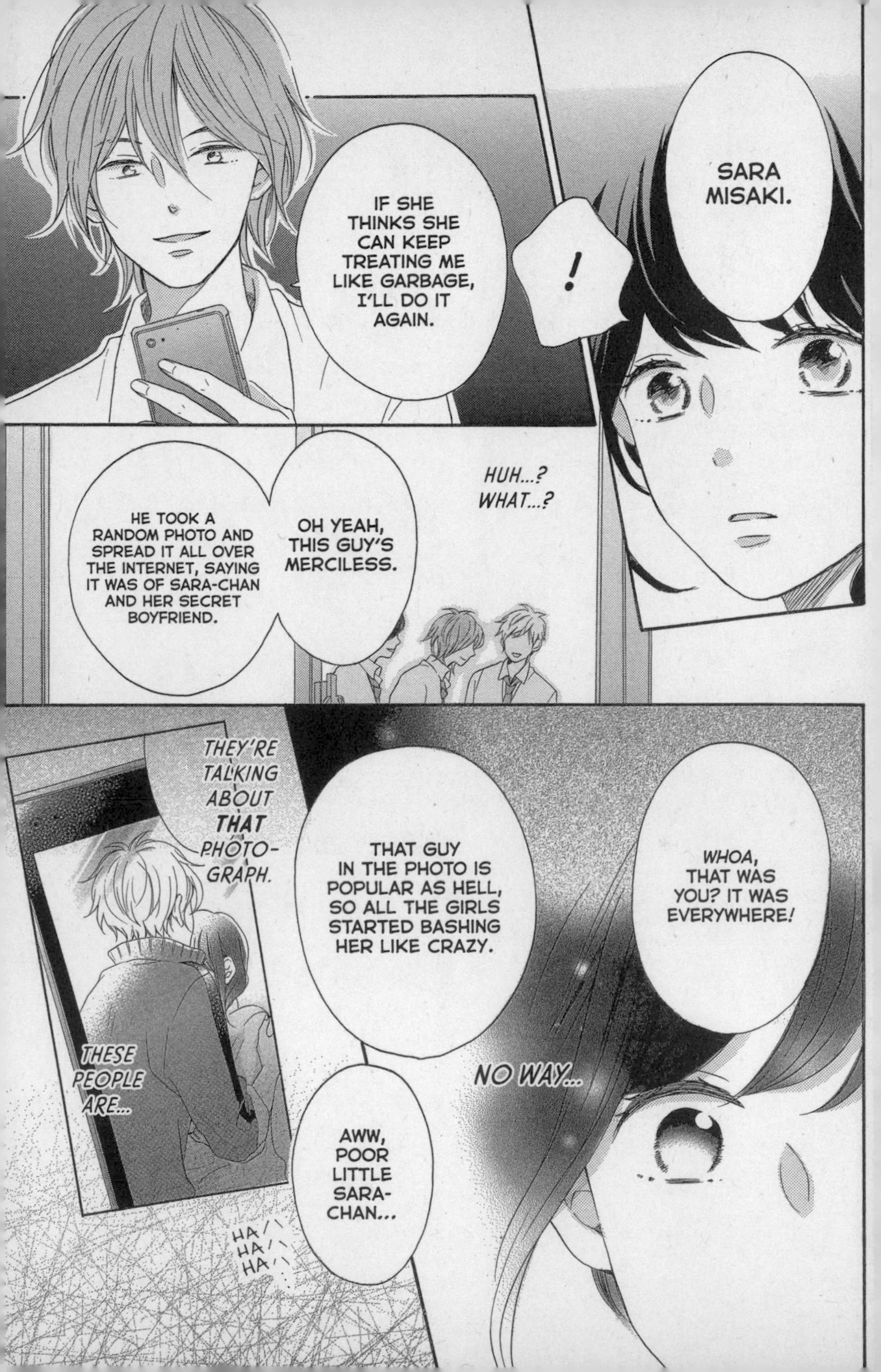
SARA MISAKI.
!
IF SHE THINKS SHE CAN KEEP TREATING ME LIKE GARBAGE, I'LL DO IT AGAIN.
HUH...? WHAT...?
OH YEAH, THIS GUY'S MERCILESS.
HE TOOK A RANDOM PHOTO AND SPREAD IT ALL OVER THE INTERNET, SAYING IT WAS OF SARA-CHAN AND HER SECRET BOYFRIEND.
WHOA, THAT WAS YOU? IT WAS EVERYWHERE!
NO WAY...
THAT GUY IN THE PHOTO IS POPULAR AS HELL, SO ALL THE GIRLS STARTED BASHING HER LIKE CRAZY.
AWW, POOR LITTLE SARA-CHAN...
THEY'RE TALKING ABOUT THAT PHOTOGRAPH.
THESE PEOPLE ARE...
HA HA HA

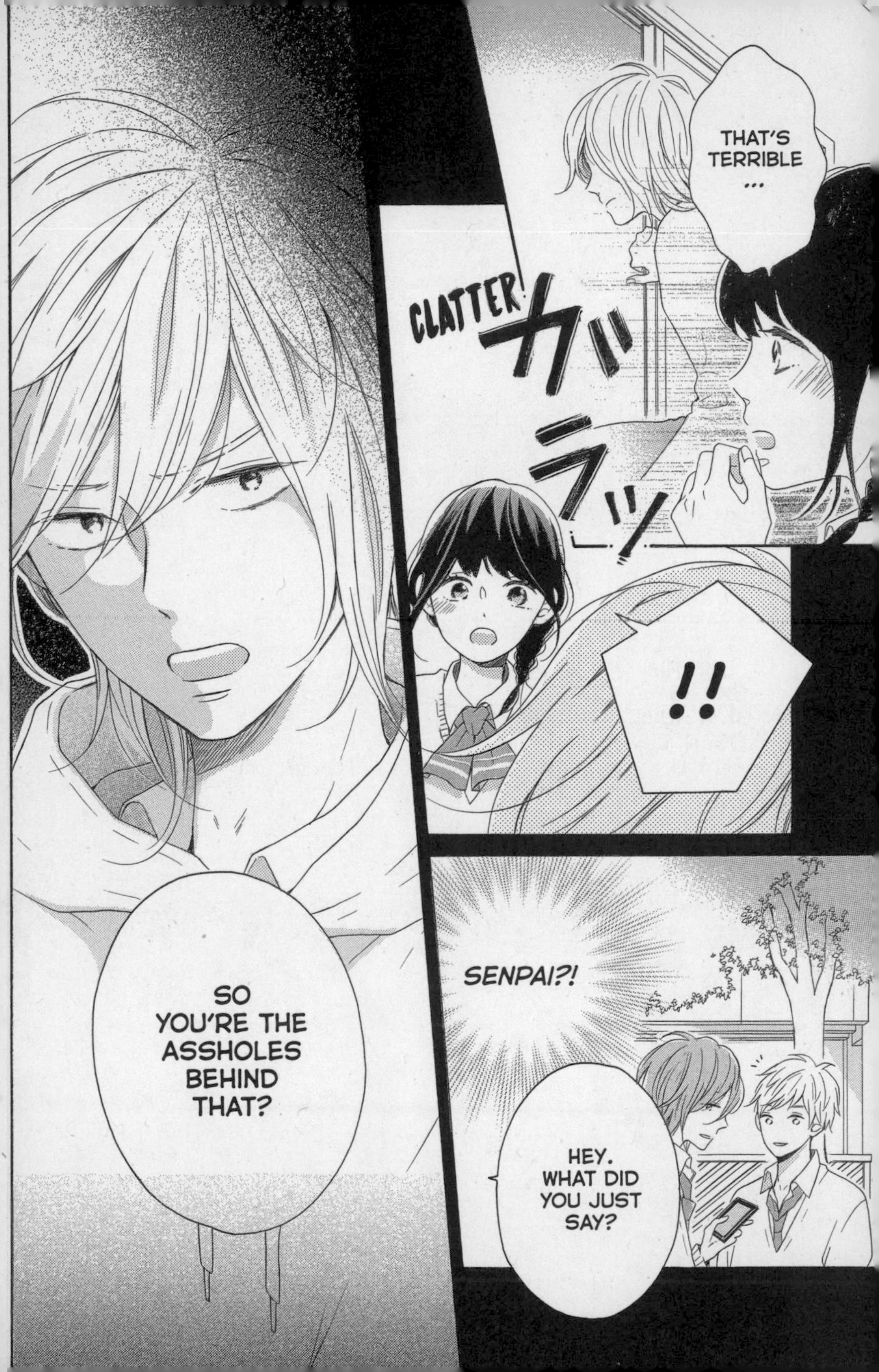
THAT'S TERRIBLE ...
CLATTER
ガラッ
!!
SENPAI?!
HEY. WHAT DID YOU JUST SAY?
SO YOU'RE THE ASSHOLES BEHIND THAT?

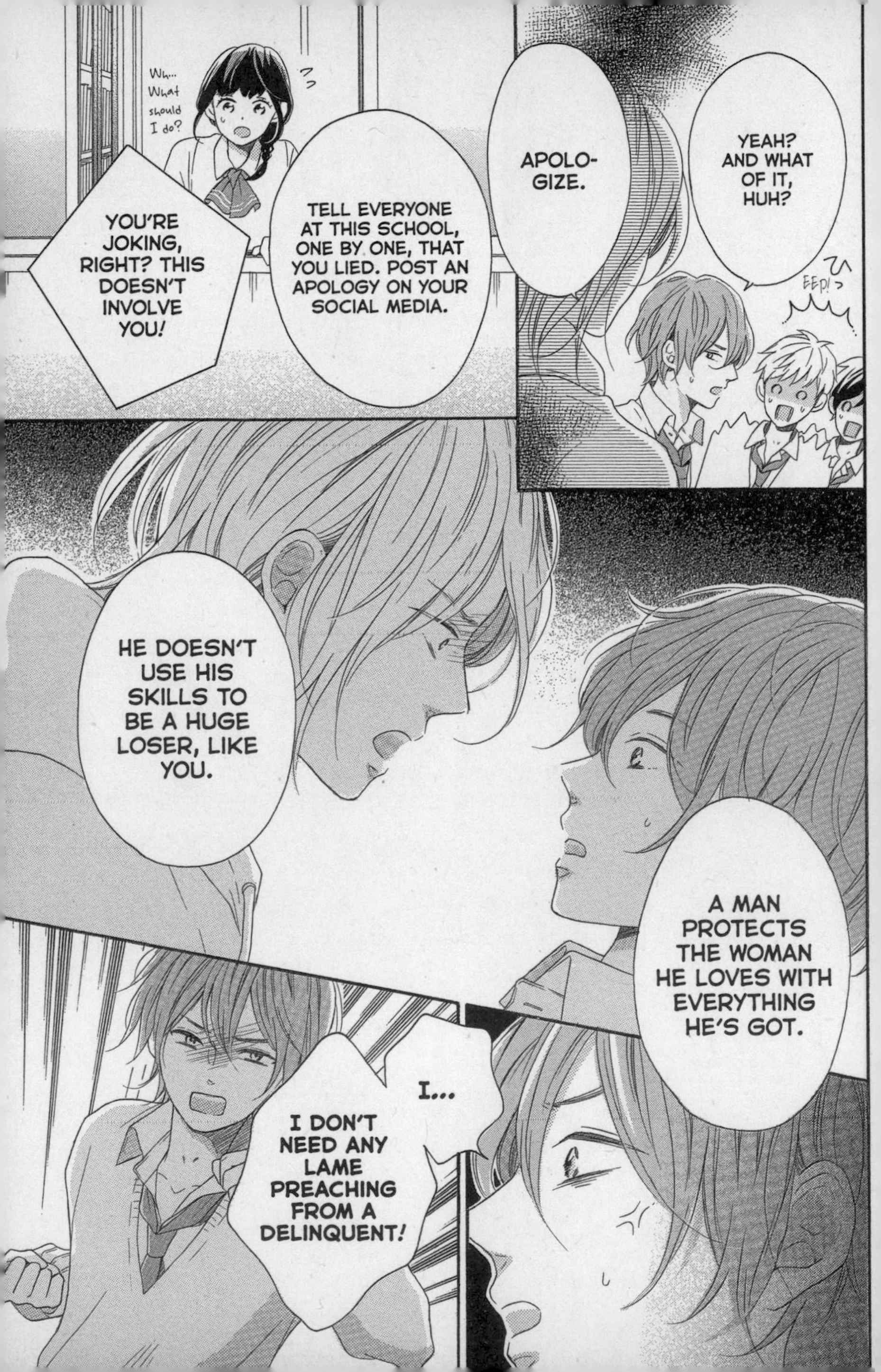
YEAH? AND WHAT OF IT, HUH?
APOLOGIZE.
EEP!
TELL EVERYONE AT THIS SCHOOL, ONE BY ONE, THAT YOU LIED. POST AN APOLOGY ON YOUR SOCIAL MEDIA.
Wh... What should I do?
YOU'RE JOKING, RIGHT? THIS DOESN'T INVOLVE YOU!
A MAN PROTECTS THE WOMAN HE LOVES WITH EVERYTHING HE'S GOT.
HE DOESN'T USE HIS SKILLS TO BE A HUGE LOSER, LIKE YOU.
I...
I DON'T NEED ANY LAME PREACHING FROM A DELINQUENT!

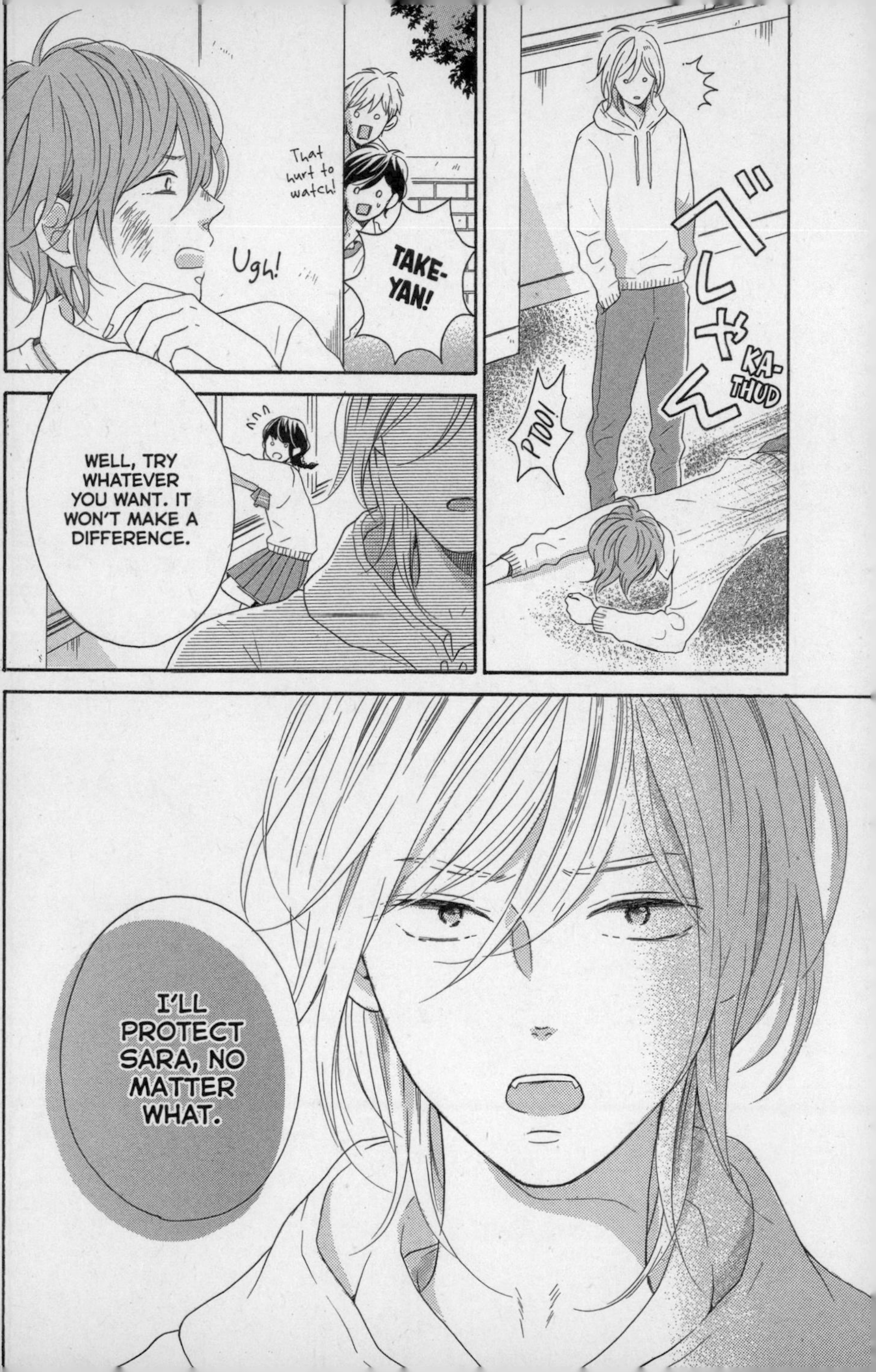
べしゃん
KA-THUD
PTOO!
That hurt to watch!
TAKE-YAN!
Ugh!
WELL, TRY WHATEVER YOU WANT. IT WON'T MAKE A DIFFERENCE.
I'LL PROTECT SARA, NO MATTER WHAT.

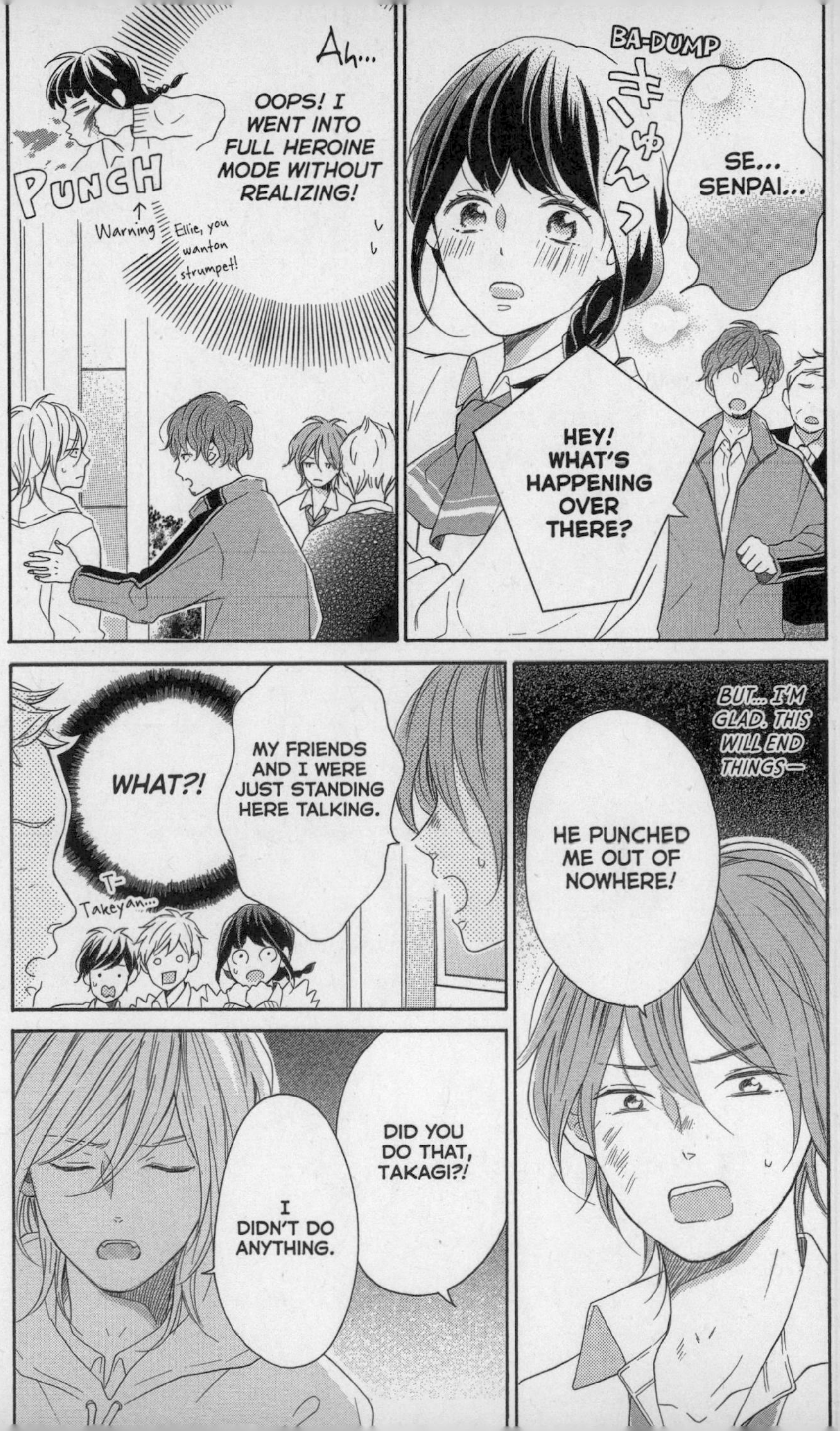
BA-DUMP
きゅんっ
SE... SENPAI...
HEY! WHAT'S HAPPENING OVER THERE?
Ah...
OOPS! I WENT INTO FULL HEROINE MODE WITHOUT REALIZING!
PUNCH
Warning
Ellie, you wanton strumpet!
BUT... I'M GLAD. THIS WILL END THINGS—
HE PUNCHED ME OUT OF NOWHERE!
MY FRIENDS AND I WERE JUST STANDING HERE TALKING.
WHAT?!
T-
Takeyan...
DID YOU DO THAT, TAKAGI?!
I DIDN'T DO ANYTHING.

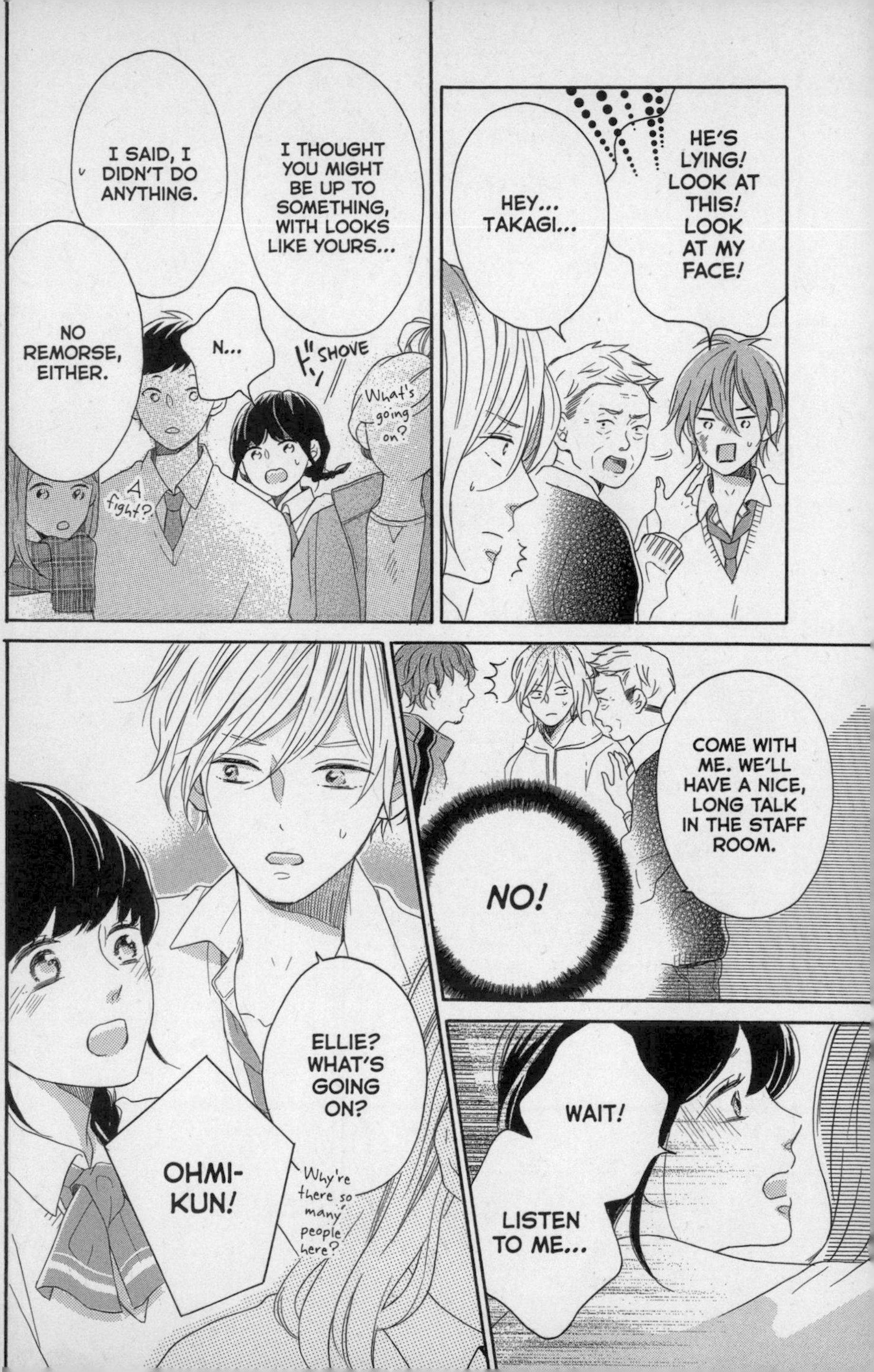
HE'S LYING! LOOK AT THIS! LOOK AT MY FACE!
HEY... TAKAGI...
I THOUGHT YOU MIGHT BE UP TO SOMETHING, WITH LOOKS LIKE YOURS...
I SAID, I DIDN'T DO ANYTHING.
SHOVE
What's going on?
N...
NO REMORSE, EITHER.
A fight?
COME WITH ME. WE'LL HAVE A NICE, LONG TALK IN THE STAFF ROOM.
NO!
WAIT!
LISTEN TO ME...
ELLIE? WHAT'S GOING ON?
Why're there so many people here?
OHMI-KUN!

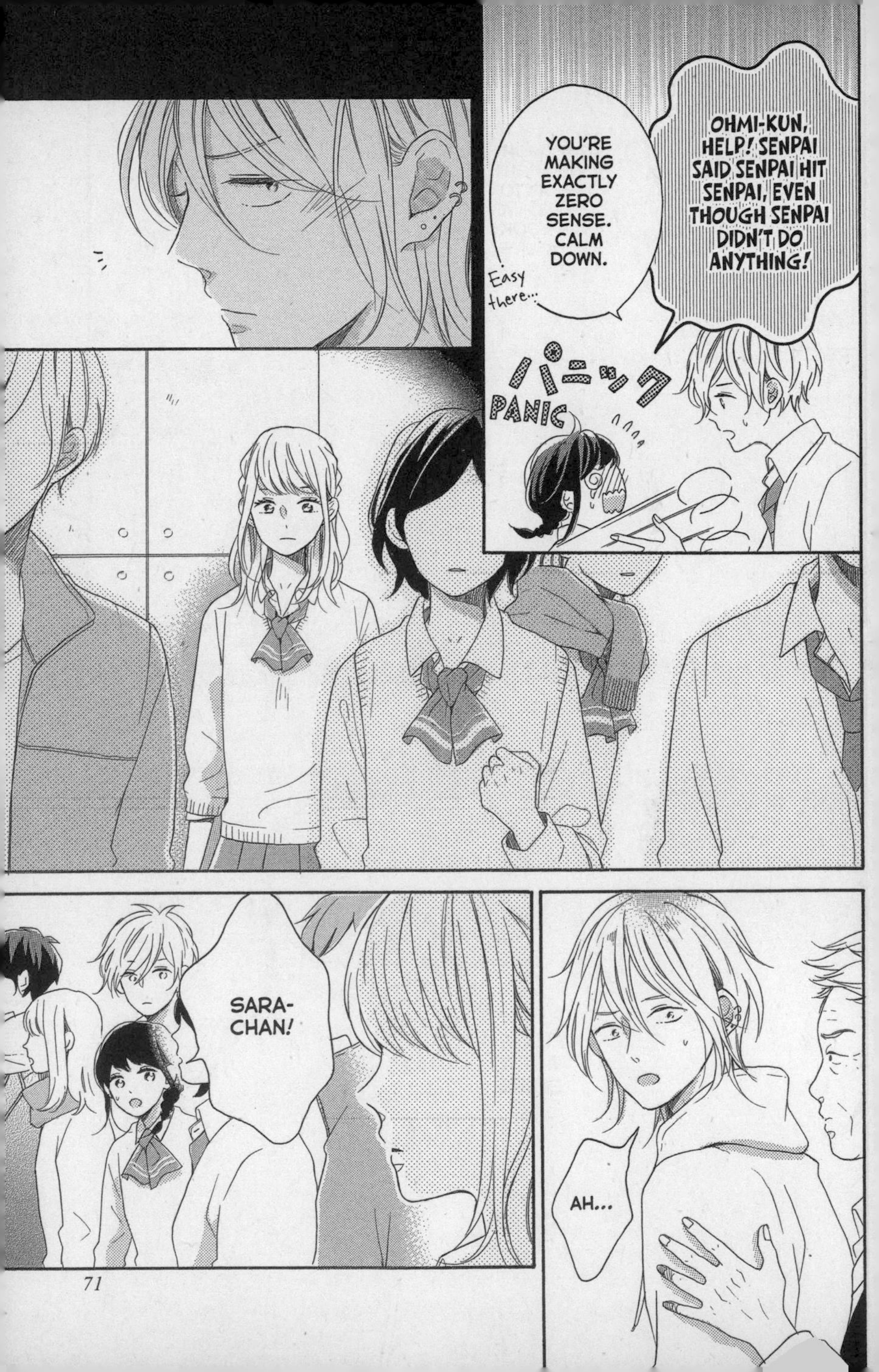
OHMI-KUN, HELP! SENPAI SAID SENPAI HIT SENPAI, EVEN THOUGH SENPAI DIDN'T DO ANYTHING!
YOU'RE MAKING EXACTLY ZERO SENSE. CALM DOWN.
Easy there...
パニック
PANIC
AH...
SARA-CHAN!

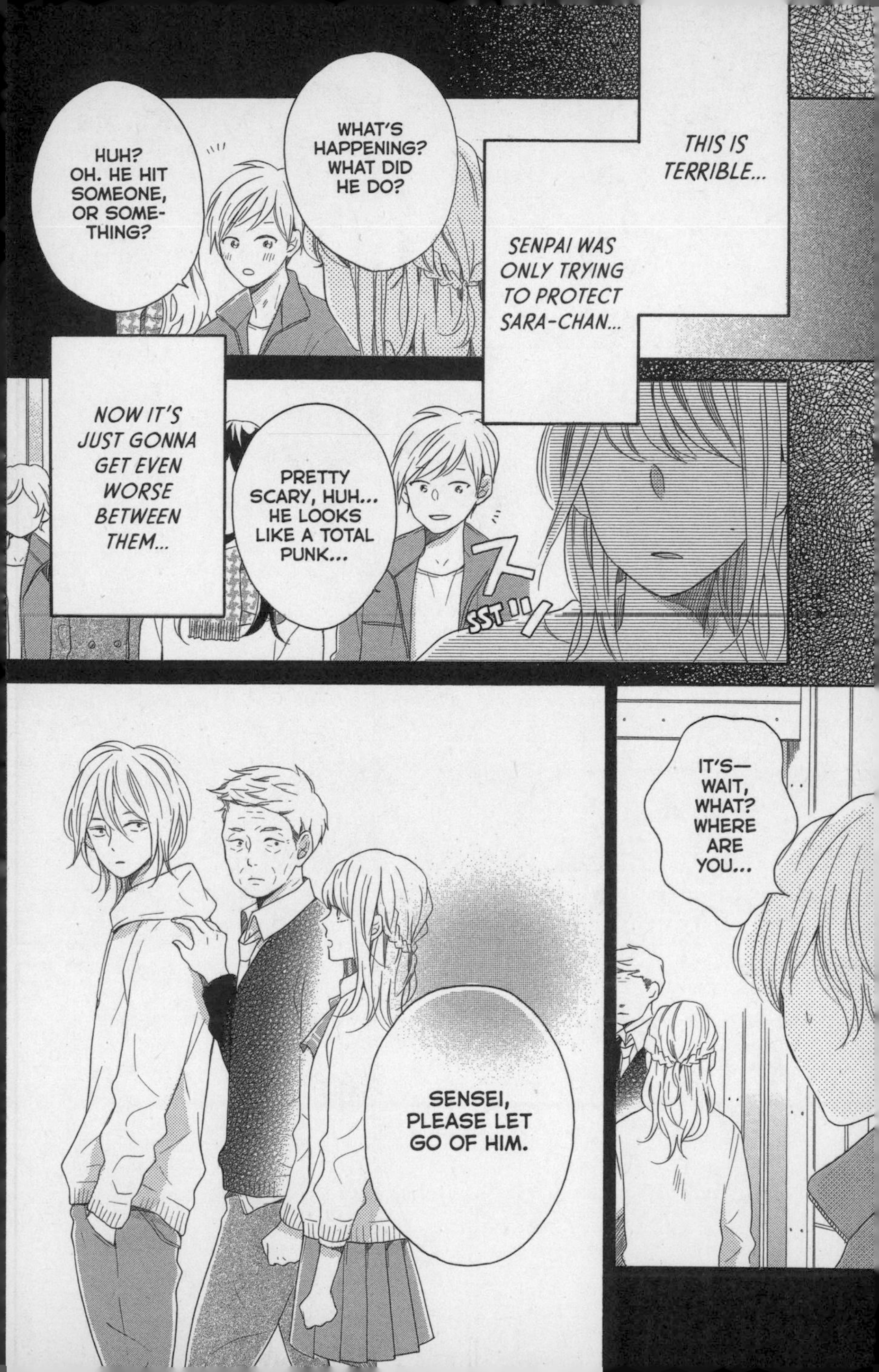
THIS IS TERRIBLE...
SENPAI WAS ONLY TRYING TO PROTECT SARA-CHAN...
WHAT'S HAPPENING? WHAT DID HE DO?
HUH? OH. HE HIT SOMEONE, OR SOME-THING?
SST
PRETTY SCARY, HUH... HE LOOKS LIKE A TOTAL PUNK...
NOW IT'S JUST GONNA GET EVEN WORSE BETWEEN THEM...
IT'S— WAIT, WHAT? WHERE ARE YOU...
SENSEI, PLEASE LET GO OF HIM.

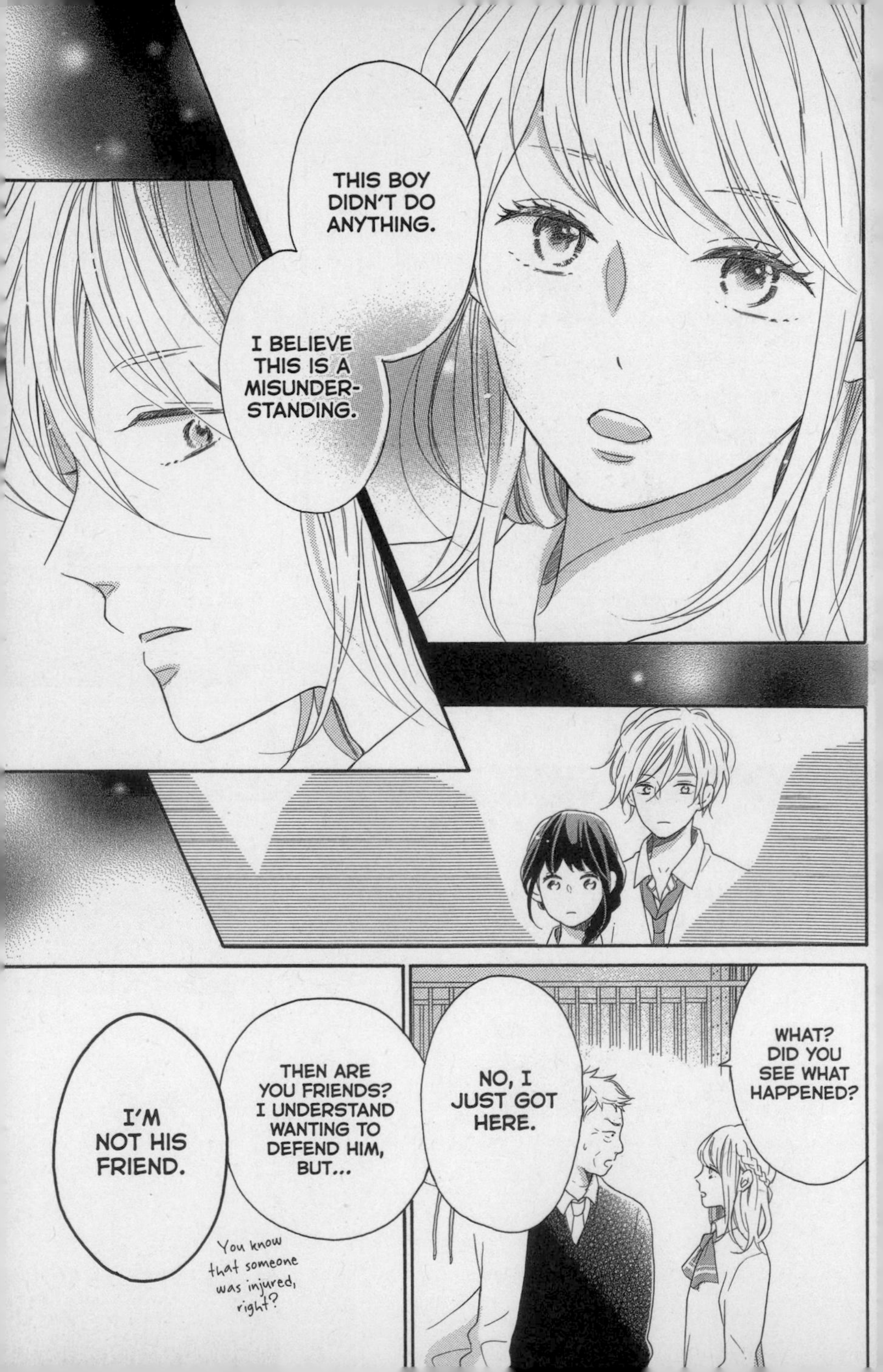
THIS BOY DIDN'T DO ANYTHING.
I BELIEVE THIS IS A MISUNDER-STANDING.
WHAT? DID YOU SEE WHAT HAPPENED?
NO, I JUST GOT HERE.
THEN ARE YOU FRIENDS? I UNDERSTAND WANTING TO DEFEND HIM, BUT...
You know that someone was injured, right?
I'M NOT HIS FRIEND.

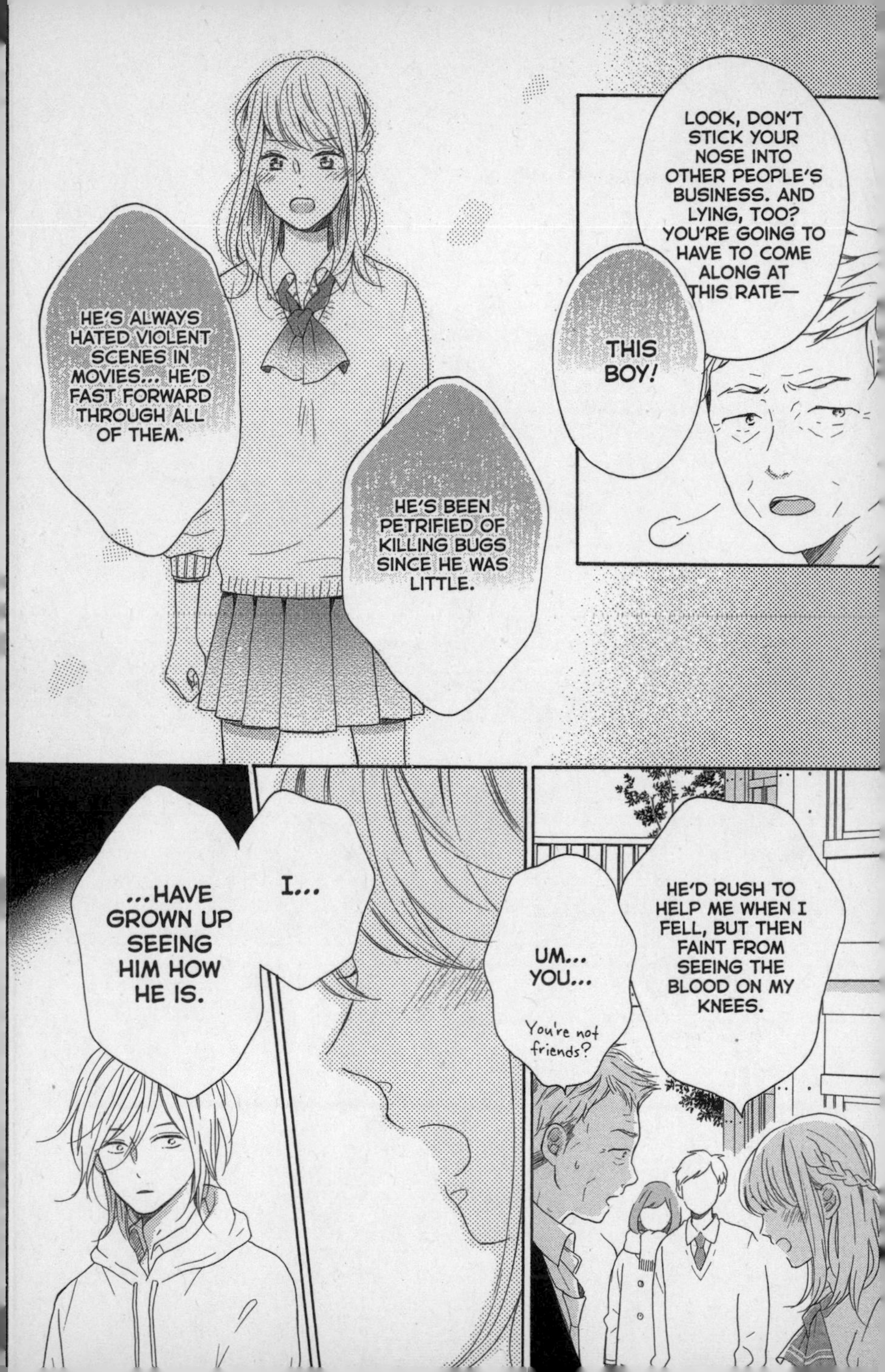
LOOK, DON'T STICK YOUR NOSE INTO OTHER PEOPLE'S BUSINESS. AND LYING, TOO? YOU'RE GOING TO HAVE TO COME ALONG AT THIS RATE—
THIS BOY!
HE'S ALWAYS HATED VIOLENT SCENES IN MOVIES... HE'D FAST FORWARD THROUGH ALL OF THEM.
HE'S BEEN PETRIFIED OF KILLING BUGS SINCE HE WAS LITTLE.
HE'D RUSH TO HELP ME WHEN I FELL, BUT THEN FAINT FROM SEEING THE BLOOD ON MY KNEES.
UM... YOU...
You're not friends?
I...
...HAVE GROWN UP SEEING HIM HOW HE IS.

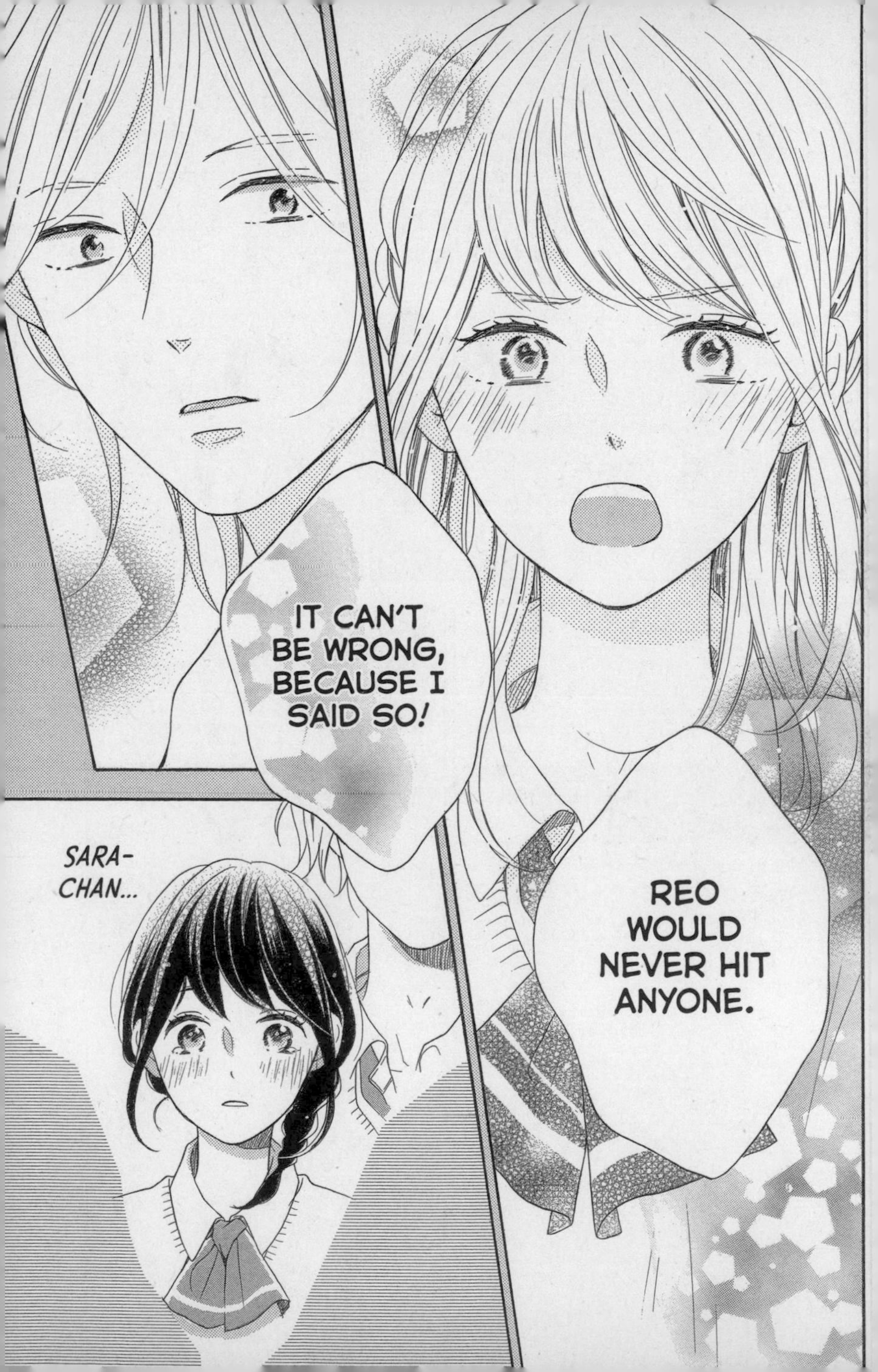
IT CAN'T BE WRONG, BECAUSE I SAID SO!
REO WOULD NEVER HIT ANYONE.
SARA-CHAN...

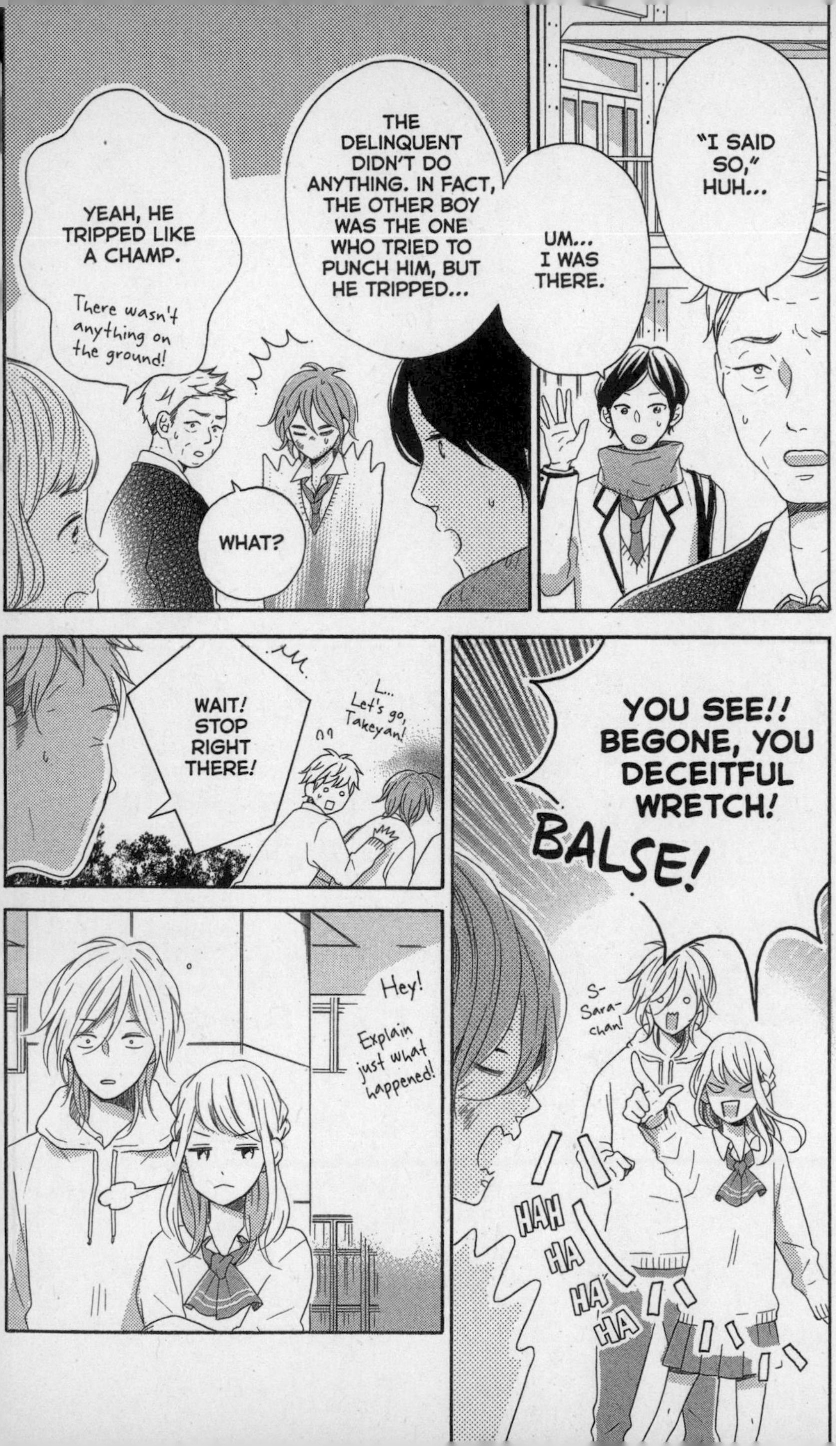
"I SAID SO," HUH...
UM... I WAS THERE.
THE DELINQUENT DIDN'T DO ANYTHING. IN FACT, THE OTHER BOY WAS THE ONE WHO TRIED TO PUNCH HIM, BUT HE TRIPPED...
YEAH, HE TRIPPED LIKE A CHAMP.
There wasn't anything on the ground!
WHAT?
YOU SEE!! BEGONE, YOU DECEITFUL WRETCH!
BALSE!
S-Sara-chan!
HAH HA HA HA
WAIT! STOP RIGHT THERE!
L... Let's go, Takeyan!
Hey!
Explain just what happened!

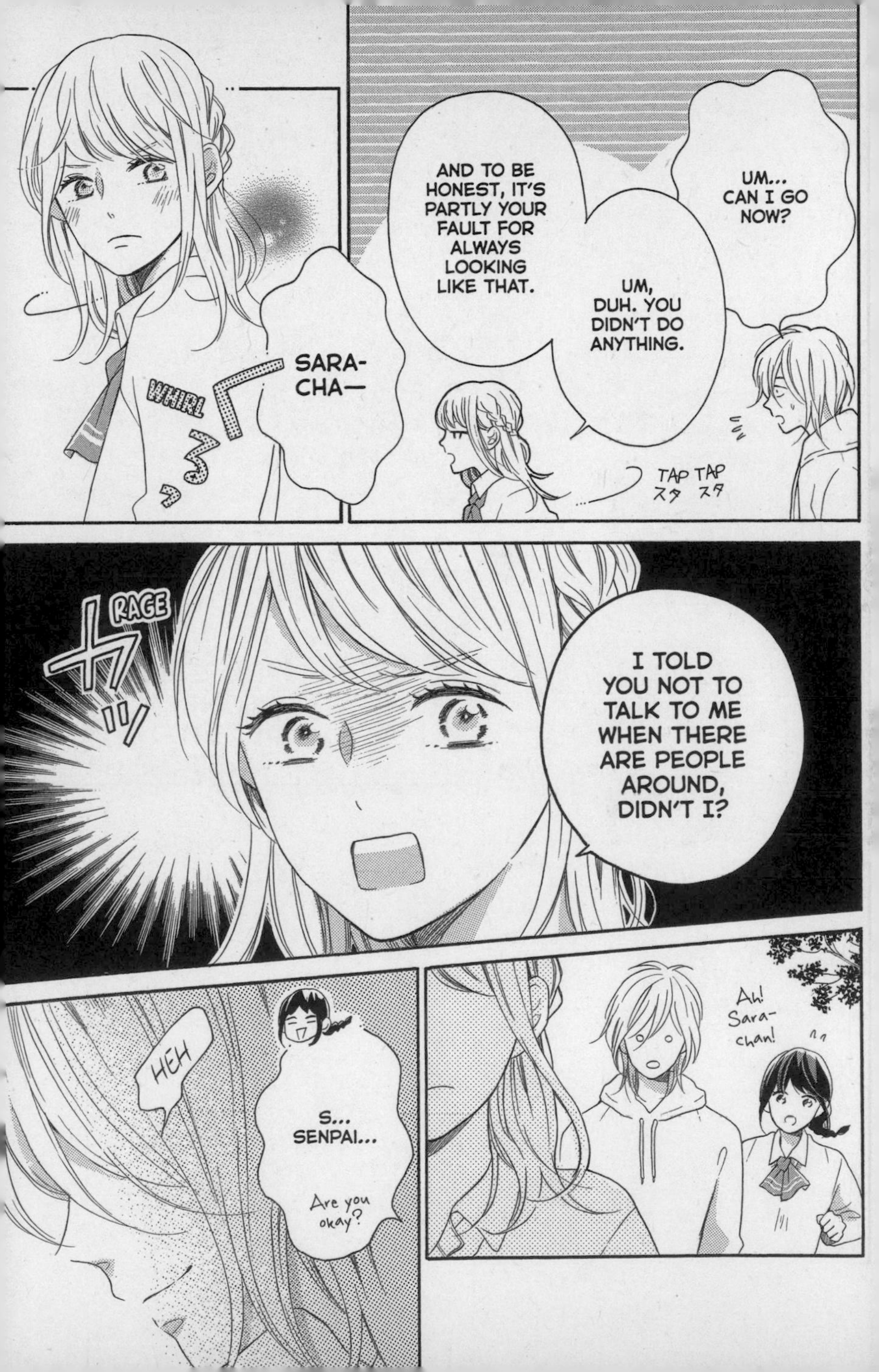
UM... CAN I GO NOW?
UM, DUH. YOU DIDN'T DO ANYTHING.
AND TO BE HONEST, IT'S PARTLY YOUR FAULT FOR ALWAYS LOOKING LIKE THAT.
TAP TAP
スタ スタ
SARA-CHA—
WHIRL
RAGE
I TOLD YOU NOT TO TALK TO ME WHEN THERE ARE PEOPLE AROUND, DIDN'T I?
Ah! Sara-chan!
S... SENPAI...
Are you okay?
HEH

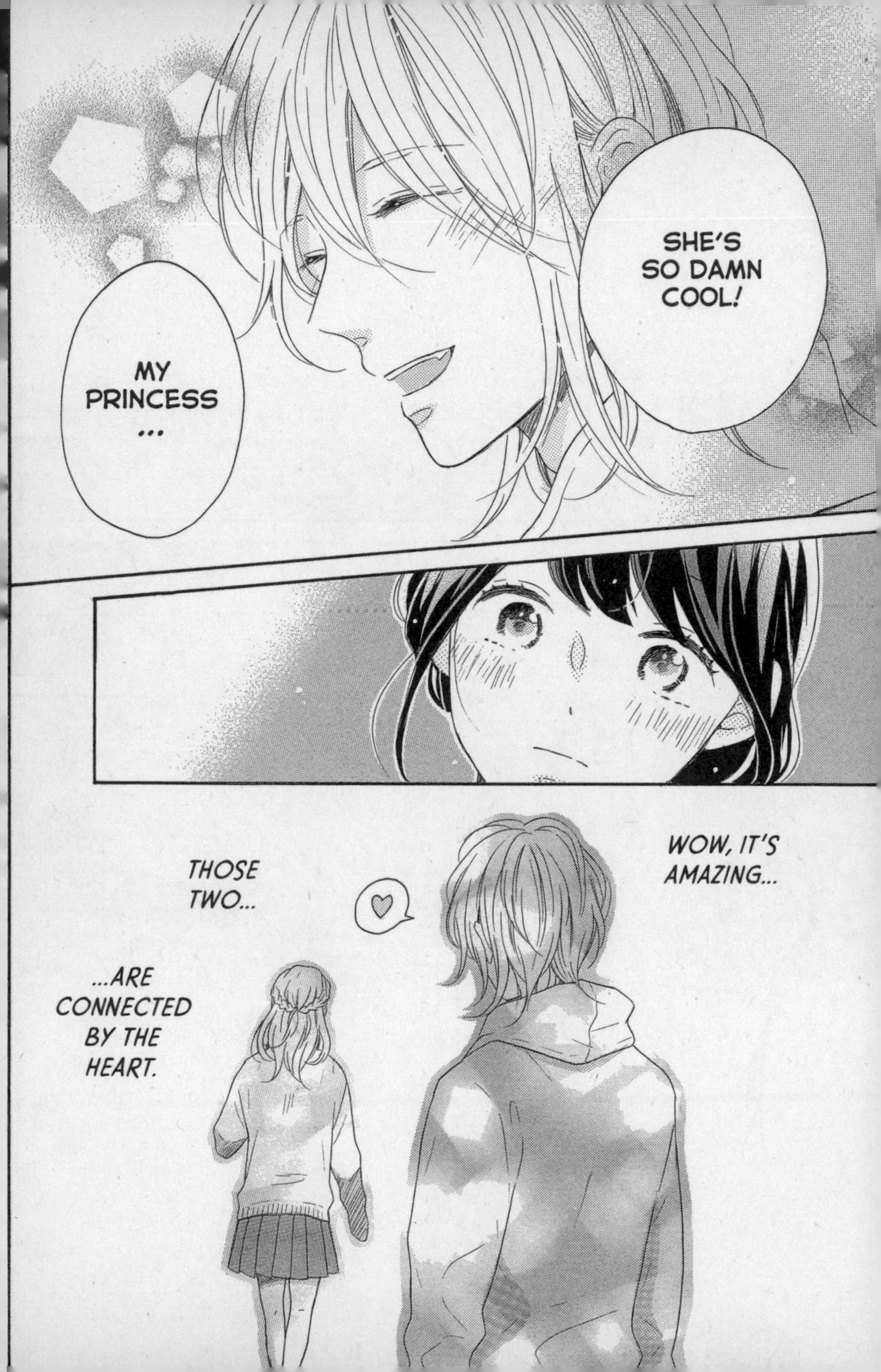
SHE'S SO DAMN COOL!
MY PRINCESS ...
WOW, IT'S AMAZING...
THOSE TWO...
...ARE CONNECTED BY THE HEART.

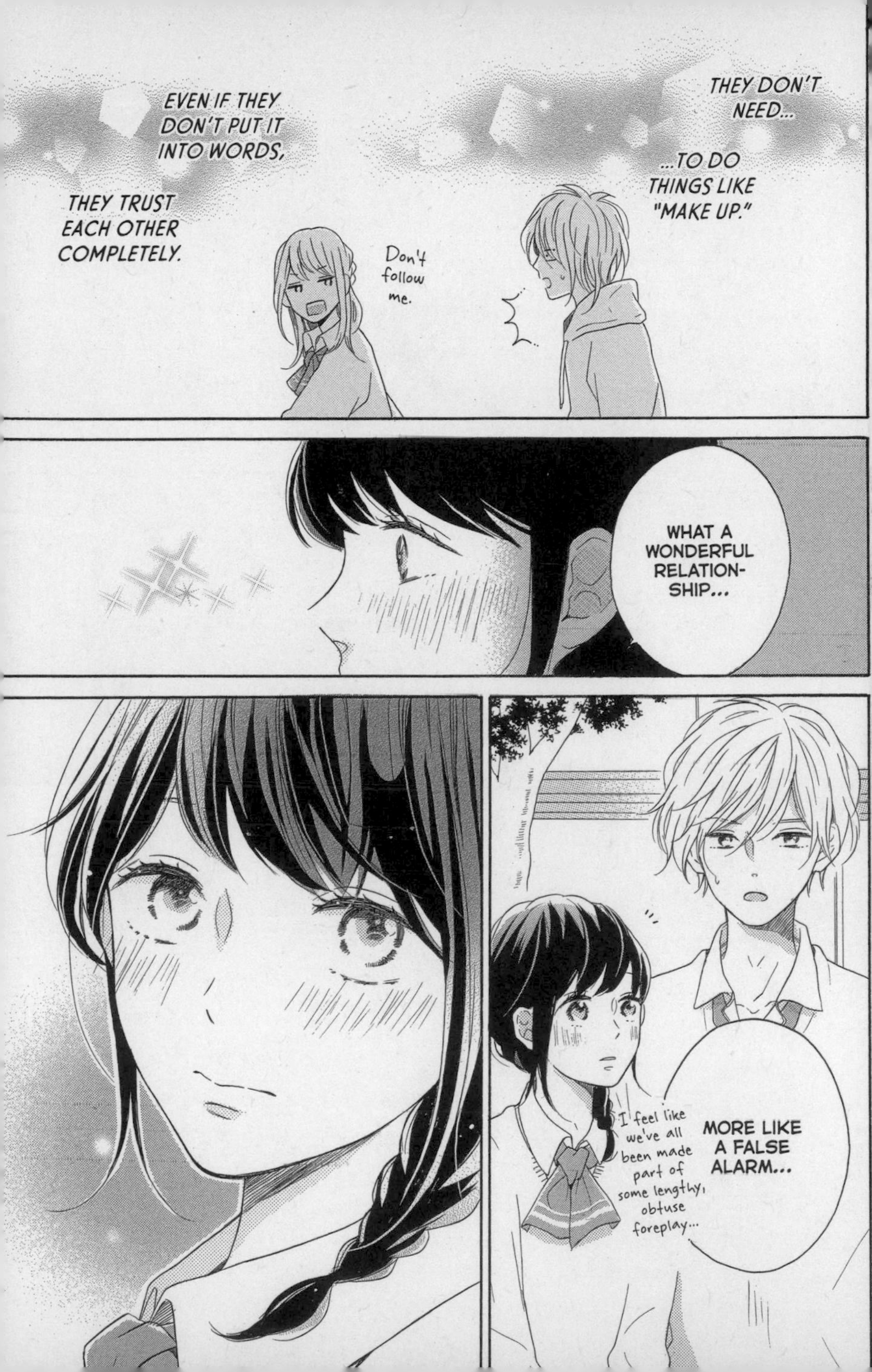
THEY DON'T NEED...
...TO DO THINGS LIKE "MAKE UP."
EVEN IF THEY DON'T PUT IT INTO WORDS,
THEY TRUST EACH OTHER COMPLETELY.
Don't follow me.
WHAT A WONDERFUL RELATION-SHIP...
MORE LIKE A FALSE ALARM...
I feel like we've all been made part of some lengthy, obtuse foreplay...

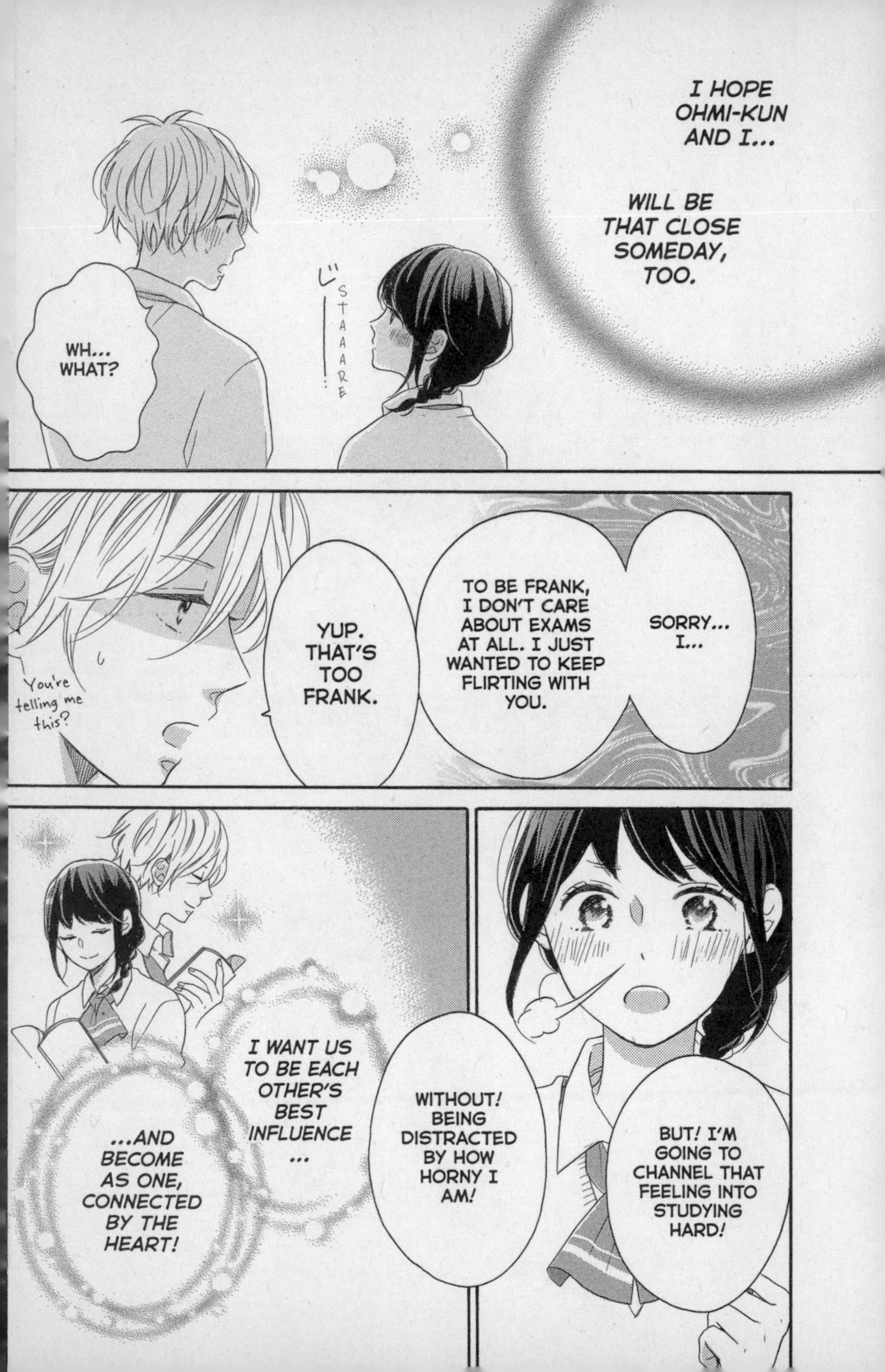
I HOPE OHMI-KUN AND I...
WILL BE THAT CLOSE SOMEDAY, TOO.
ジ
STAAARE
WH... WHAT?
SORRY... I...
TO BE FRANK, I DON'T CARE ABOUT EXAMS AT ALL. I JUST WANTED TO KEEP FLIRTING WITH YOU.
YUP. THAT'S TOO FRANK.
You're telling me this?
BUT! I'M GOING TO CHANNEL THAT FEELING INTO STUDYING HARD!
WITHOUT! BEING DISTRACTED BY HOW HORNY I AM!
I WANT US TO BE EACH OTHER'S BEST INFLUENCE ...
...AND BECOME AS ONE, CONNECTED BY THE HEART!

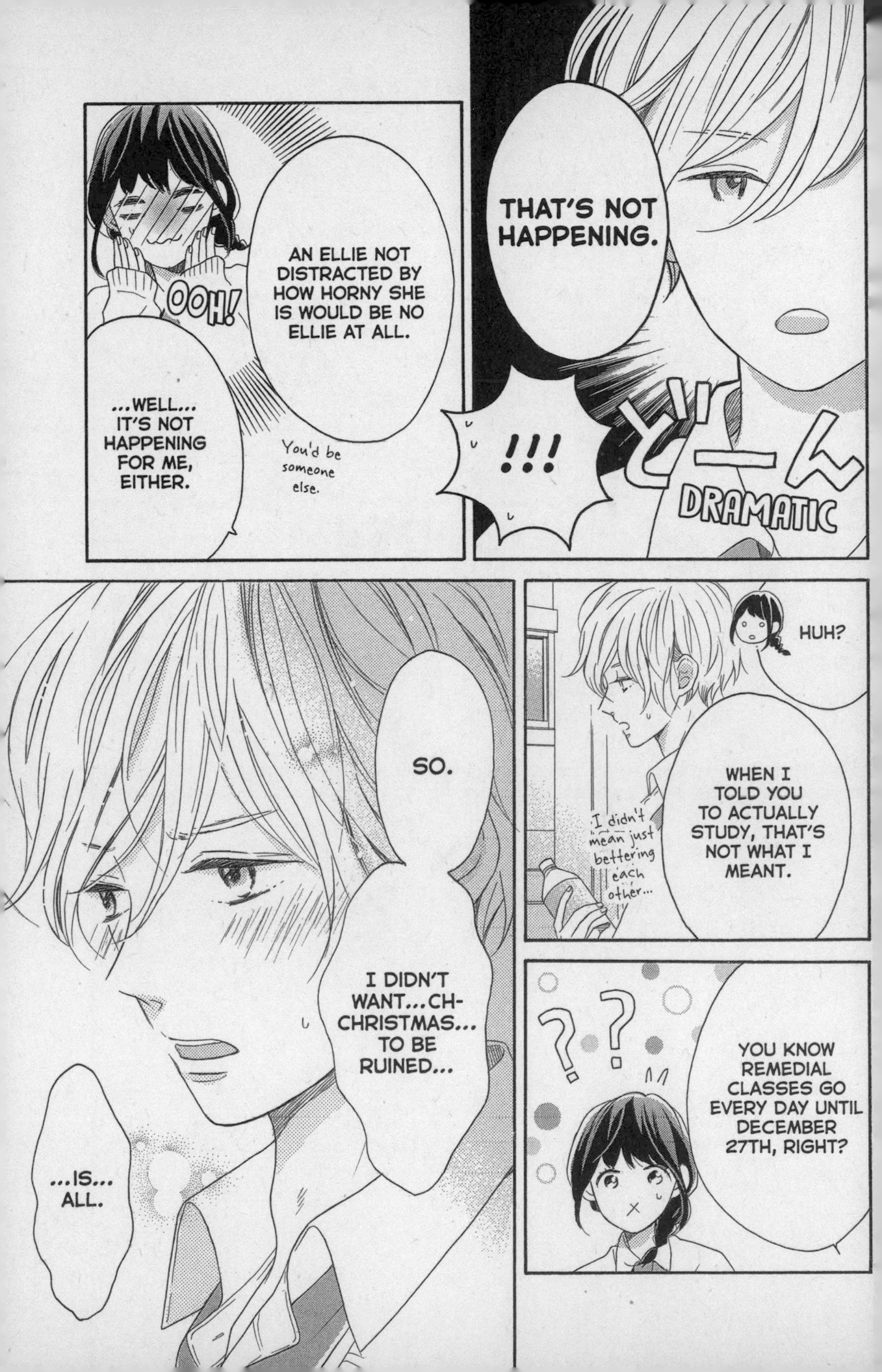
THAT'S NOT HAPPENING.
!!!
どーん
DRAMATIC
AN ELLIE NOT DISTRACTED BY HOW HORNY SHE IS WOULD BE NO ELLIE AT ALL.
You'd be someone else.
OOH!
...WELL... IT'S NOT HAPPENING FOR ME, EITHER.
HUH?
WHEN I TOLD YOU TO ACTUALLY STUDY, THAT'S NOT WHAT I MEANT.
I didn't mean just bettering each other...
YOU KNOW REMEDIAL CLASSES GO EVERY DAY UNTIL DECEMBER 27TH, RIGHT?
SO.
I DIDN'T WANT...CH-CHRISTMAS... TO BE RUINED...
...IS... ALL.

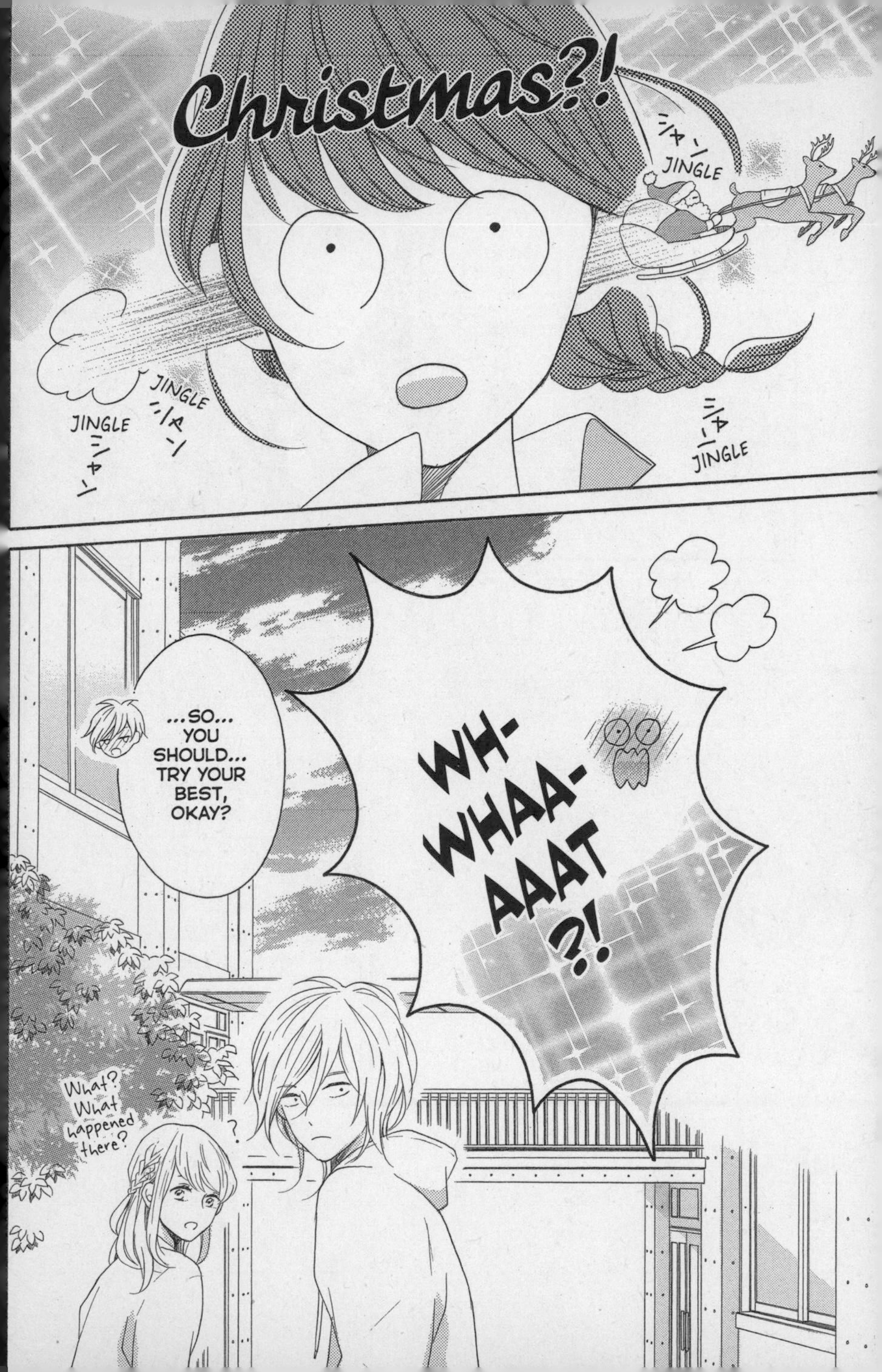
Christmas?!
シャン JINGLE
シャン JINGLE
JINGLE シャン
JINGLE シャン
WH-WHAA-AAAT?!
...SO... YOU SHOULD... TRY YOUR BEST, OKAY?
What? What happened there?
?

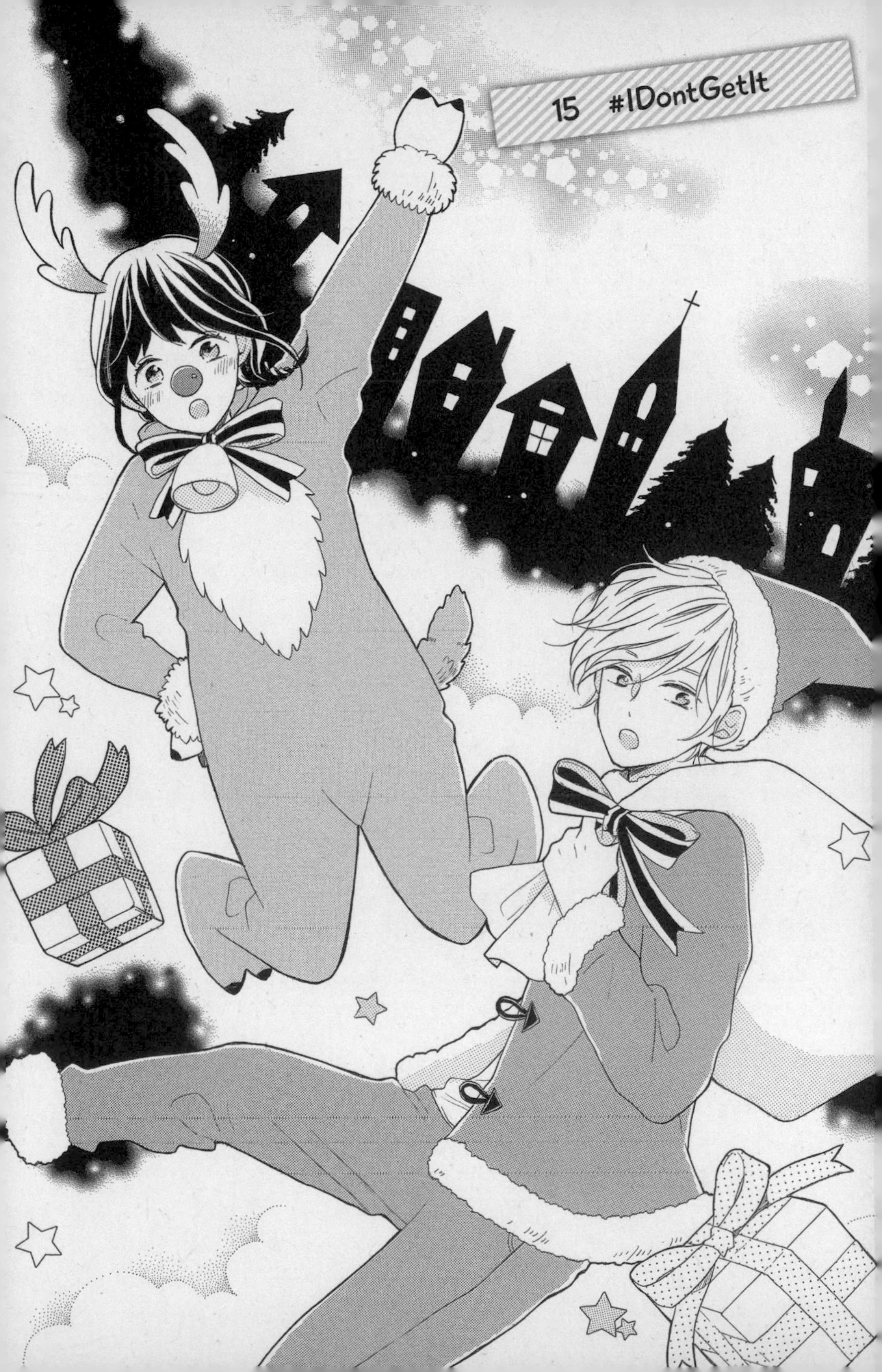
15 #IDontGetIt

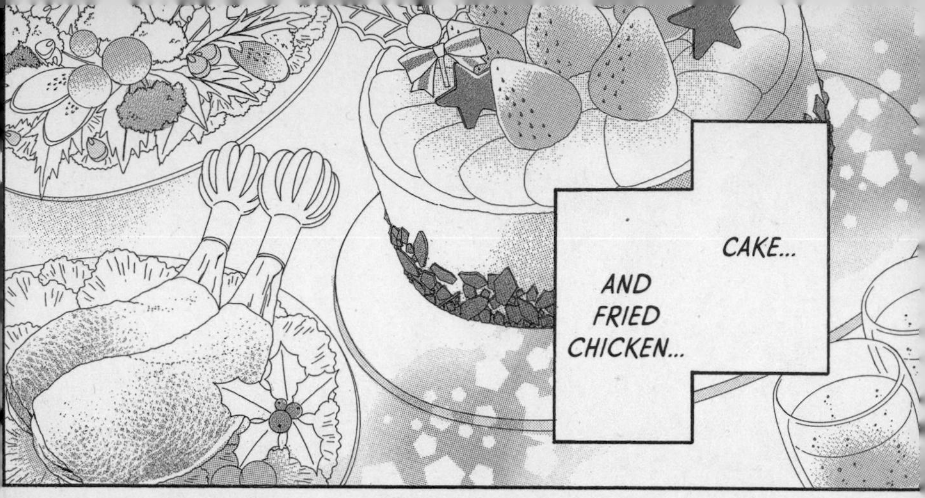
CAKE...
AND FRIED CHICKEN...

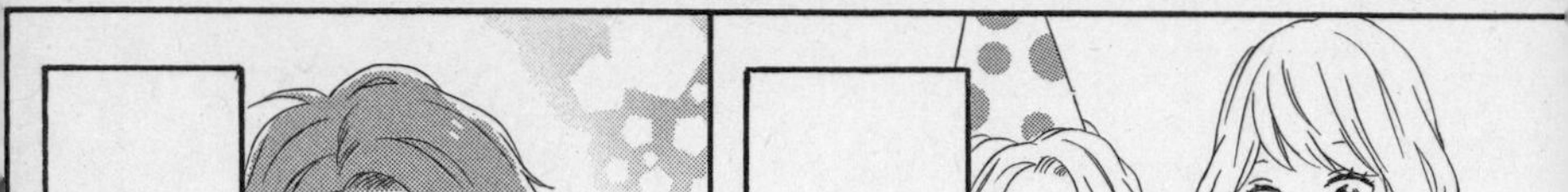
MY FAMILY'S SMILES...
AND PRESENTS.
BUT...

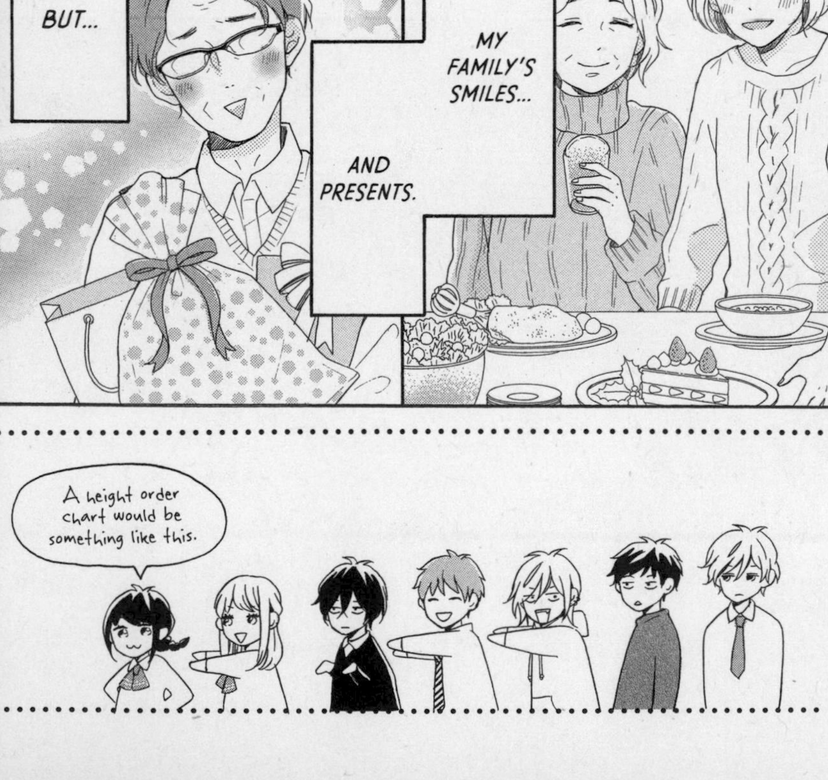
A height order chart would be something like this.

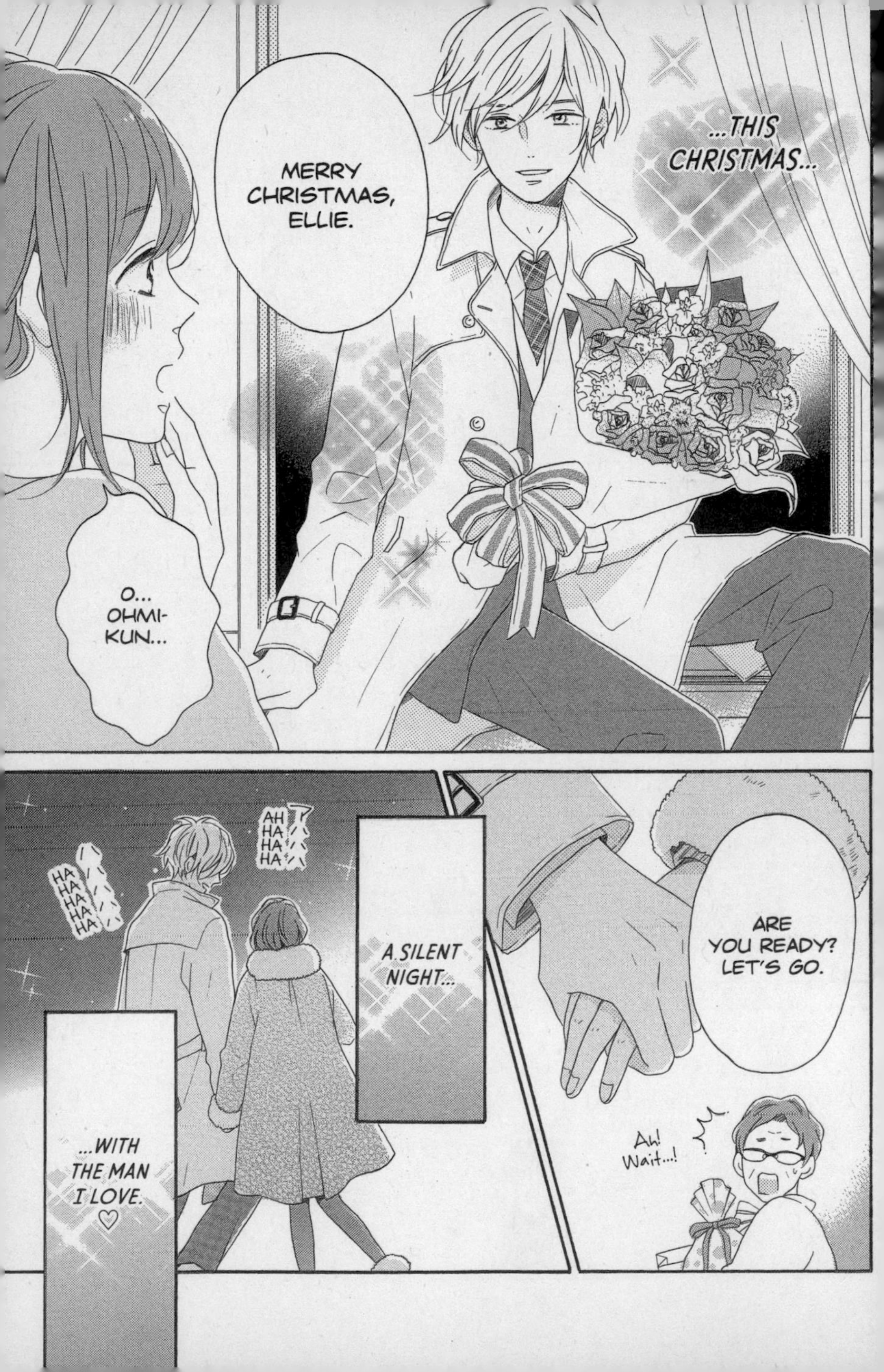
...THIS CHRISTMAS...
MERRY CHRISTMAS, ELLIE.
O... OHMI-KUN...
ARE YOU READY? LET'S GO.
Ah! Wait...!
A SILENT NIGHT...
AH HA HA HA HA
HA HA HA HA HA HA
...WITH THE MAN I LOVE. ♡

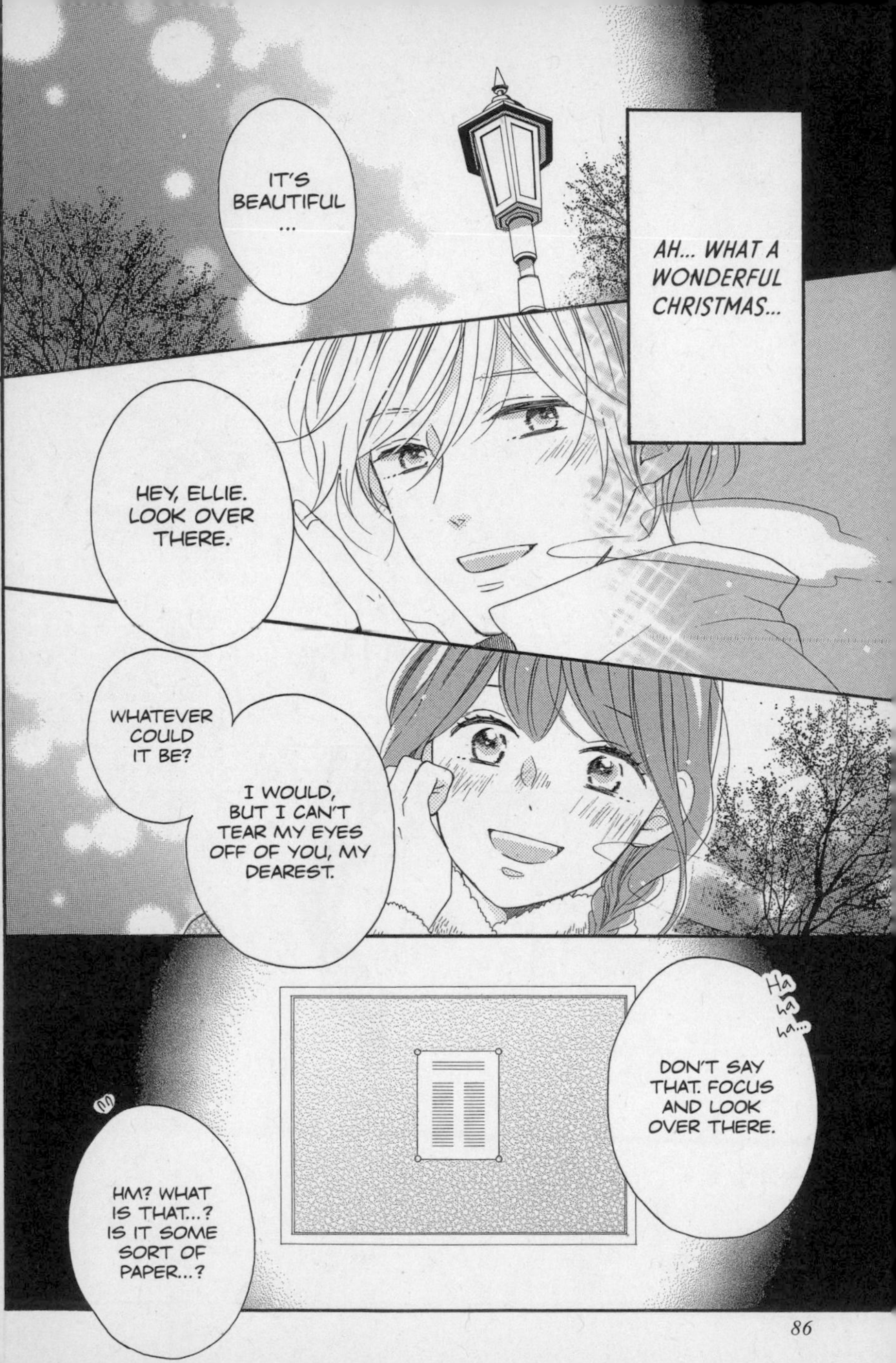
AH... WHAT A WONDERFUL CHRISTMAS...
IT'S BEAUTIFUL ...
HEY, ELLIE. LOOK OVER THERE.
WHATEVER COULD IT BE?
I WOULD, BUT I CAN'T TEAR MY EYES OFF OF YOU, MY DEAREST.
Ha ha ha...
DON'T SAY THAT. FOCUS AND LOOK OVER THERE.
HM? WHAT IS THAT...? IS IT SOME SORT OF PAPER...?

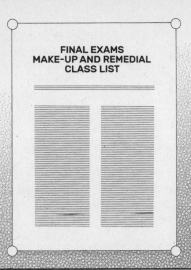

**FINAL EXAMS
MAKE-UP AND REMEDIAL
CLASS LIST**

# Eriko Ichimura (Physics)

E...
ERITSUIN...

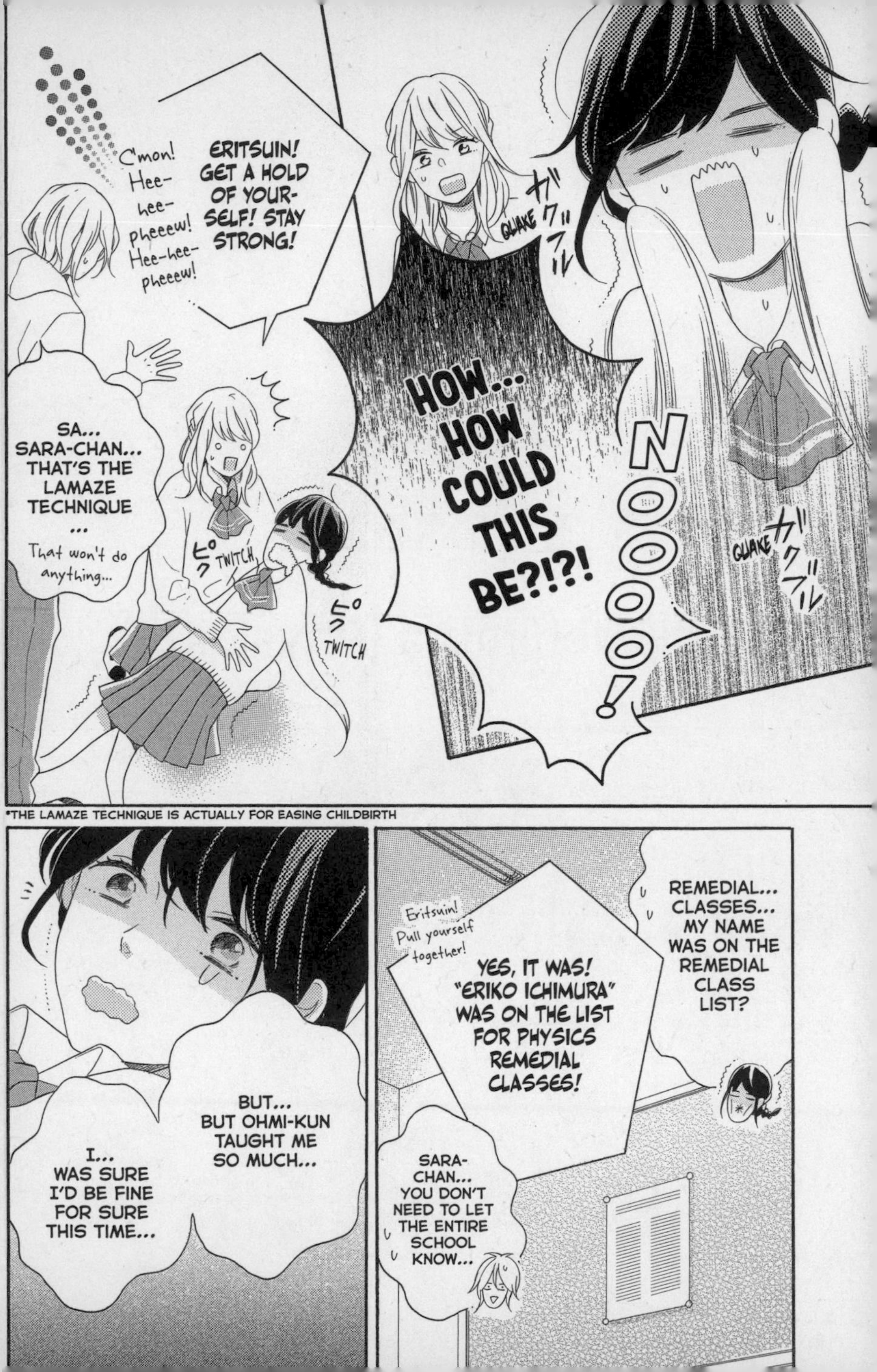
NOOOOO!
QUAKE
QUAKE
HOW... HOW COULD THIS BE?!?!
ERITSUIN! GET A HOLD OF YOURSELF! STAY STRONG!
C'mon! Hee-hee-pheeew! Hee-hee-pheeew!
SA... SARA-CHAN... THAT'S THE LAMAZE TECHNIQUE...
That won't do anything...
TWITCH
TWITCH
*THE LAMAZE TECHNIQUE IS ACTUALLY FOR EASING CHILDBIRTH
REMEDIAL... CLASSES... MY NAME WAS ON THE REMEDIAL CLASS LIST?
YES, IT WAS! "ERIKO ICHIMURA" WAS ON THE LIST FOR PHYSICS REMEDIAL CLASSES!
Eritsuin! Pull yourself together!
SARA-CHAN... YOU DON'T NEED TO LET THE ENTIRE SCHOOL KNOW...
BUT... BUT OHMI-KUN TAUGHT ME SO MUCH...
I... WAS SURE I'D BE FINE FOR SURE THIS TIME...

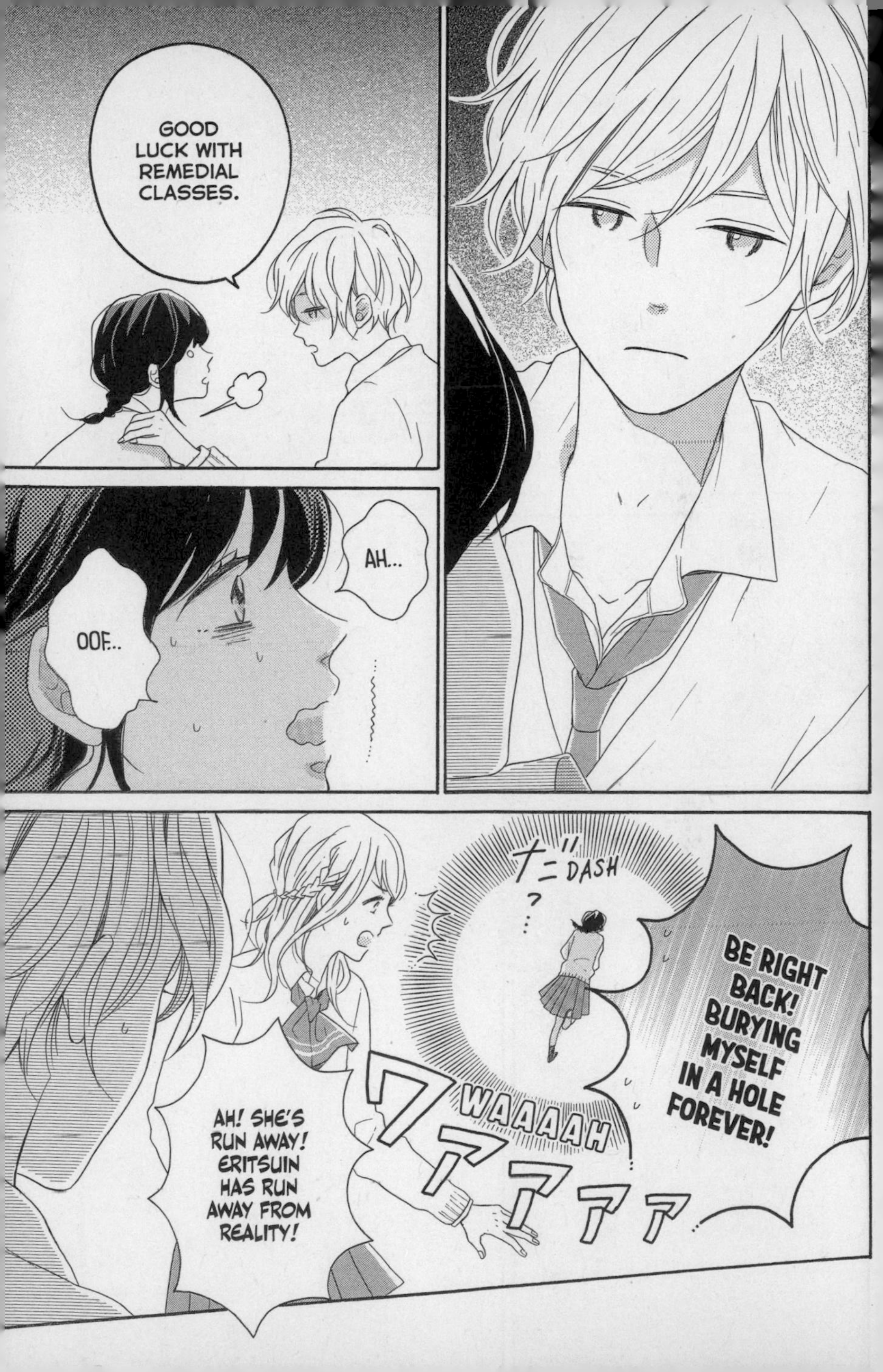

GOOD LUCK WITH REMEDIAL CLASSES.
AH...
OOF...
BE RIGHT BACK! BURYING MYSELF IN A HOLE FOREVER!
DASH
WAAAAH
AH! SHE'S RUN AWAY! ERITSUIN HAS RUN AWAY FROM REALITY!

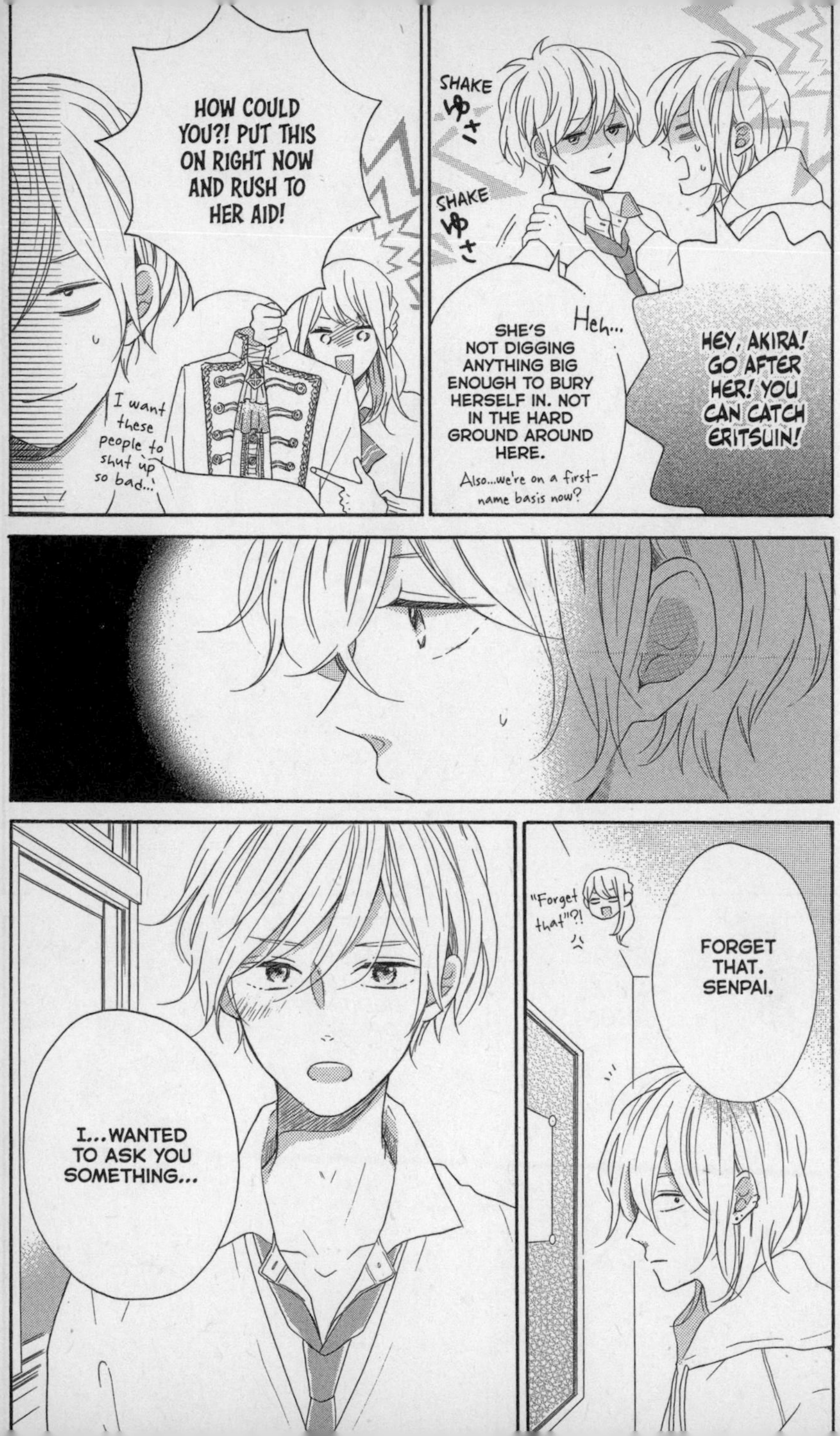
SHAKE ゆさ
SHAKE ゆさ
HEY, AKIRA! GO AFTER HER! YOU CAN CATCH ERITSUIN!
Heh...
SHE'S NOT DIGGING ANYTHING BIG ENOUGH TO BURY HERSELF IN. NOT IN THE HARD GROUND AROUND HERE.
Also...we're on a first-name basis now?
HOW COULD YOU?! PUT THIS ON RIGHT NOW AND RUSH TO HER AID!
I want these people to shut up so bad...
FORGET THAT. SENPAI.
"Forget that"?!
I...WANTED TO ASK YOU SOMETHING...

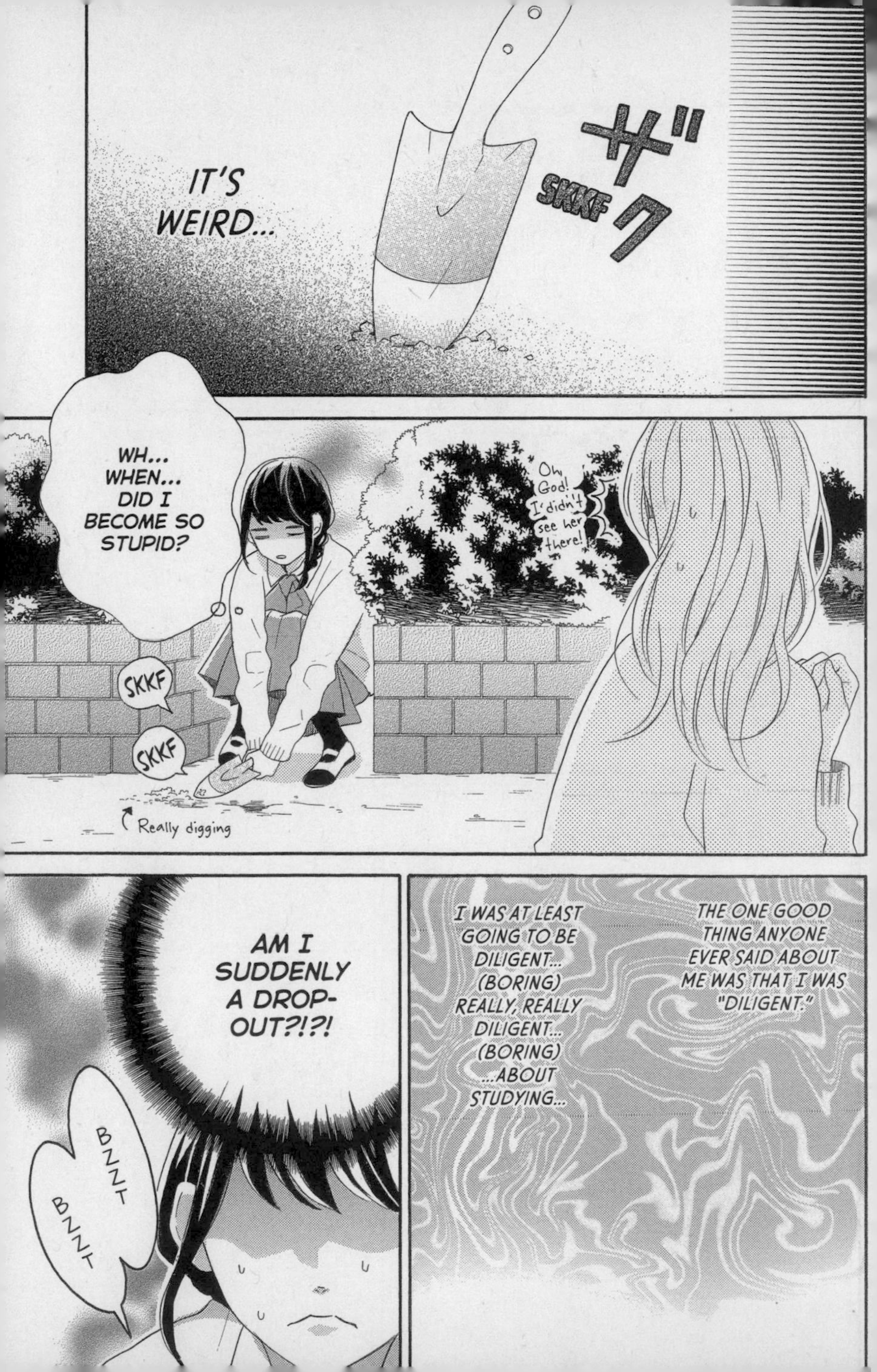

IT'S WEIRD...
ザク
SKKF
Oh, God! I didn't see her there!
WH... WHEN... DID I BECOME SO STUPID?
SKKF
SKKF
Really digging
THE ONE GOOD THING ANYONE EVER SAID ABOUT ME WAS THAT I WAS "DILIGENT."
I WAS AT LEAST GOING TO BE DILIGENT... (BORING) REALLY, REALLY DILIGENT... (BORING) ...ABOUT STUDYING...
AM I SUDDENLY A DROP-OUT?!?!
BZZT BZZT

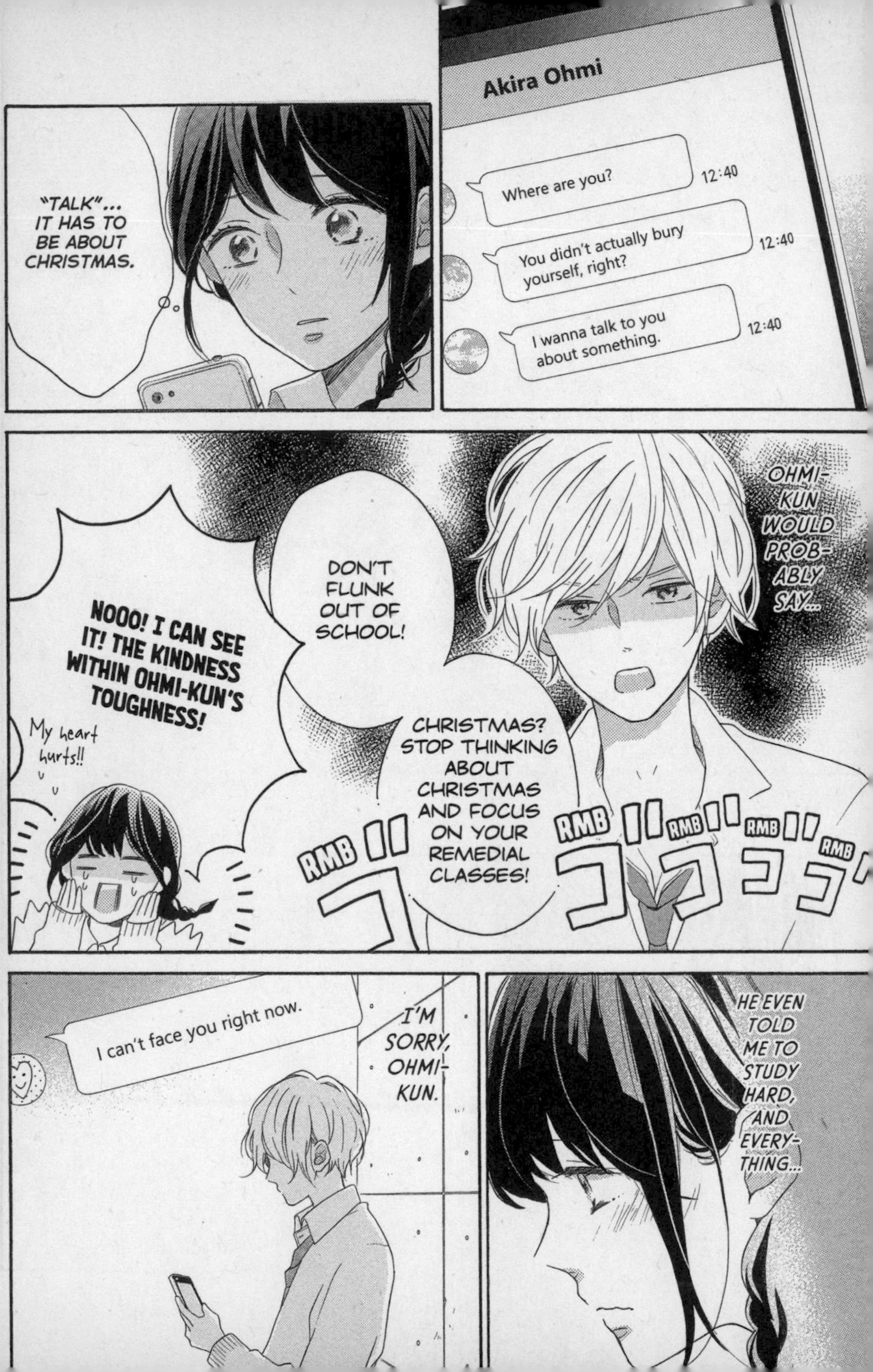
Akira Ohmi
Where are you? 12:40
You didn't actually bury yourself, right? 12:40
I wanna talk to you about something. 12:40
"TALK"... IT HAS TO BE ABOUT CHRISTMAS.
OHMI-KUN WOULD PROB-ABLY SAY...
DON'T FLUNK OUT OF SCHOOL!
CHRISTMAS? STOP THINKING ABOUT CHRISTMAS AND FOCUS ON YOUR REMEDIAL CLASSES!
RMB RMB RMB RMB RMB
NOOO! I CAN SEE IT! THE KINDNESS WITHIN OHMI-KUN'S TOUGHNESS!
My heart hurts!!
HE EVEN TOLD ME TO STUDY HARD, AND EVERY-THING...
I'M SORRY, OHMI-KUN.
I can't face you right now.

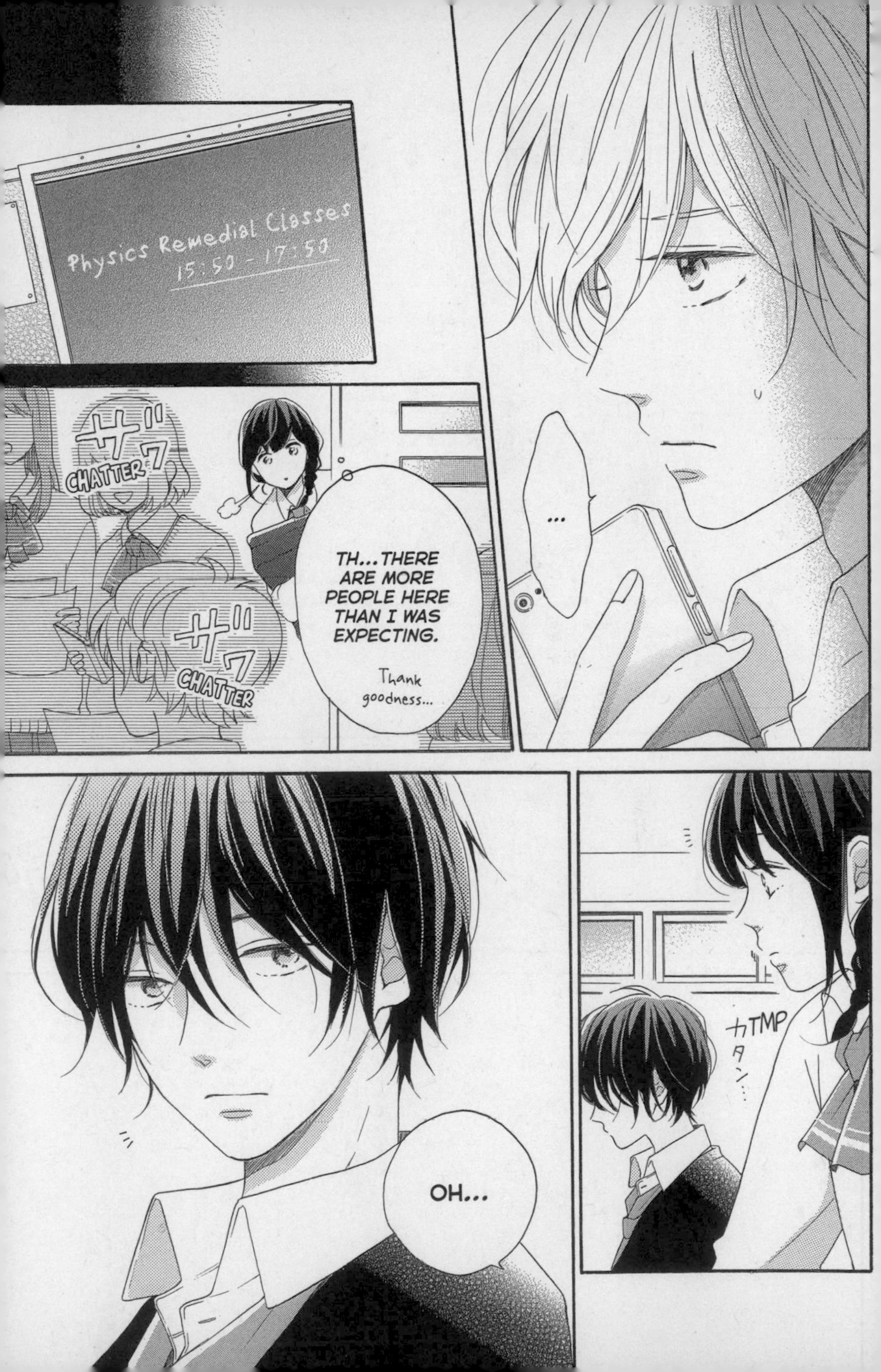
...
Physics Remedial Classes
15:50 - 17:50
TH...THERE ARE MORE PEOPLE HERE THAN I WAS EXPECTING.
Thank goodness...
ザワ CHATTER
ザワ CHATTER
カタン… TMP
OH...

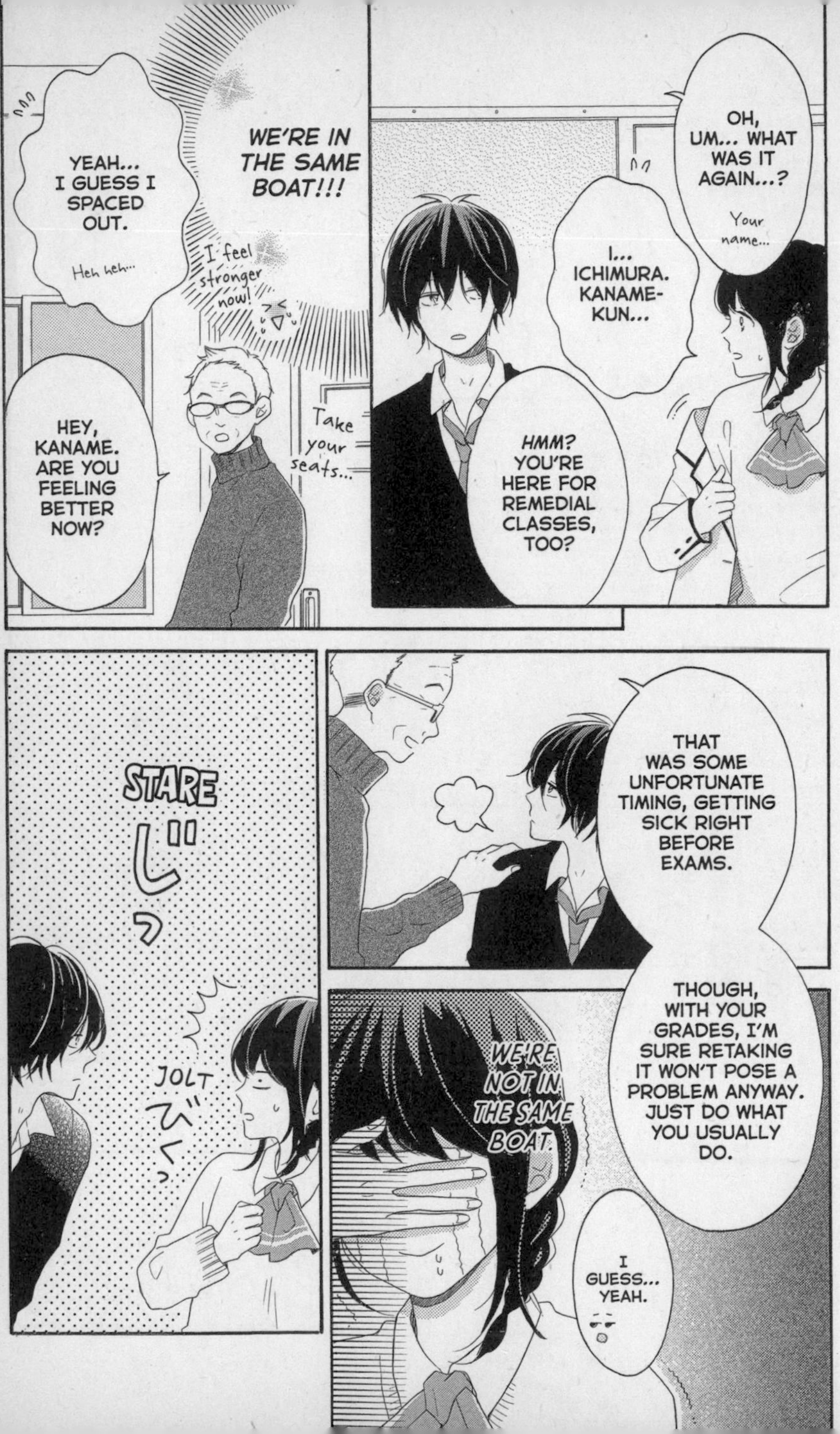
OH, UM... WHAT WAS IT AGAIN...?
Your name...
I... ICHIMURA. KANAME-KUN...
HMM? YOU'RE HERE FOR REMEDIAL CLASSES, TOO?
WE'RE IN THE SAME BOAT!!!
I feel stronger now!
YEAH... I GUESS I SPACED OUT.
Heh heh...
HEY, KANAME. ARE YOU FEELING BETTER NOW?
Take your seats...
THAT WAS SOME UNFORTUNATE TIMING, GETTING SICK RIGHT BEFORE EXAMS.
THOUGH, WITH YOUR GRADES, I'M SURE RETAKING IT WON'T POSE A PROBLEM ANYWAY. JUST DO WHAT YOU USUALLY DO.
WE'RE NOT IN THE SAME BOAT.
I GUESS... YEAH.
STARE
JOLT

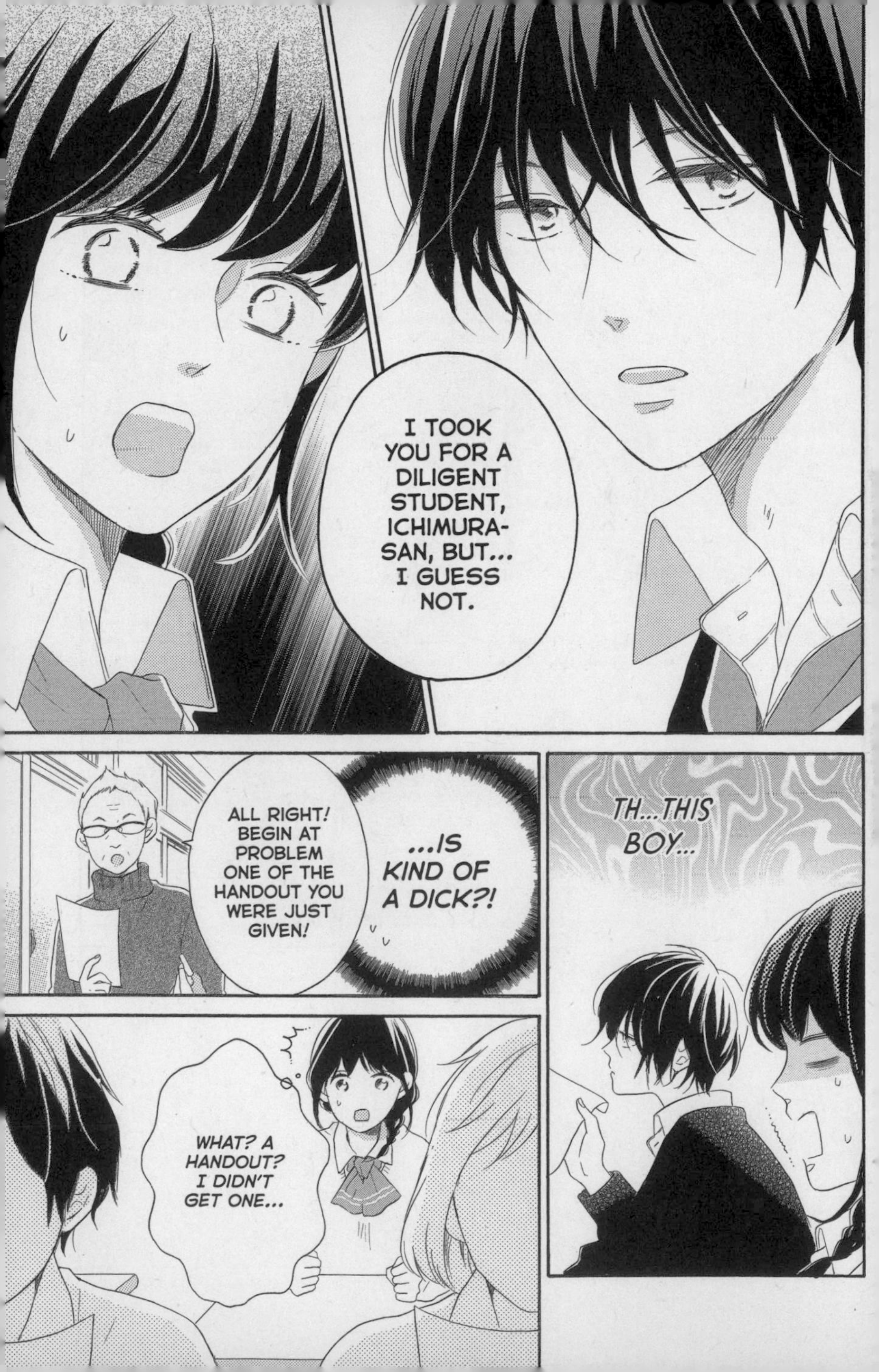
I TOOK YOU FOR A DILIGENT STUDENT, ICHIMURA-SAN, BUT... I GUESS NOT.
TH...THIS BOY...
...IS KIND OF A DICK?!
ALL RIGHT! BEGIN AT PROBLEM ONE OF THE HANDOUT YOU WERE JUST GIVEN!
WHAT? A HANDOUT? I DIDN'T GET ONE...

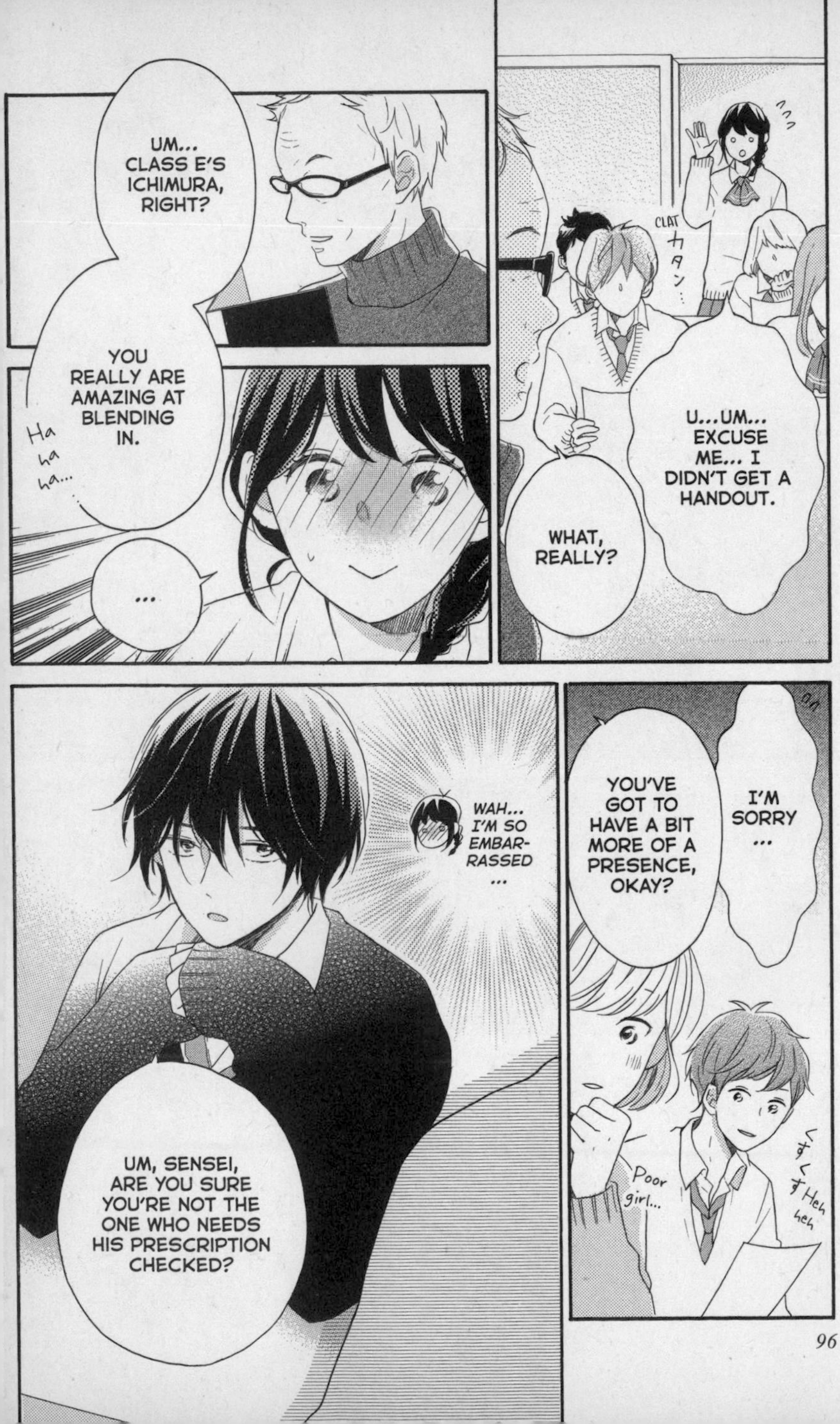
CLAT カタン…
U…UM… EXCUSE ME… I DIDN'T GET A HANDOUT.
WHAT, REALLY?
UM… CLASS E'S ICHIMURA, RIGHT?
YOU REALLY ARE AMAZING AT BLENDING IN.
Ha ha ha…
…
I'M SORRY…
YOU'VE GOT TO HAVE A BIT MORE OF A PRESENCE, OKAY?
Poor girl…
くすくす Heh heh
WAH… I'M SO EMBARRASSED…
UM, SENSEI, ARE YOU SURE YOU'RE NOT THE ONE WHO NEEDS HIS PRESCRIPTION CHECKED?

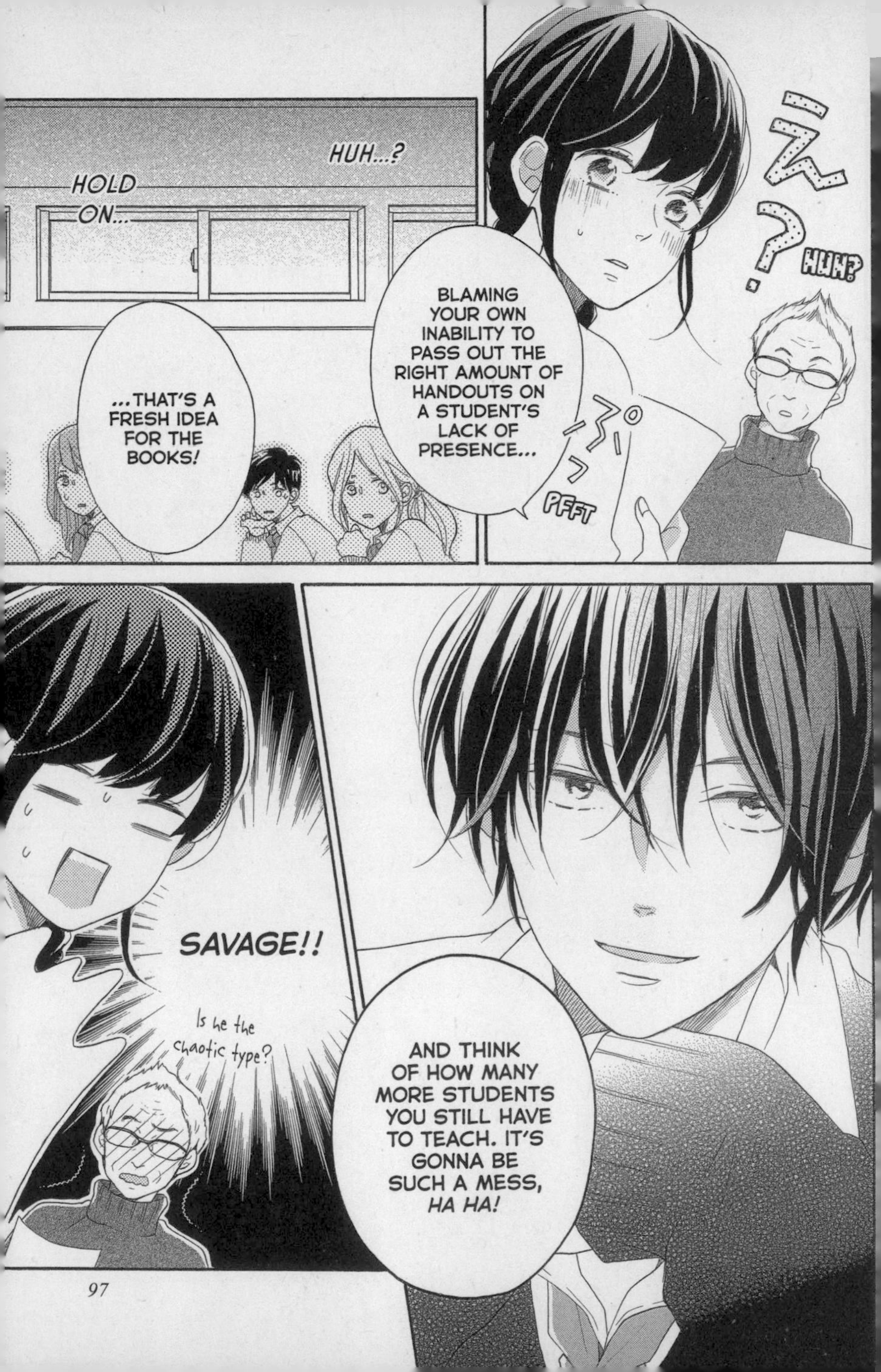

え?
HUH?
BLAMING YOUR OWN INABILITY TO PASS OUT THE RIGHT AMOUNT OF HANDOUTS ON A STUDENT'S LACK OF PRESENCE...
ぷっ
PFFT
HUH...?
HOLD ON...
...THAT'S A FRESH IDEA FOR THE BOOKS!
AND THINK OF HOW MANY MORE STUDENTS YOU STILL HAVE TO TEACH. IT'S GONNA BE SUCH A MESS, *HA HA!*
SAVAGE!!
Is he the chaotic type?

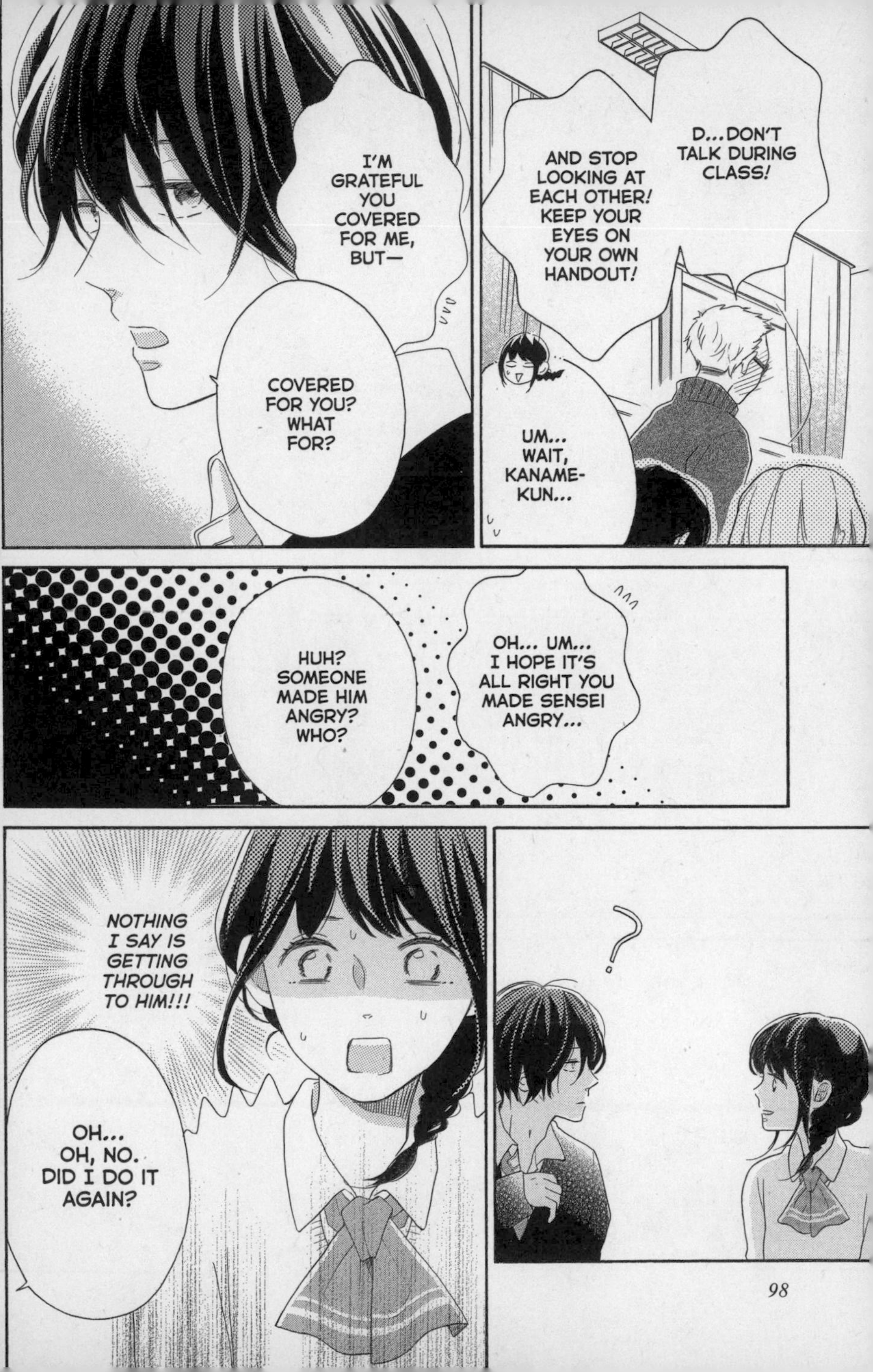
D...DON'T TALK DURING CLASS!
AND STOP LOOKING AT EACH OTHER! KEEP YOUR EYES ON YOUR OWN HANDOUT!
UM... WAIT, KANAME-KUN...
I'M GRATEFUL YOU COVERED FOR ME, BUT—
COVERED FOR YOU? WHAT FOR?
OH... UM... I HOPE IT'S ALL RIGHT YOU MADE SENSEI ANGRY...
HUH? SOMEONE MADE HIM ANGRY? WHO?
?
NOTHING I SAY IS GETTING THROUGH TO HIM!!!
OH... OH, NO. DID I DO IT AGAIN?

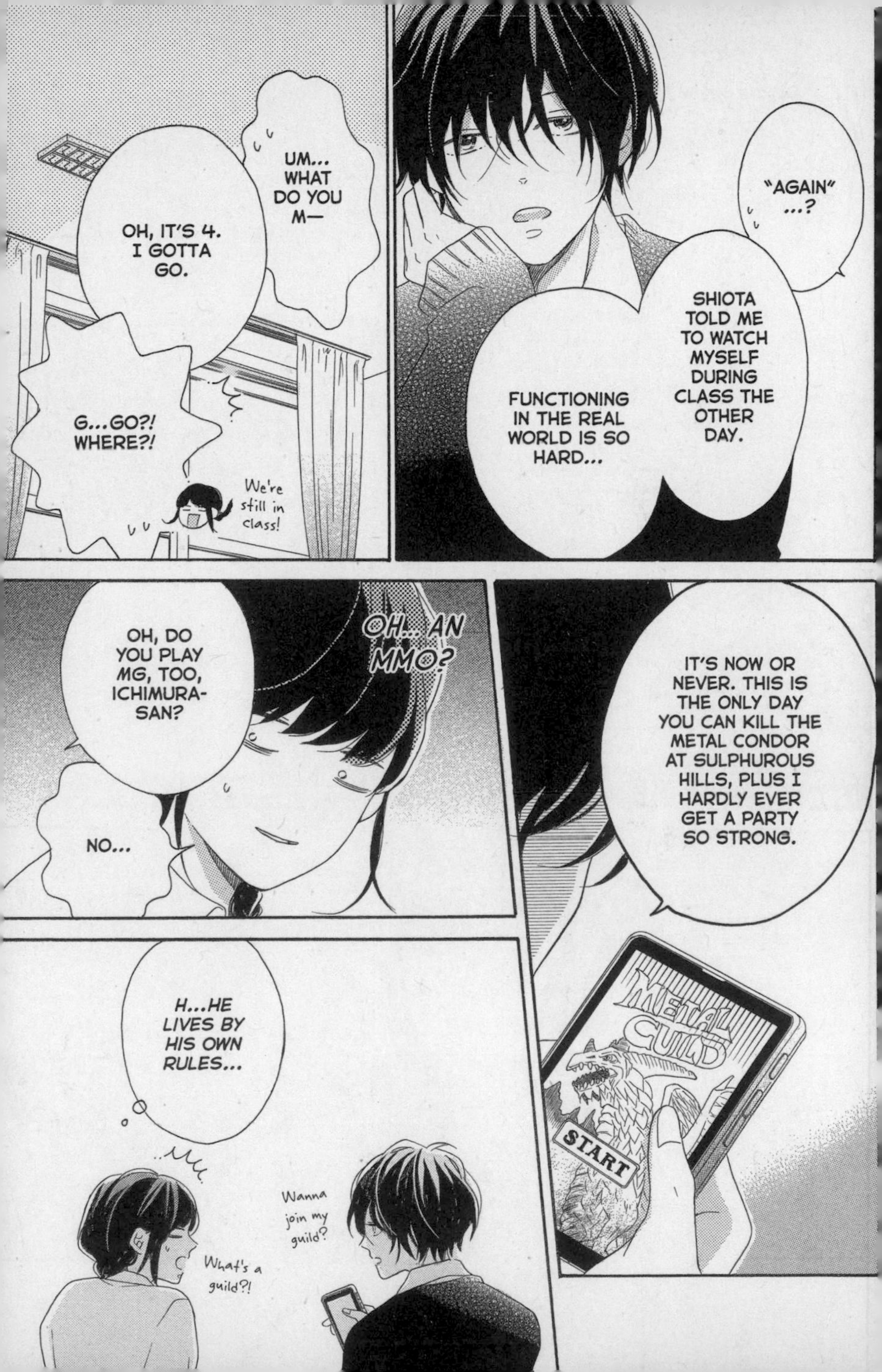
"AGAIN" ...?
SHIOTA TOLD ME TO WATCH MYSELF DURING CLASS THE OTHER DAY.
FUNCTIONING IN THE REAL WORLD IS SO HARD...
UM... WHAT DO YOU M—
OH, IT'S 4. I GOTTA GO.
G...GO?! WHERE?!
We're still in class!
IT'S NOW OR NEVER. THIS IS THE ONLY DAY YOU CAN KILL THE METAL CONDOR AT SULPHUROUS HILLS, PLUS I HARDLY EVER GET A PARTY SO STRONG.
METAL GUILD
START
OH... AN MMO?
OH, DO YOU PLAY MG, TOO, ICHIMURA-SAN?
NO...
H...HE LIVES BY HIS OWN RULES...
Wanna join my guild?
What's a guild?!

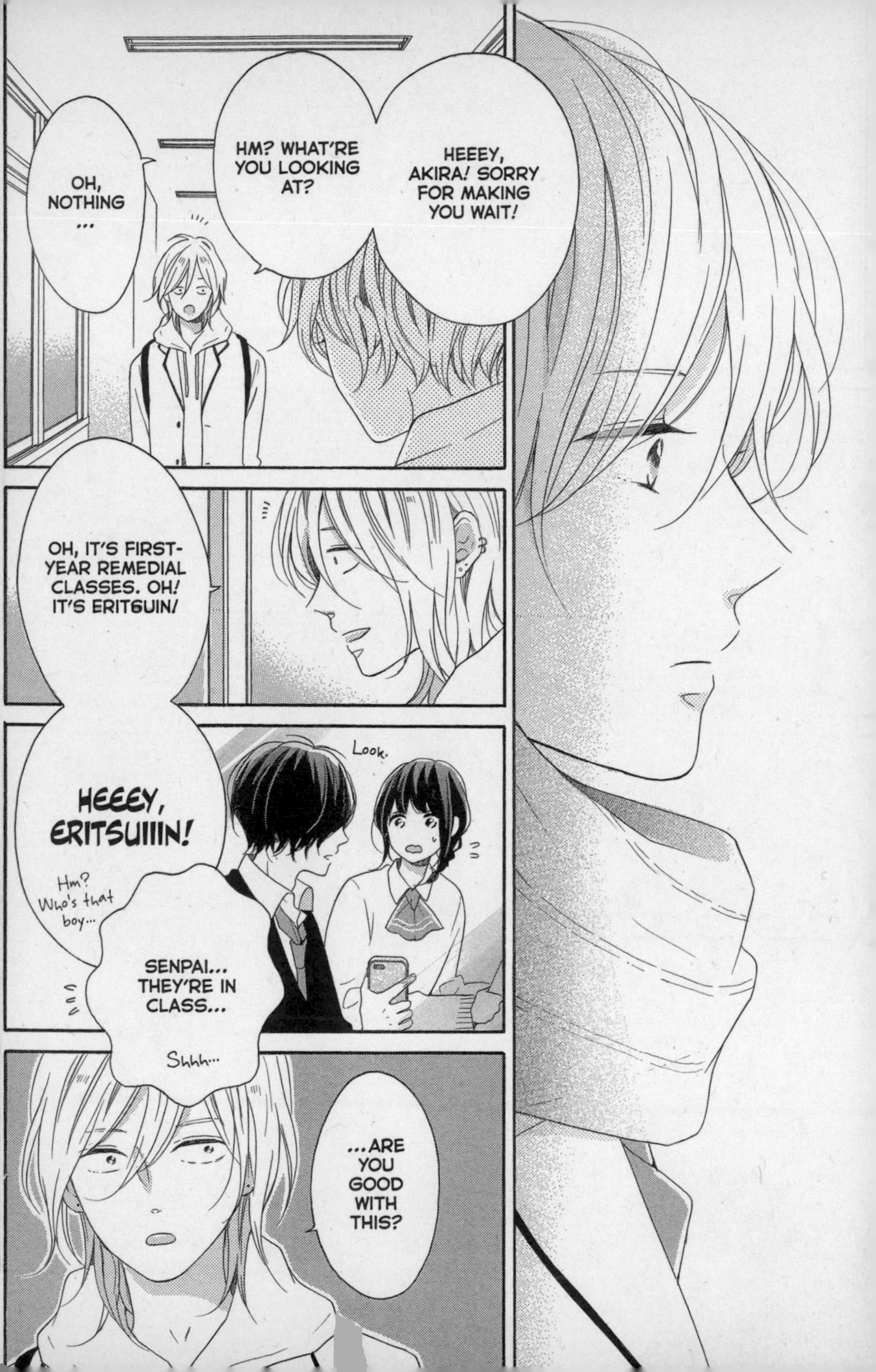

HEEEY, AKIRA! SORRY FOR MAKING YOU WAIT!
HM? WHAT'RE YOU LOOKING AT?
OH, NOTHING ...
OH, IT'S FIRST-YEAR REMEDIAL CLASSES. OH! IT'S ERITSUIN!
HEEEY, ERITSUIIIN!
Look.
Hm? Who's that boy...
SENPAI... THEY'RE IN CLASS...
Shhh...
...ARE YOU GOOD WITH THIS?

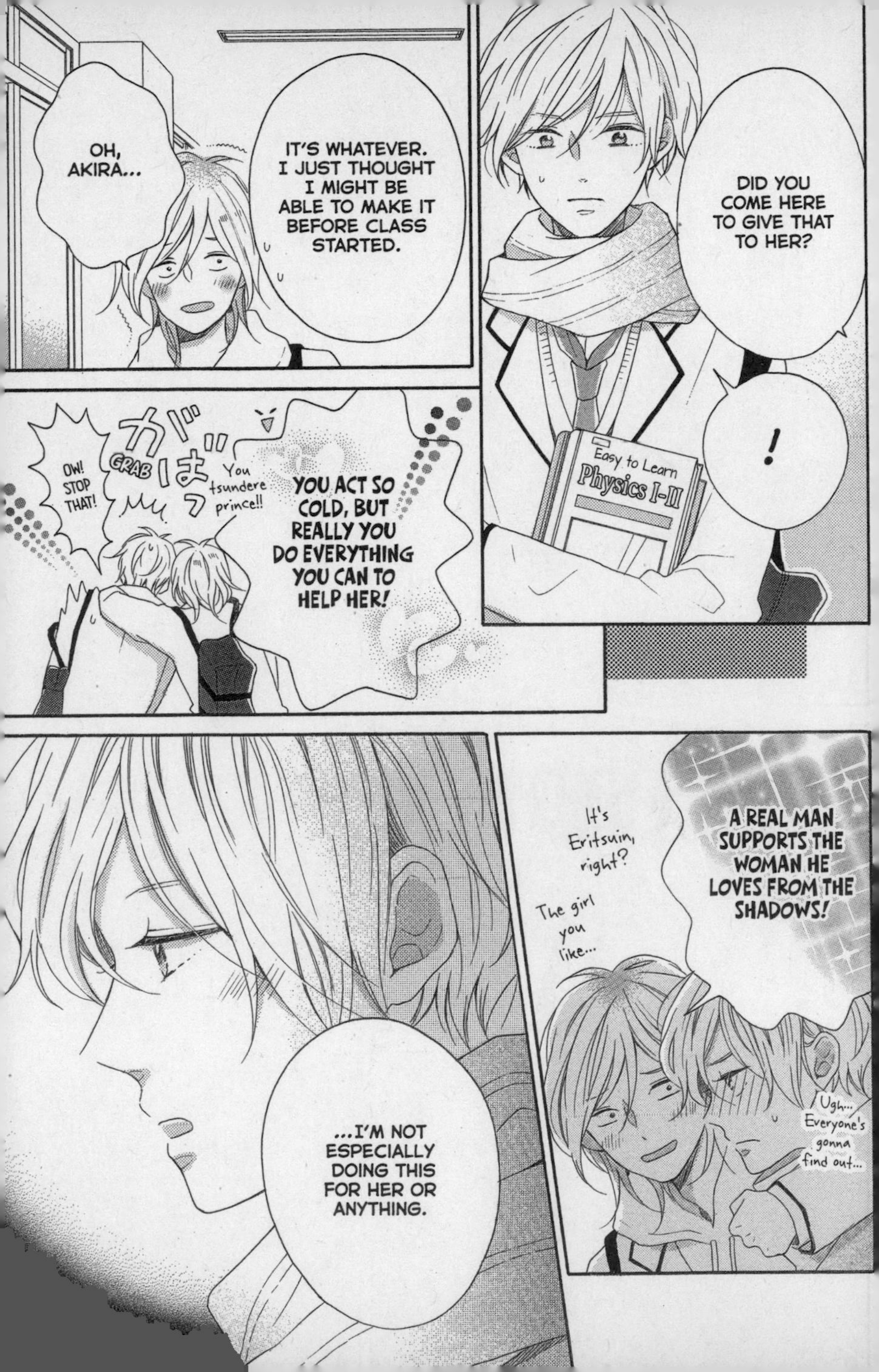
DID YOU COME HERE TO GIVE THAT TO HER?
!
Easy to Learn
Physics I-II
IT'S WHATEVER. I JUST THOUGHT I MIGHT BE ABLE TO MAKE IT BEFORE CLASS STARTED.
OH, AKIRA...
YOU ACT SO COLD, BUT REALLY YOU DO EVERYTHING YOU CAN TO HELP HER!
You tsundere prince!!
がばっ
GRAB
OW! STOP THAT!
A REAL MAN SUPPORTS THE WOMAN HE LOVES FROM THE SHADOWS!
It's Eritsuin, right?
The girl you like...
Ugh... Everyone's gonna find out...
...I'M NOT ESPECIALLY DOING THIS FOR HER OR ANYTHING.

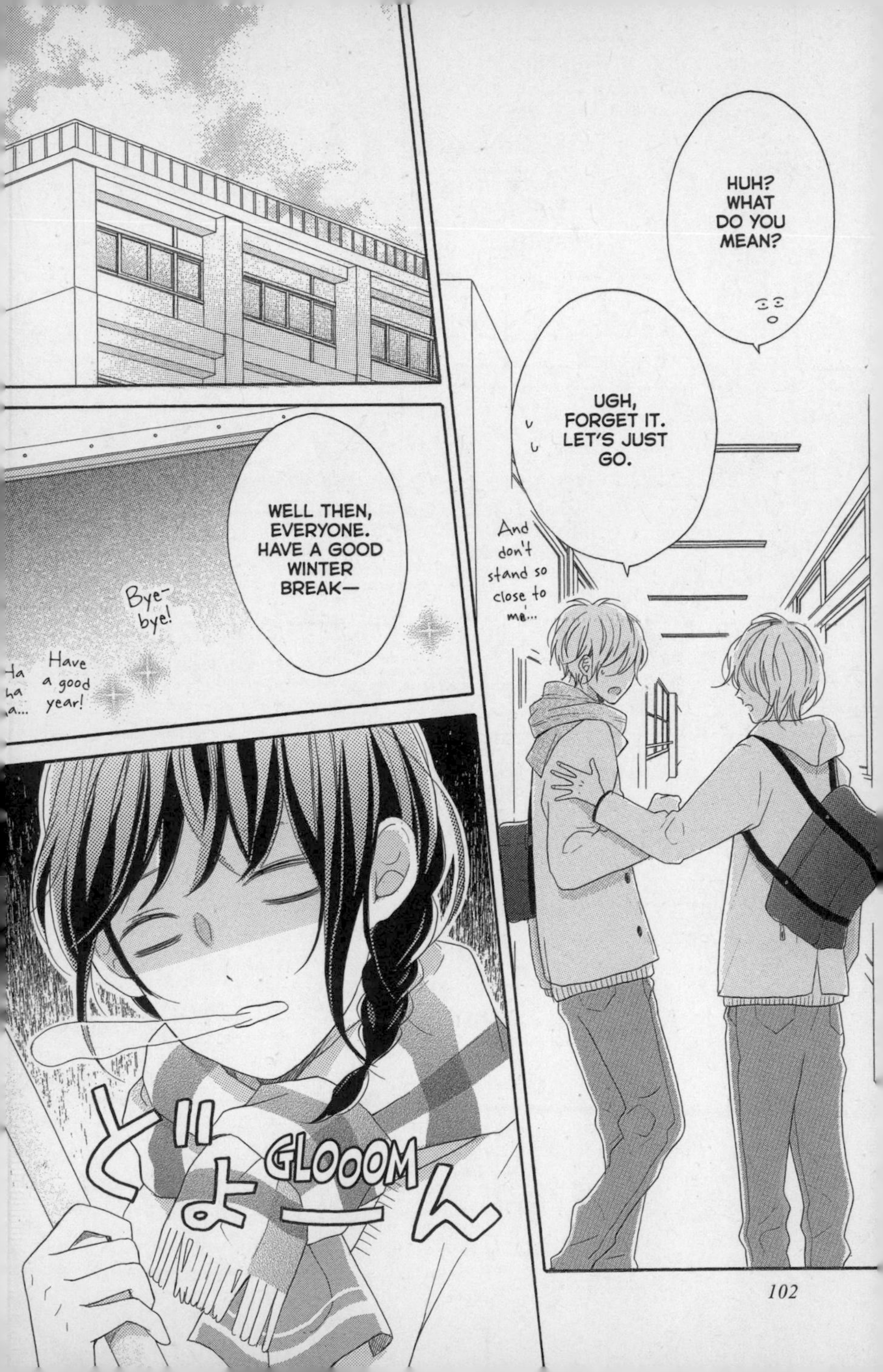
HUH? WHAT DO YOU MEAN?
UGH, FORGET IT. LET'S JUST GO.
And don't stand so close to me...
WELL THEN, EVERYONE. HAVE A GOOD WINTER BREAK—
Bye-bye!
Have a good year!
どよーん
GLOOOM

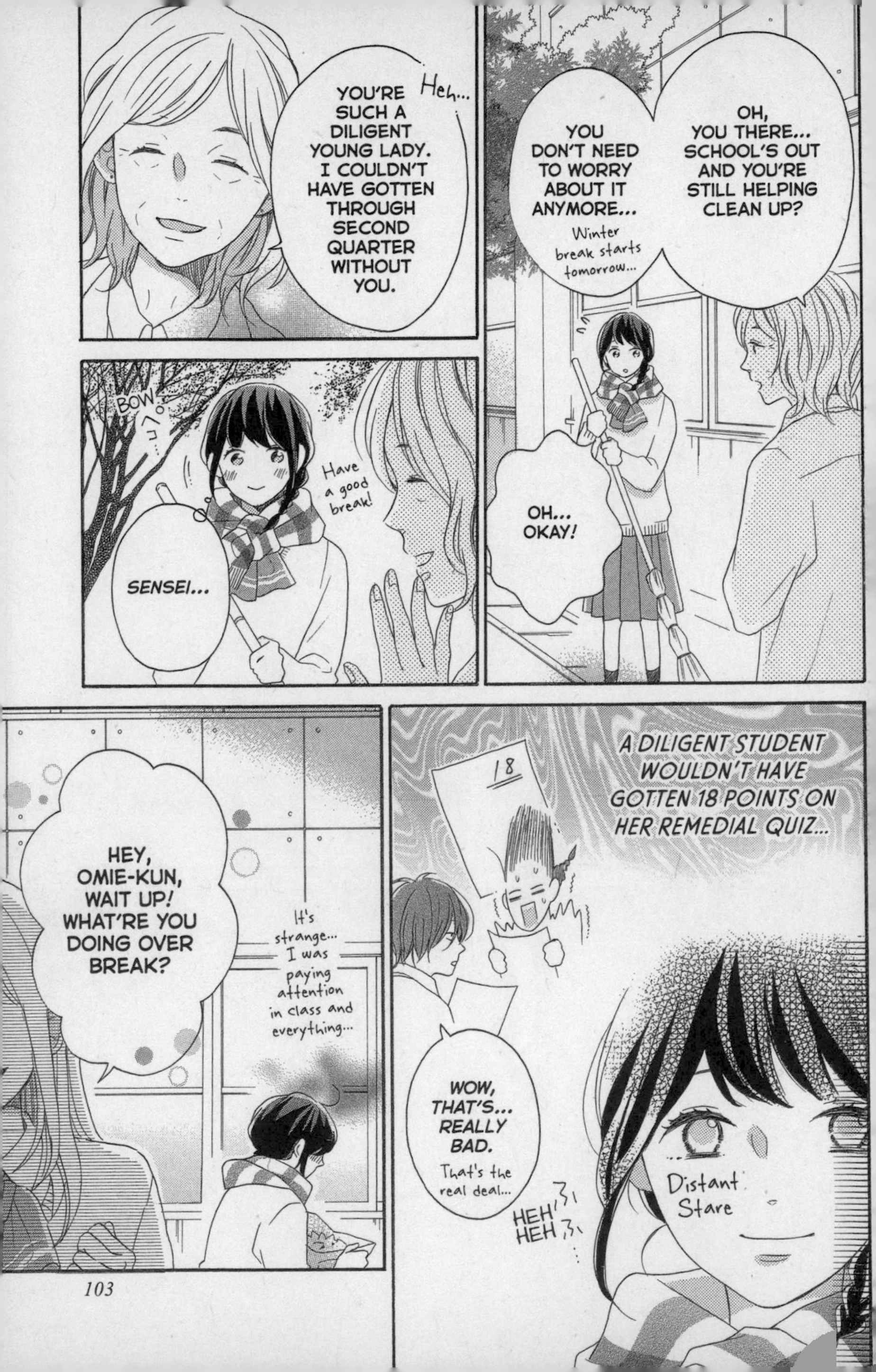
OH, YOU THERE... SCHOOL'S OUT AND YOU'RE STILL HELPING CLEAN UP?
YOU DON'T NEED TO WORRY ABOUT IT ANYMORE...
Winter break starts tomorrow...
OH... OKAY!
Heh...
YOU'RE SUCH A DILIGENT YOUNG LADY. I COULDN'T HAVE GOTTEN THROUGH SECOND QUARTER WITHOUT YOU.
BOW
Have a good break!
SENSEI...
A DILIGENT STUDENT WOULDN'T HAVE GOTTEN 18 POINTS ON HER REMEDIAL QUIZ...
18
WOW, THAT'S... REALLY BAD.
That's the real deal...
HEH HEH
Distant Stare
HEY, OMIE-KUN, WAIT UP! WHAT'RE YOU DOING OVER BREAK?
It's strange... I was paying attention in class and everything...

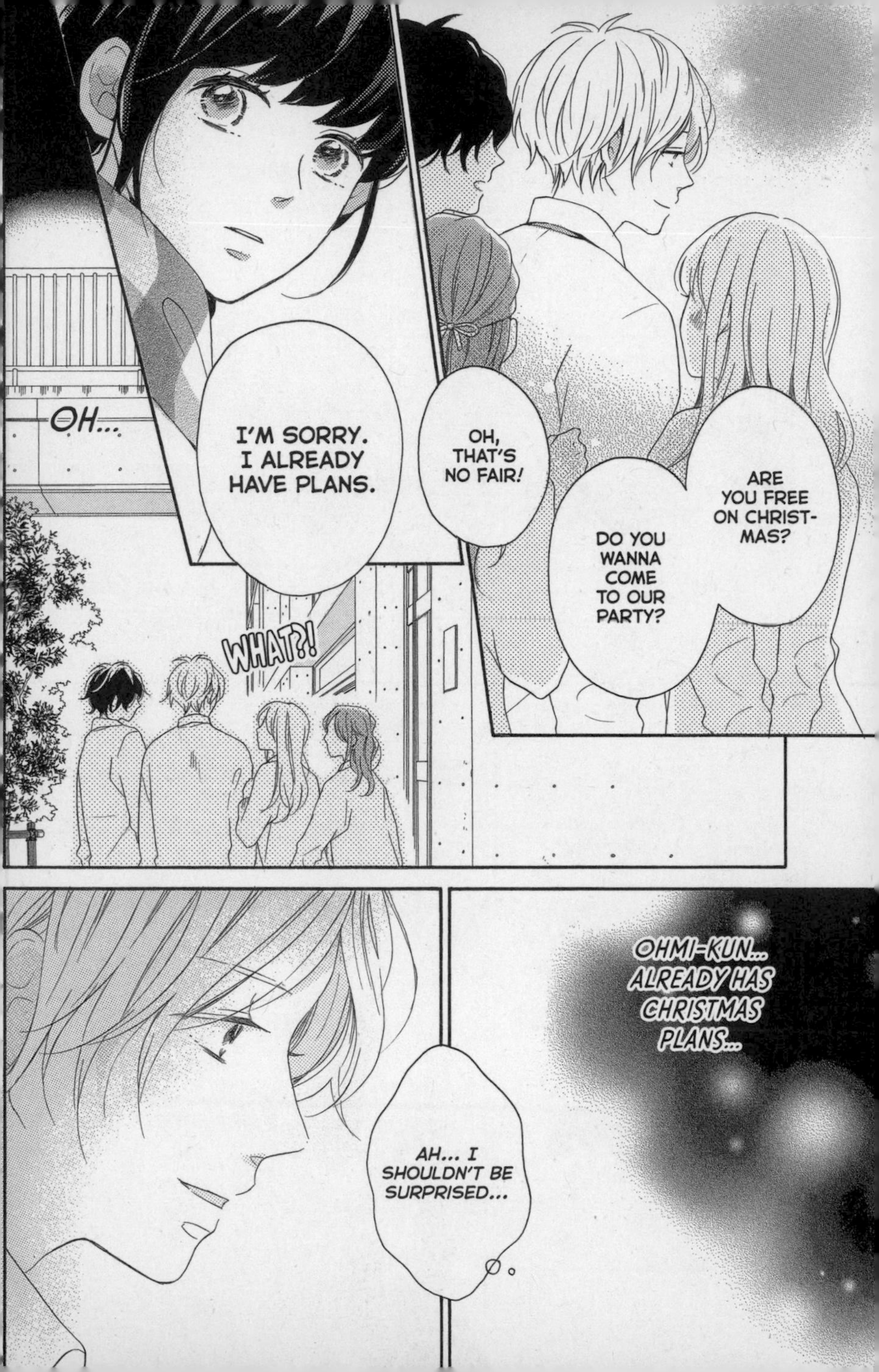
ARE YOU FREE ON CHRIST-MAS?
DO YOU WANNA COME TO OUR PARTY?
OH, THAT'S NO FAIR!
I'M SORRY. I ALREADY HAVE PLANS.
WHAT?!
OH...
OHMI-KUN... ALREADY HAS CHRISTMAS PLANS...
AH... I SHOULDN'T BE SURPRISED...

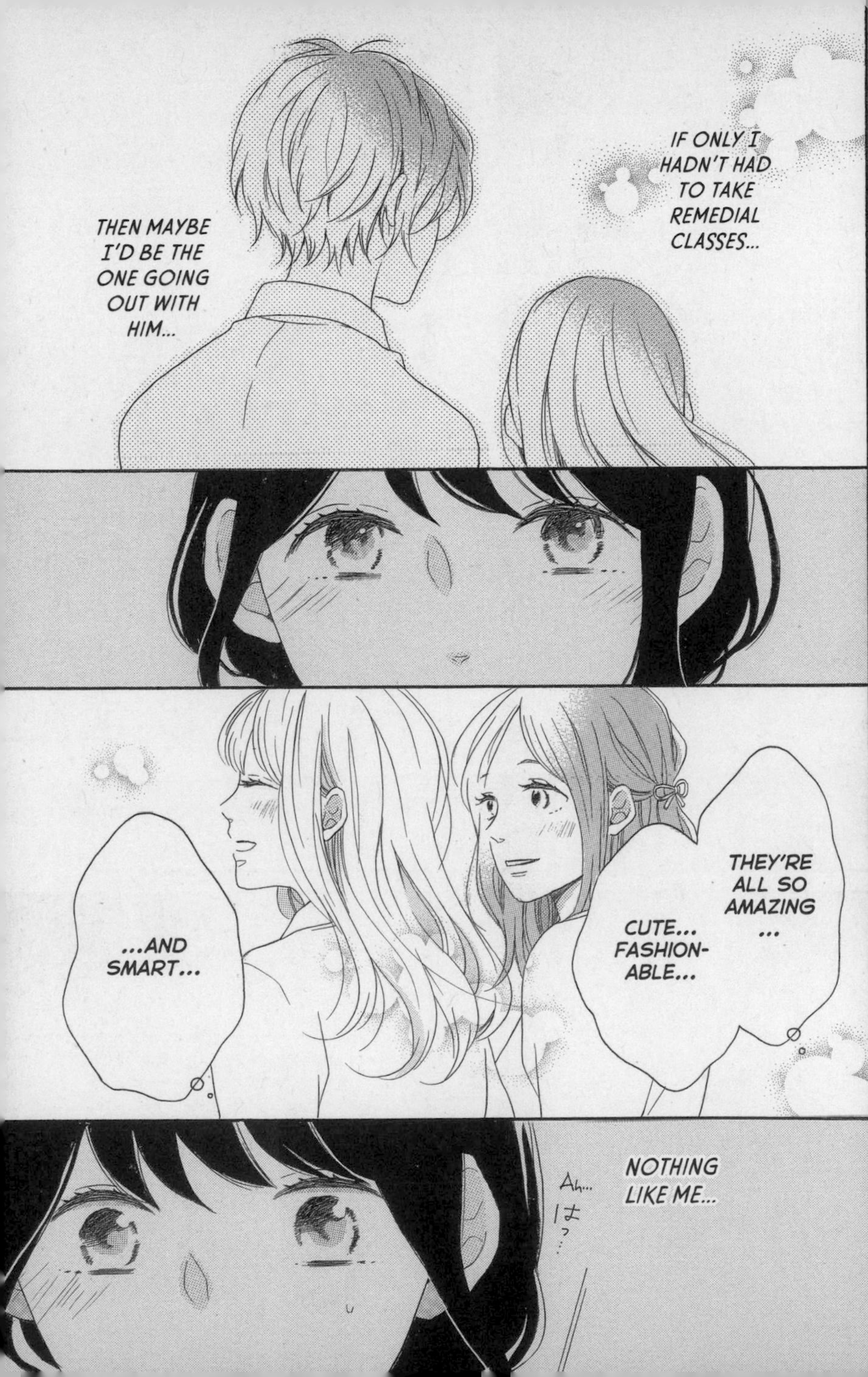
IF ONLY I HADN'T HAD TO TAKE REMEDIAL CLASSES...
THEN MAYBE I'D BE THE ONE GOING OUT WITH HIM...
THEY'RE ALL SO AMAZING ...
CUTE... FASHION-ABLE...
...AND SMART...
NOTHING LIKE ME...
Ah...
はっ...

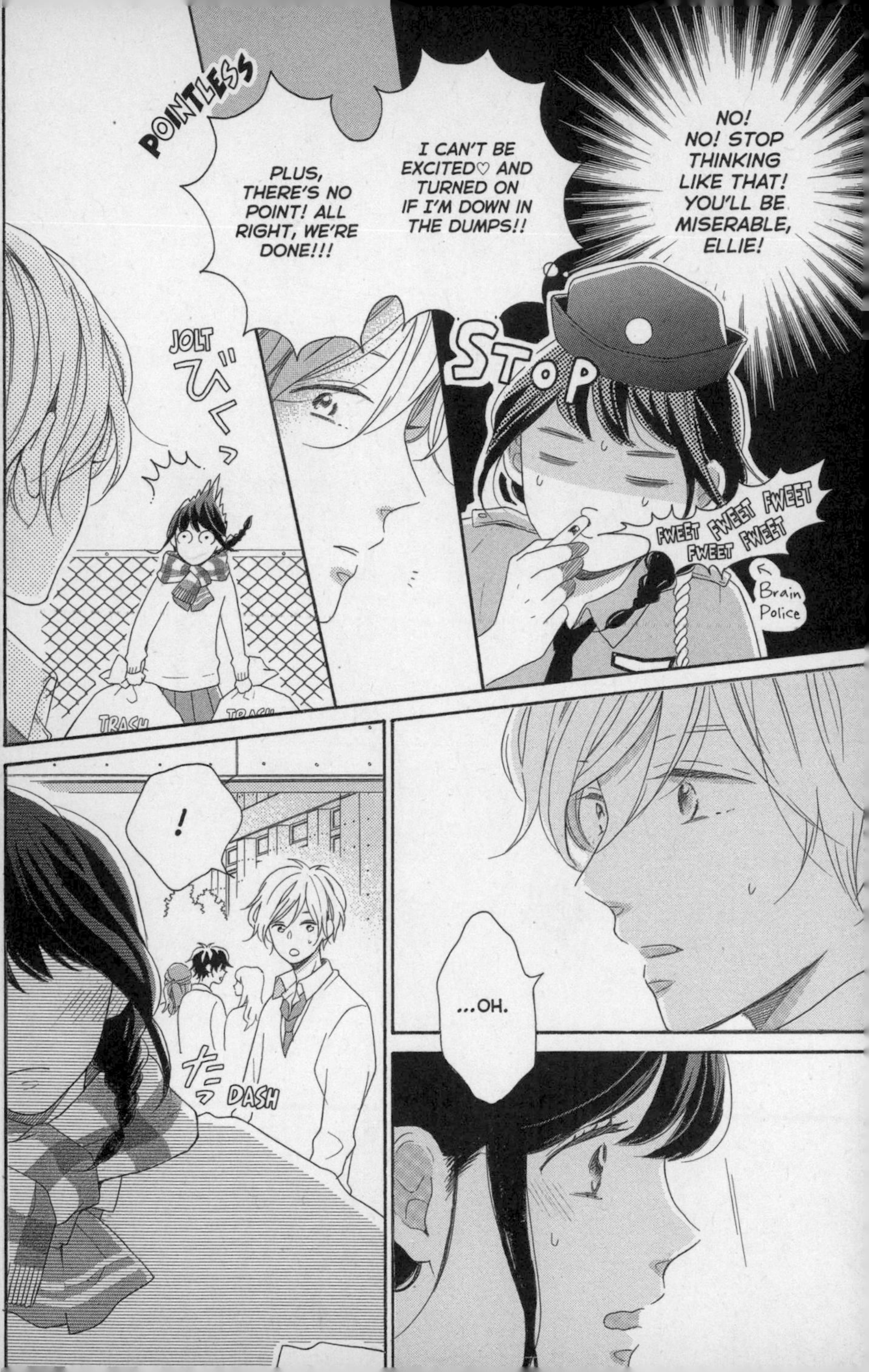
NO! NO! STOP THINKING LIKE THAT! YOU'LL BE MISERABLE, ELLIE!
I CAN'T BE EXCITED♡ AND TURNED ON IF I'M DOWN IN THE DUMPS!!
PLUS, THERE'S NO POINT! ALL RIGHT, WE'RE DONE!!!
POINTLESS
STOP
FWEET FWEET FWEET FWEET FWEET FWEET
← Brain Police
JOLT
びくっ
TRASH
TRASH
...OH.
!
たっ
DASH

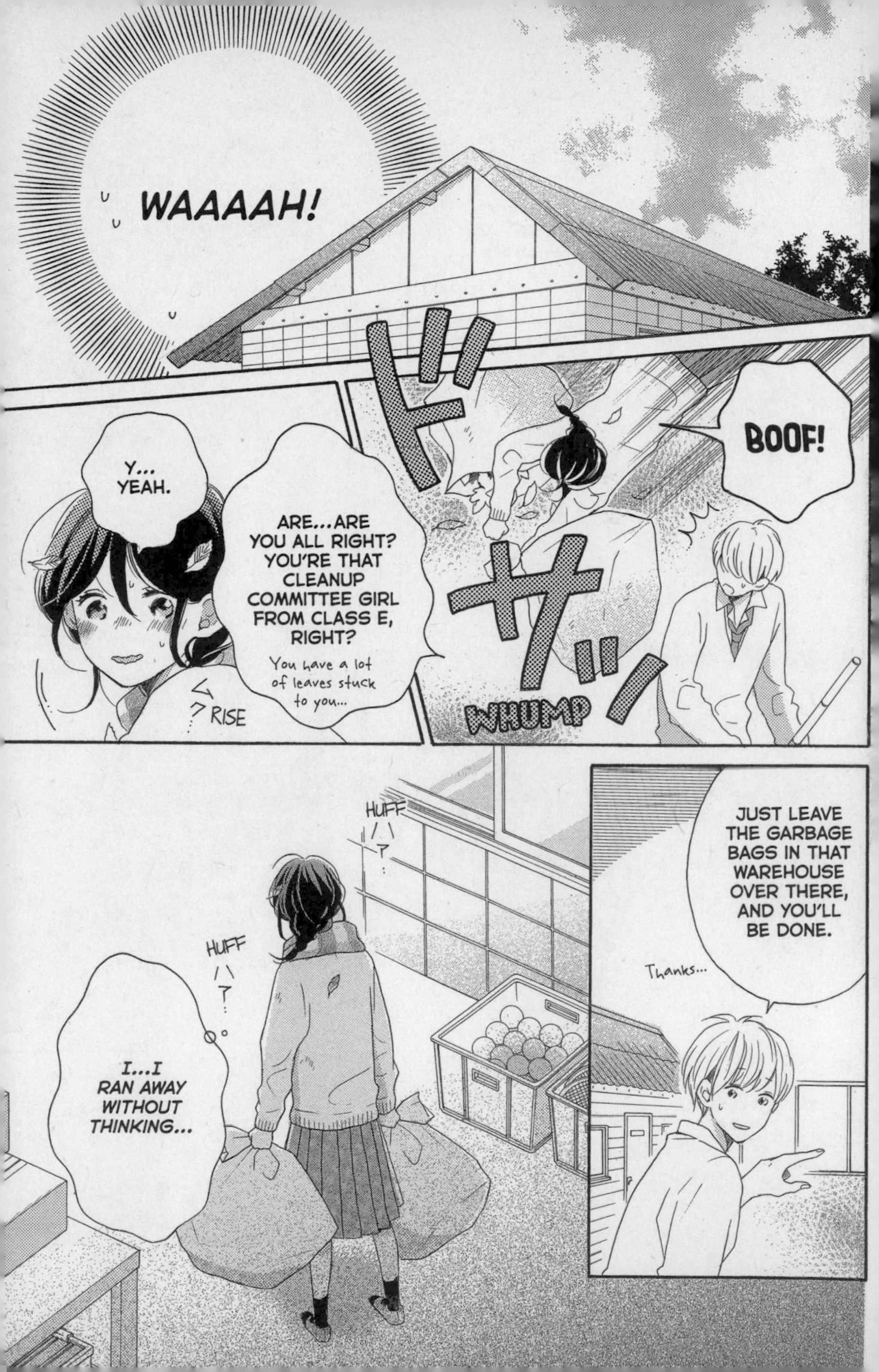
WAAAAH!
BOOF!
ドサッ
WHUMP
ARE...ARE YOU ALL RIGHT? YOU'RE THAT CLEANUP COMMITTEE GIRL FROM CLASS E, RIGHT?
You have a lot of leaves stuck to you...
Y... YEAH.
RISE
JUST LEAVE THE GARBAGE BAGS IN THAT WAREHOUSE OVER THERE, AND YOU'LL BE DONE.
Thanks...
HUFF
HUFF
I...I RAN AWAY WITHOUT THINKING...

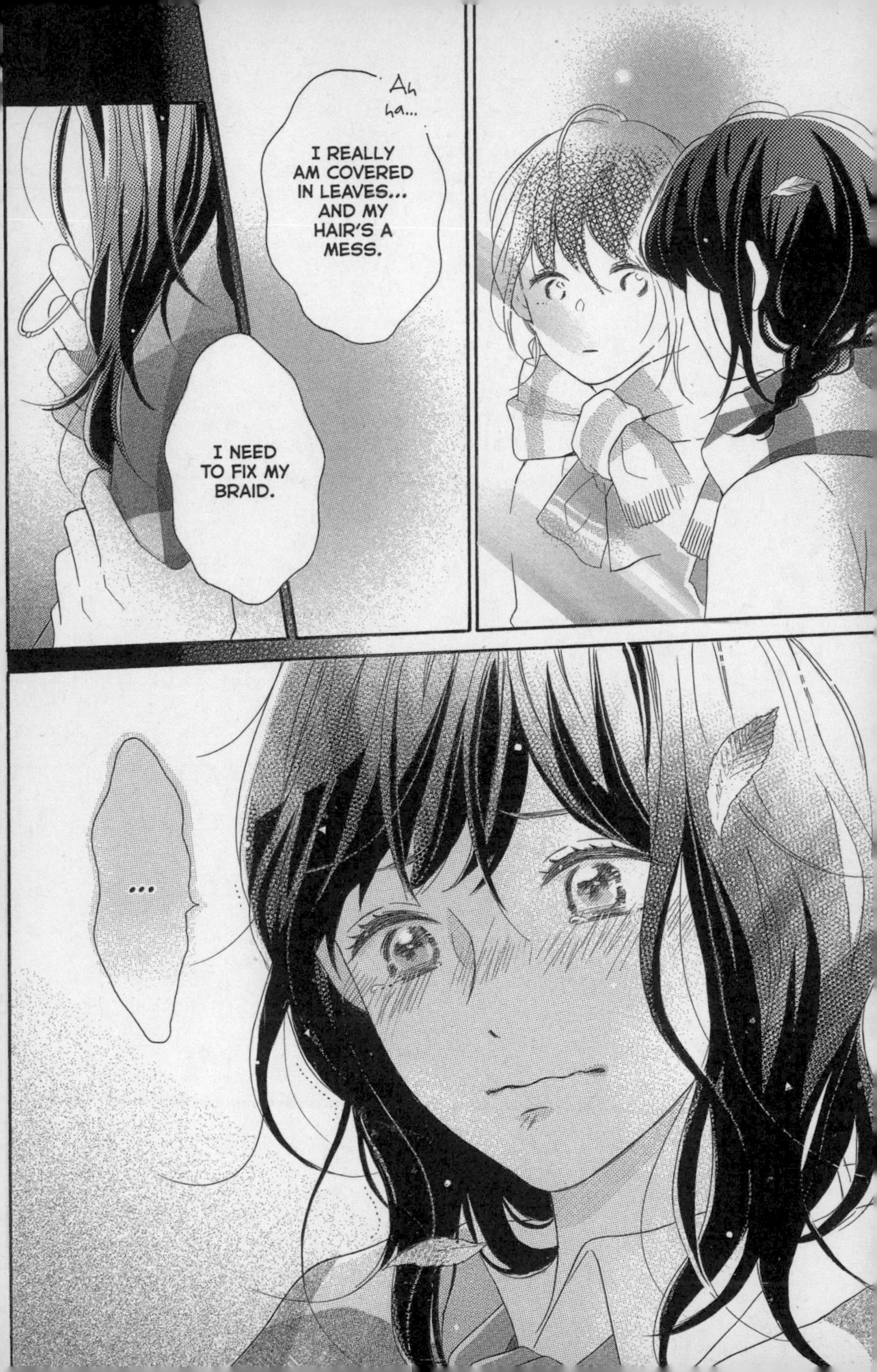
Ah ha...
I REALLY AM COVERED IN LEAVES... AND MY HAIR'S A MESS.
I NEED TO FIX MY BRAID.
...

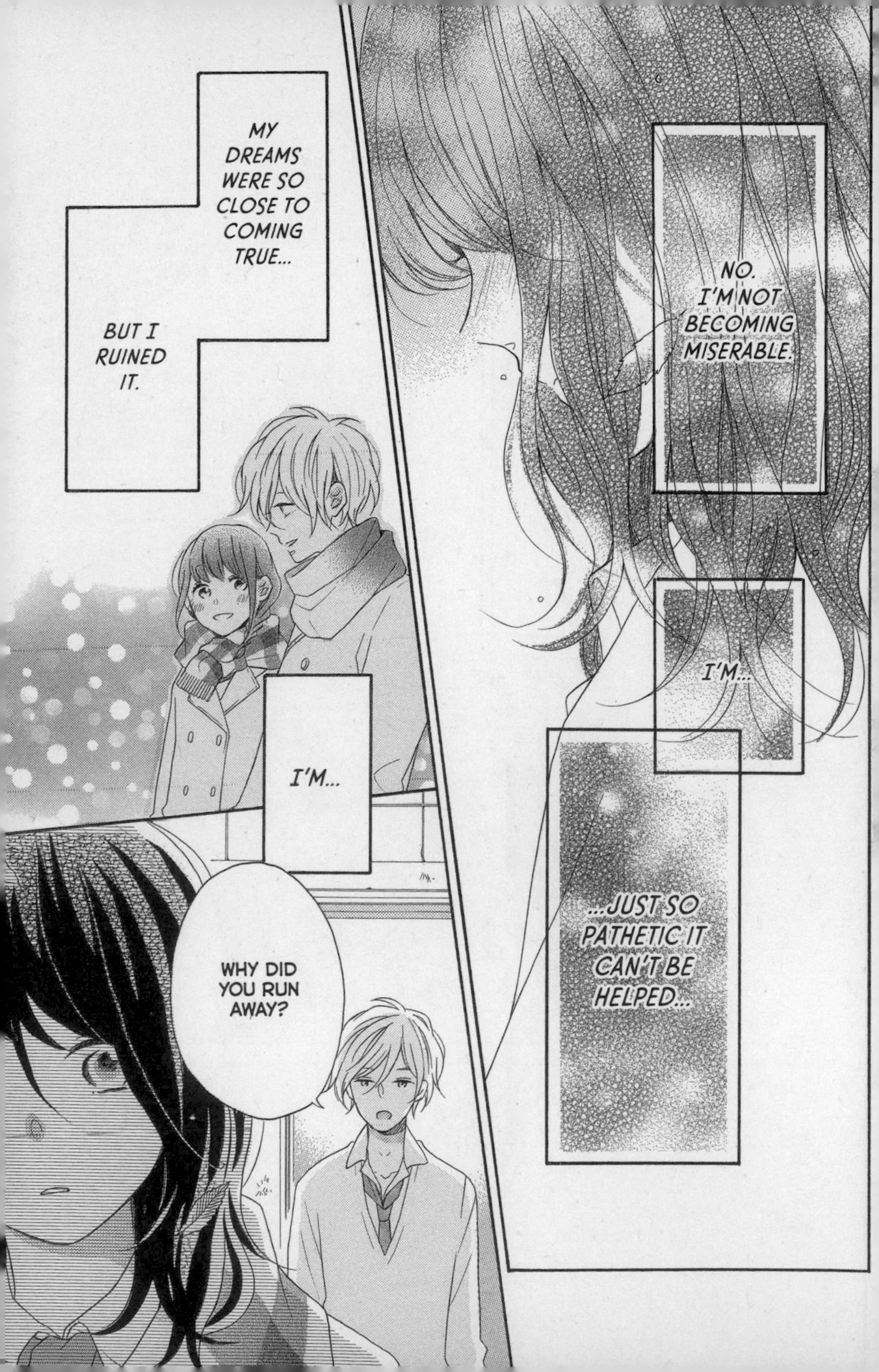
MY DREAMS WERE SO CLOSE TO COMING TRUE...
BUT I RUINED IT.
I'M...
NO. I'M NOT BECOMING MISERABLE.
I'M...
...JUST SO PATHETIC IT CAN'T BE HELPED...
WHY DID YOU RUN AWAY?

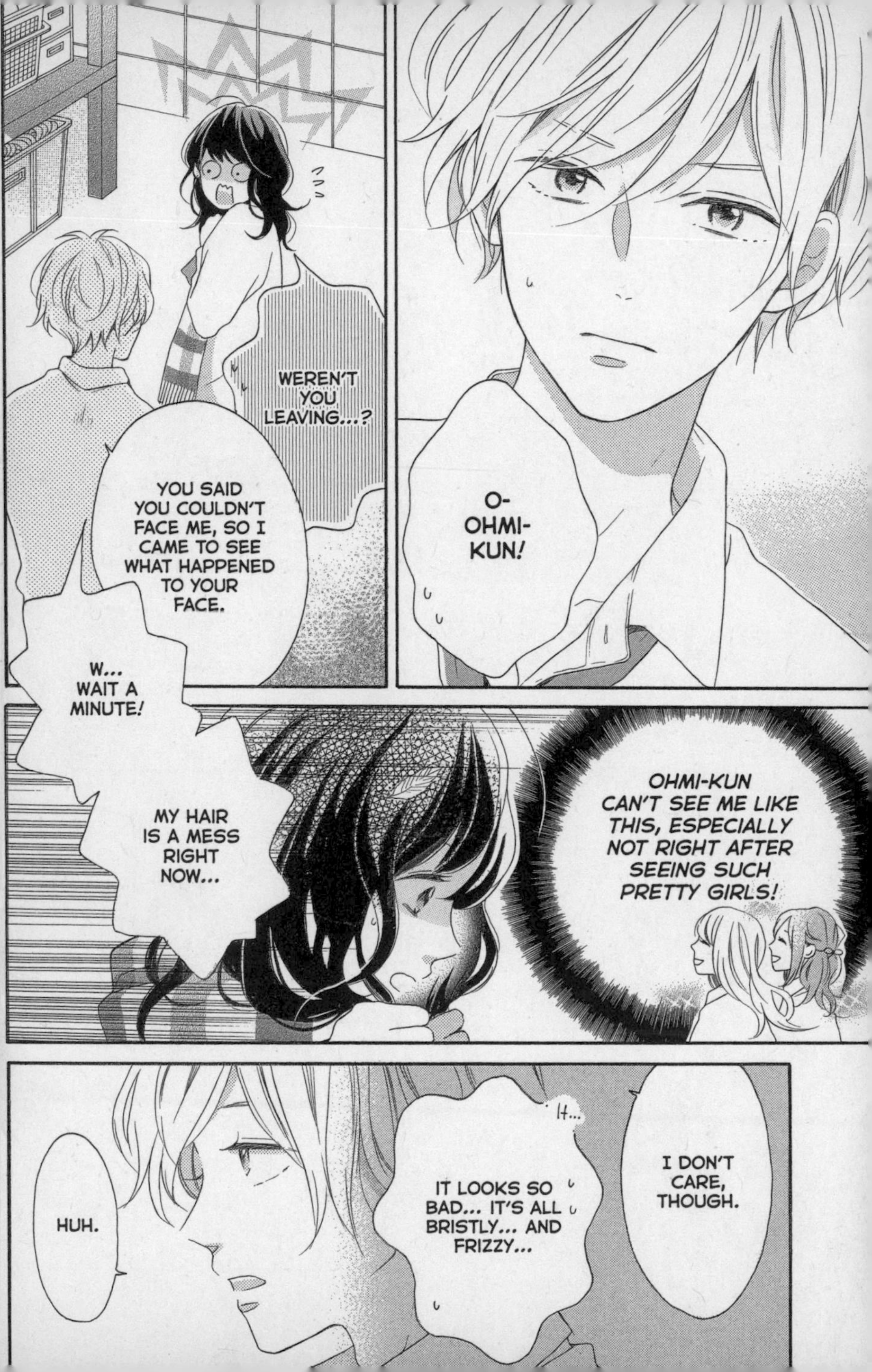
O- OHMI-KUN!
WEREN'T YOU LEAVING...?
YOU SAID YOU COULDN'T FACE ME, SO I CAME TO SEE WHAT HAPPENED TO YOUR FACE.
W... WAIT A MINUTE!
MY HAIR IS A MESS RIGHT NOW...
OHMI-KUN CAN'T SEE ME LIKE THIS, ESPECIALLY NOT RIGHT AFTER SEEING SUCH PRETTY GIRLS!
It...
IT LOOKS SO BAD... IT'S ALL BRISTLY... AND FRIZZY...
I DON'T CARE, THOUGH.
HUH.

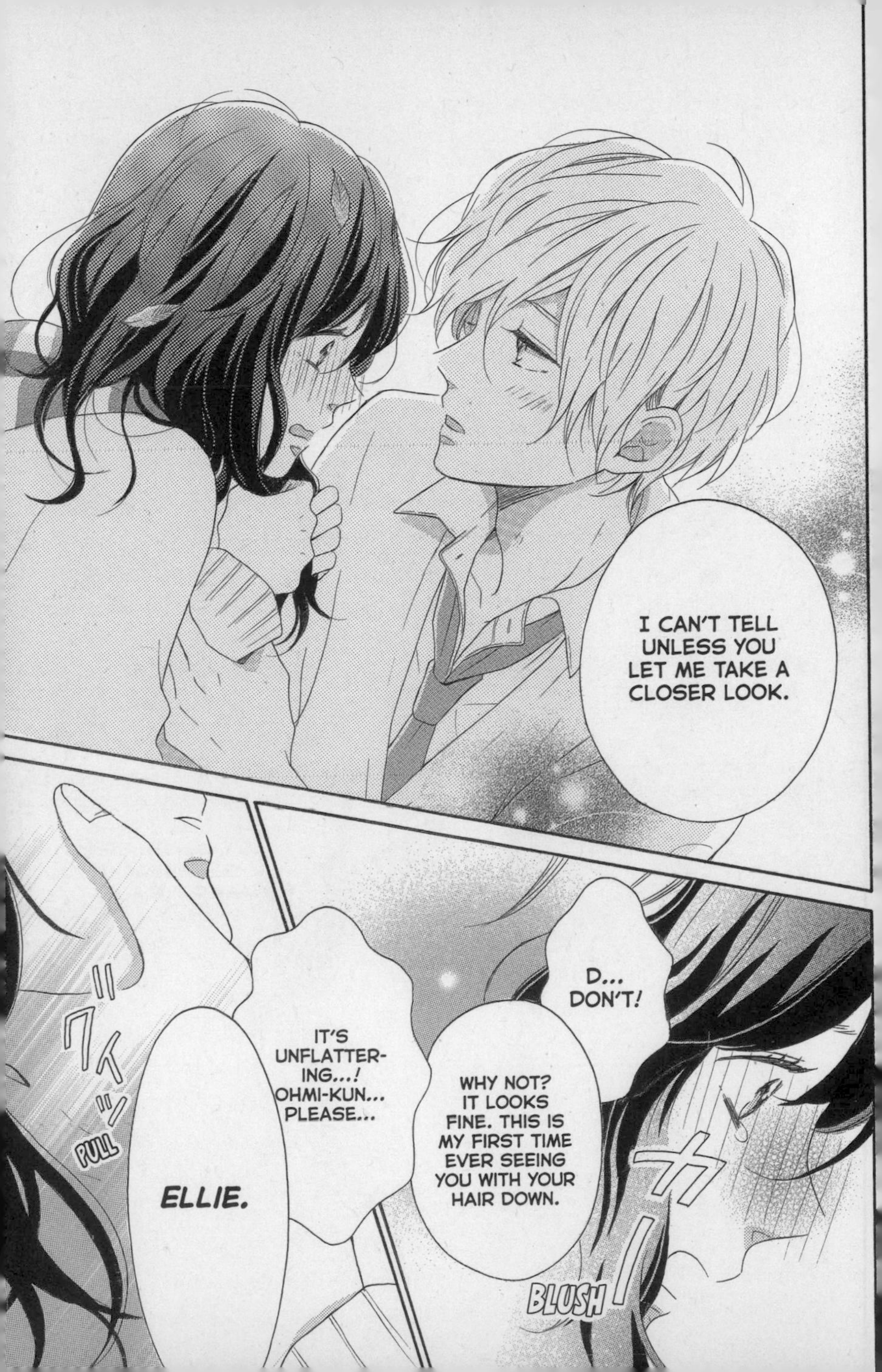
I CAN'T TELL UNLESS YOU LET ME TAKE A CLOSER LOOK.
D... DON'T!
WHY NOT? IT LOOKS FINE. THIS IS MY FIRST TIME EVER SEEING YOU WITH YOUR HAIR DOWN.
BLUSH
IT'S UNFLATTERING...! OHMI-KUN... PLEASE...
ELLIE.
PULL

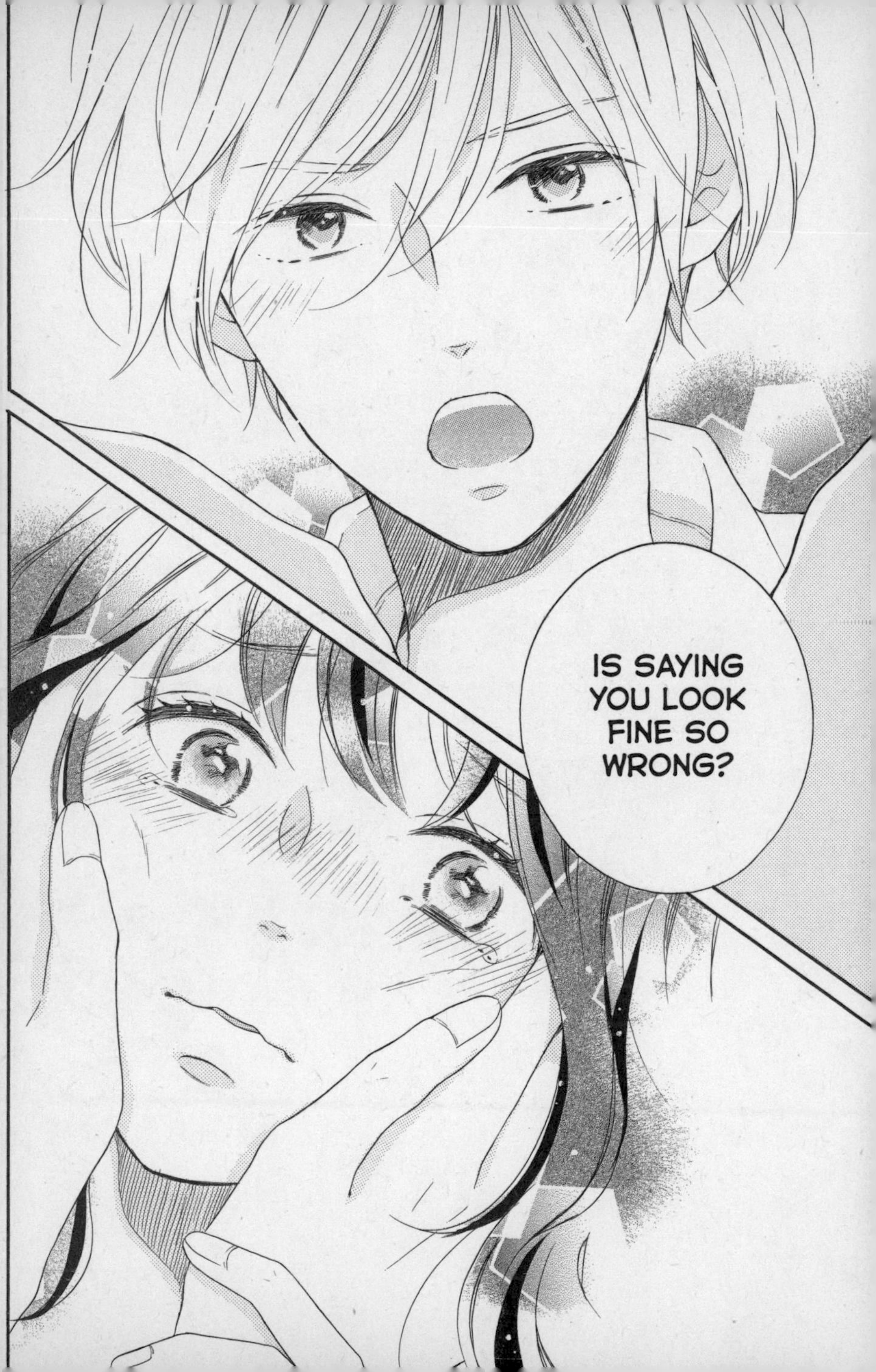
IS SAYING YOU LOOK FINE SO WRONG?

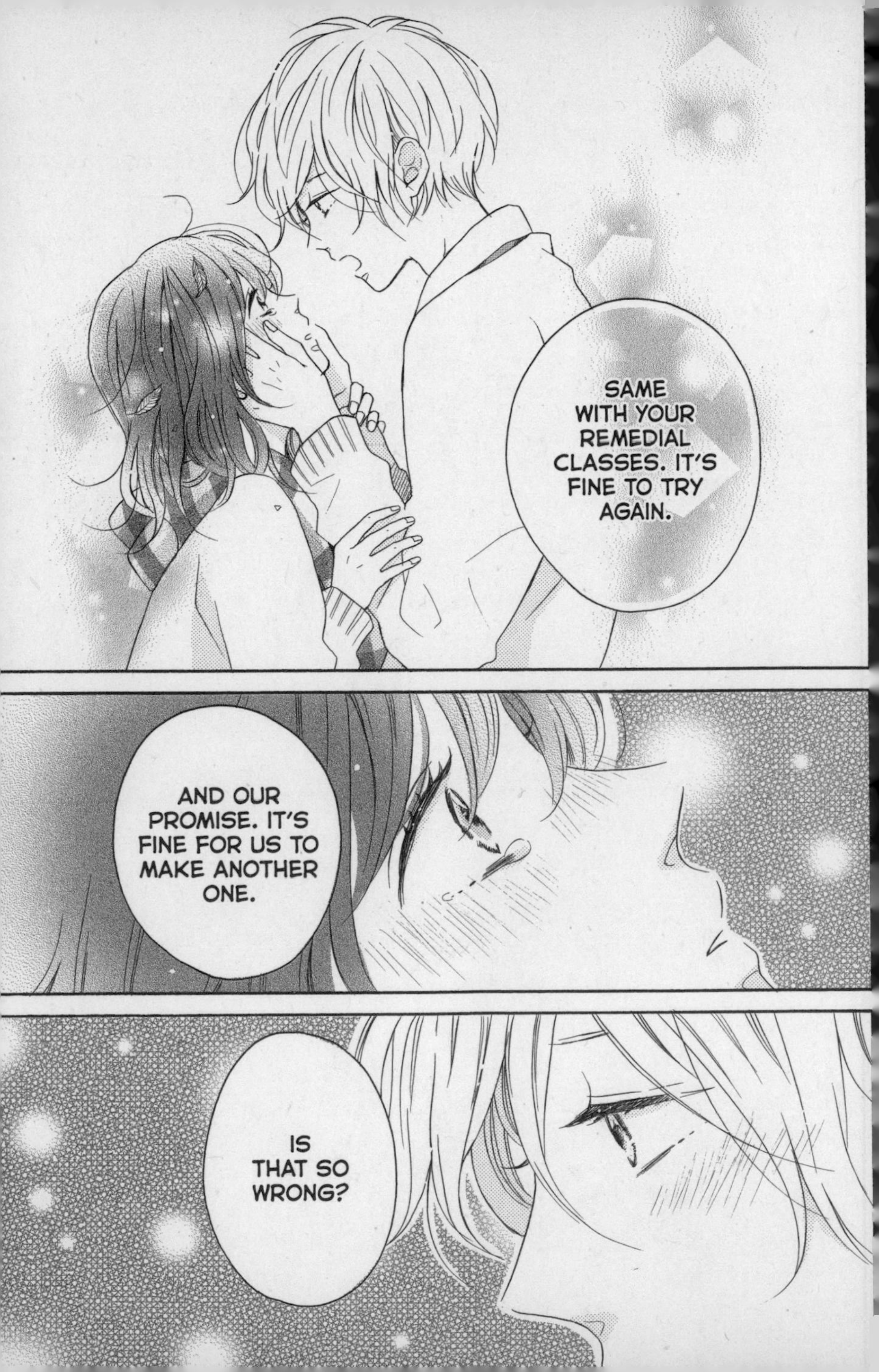
SAME WITH YOUR REMEDIAL CLASSES. IT'S FINE TO TRY AGAIN.
AND OUR PROMISE. IT'S FINE FOR US TO MAKE ANOTHER ONE.
IS THAT SO WRONG?

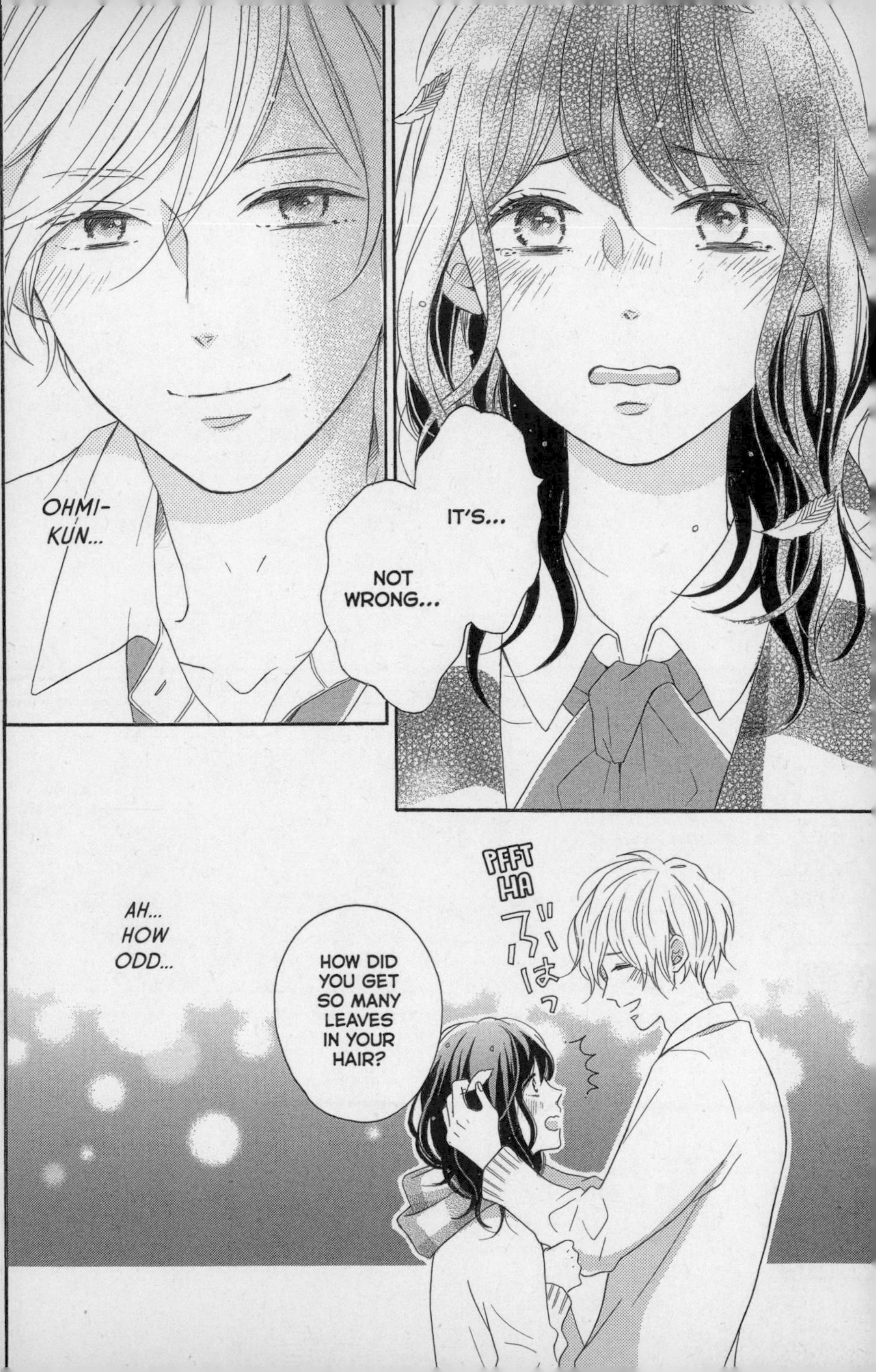

IT'S... NOT WRONG...
OHMI-KUN...
PFFT HA
ぶはっ
AH... HOW ODD...
HOW DID YOU GET SO MANY LEAVES IN YOUR HAIR?

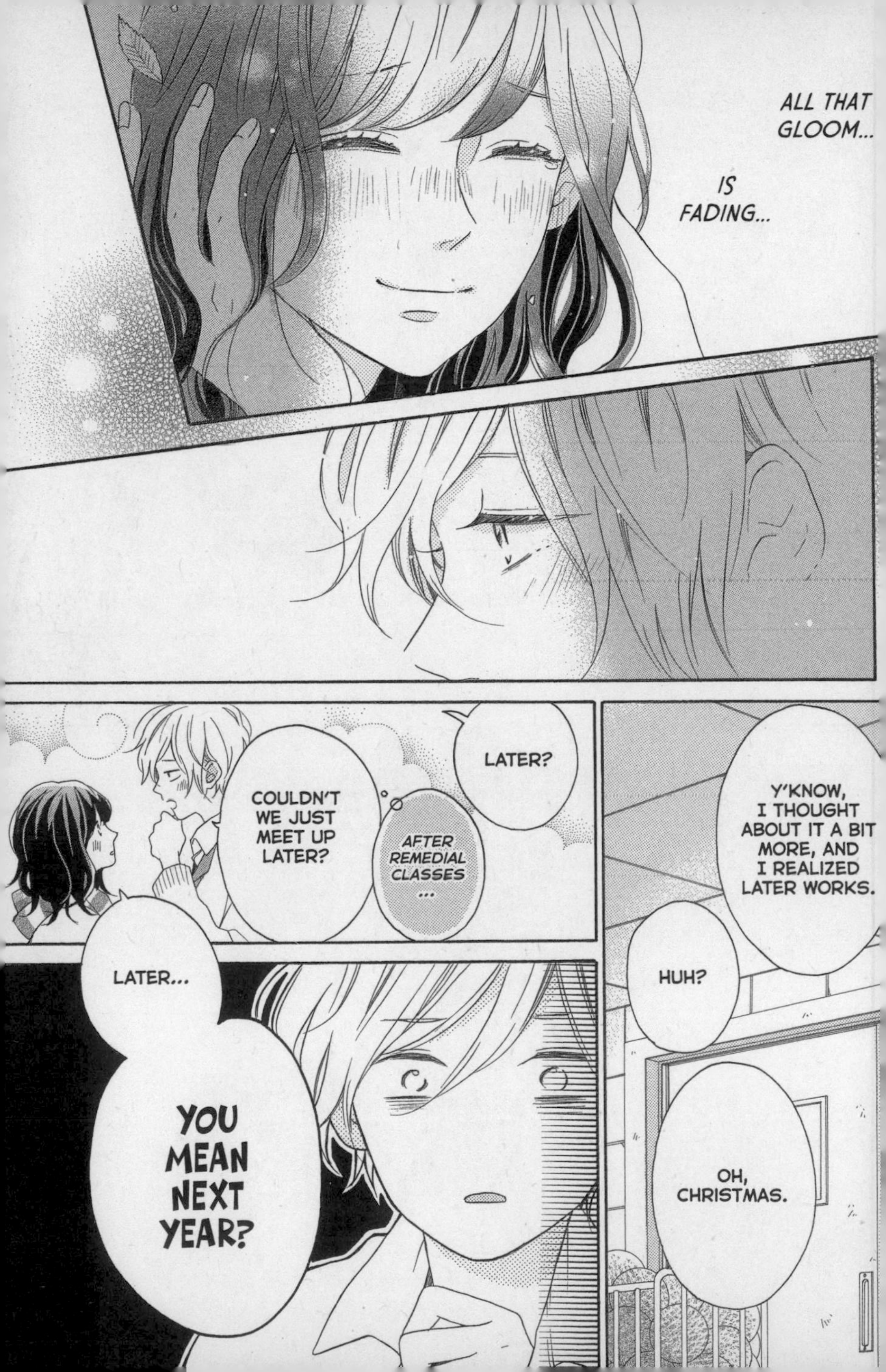
ALL THAT GLOOM...
IS FADING...
Y'KNOW, I THOUGHT ABOUT IT A BIT MORE, AND I REALIZED LATER WORKS.
HUH?
OH, CHRISTMAS.
LATER?
COULDN'T WE JUST MEET UP LATER?
AFTER REMEDIAL CLASSES ...
LATER...
YOU MEAN NEXT YEAR?

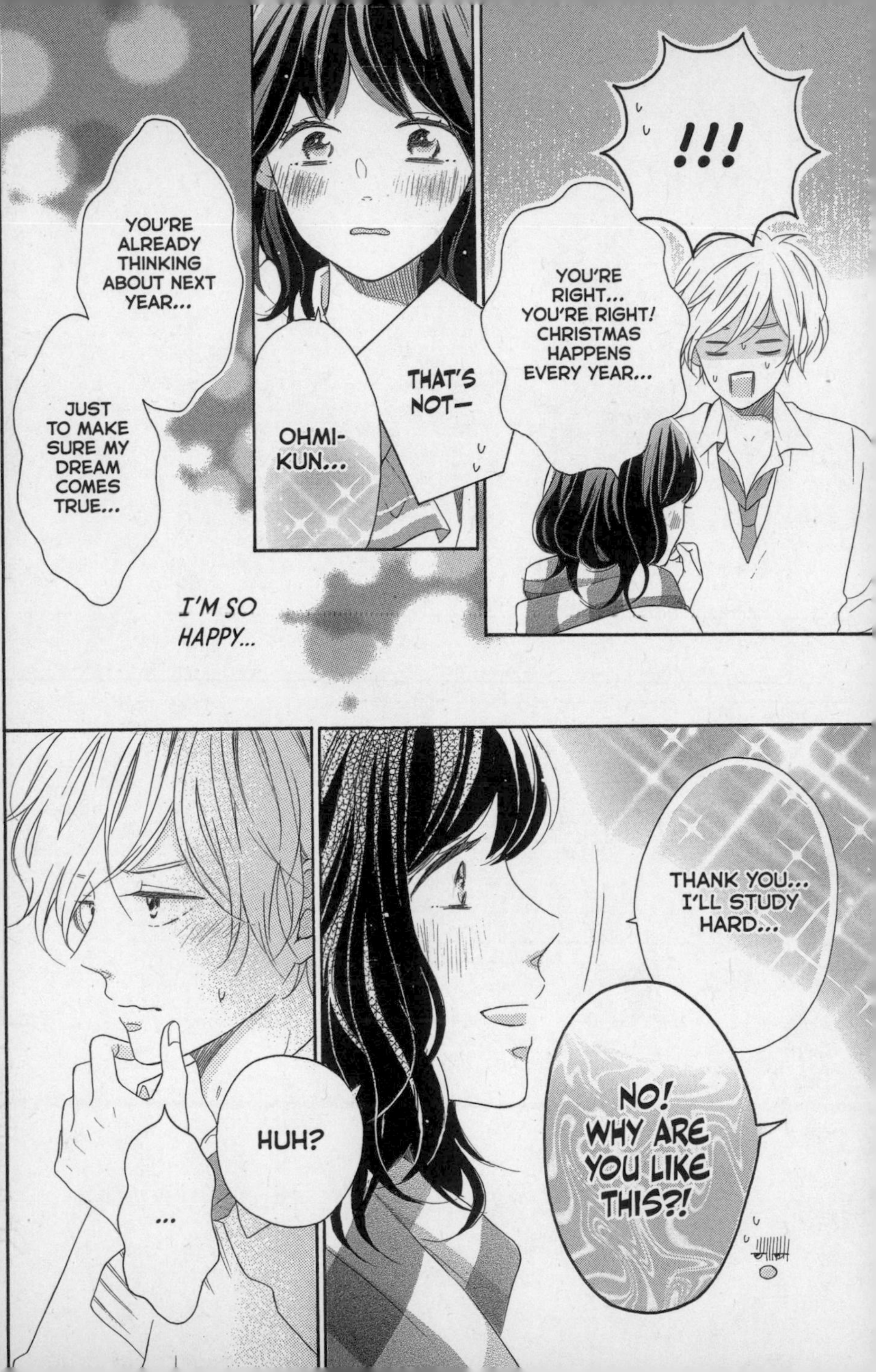
!!!
YOU'RE RIGHT... YOU'RE RIGHT! CHRISTMAS HAPPENS EVERY YEAR...
THAT'S NOT—
OHMI-KUN...
YOU'RE ALREADY THINKING ABOUT NEXT YEAR...
JUST TO MAKE SURE MY DREAM COMES TRUE...
I'M SO HAPPY...
THANK YOU... I'LL STUDY HARD...
NO! WHY ARE YOU LIKE THIS?!
HUH?
...

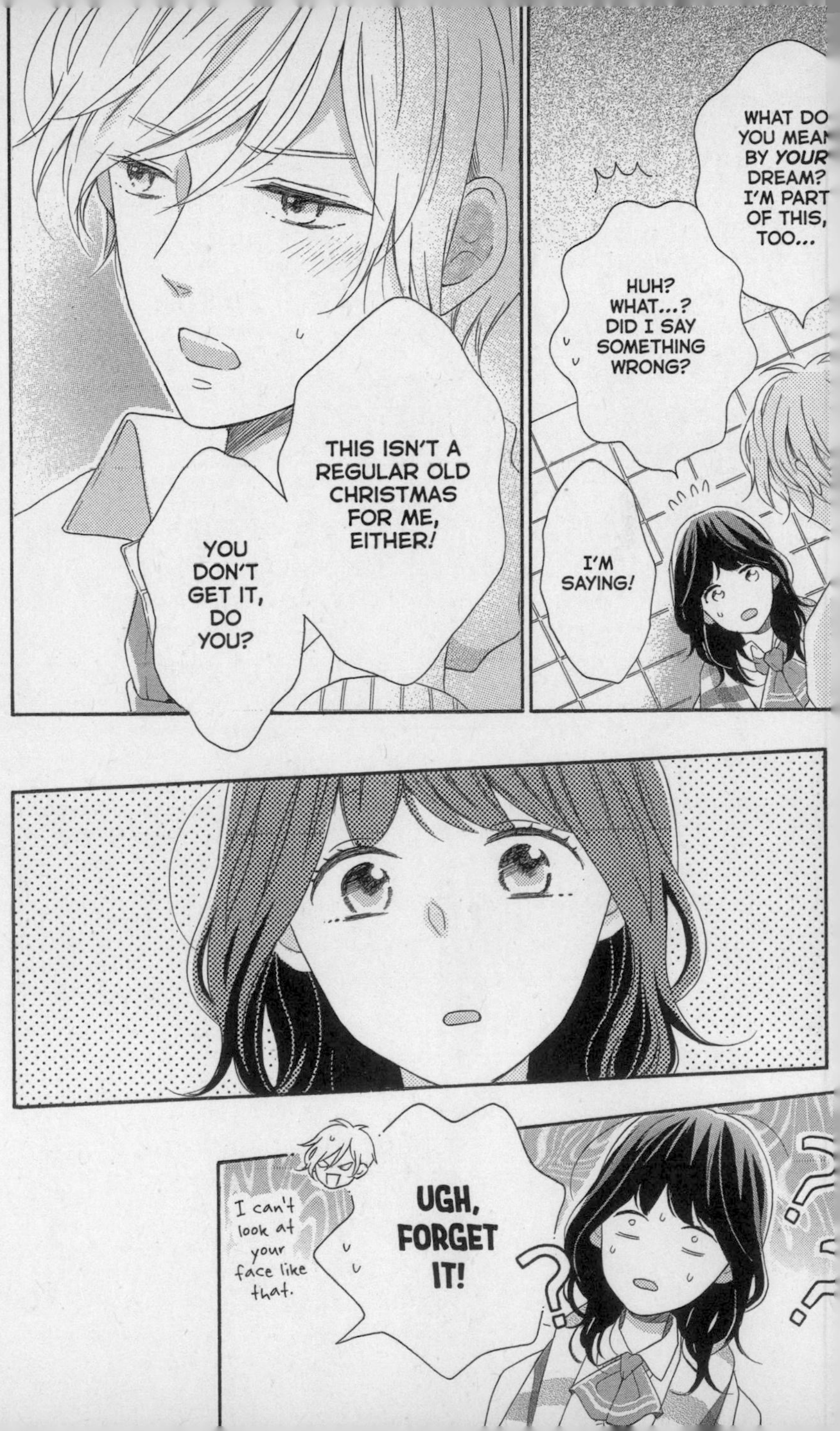
WHAT DO YOU MEAN BY *YOUR* DREAM? I'M PART OF THIS, TOO...
HUH? WHAT...? DID I SAY SOMETHING WRONG?
I'M SAYING!
THIS ISN'T A REGULAR OLD CHRISTMAS FOR ME, EITHER!
YOU DON'T GET IT, DO YOU?
UGH, FORGET IT!
I can't look at your face like that.

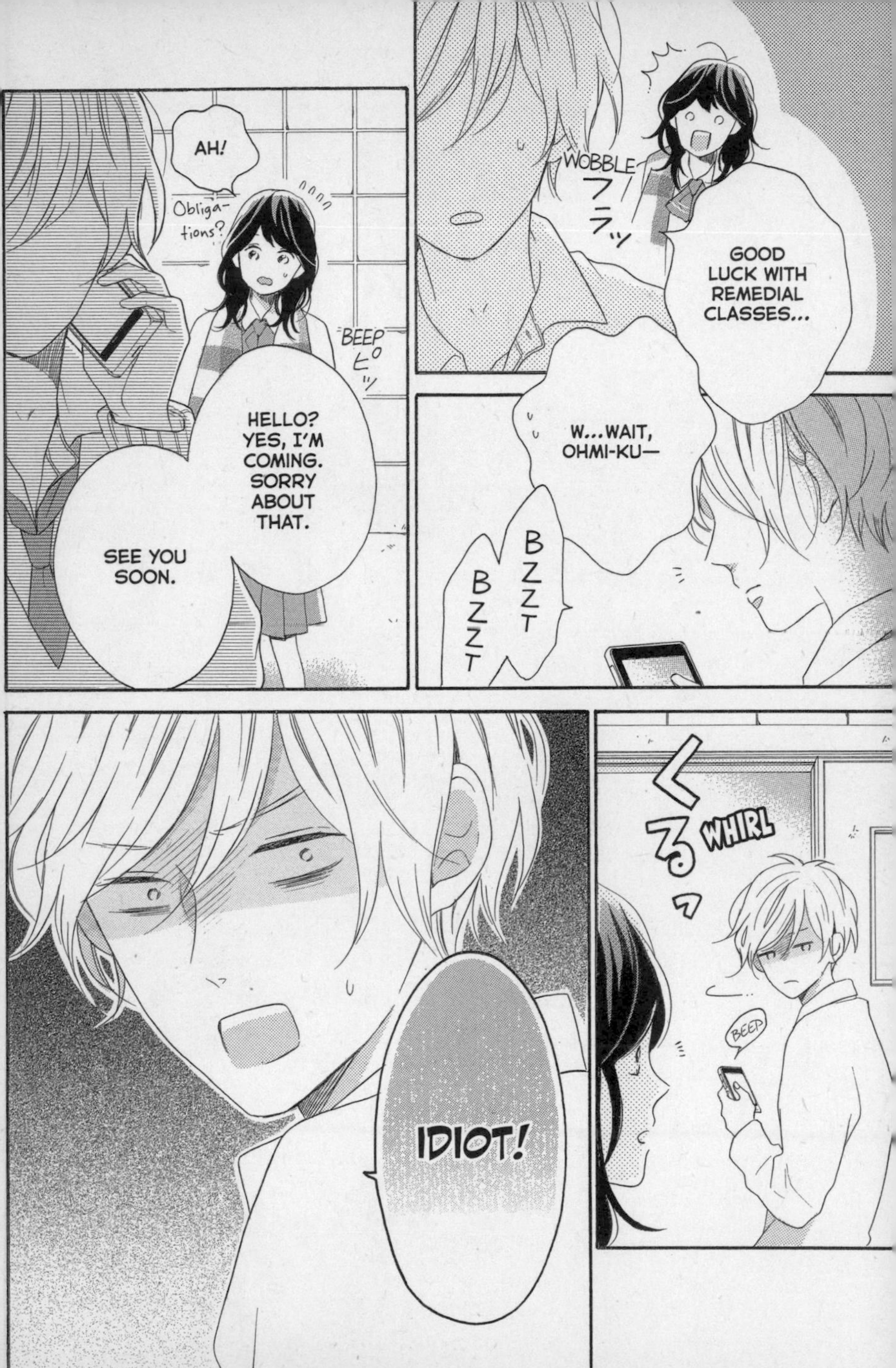
WOBBLE
フラッ
GOOD LUCK WITH REMEDIAL CLASSES...
W...WAIT, OHMI-KU—
BZZT
BZZT
AH!
Obliga-tions?
BEEP
ピッ
HELLO? YES, I'M COMING. SORRY ABOUT THAT.
SEE YOU SOON.
くるっ
WHIRL
BEEP
IDIOT!

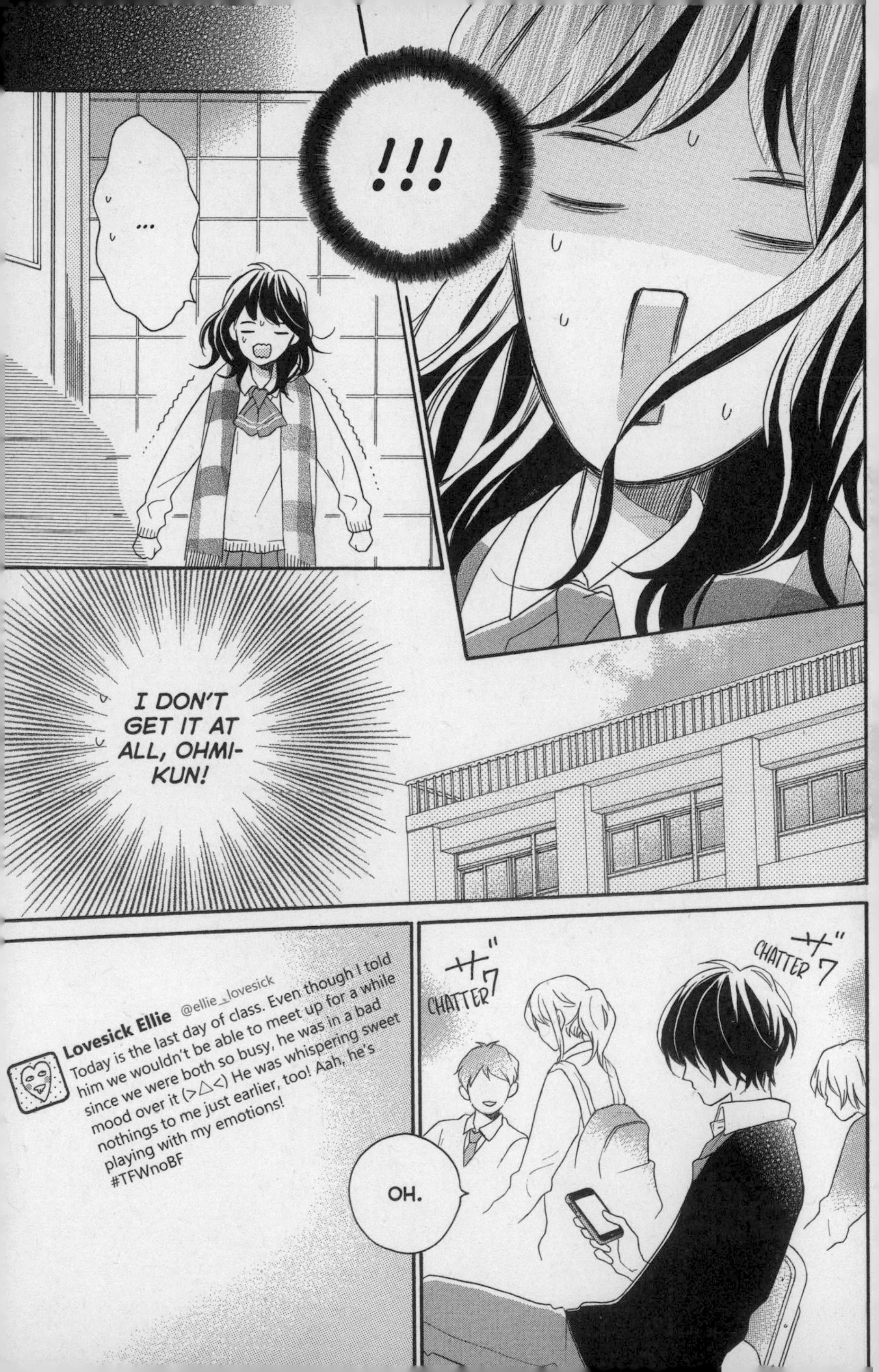
!!!
...
I DON'T GET IT AT ALL, OHMI-KUN!
CHATTER
CHATTER
OH.
Lovesick Ellie @ellie_lovesick
Today is the last day of class. Even though I told him we wouldn't be able to meet up for a while since we were both so busy, he was in a bad mood over it (>△<) He was whispering sweet nothings to me just earlier, too! Aah, he's playing with my emotions!
#TFWnoBF

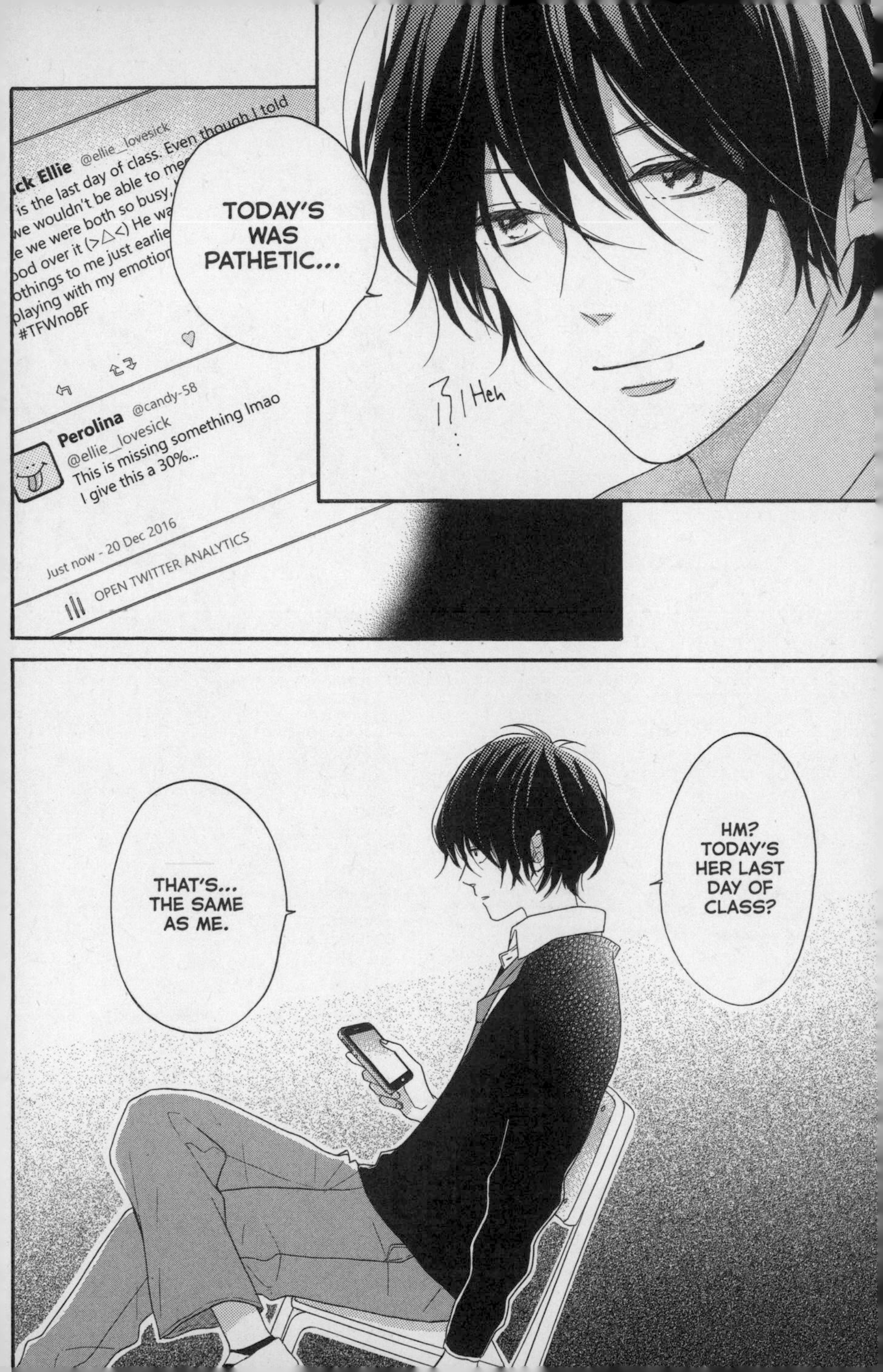
TODAY'S WAS PATHETIC...
Heh
ick Ellie @ellie__lovesick
is the last day of class. Even though I told
we wouldn't be able to me
e we were both so busy,
ood over it (>△<) He wa
othings to me just earlie
playing with my emotio
#TFWnoBF
Perolina @candy-58
@ellie__lovesick
This is missing something lmao
I give this a 30%...
Just now - 20 Dec 2016
OPEN TWITTER ANALYTICS
HM? TODAY'S HER LAST DAY OF CLASS?
THAT'S... THE SAME AS ME.

# Lovesick
# Ellie

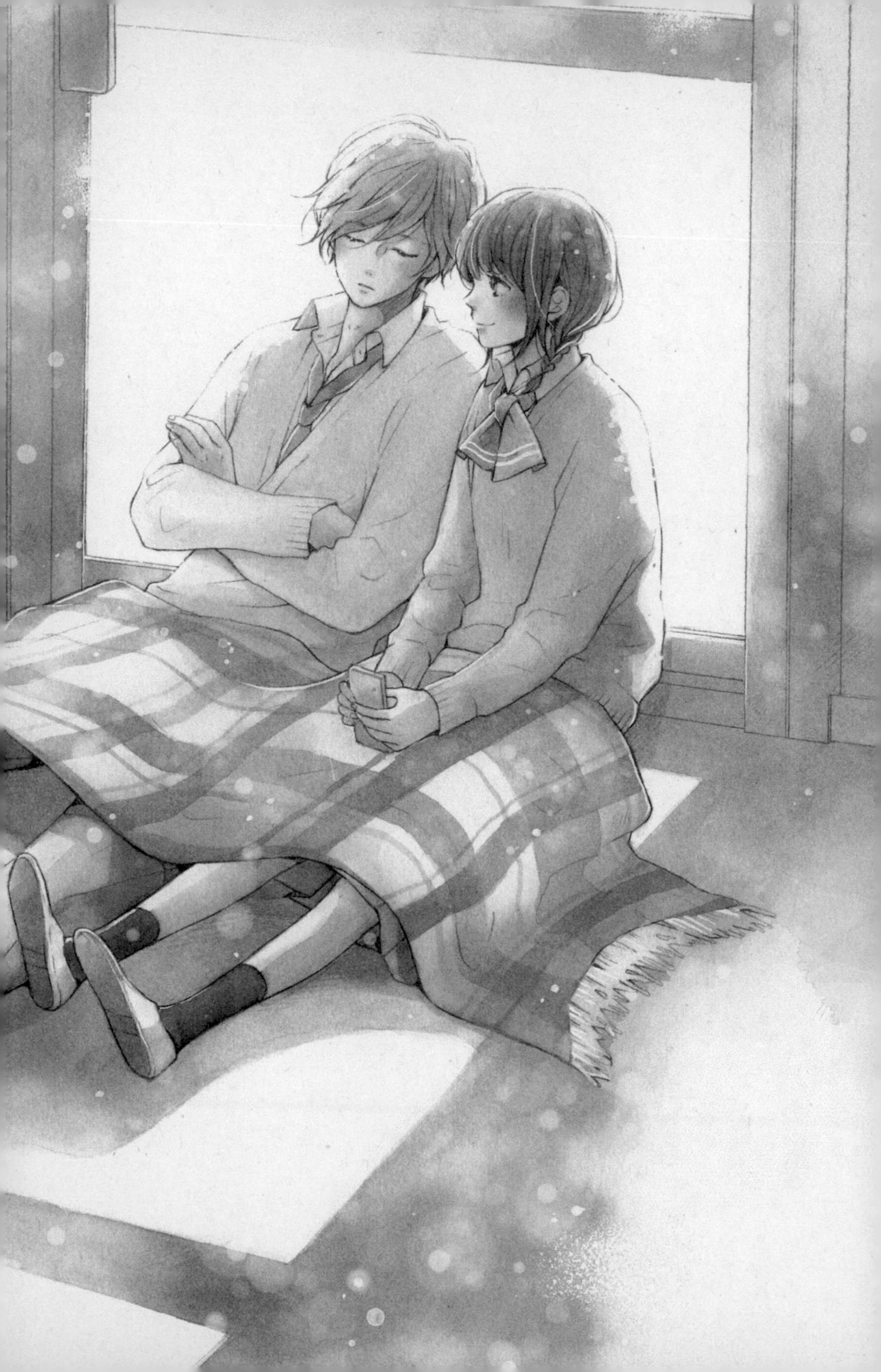

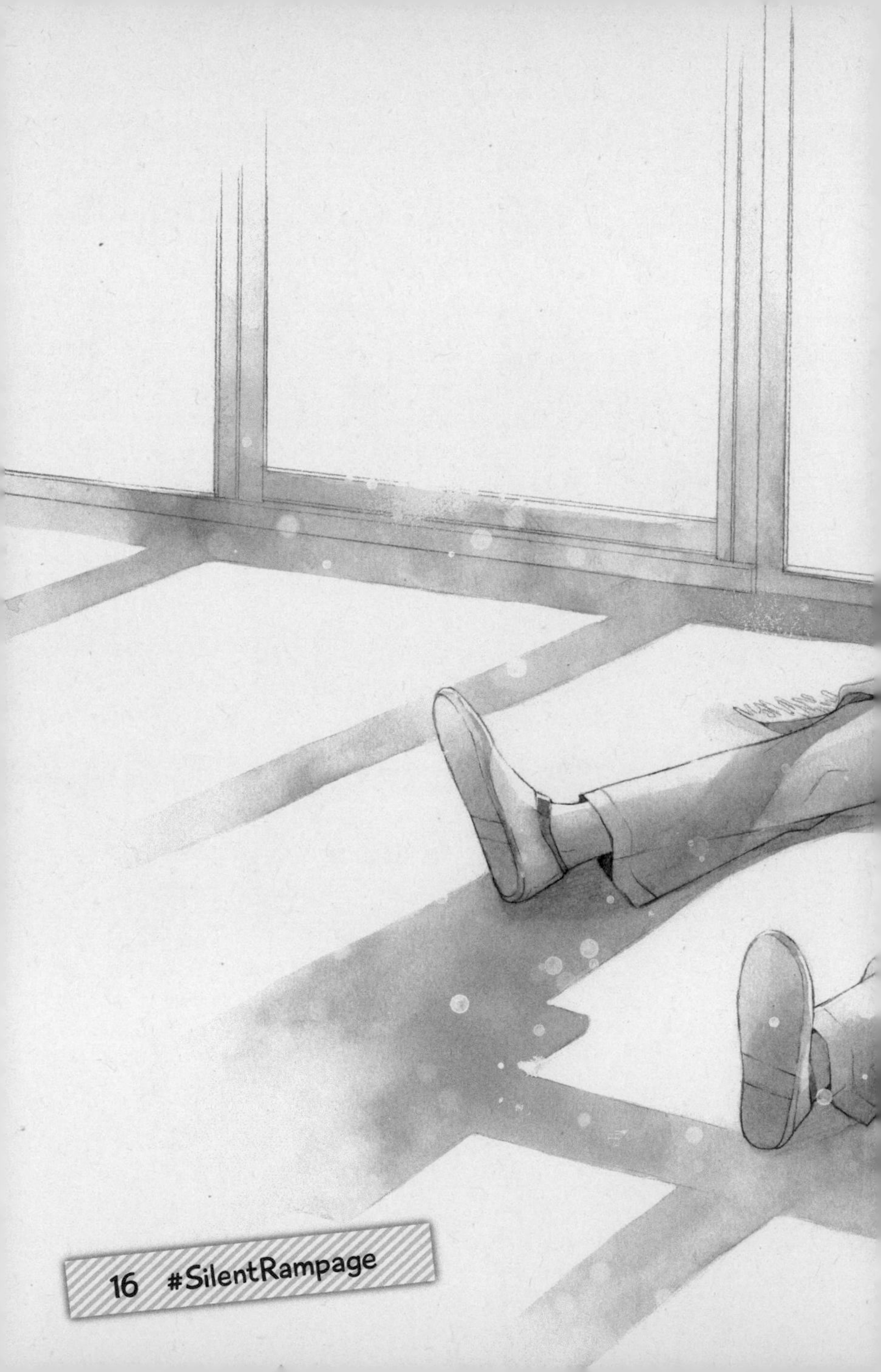

# 16 #SilentRampage

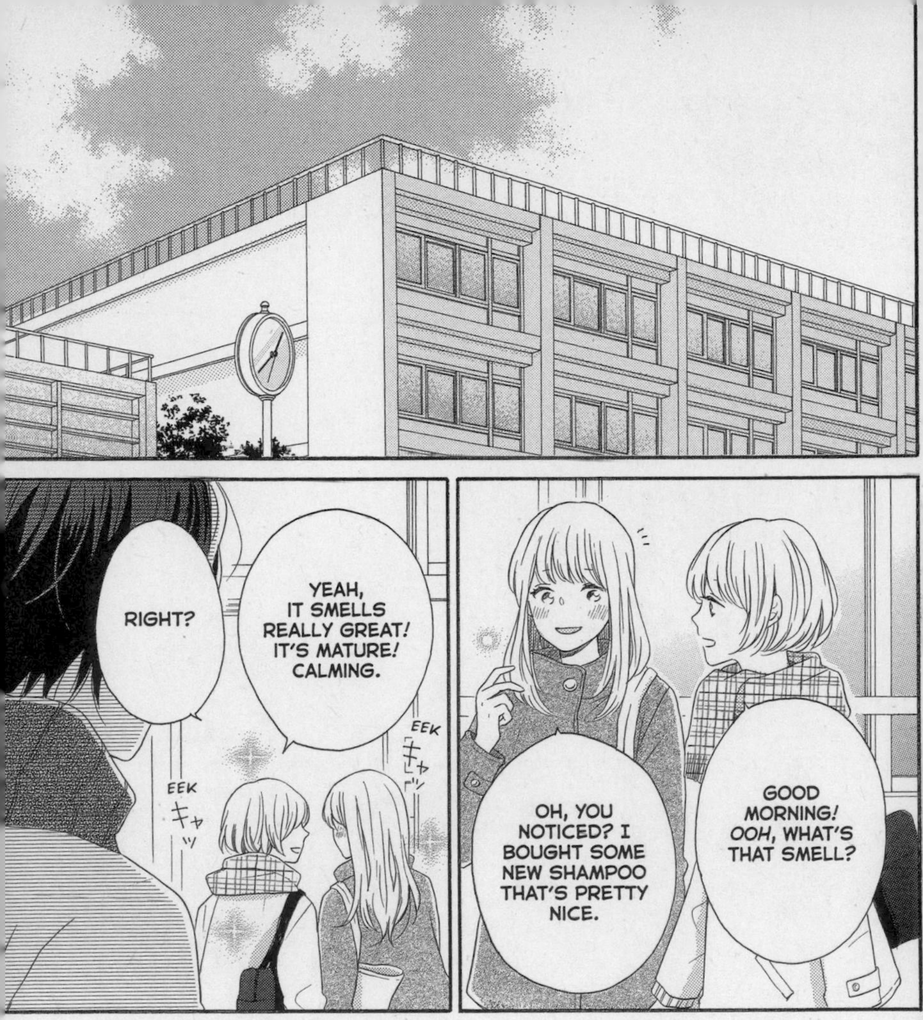
GOOD MORNING! *OOH*, WHAT'S THAT SMELL?
OH, YOU NOTICED? I BOUGHT SOME NEW SHAMPOO THAT'S PRETTY NICE.
YEAH, IT SMELLS REALLY GREAT! IT'S MATURE! CALMING.
EEK
RIGHT?
EEK

I don't know how we got here, but we're going into our fifth volume! Every chapter's a struggle, so I'm still surprised every time it keeps going. I still don't feel like I can relax (psychologically).

Special Thanks

Kuumii

Nagasaki, Chiaki, Okumura

Editor Minchi    Designer Osawa

Everyone at *Dessert* Publishing

And all my readers

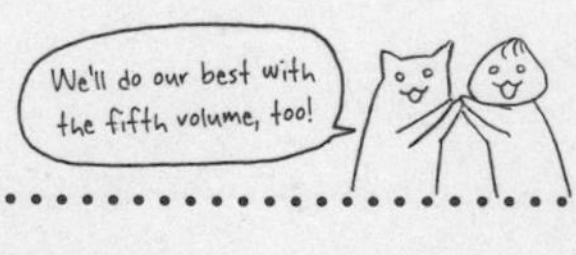
We'll do our best with the fifth volume, too!

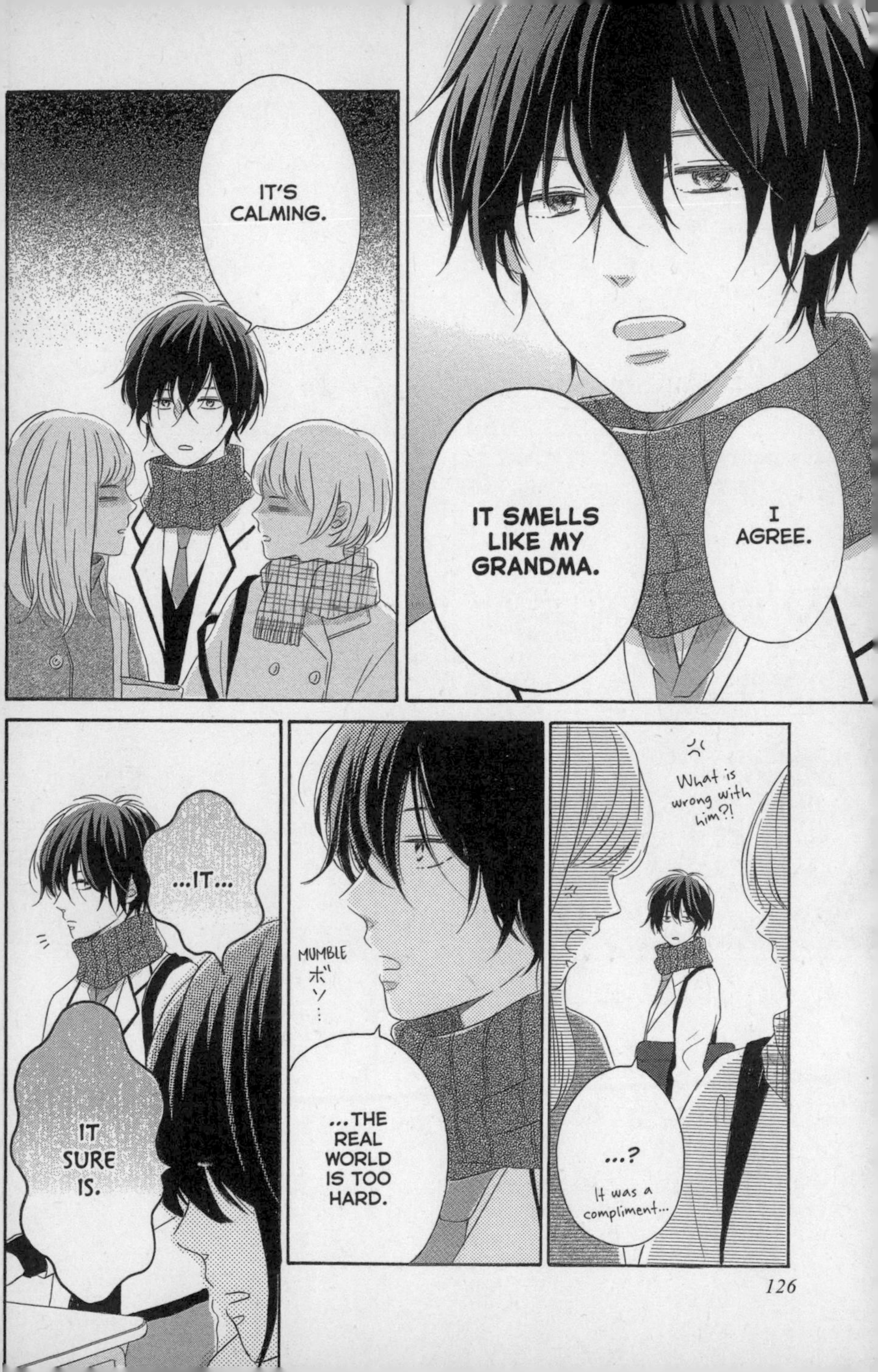
I AGREE.
IT SMELLS LIKE MY GRANDMA.
IT'S CALMING.
What is wrong with him?!
...?
It was a compliment...
MUMBLE ボソ…
...THE REAL WORLD IS TOO HARD.
...IT...
IT SURE IS.

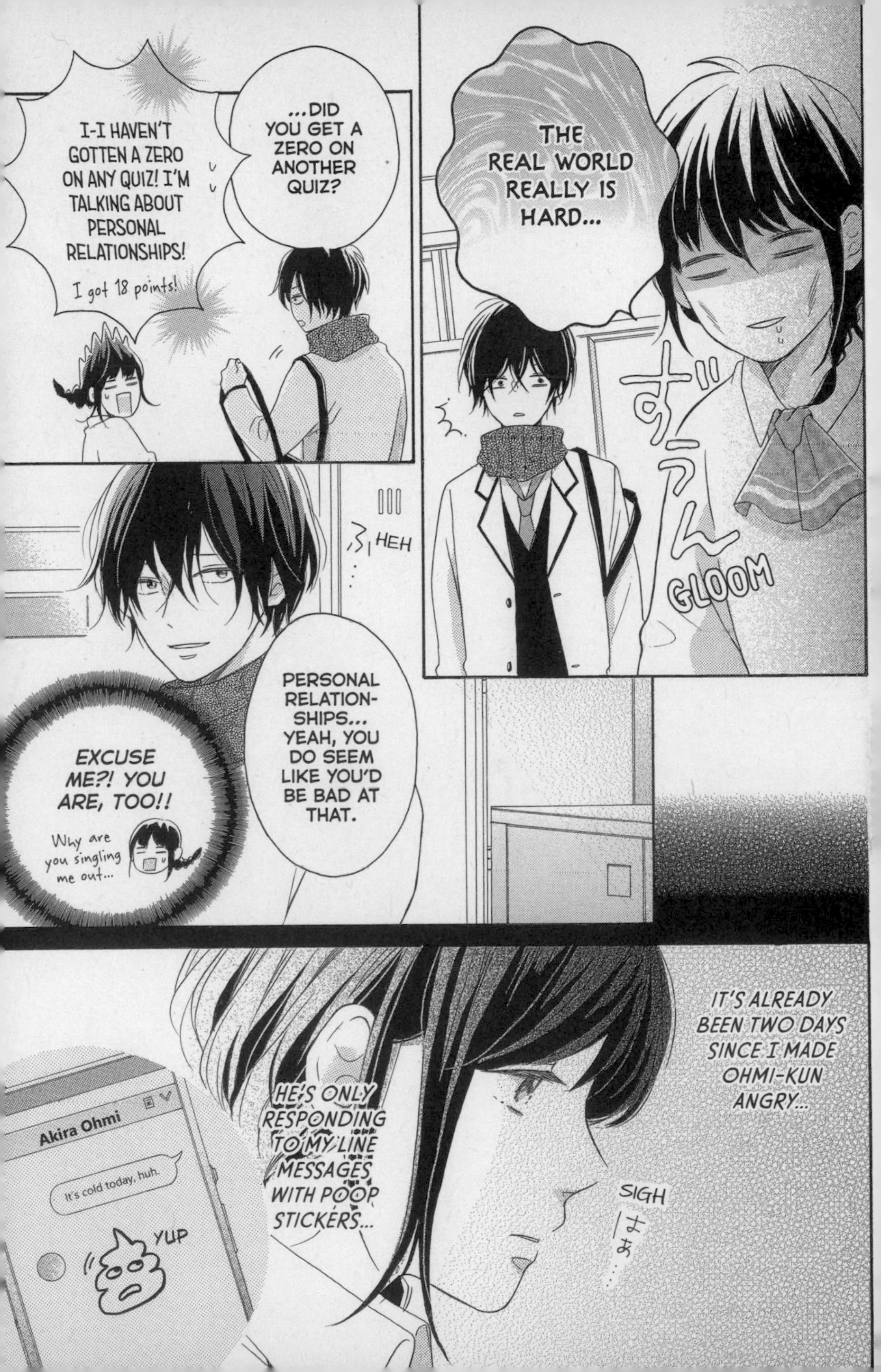
THE REAL WORLD REALLY IS HARD...
ずうん
GLOOM
...DID YOU GET A ZERO ON ANOTHER QUIZ?
I-I HAVEN'T GOTTEN A ZERO ON ANY QUIZ! I'M TALKING ABOUT PERSONAL RELATIONSHIPS!
I got 18 points!
ふ
HEH
PERSONAL RELATION-SHIPS... YEAH, YOU DO SEEM LIKE YOU'D BE BAD AT THAT.
EXCUSE ME?! YOU ARE, TOO!!
Why are you singling me out...
IT'S ALREADY BEEN TWO DAYS SINCE I MADE OHMI-KUN ANGRY...
SIGH
はぁ…
HE'S ONLY RESPONDING TO MY LINE MESSAGES WITH POOP STICKERS...
Akira Ohmi
It's cold today, huh.
YUP

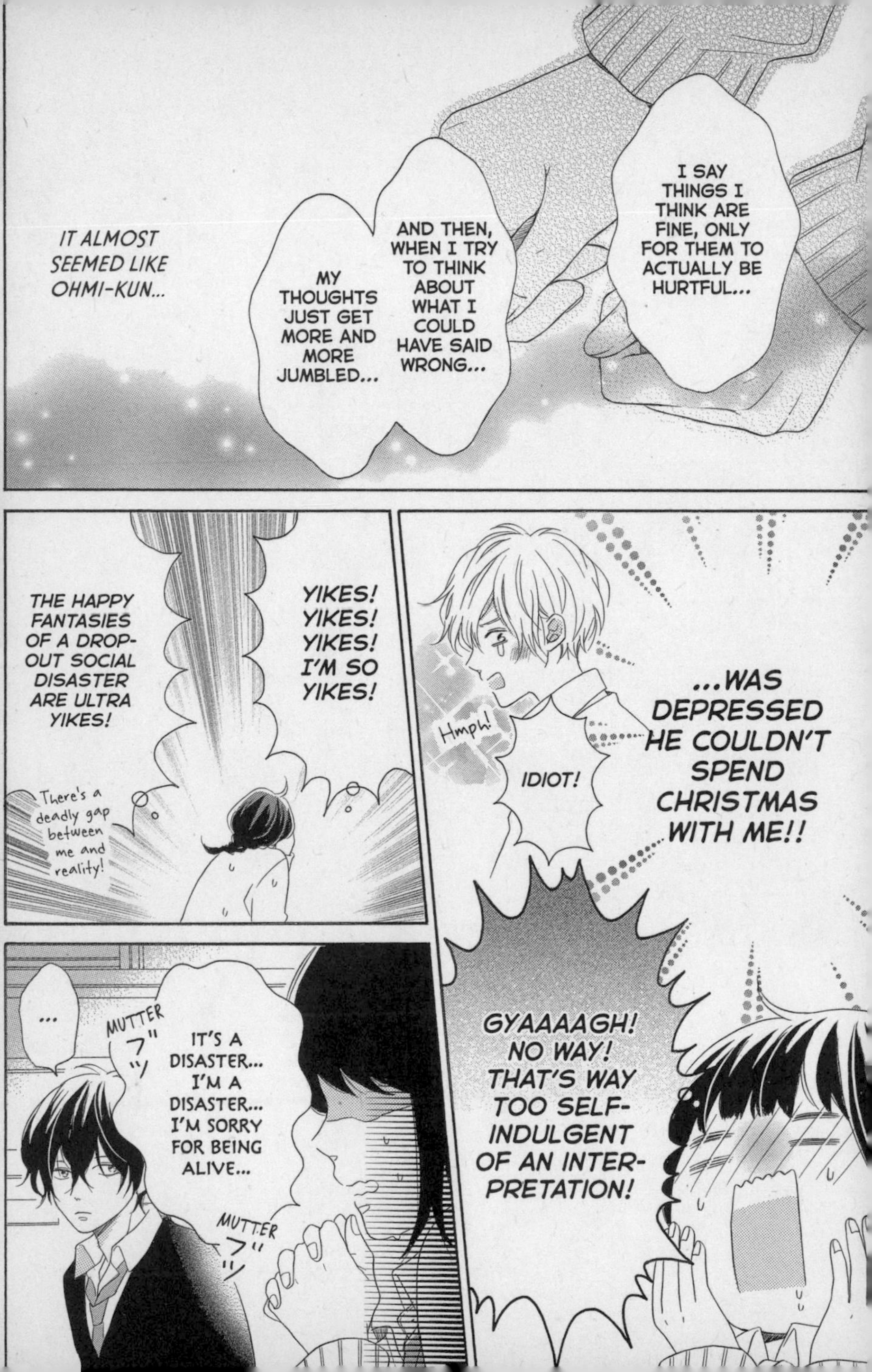
I SAY THINGS I THINK ARE FINE, ONLY FOR THEM TO ACTUALLY BE HURTFUL...
AND THEN, WHEN I TRY TO THINK ABOUT WHAT I COULD HAVE SAID WRONG...
MY THOUGHTS JUST GET MORE AND MORE JUMBLED...
IT ALMOST SEEMED LIKE OHMI-KUN...
...WAS DEPRESSED HE COULDN'T SPEND CHRISTMAS WITH ME!!
Hmph!
IDIOT!
GYAAAAGH! NO WAY! THAT'S WAY TOO SELF-INDULGENT OF AN INTER-PRETATION!
YIKES! YIKES! YIKES! I'M SO YIKES!
THE HAPPY FANTASIES OF A DROP-OUT SOCIAL DISASTER ARE ULTRA YIKES!
There's a deadly gap between me and reality!
...
MUTTER
IT'S A DISASTER... I'M A DISASTER... I'M SORRY FOR BEING ALIVE...
MUTTER

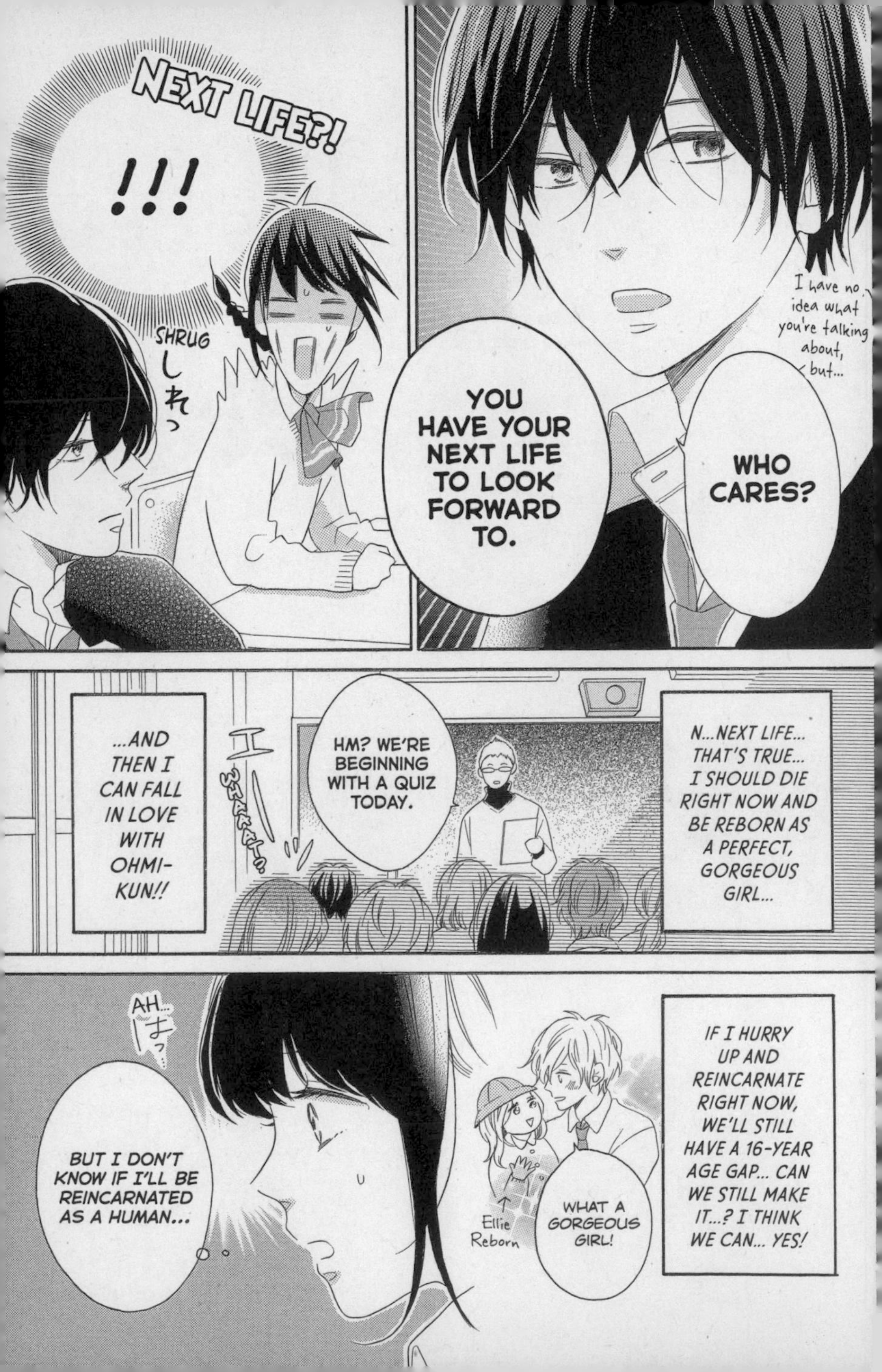
I have no idea what you're talking about, but...
WHO CARES?
YOU HAVE YOUR NEXT LIFE TO LOOK FORWARD TO.
NEXT LIFE?!
!!!
SHRUG
しれっ
N...NEXT LIFE... THAT'S TRUE... I SHOULD DIE RIGHT NOW AND BE REBORN AS A PERFECT, GORGEOUS GIRL...
HM? WE'RE BEGINNING WITH A QUIZ TODAY.
...AND THEN I CAN FALL IN LOVE WITH OHMI-KUN!!
IF I HURRY UP AND REINCARNATE RIGHT NOW, WE'LL STILL HAVE A 16-YEAR AGE GAP... CAN WE STILL MAKE IT...? I THINK WE CAN... YES!
WHAT A GORGEOUS GIRL!
Ellie Reborn
AH...
はっ
BUT I DON'T KNOW IF I'LL BE REINCARNATED AS A HUMAN...

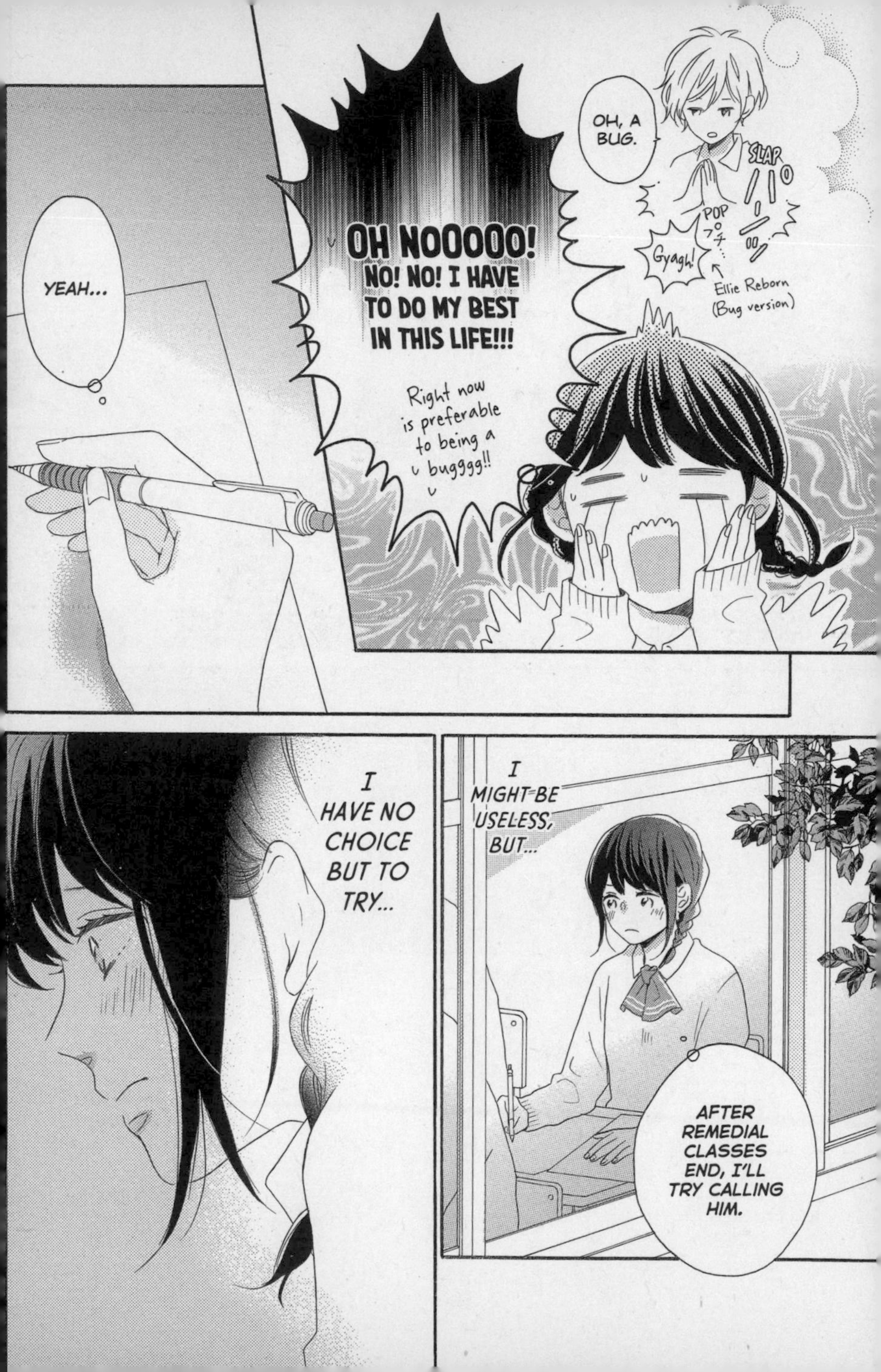
OH, A BUG.
SLAP
POP
Gyagh!
Ellie Reborn (Bug version)
OH NOOOOO! NO! NO! I HAVE TO DO MY BEST IN THIS LIFE!!!
Right now is preferable to being a bugggg!!
YEAH...
I MIGHT BE USELESS, BUT...
AFTER REMEDIAL CLASSES END, I'LL TRY CALLING HIM.
I HAVE NO CHOICE BUT TO TRY...

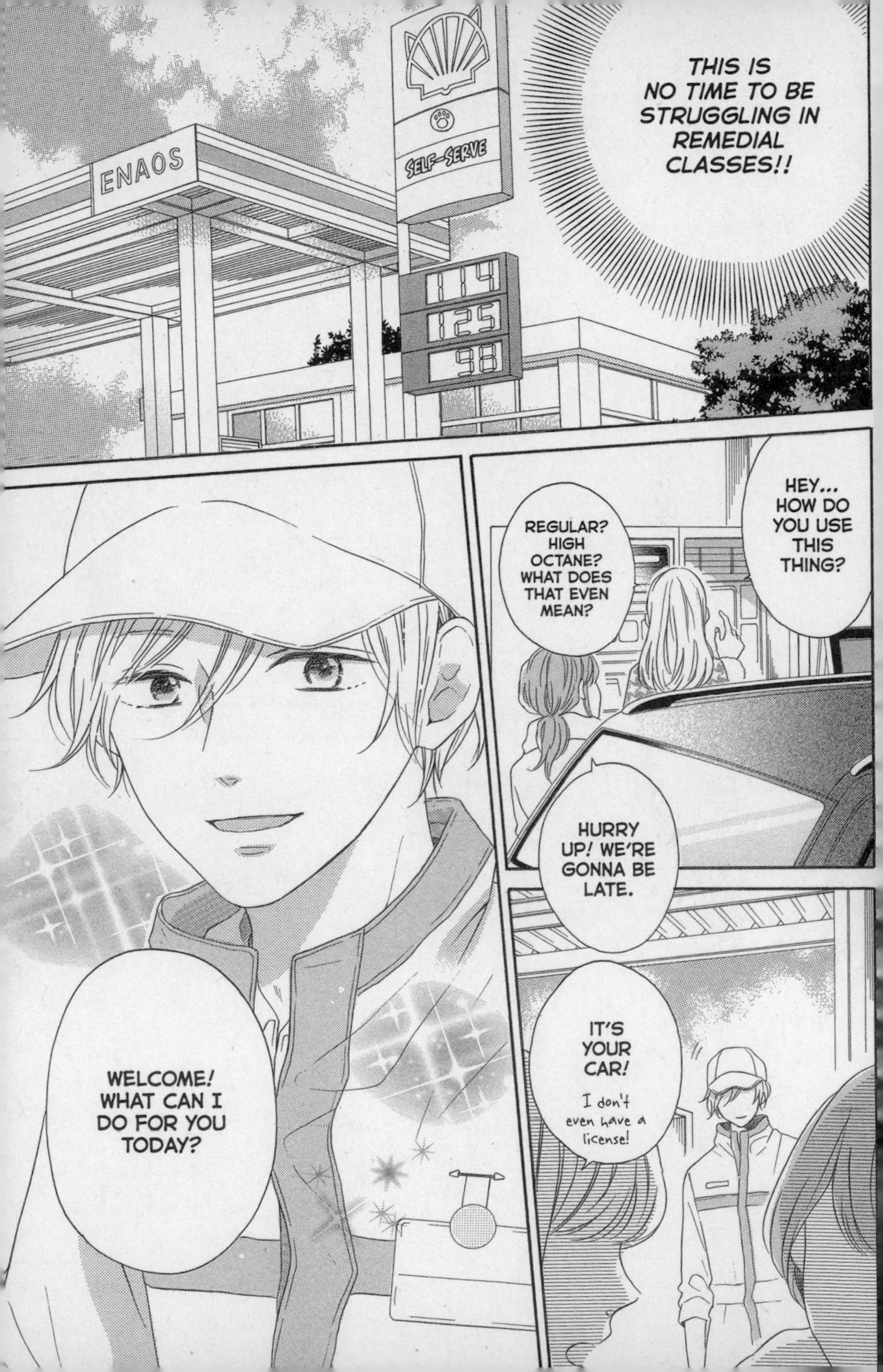
THIS IS NO TIME TO BE STRUGGLING IN REMEDIAL CLASSES!!
SELF-SERVE
114
125
98
ENAOS
HEY... HOW DO YOU USE THIS THING?
REGULAR? HIGH OCTANE? WHAT DOES THAT EVEN MEAN?
HURRY UP! WE'RE GONNA BE LATE.
IT'S YOUR CAR!
I don't even have a license!
WELCOME! WHAT CAN I DO FOR YOU TODAY?

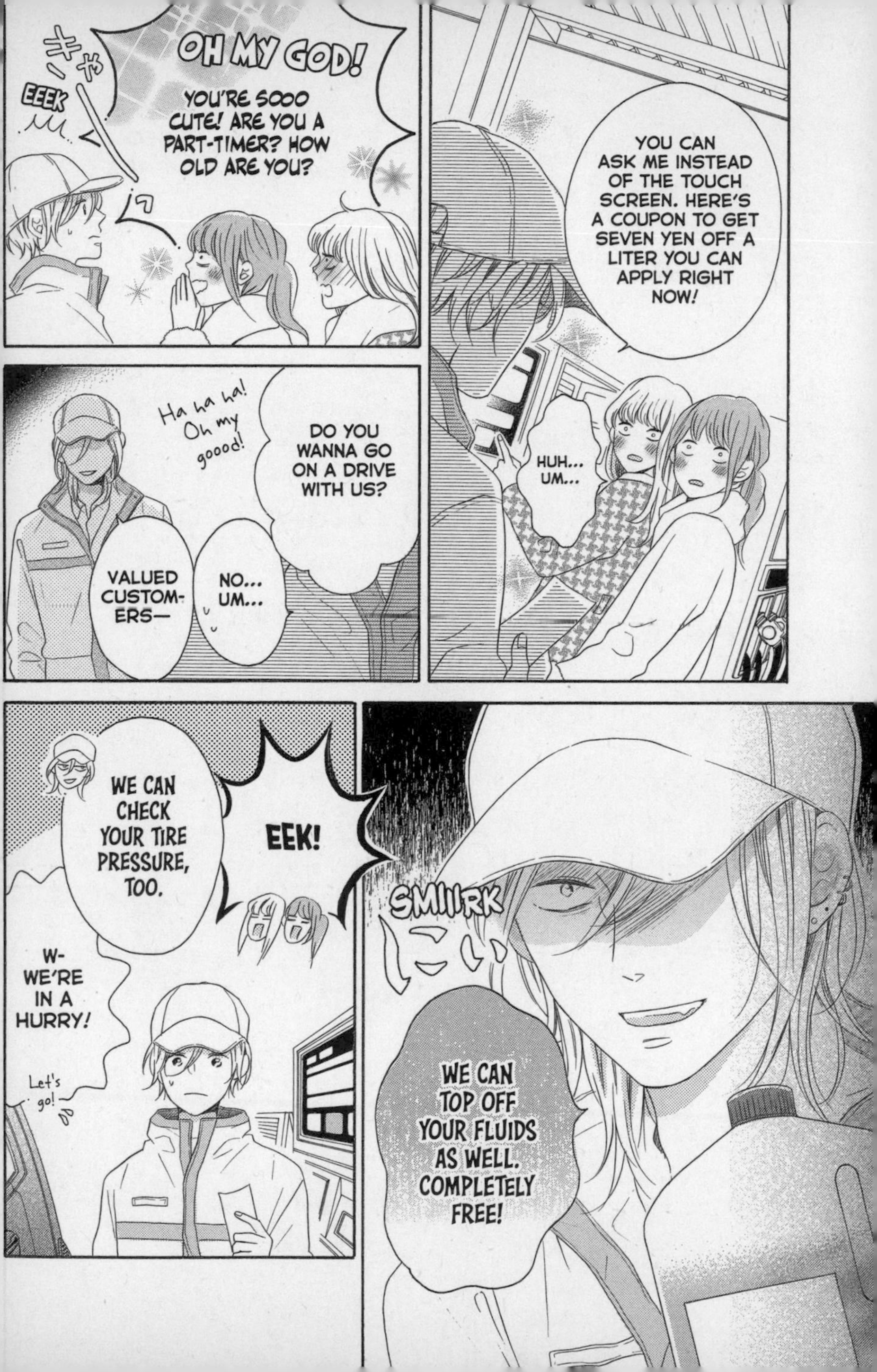
YOU CAN ASK ME INSTEAD OF THE TOUCH SCREEN. HERE'S A COUPON TO GET SEVEN YEN OFF A LITER YOU CAN APPLY RIGHT NOW!
HUH... UM...
OH MY GOD!
YOU'RE SOOO CUTE! ARE YOU A PART-TIMER? HOW OLD ARE YOU?
EEEK
DO YOU WANNA GO ON A DRIVE WITH US?
Ha ha ha! Oh my goood!
NO... UM...
VALUED CUSTOM-ERS—
SMIIIRK
WE CAN TOP OFF YOUR FLUIDS AS WELL. COMPLETELY FREE!
EEK!
WE CAN CHECK YOUR TIRE PRESSURE, TOO.
W-WE'RE IN A HURRY!
Let's go!

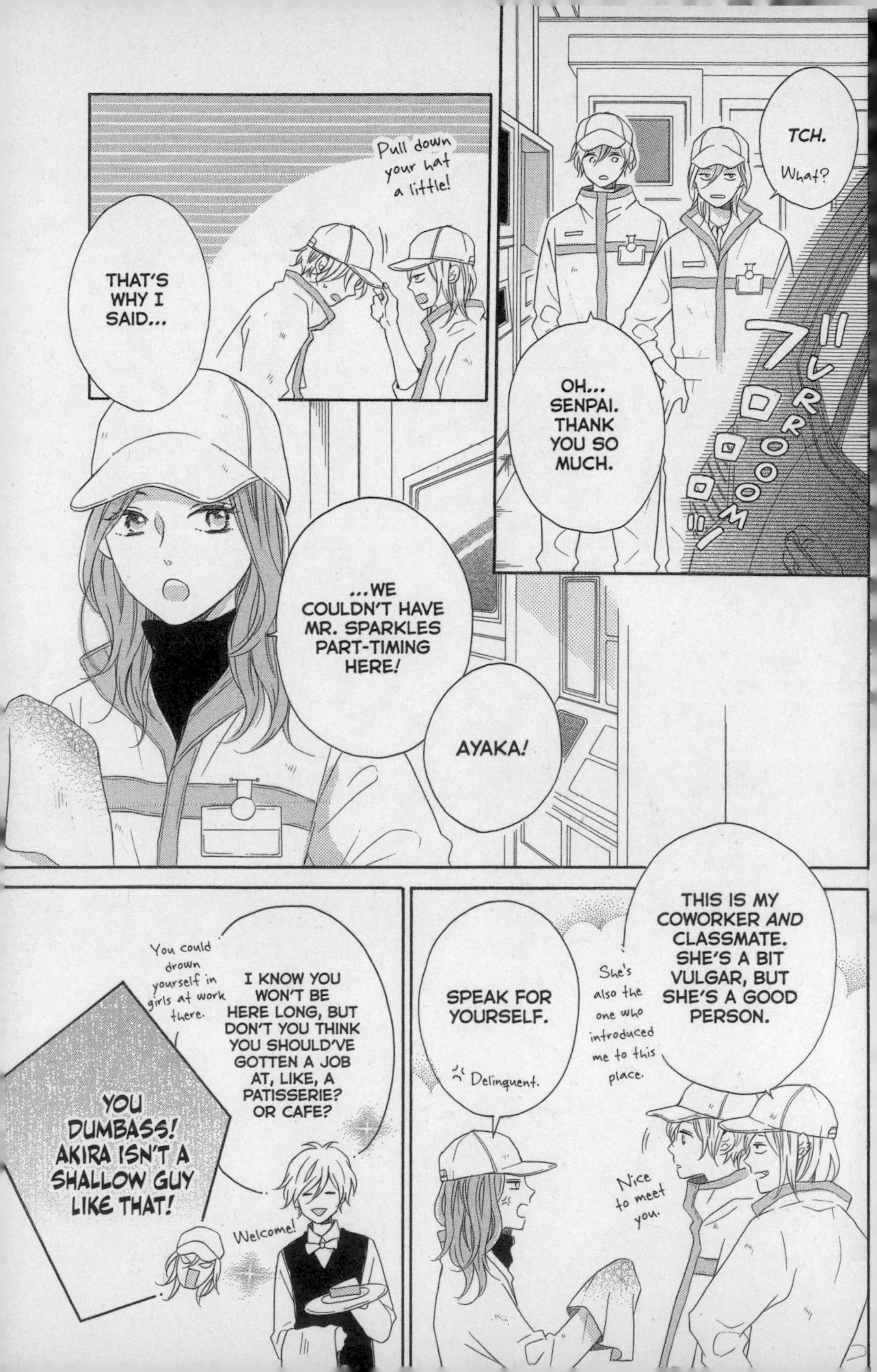
TCH.
What?
OH... SENPAI. THANK YOU SO MUCH.
VROOOOM!!
Pull down your hat a little!
THAT'S WHY I SAID...
...WE COULDN'T HAVE MR. SPARKLES PART-TIMING HERE!
AYAKA!
THIS IS MY COWORKER AND CLASSMATE. SHE'S A BIT VULGAR, BUT SHE'S A GOOD PERSON.
She's also the one who introduced me to this place.
Nice to meet you.
SPEAK FOR YOURSELF.
Delinquent.
I KNOW YOU WON'T BE HERE LONG, BUT DON'T YOU THINK YOU SHOULD'VE GOTTEN A JOB AT, LIKE, A PATISSERIE? OR CAFE?
You could drown yourself in girls at work there.
YOU DUMBASS! AKIRA ISN'T A SHALLOW GUY LIKE THAT!
Welcome!

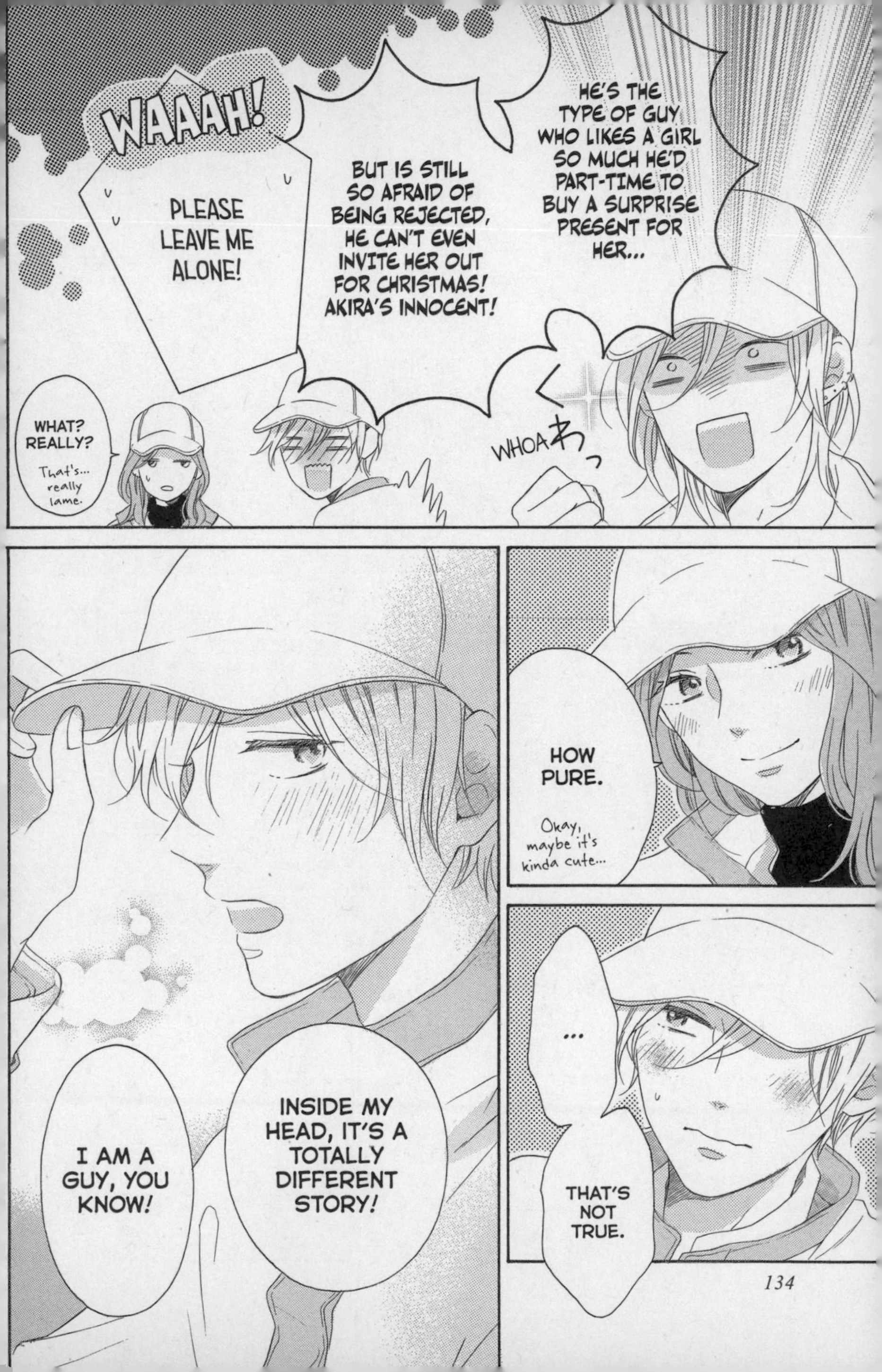
HE'S THE TYPE OF GUY WHO LIKES A GIRL SO MUCH HE'D PART-TIME TO BUY A SURPRISE PRESENT FOR HER...
BUT IS STILL SO AFRAID OF BEING REJECTED, HE CAN'T EVEN INVITE HER OUT FOR CHRISTMAS! AKIRA'S INNOCENT!
WHOA
WAAAH!
PLEASE LEAVE ME ALONE!
WHAT? REALLY?
That's... really lame.
HOW PURE.
Okay, maybe it's kinda cute...
...
THAT'S NOT TRUE.
INSIDE MY HEAD, IT'S A TOTALLY DIFFERENT STORY!
I AM A GUY, YOU KNOW!

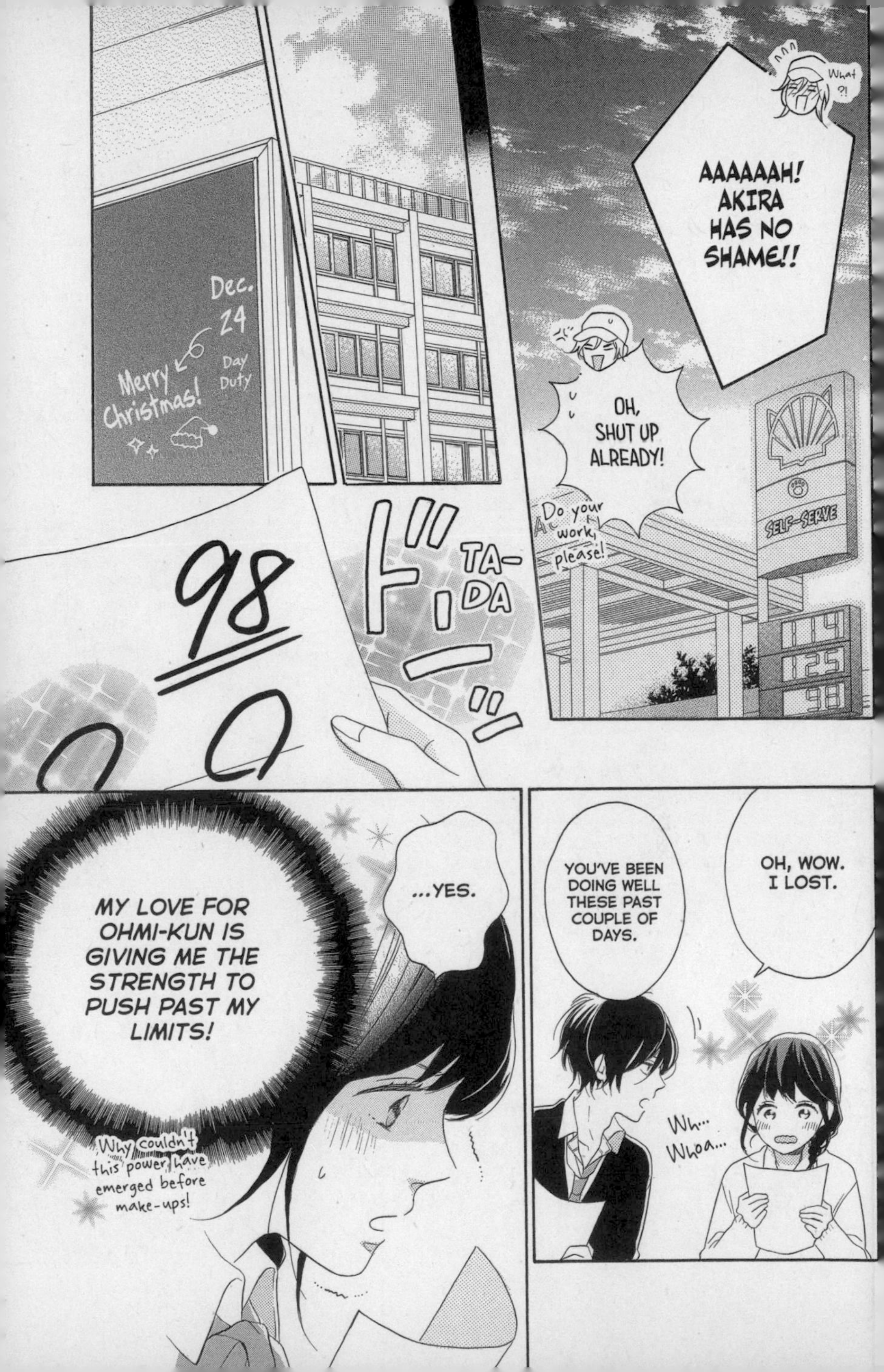
What?!
AAAAAAH! AKIRA HAS NO SHAME!!
OH, SHUT UP ALREADY!
Do your work, please!
SELF-SERVE
Dec. 24
Day Duty
Merry Christmas!
98
TA-DA
OH, WOW. I LOST.
YOU'VE BEEN DOING WELL THESE PAST COUPLE OF DAYS.
Wh... Whoa...
...YES.
MY LOVE FOR OHMI-KUN IS GIVING ME THE STRENGTH TO PUSH PAST MY LIMITS!
Why couldn't this power have emerged before make-ups!

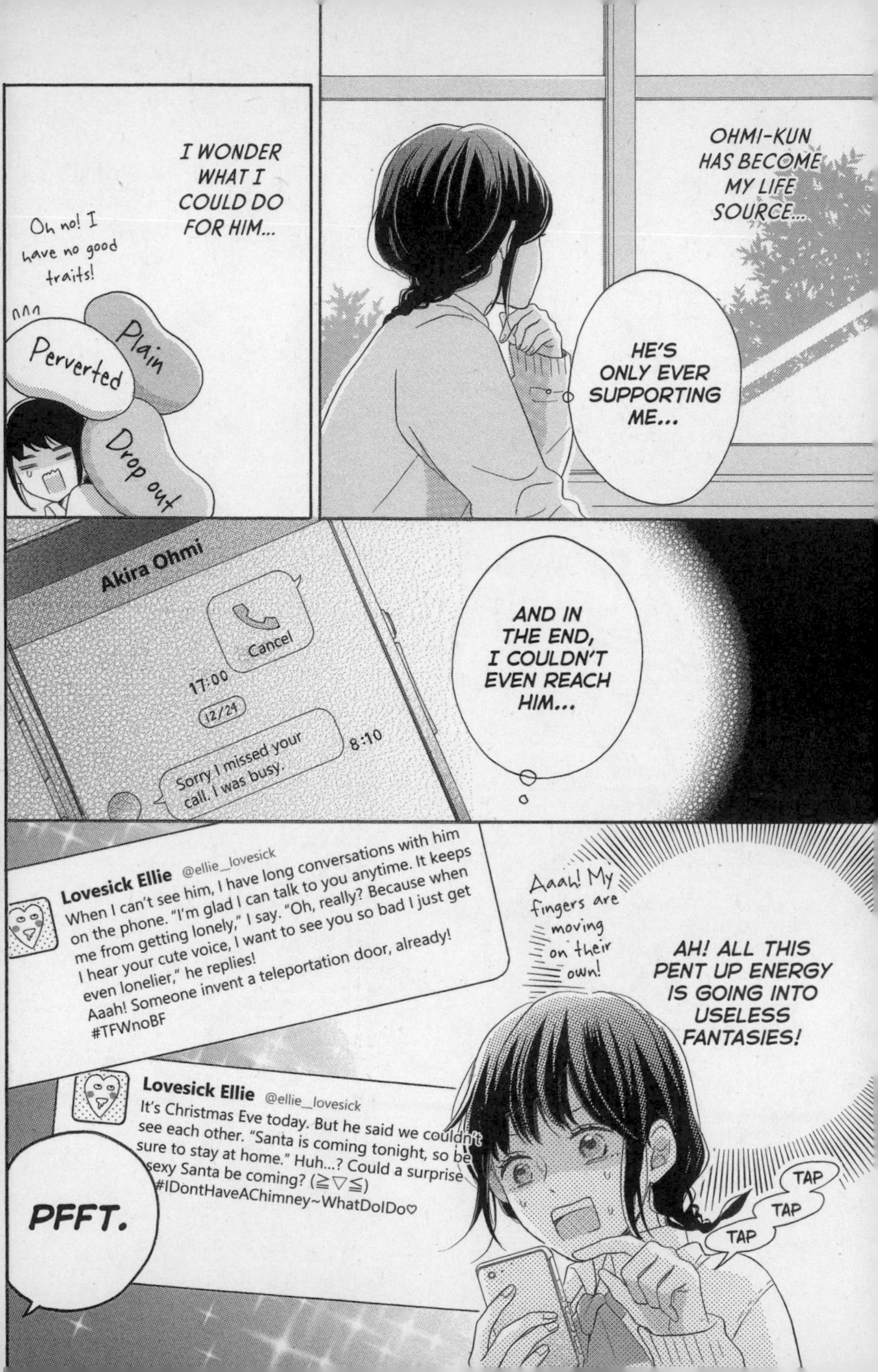
OHMI-KUN HAS BECOME MY LIFE SOURCE...
HE'S ONLY EVER SUPPORTING ME...
I WONDER WHAT I COULD DO FOR HIM...
Oh no! I have no good traits!
Plain
Perverted
Drop out
AND IN THE END, I COULDN'T EVEN REACH HIM...
Akira Ohmi
Cancel
17:00
12/24
Sorry I missed your call. I was busy.
8:10
Aaah! My fingers are moving on their own!
AH! ALL THIS PENT UP ENERGY IS GOING INTO USELESS FANTASIES!
Lovesick Ellie @ellie__lovesick
When I can't see him, I have long conversations with him on the phone. "I'm glad I can talk to you anytime. It keeps me from getting lonely," I say. "Oh, really? Because when I hear your cute voice, I want to see you so bad I just get even lonelier," he replies! Aaah! Someone invent a teleportation door, already! #TFWnoBF
Lovesick Ellie @ellie__lovesick
It's Christmas Eve today. But he said we couldn't see each other. "Santa is coming tonight, so be sure to stay at home." Huh...? Could a surprise sexy Santa be coming? (≧▽≦) #IDontHaveAChimney~WhatDoIDo♡
TAP
TAP
TAP
PFFT.

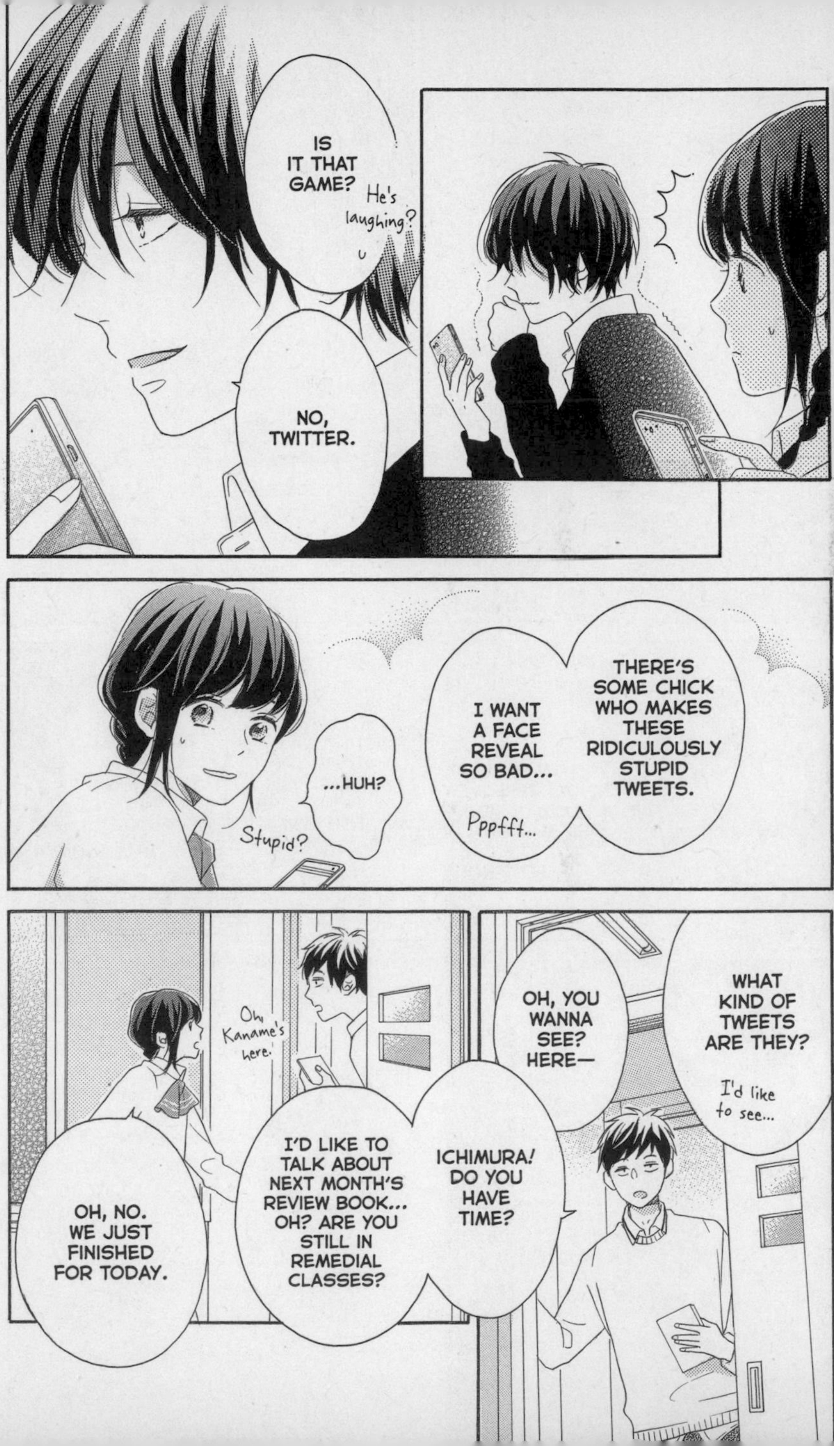
IS IT THAT GAME?
He's laughing?
NO, TWITTER.
THERE'S SOME CHICK WHO MAKES THESE RIDICULOUSLY STUPID TWEETS.
I WANT A FACE REVEAL SO BAD...
Pppfft...
...HUH?
Stupid?
WHAT KIND OF TWEETS ARE THEY?
I'd like to see...
OH, YOU WANNA SEE? HERE—
ICHIMURA! DO YOU HAVE TIME?
I'D LIKE TO TALK ABOUT NEXT MONTH'S REVIEW BOOK... OH? ARE YOU STILL IN REMEDIAL CLASSES?
Oh Kaname's here.
OH, NO. WE JUST FINISHED FOR TODAY.

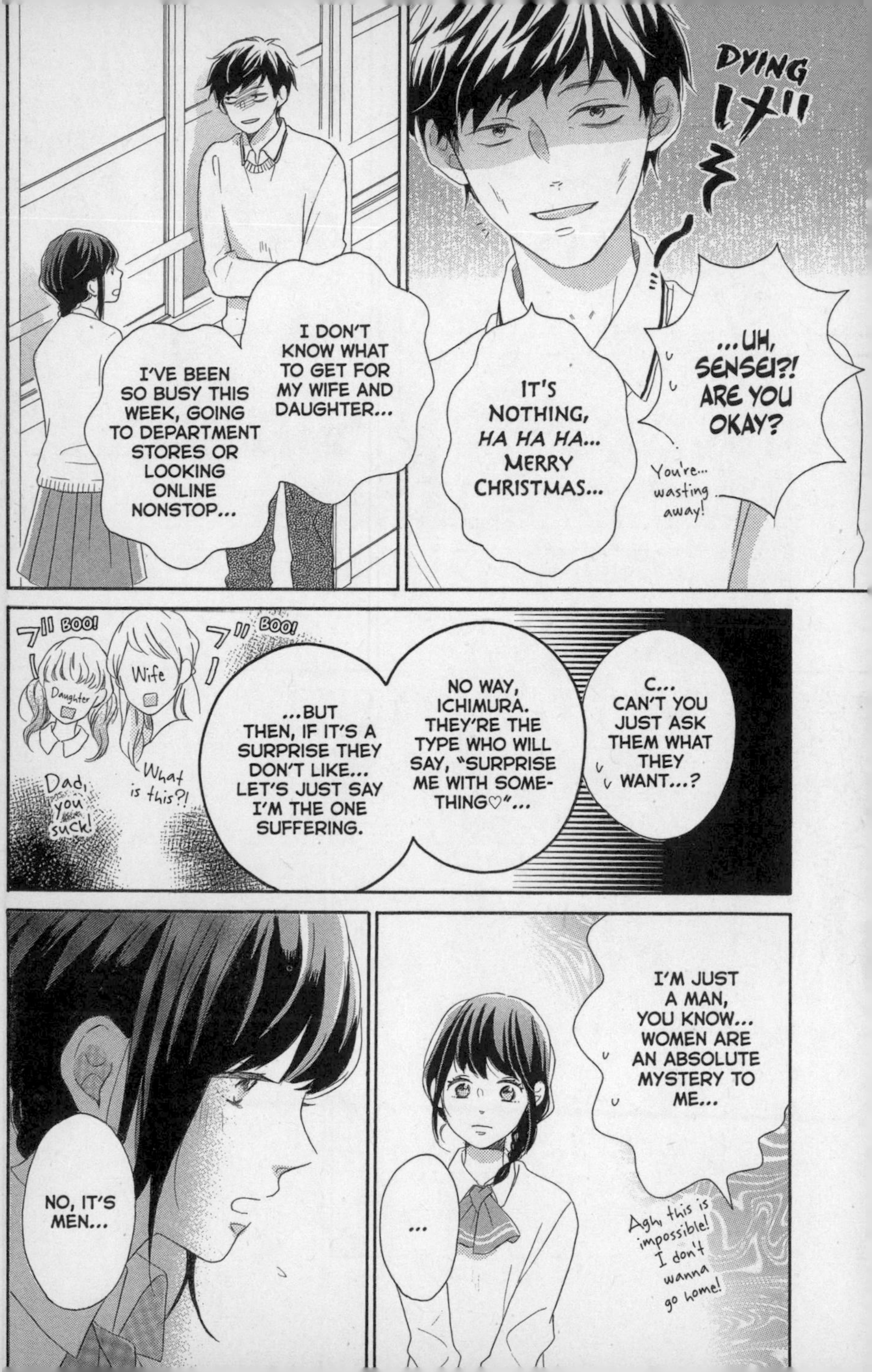
DYING
...UH, SENSEI?! ARE YOU OKAY?
You're... wasting away!
IT'S NOTHING, *HA HA HA*... MERRY CHRISTMAS...
I DON'T KNOW WHAT TO GET FOR MY WIFE AND DAUGHTER...
I'VE BEEN SO BUSY THIS WEEK, GOING TO DEPARTMENT STORES OR LOOKING ONLINE NONSTOP...
C... CAN'T YOU JUST ASK THEM WHAT THEY WANT...?
NO WAY, ICHIMURA. THEY'RE THE TYPE WHO WILL SAY, "SURPRISE ME WITH SOME-THING♡"...
...BUT THEN, IF IT'S A SURPRISE THEY DON'T LIKE... LET'S JUST SAY I'M THE ONE SUFFERING.
BOO!
BOO!
Wife
Daughter
What is this?!
Dad, you suck!
I'M JUST A MAN, YOU KNOW... WOMEN ARE AN ABSOLUTE MYSTERY TO ME...
Agh, this is impossible! I don't wanna go home!
...
NO, IT'S MEN...

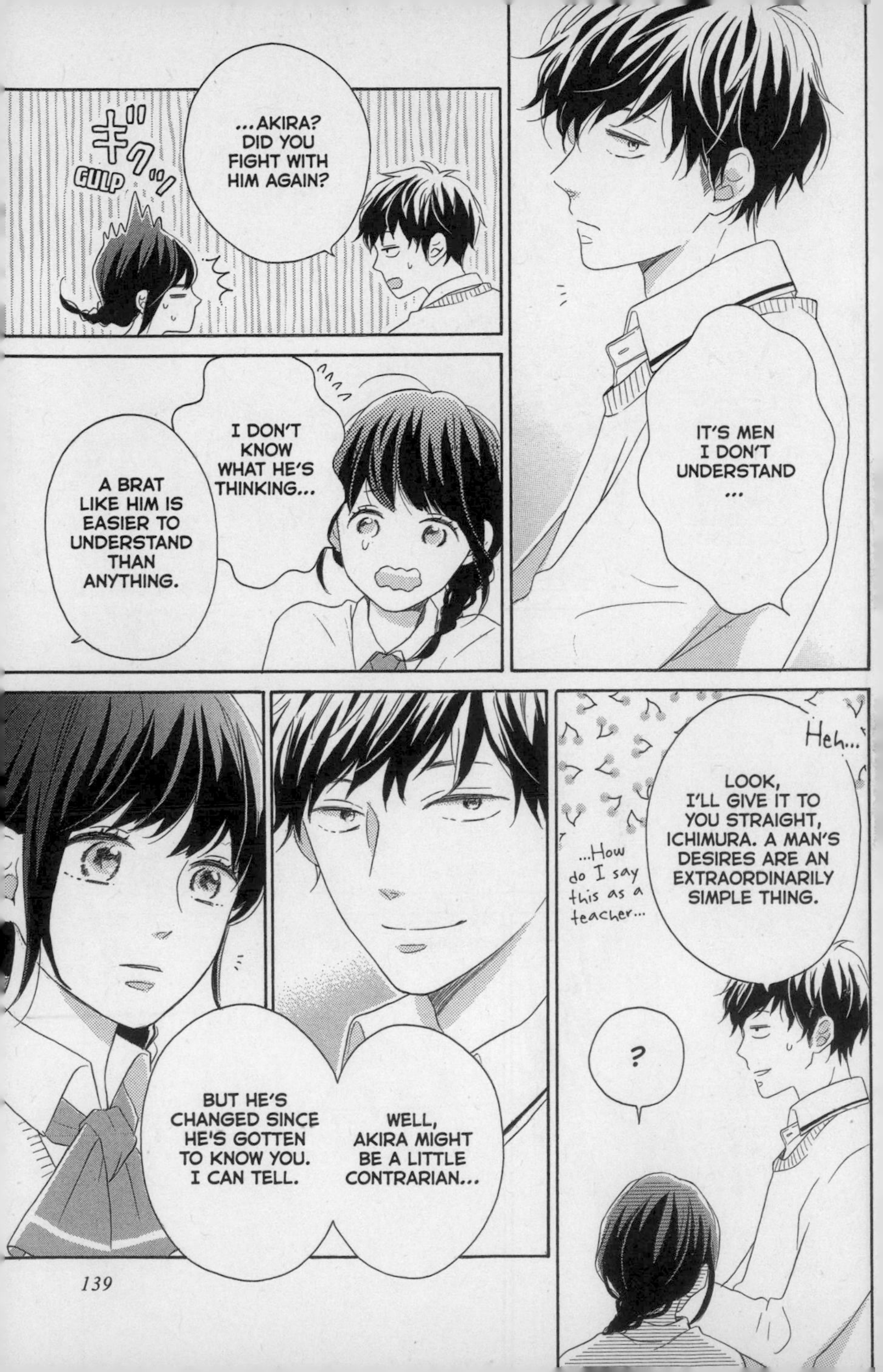
IT'S MEN I DON'T UNDERSTAND ...
...AKIRA? DID YOU FIGHT WITH HIM AGAIN?
ギクッ
GULP
I DON'T KNOW WHAT HE'S THINKING...
A BRAT LIKE HIM IS EASIER TO UNDERSTAND THAN ANYTHING.
Heh...
LOOK, I'LL GIVE IT TO YOU STRAIGHT, ICHIMURA. A MAN'S DESIRES ARE AN EXTRAORDINARILY SIMPLE THING.
...How do I say this as a teacher...
?
WELL, AKIRA MIGHT BE A LITTLE CONTRARIAN...
BUT HE'S CHANGED SINCE HE'S GOTTEN TO KNOW YOU. I CAN TELL.

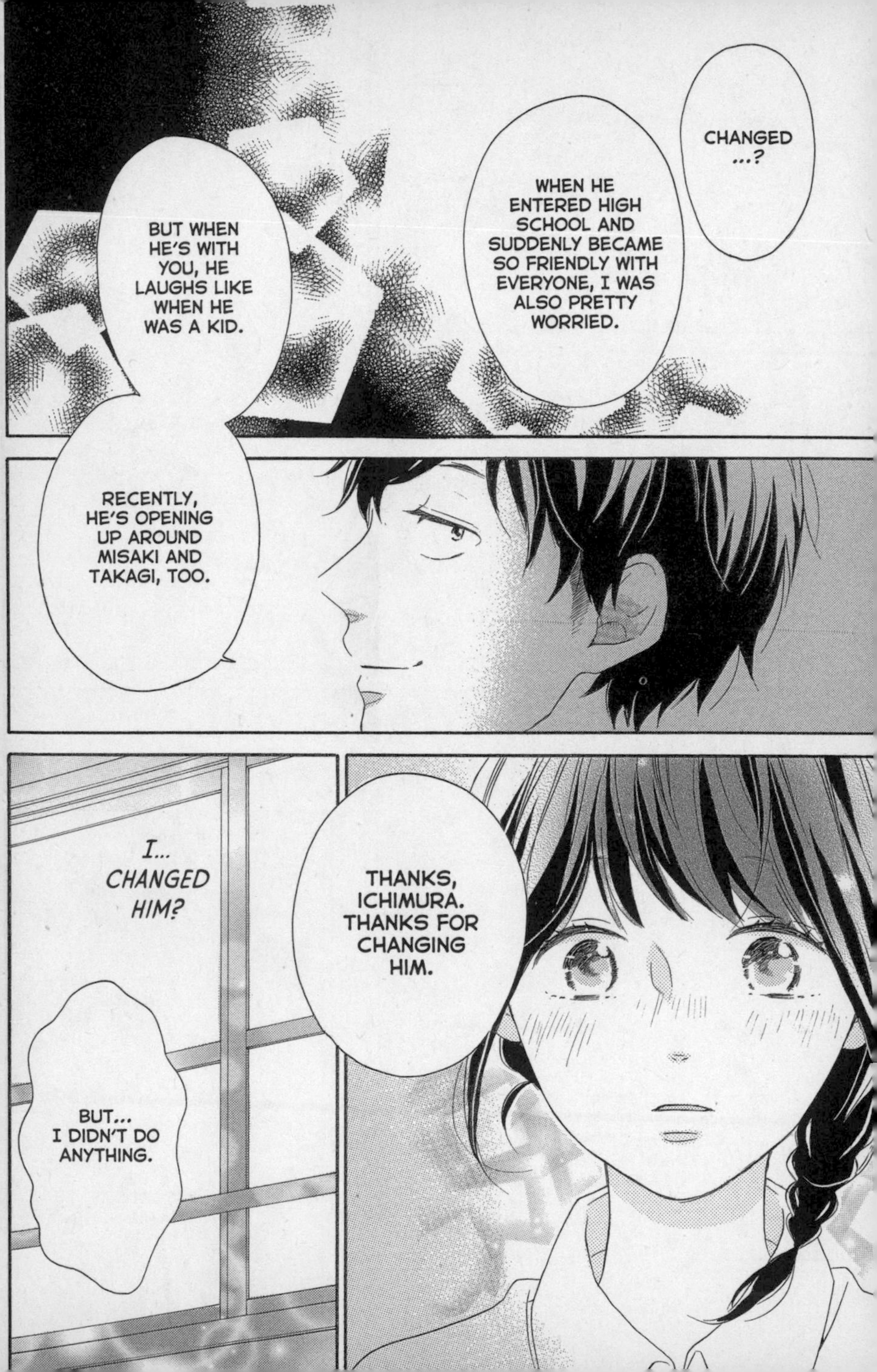
CHANGED ...?
WHEN HE ENTERED HIGH SCHOOL AND SUDDENLY BECAME SO FRIENDLY WITH EVERYONE, I WAS ALSO PRETTY WORRIED.
BUT WHEN HE'S WITH YOU, HE LAUGHS LIKE WHEN HE WAS A KID.
RECENTLY, HE'S OPENING UP AROUND MISAKI AND TAKAGI, TOO.
THANKS, ICHIMURA. THANKS FOR CHANGING HIM.
I... CHANGED HIM?
BUT... I DIDN'T DO ANYTHING.

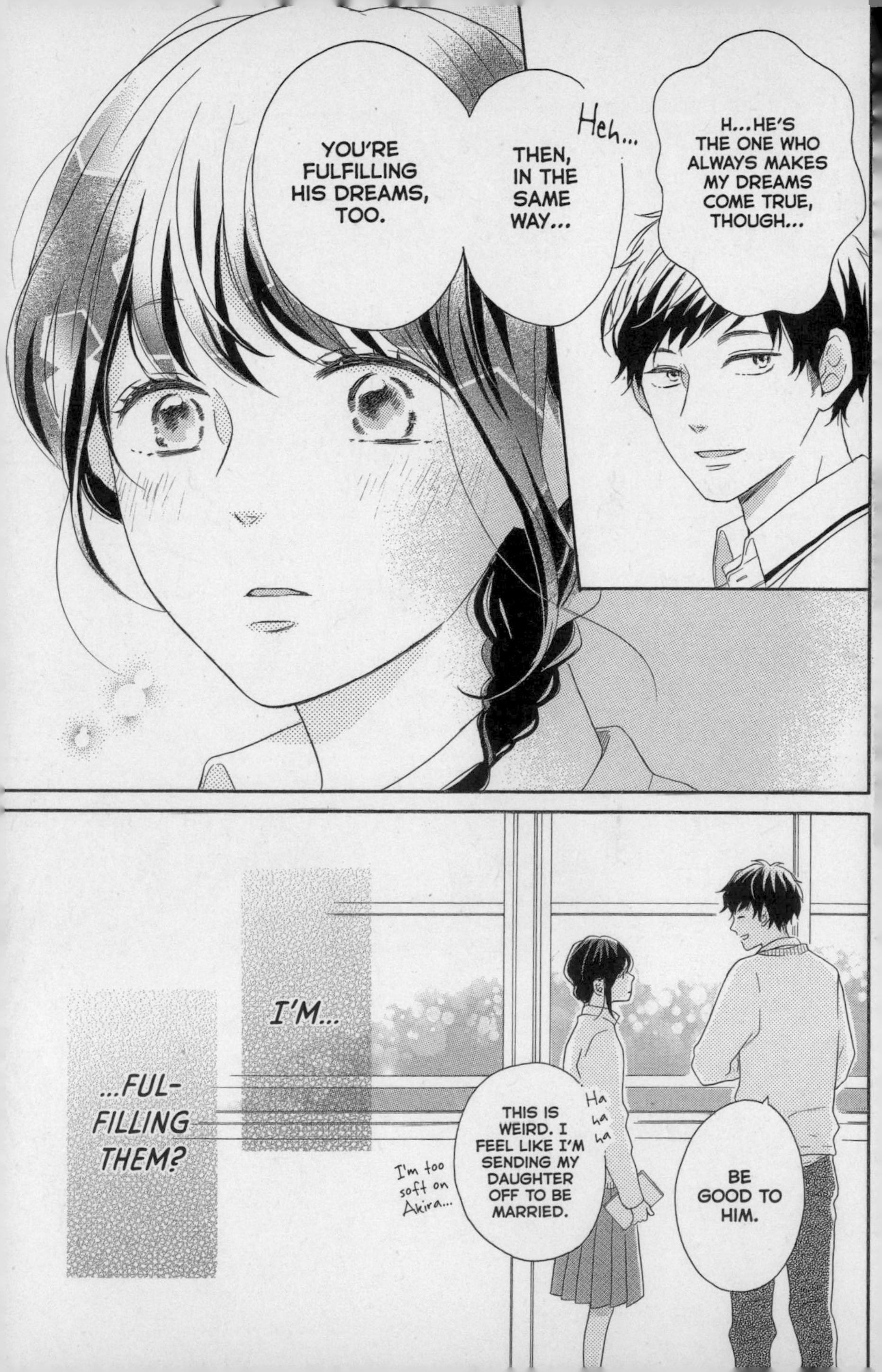
H...HE'S THE ONE WHO ALWAYS MAKES MY DREAMS COME TRUE, THOUGH...
Heh...
THEN, IN THE SAME WAY...
YOU'RE FULFILLING HIS DREAMS, TOO.
BE GOOD TO HIM.
Ha ha ha
THIS IS WEIRD. I FEEL LIKE I'M SENDING MY DAUGHTER OFF TO BE MARRIED.
I'm too soft on Akira...
I'M...
...FUL-FILLING THEM?

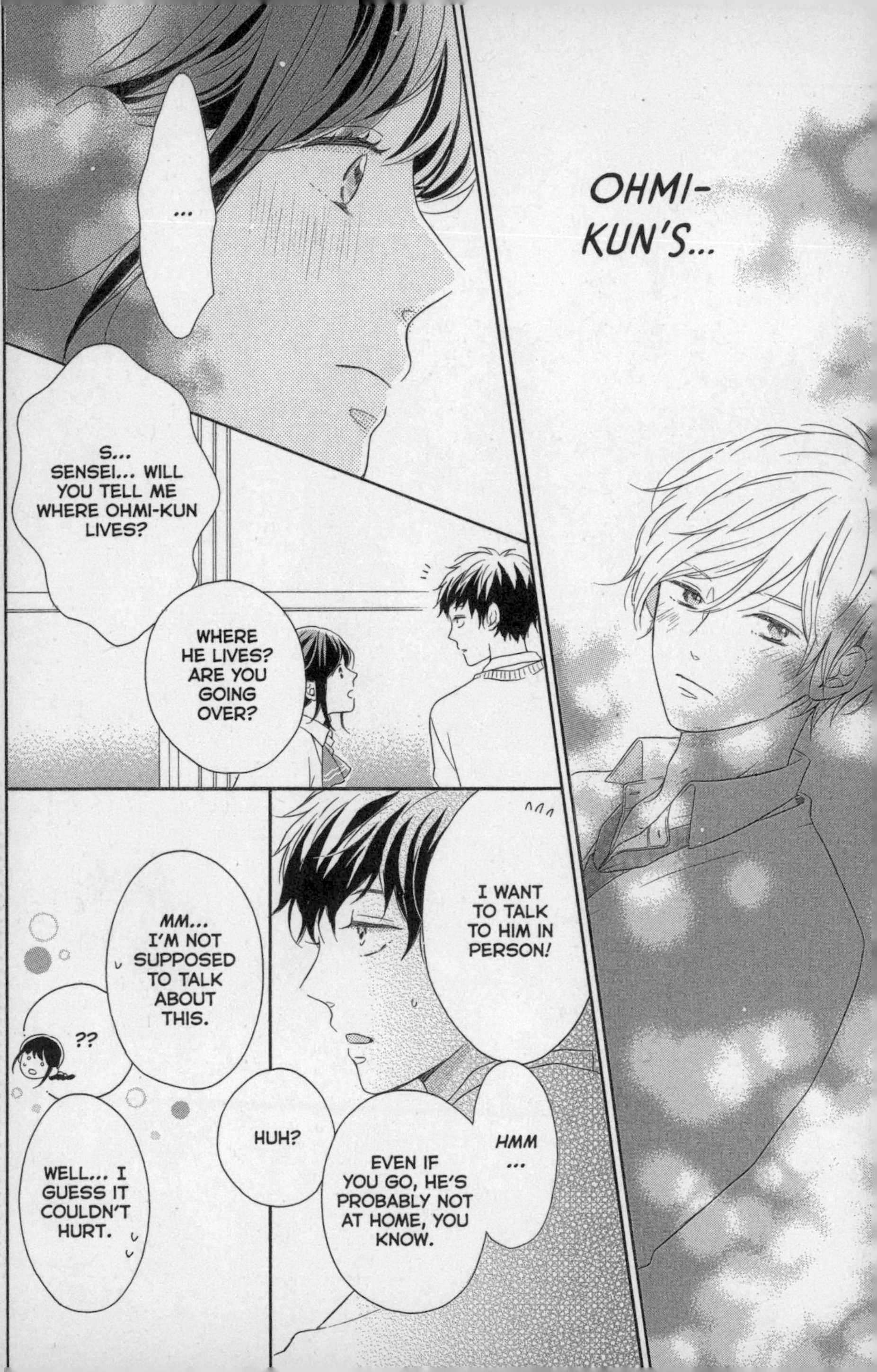
OHMI-KUN'S...
...
S... SENSEI... WILL YOU TELL ME WHERE OHMI-KUN LIVES?
WHERE HE LIVES? ARE YOU GOING OVER?
I WANT TO TALK TO HIM IN PERSON!
HMM ...
EVEN IF YOU GO, HE'S PROBABLY NOT AT HOME, YOU KNOW.
HUH?
MM... I'M NOT SUPPOSED TO TALK ABOUT THIS.
??
WELL... I GUESS IT COULDN'T HURT.

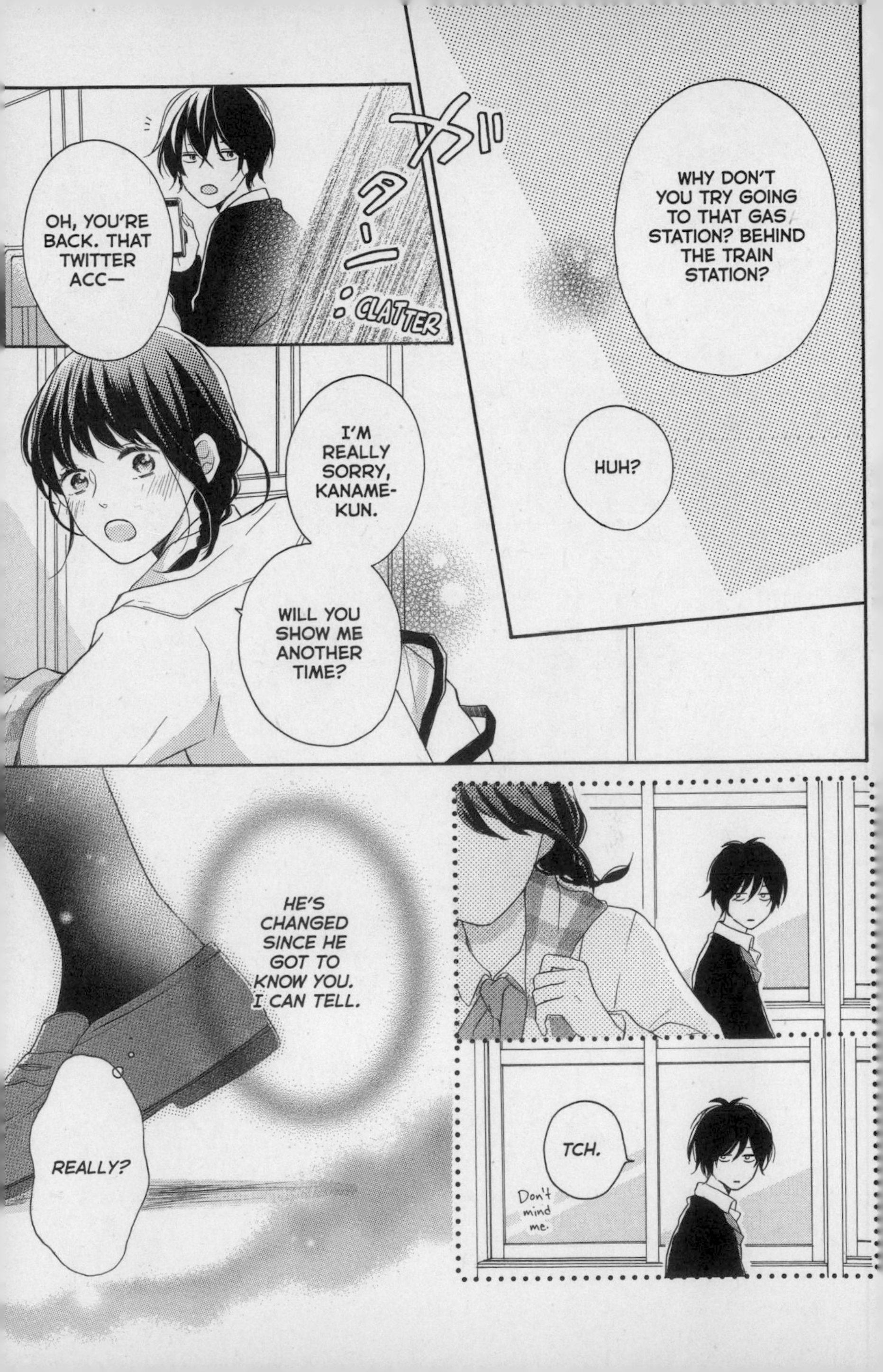
WHY DON'T YOU TRY GOING TO THAT GAS STATION? BEHIND THE TRAIN STATION?
HUH?
OH, YOU'RE BACK. THAT TWITTER ACC—
CLATTER
I'M REALLY SORRY, KANAME-KUN.
WILL YOU SHOW ME ANOTHER TIME?
TCH.
Don't mind me.
HE'S CHANGED SINCE HE GOT TO KNOW YOU. I CAN TELL.
REALLY?

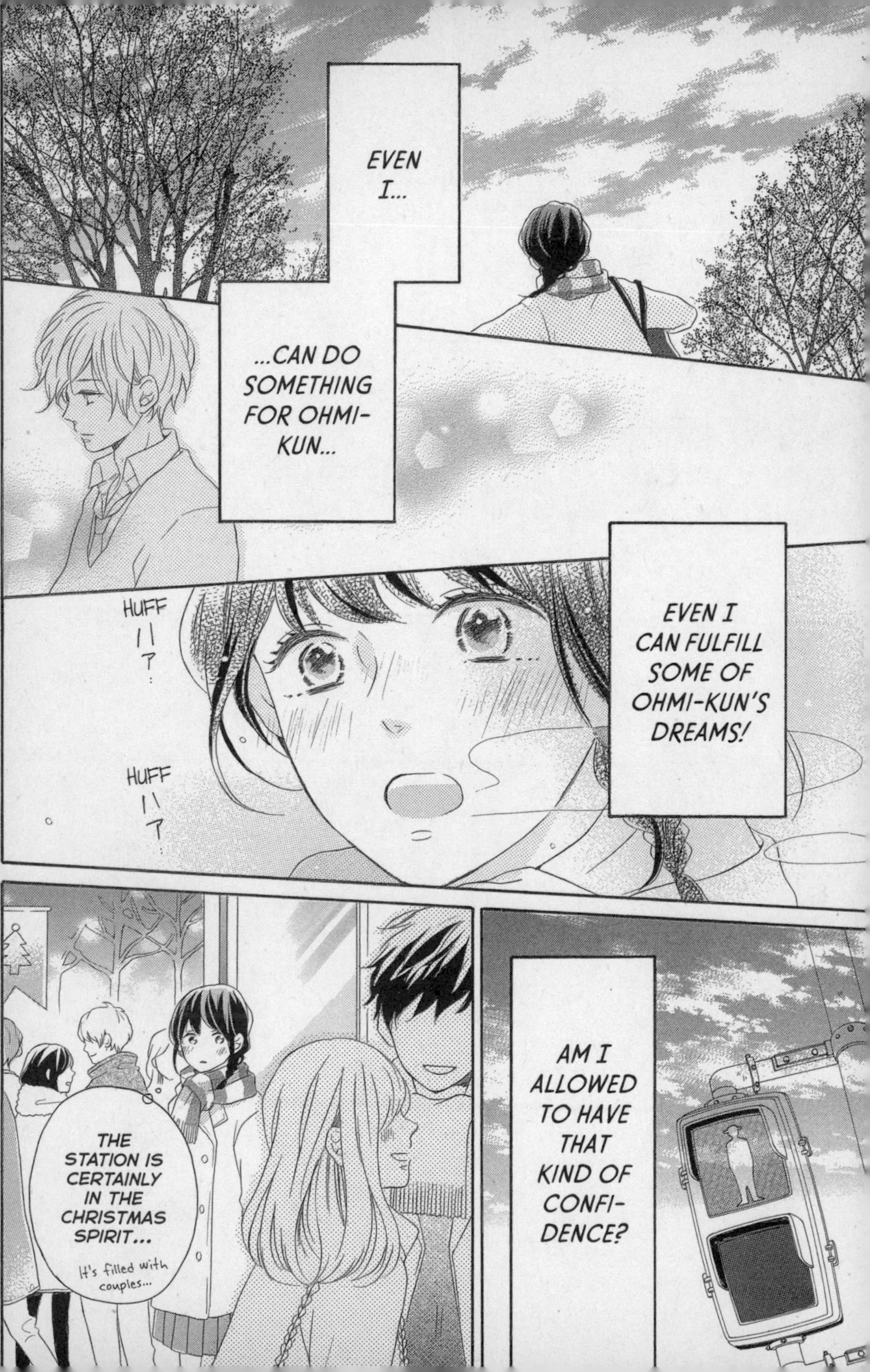
EVEN I...
...CAN DO SOMETHING FOR OHMI-KUN...
EVEN I CAN FULFILL SOME OF OHMI-KUN'S DREAMS!
HUFF
ハア
HUFF
ハア
AM I ALLOWED TO HAVE THAT KIND OF CONFI-DENCE?
THE STATION IS CERTAINLY IN THE CHRISTMAS SPIRIT...
It's filled with couples...

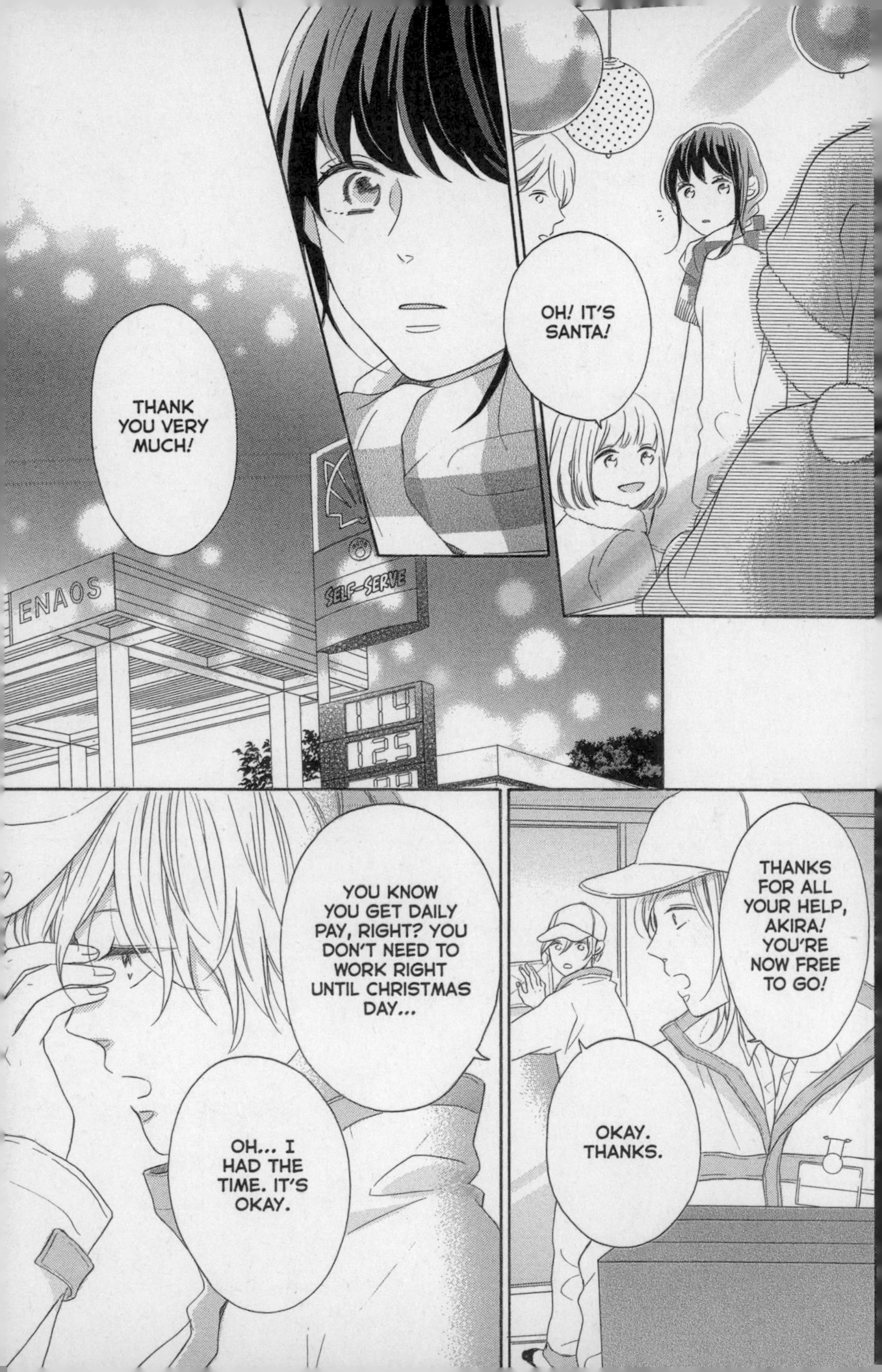
OH! IT'S SANTA!
THANK YOU VERY MUCH!
ENAOS
SELF-SERVE
THANKS FOR ALL YOUR HELP, AKIRA! YOU'RE NOW FREE TO GO!
OKAY. THANKS.
YOU KNOW YOU GET DAILY PAY, RIGHT? YOU DON'T NEED TO WORK RIGHT UNTIL CHRISTMAS DAY...
OH... I HAD THE TIME. IT'S OKAY.

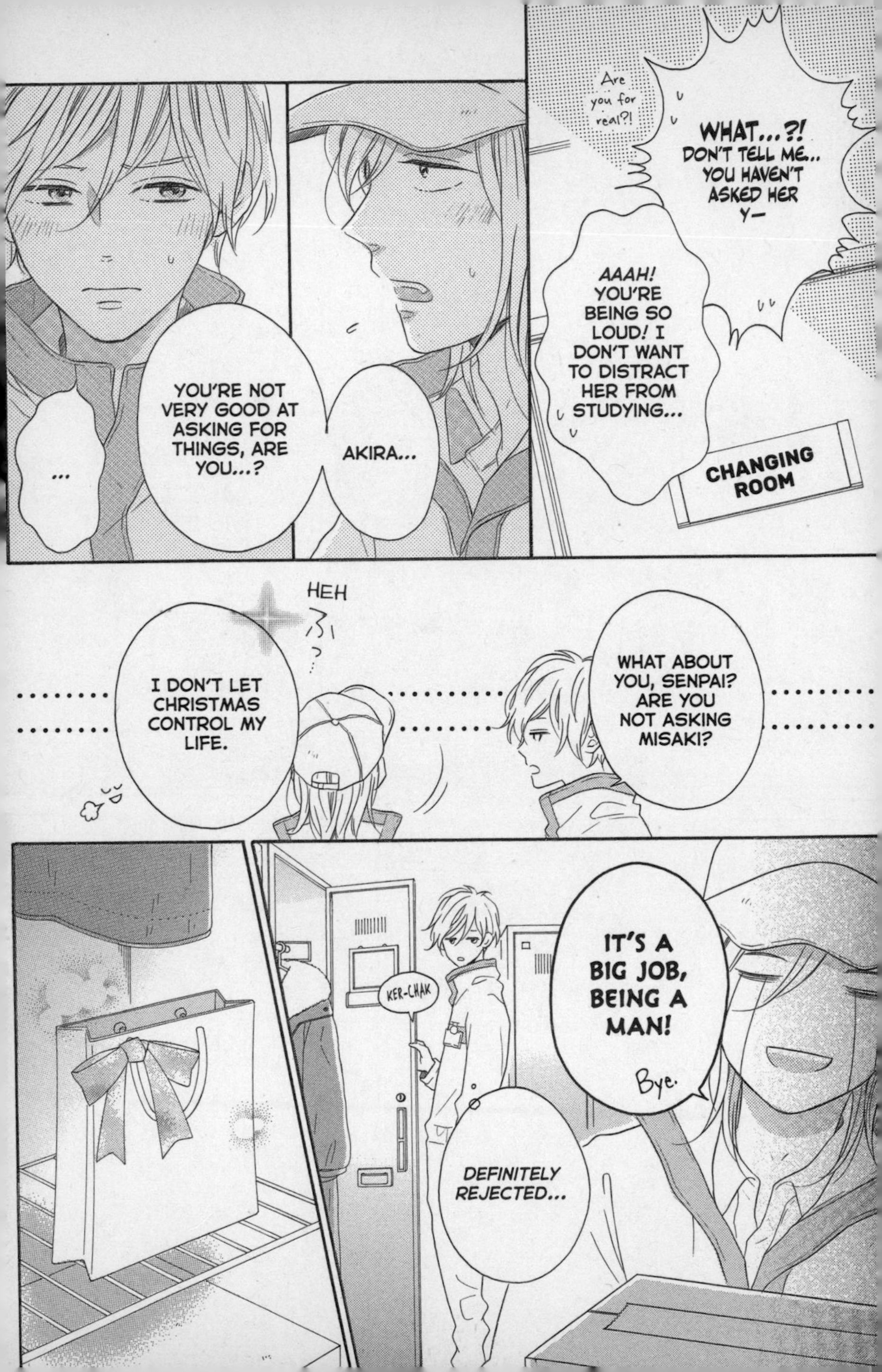
Are you for real?!
WHAT...?! DON'T TELL ME... YOU HAVEN'T ASKED HER Y—
AAAH! YOU'RE BEING SO LOUD! I DON'T WANT TO DISTRACT HER FROM STUDYING...
CHANGING ROOM
AKIRA...
YOU'RE NOT VERY GOOD AT ASKING FOR THINGS, ARE YOU...?
...
WHAT ABOUT YOU, SENPAI? ARE YOU NOT ASKING MISAKI?
HEH
ふ
I DON'T LET CHRISTMAS CONTROL MY LIFE.
IT'S A BIG JOB, BEING A MAN!
Bye.
KER-CHAK
DEFINITELY REJECTED...

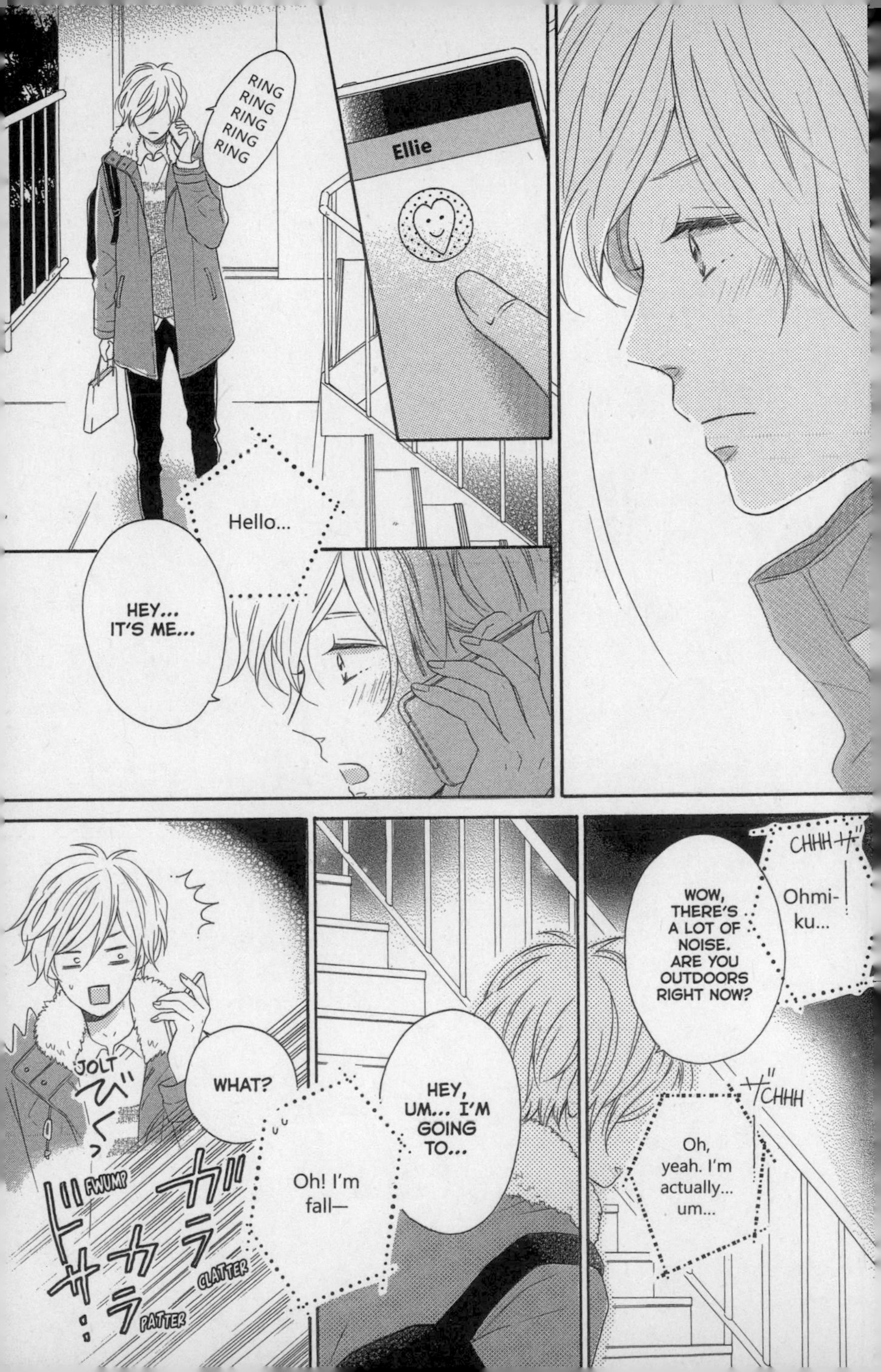
Ellie
RING RING RING RING RING
Hello...
HEY... IT'S ME...
CHHH
Ohmi-ku...
WOW, THERE'S A LOT OF NOISE. ARE YOU OUTDOORS RIGHT NOW?
CHHH
Oh, yeah. I'm actually... um...
HEY, UM... I'M GOING TO...
WHAT?
Oh! I'm fall—
JOLT
FWUMP
CLATTER
PATTER

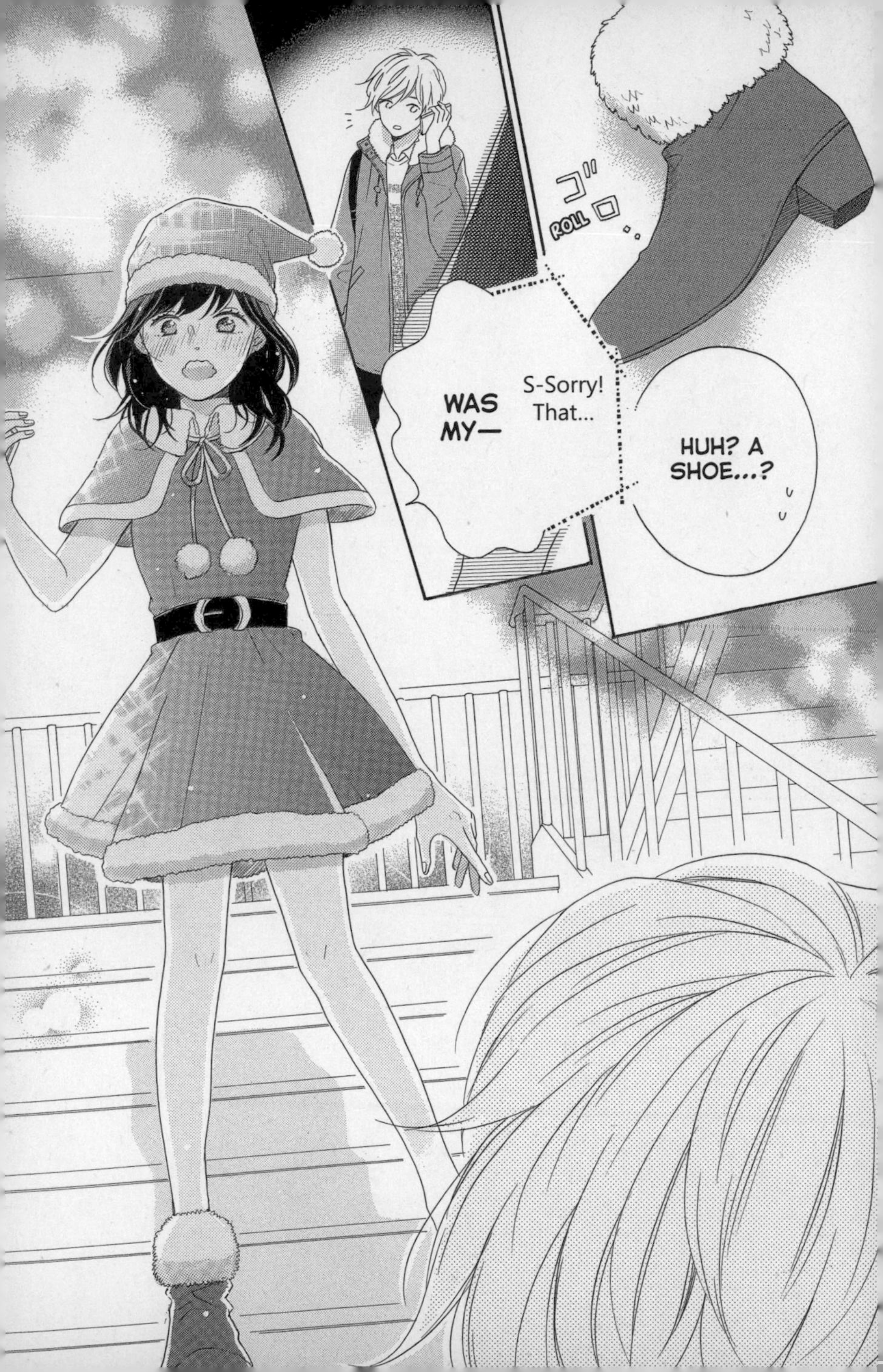
ゴロ
ROLL
HUH? A SHOE...?
S-Sorry! That...
WAS MY—

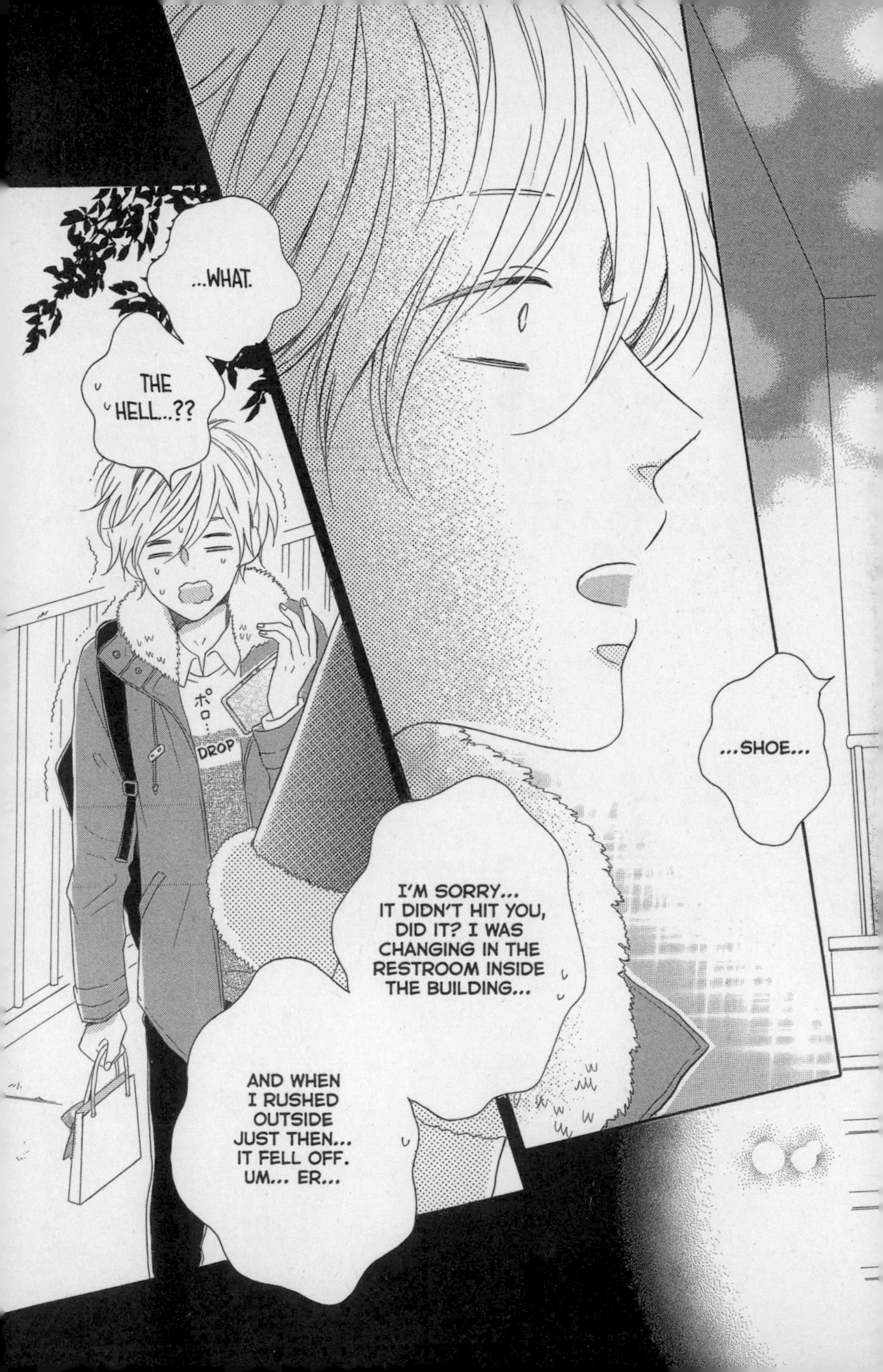
...SHOE...
I'M SORRY... IT DIDN'T HIT YOU, DID IT? I WAS CHANGING IN THE RESTROOM INSIDE THE BUILDING...
AND WHEN I RUSHED OUTSIDE JUST THEN... IT FELL OFF. UM... ER...
...WHAT.
THE HELL...??
ポロ…
DROP

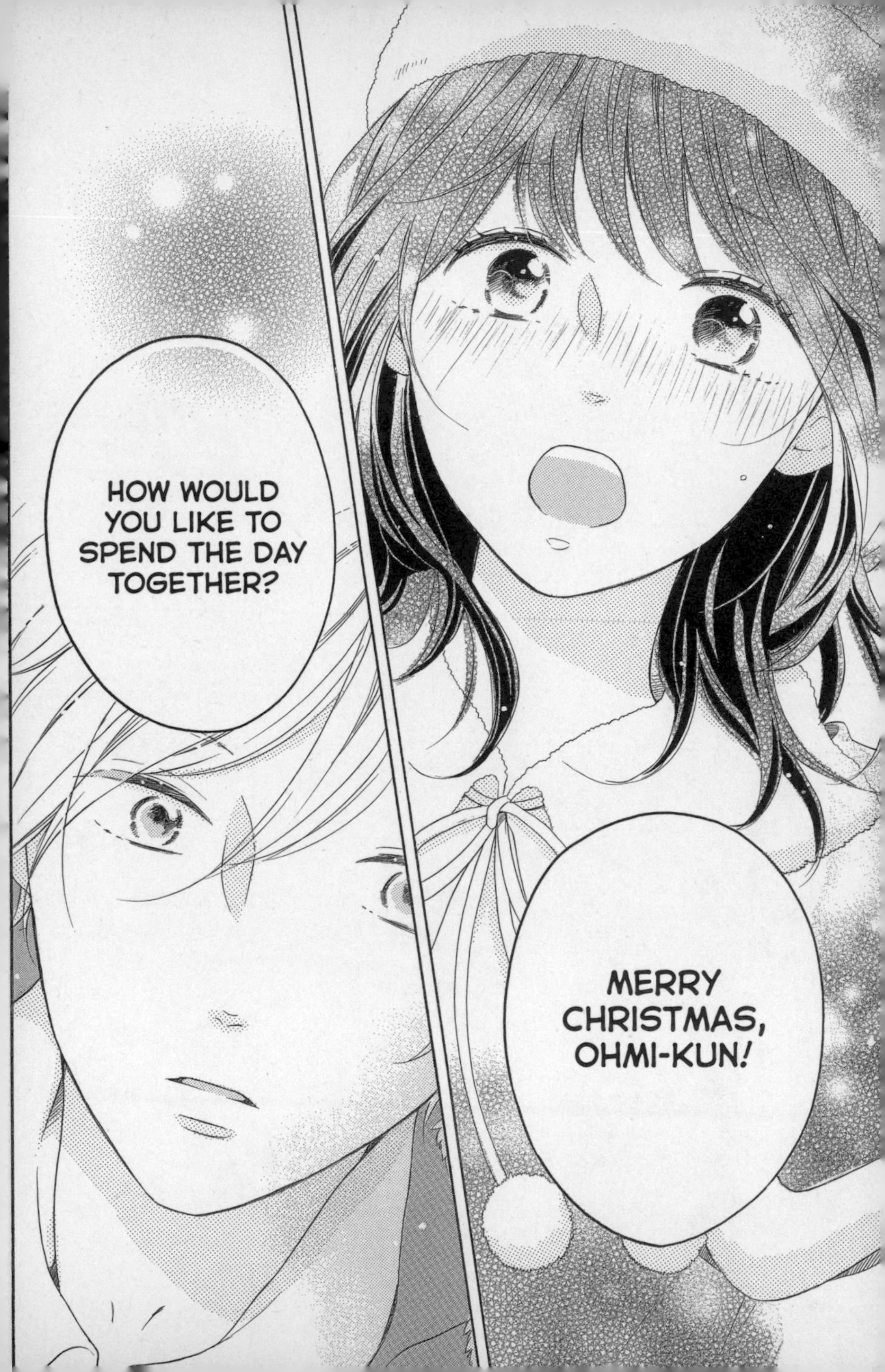
MERRY CHRISTMAS, OHMI-KUN!
HOW WOULD YOU LIKE TO SPEND THE DAY TOGETHER?

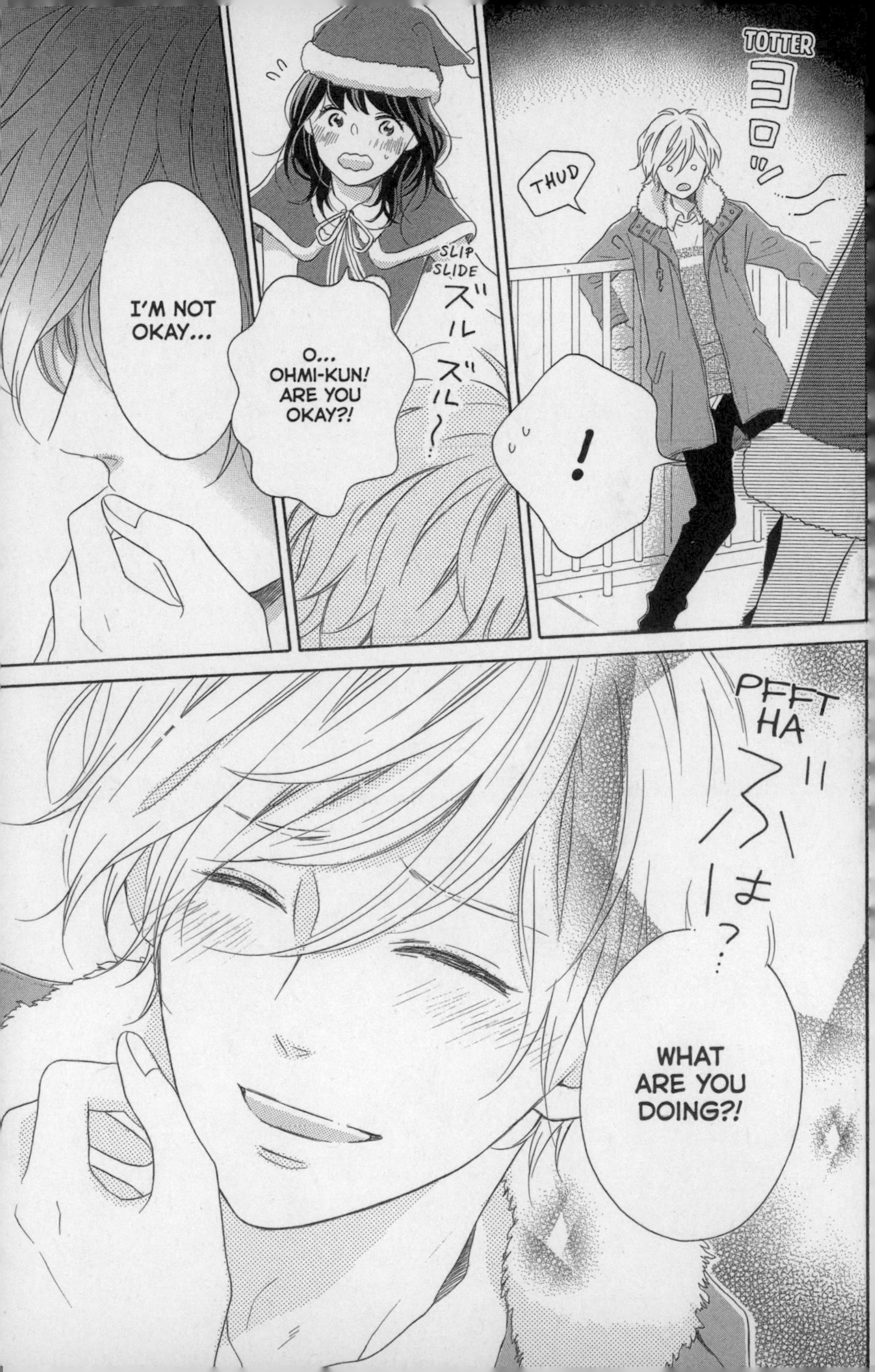
TOTTER
ヨロッ
THUD
!
SLIP SLIDE
ズルズル～
O... OHMI-KUN! ARE YOU OKAY?!
I'M NOT OKAY...
PFFT HA
ふはっ
WHAT ARE YOU DOING?!

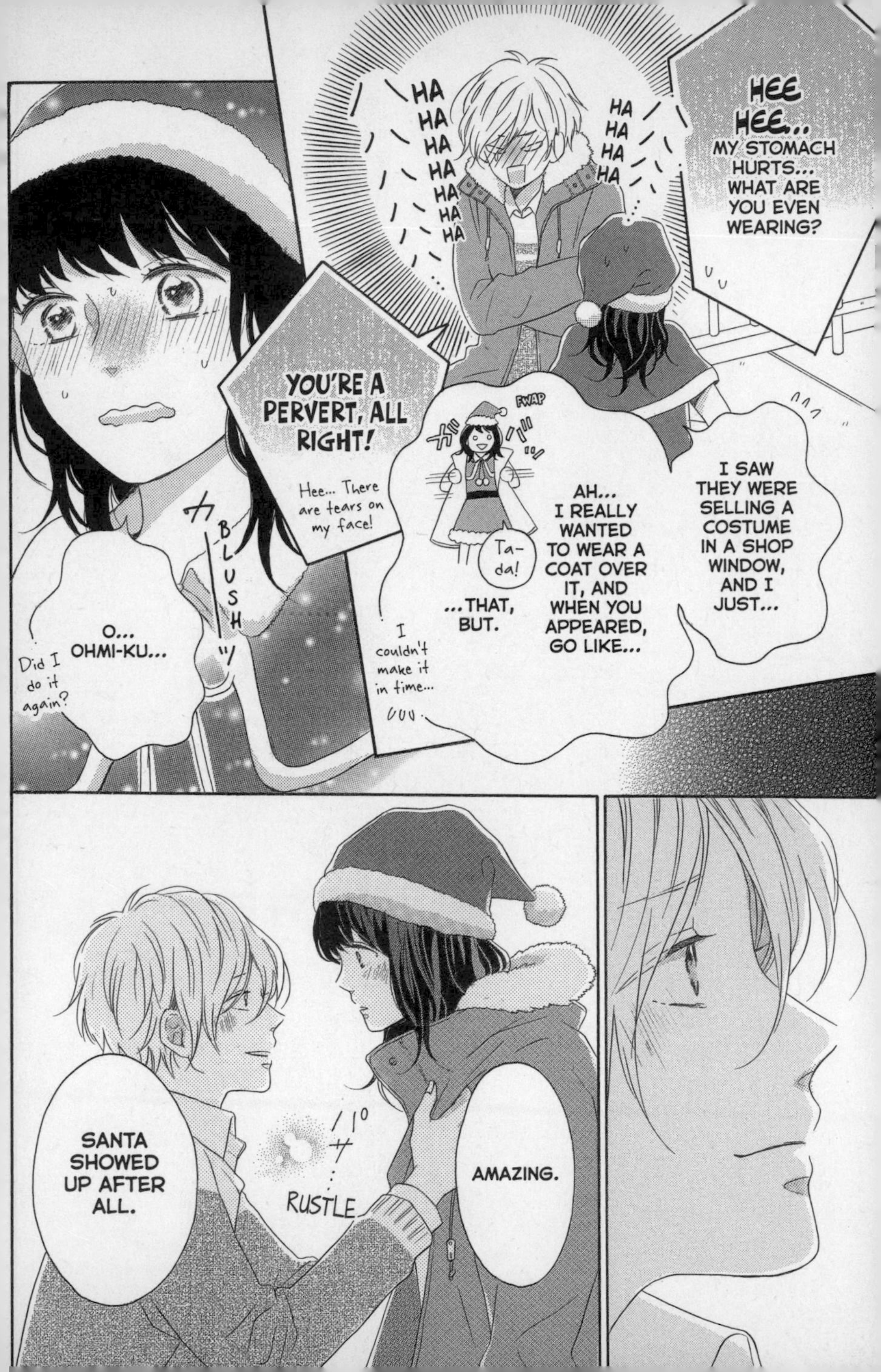
HEE HEE... MY STOMACH HURTS... WHAT ARE YOU EVEN WEARING?
HA HA HA HA
HA HA HA HA HA HA HA
I SAW THEY WERE SELLING A COSTUME IN A SHOP WINDOW, AND I JUST...
AH... I REALLY WANTED TO WEAR A COAT OVER IT, AND WHEN YOU APPEARED, GO LIKE...
FWAP
Ta-da!
...THAT, BUT.
I couldn't make it in time...
YOU'RE A PERVERT, ALL RIGHT!
Hee... There are tears on my face!
BLUSH
O... OHMI-KU...
Did I do it again?
AMAZING.
RUSTLE
SANTA SHOWED UP AFTER ALL.

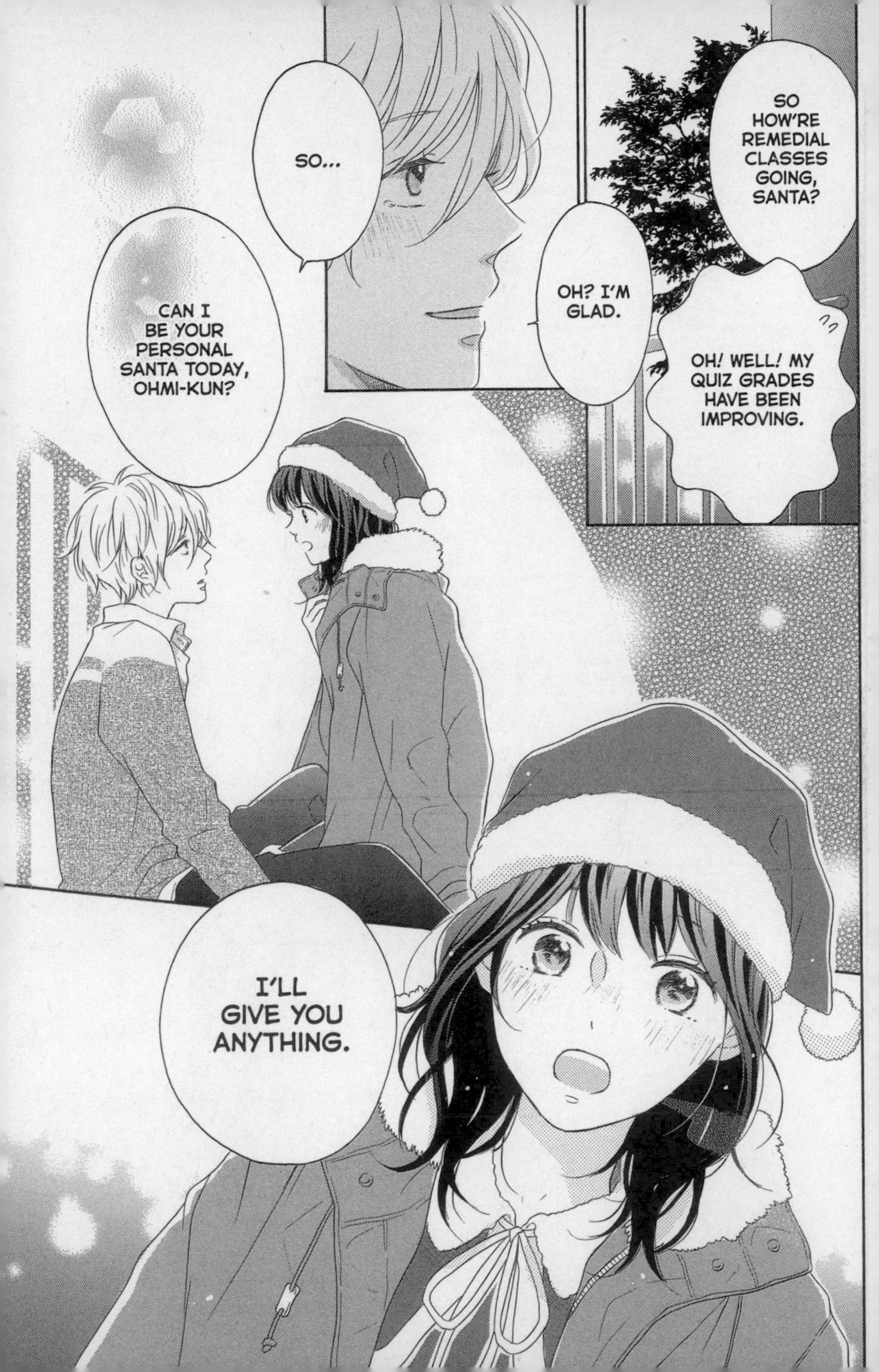
SO HOW'RE REMEDIAL CLASSES GOING, SANTA?
OH! WELL! MY QUIZ GRADES HAVE BEEN IMPROVING.
OH? I'M GLAD.
SO...
CAN I BE YOUR PERSONAL SANTA TODAY, OHMI-KUN?
I'LL GIVE YOU ANYTHING.

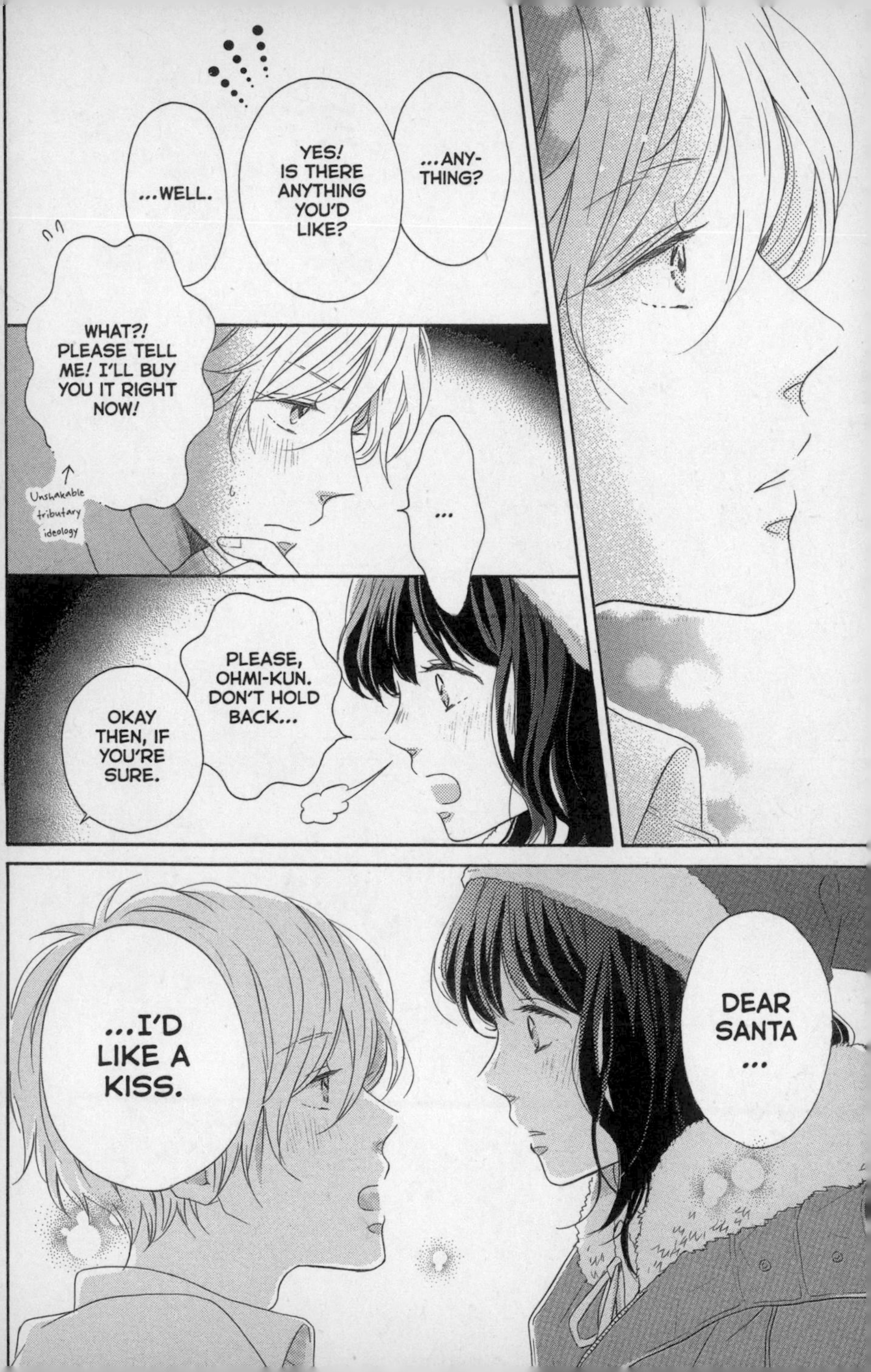
...ANY-THING?
YES! IS THERE ANYTHING YOU'D LIKE?
...WELL.
WHAT?! PLEASE TELL ME! I'LL BUY YOU IT RIGHT NOW!
Unshakable tributary ideology
...
PLEASE, OHMI-KUN. DON'T HOLD BACK...
OKAY THEN, IF YOU'RE SURE.
DEAR SANTA ...
...I'D LIKE A KISS.

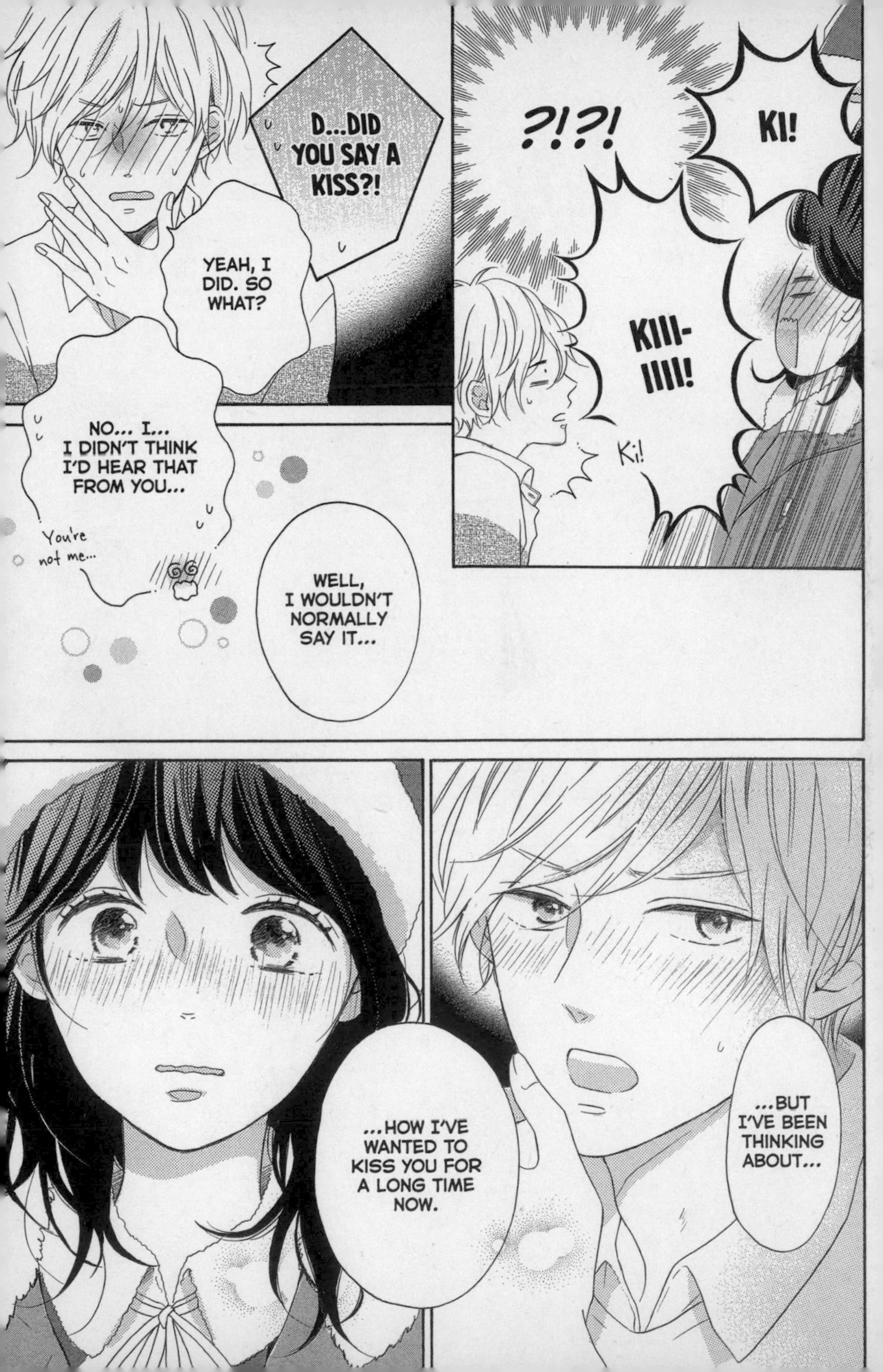
?!?!
KI!
KIII-IIII!
Ki!
D...DID YOU SAY A KISS?!
YEAH, I DID. SO WHAT?
NO... I... I DIDN'T THINK I'D HEAR THAT FROM YOU...
You're not me...
WELL, I WOULDN'T NORMALLY SAY IT...
...BUT I'VE BEEN THINKING ABOUT...
...HOW I'VE WANTED TO KISS YOU FOR A LONG TIME NOW.

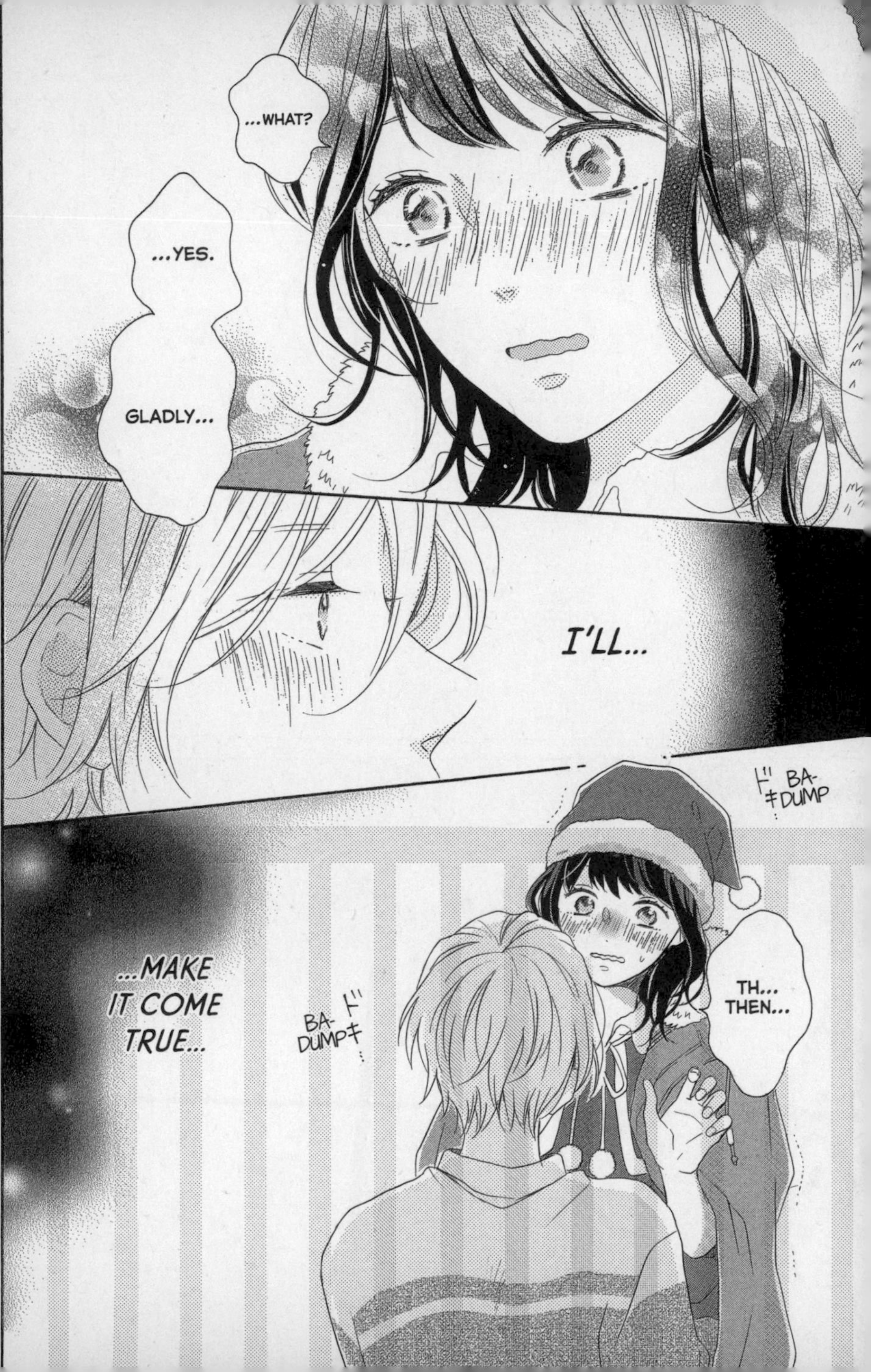
...WHAT?
...YES.
GLADLY...
I'LL...
ドキ BA-DUMP
TH... THEN...
BA-DUMP ドキ
...MAKE IT COME TRUE...

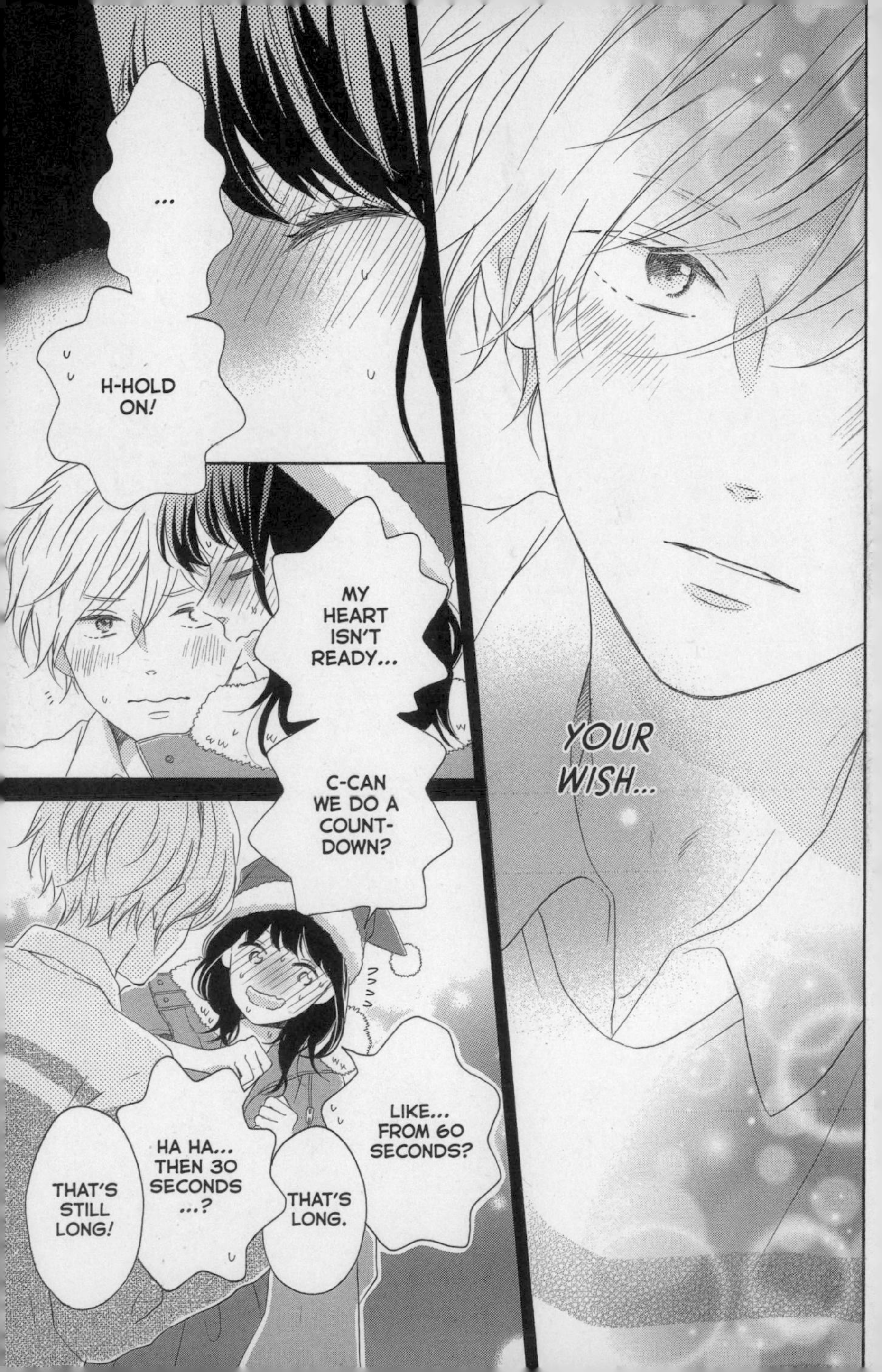
YOUR WISH...
...
H-HOLD ON!
MY HEART ISN'T READY...
C-CAN WE DO A COUNT-DOWN?
LIKE... FROM 60 SECONDS?
THAT'S LONG.
HA HA... THEN 30 SECONDS ...?
THAT'S STILL LONG!

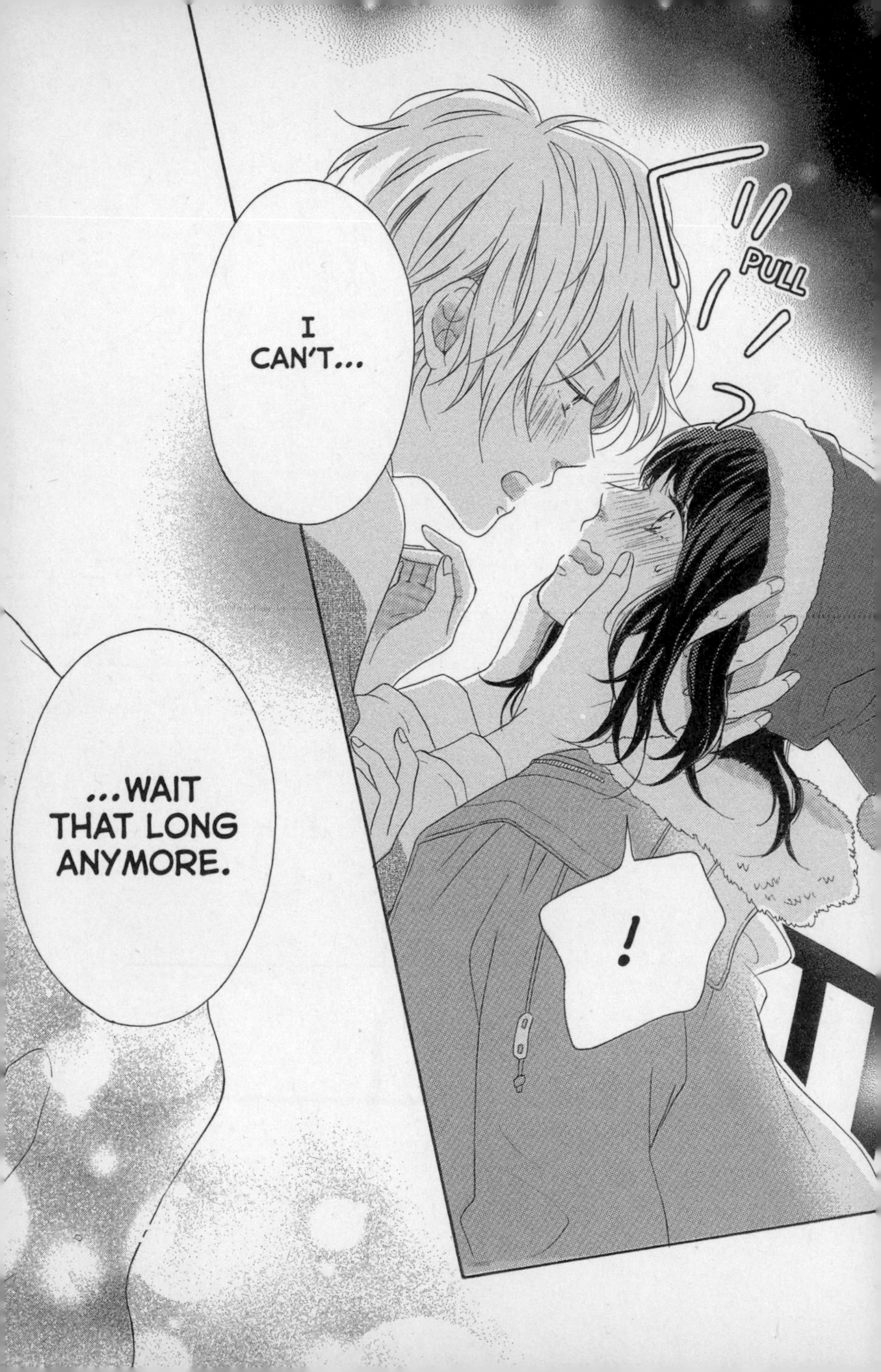
PULL
I CAN'T...
!
...WAIT THAT LONG ANYMORE.

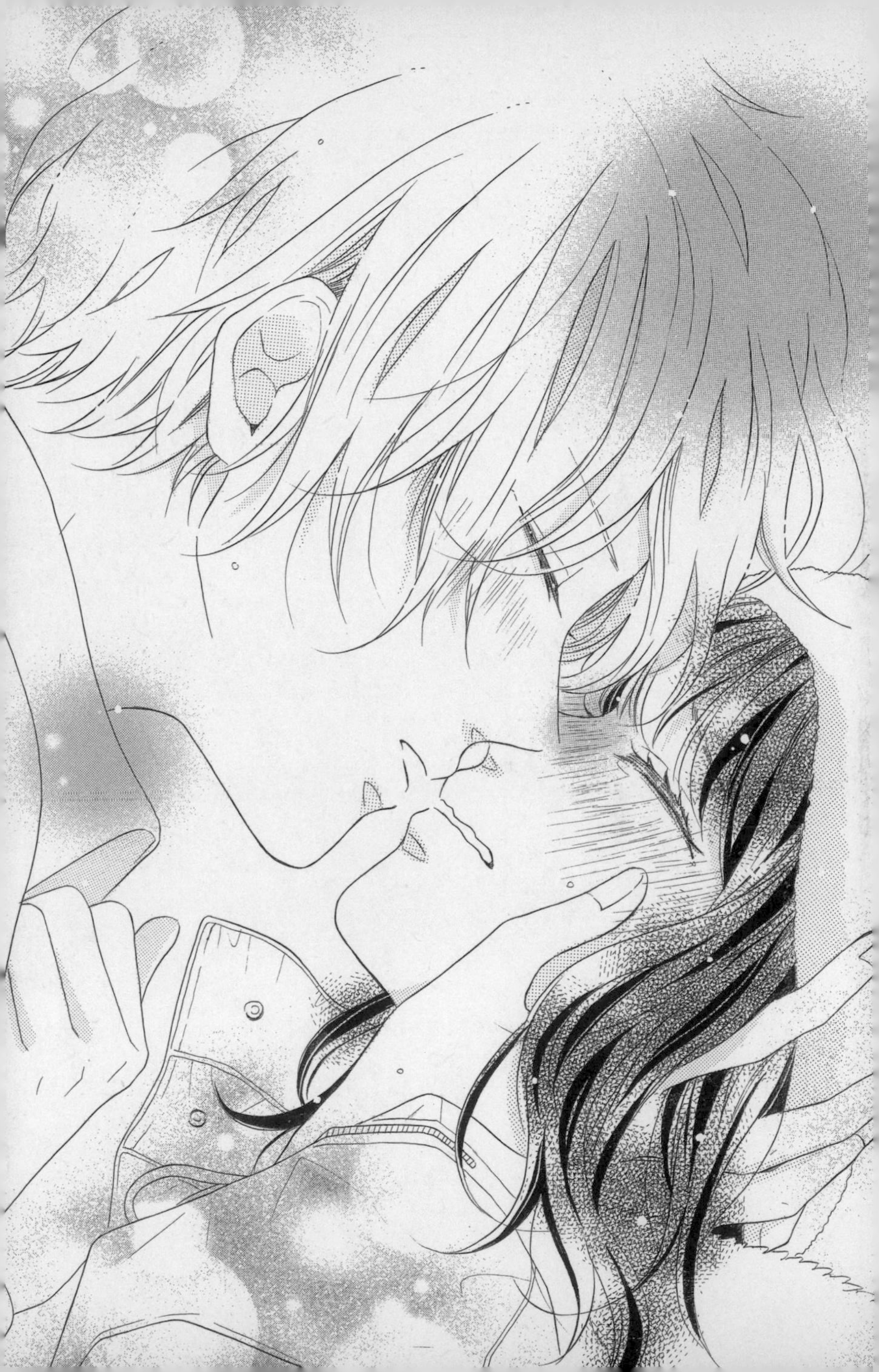

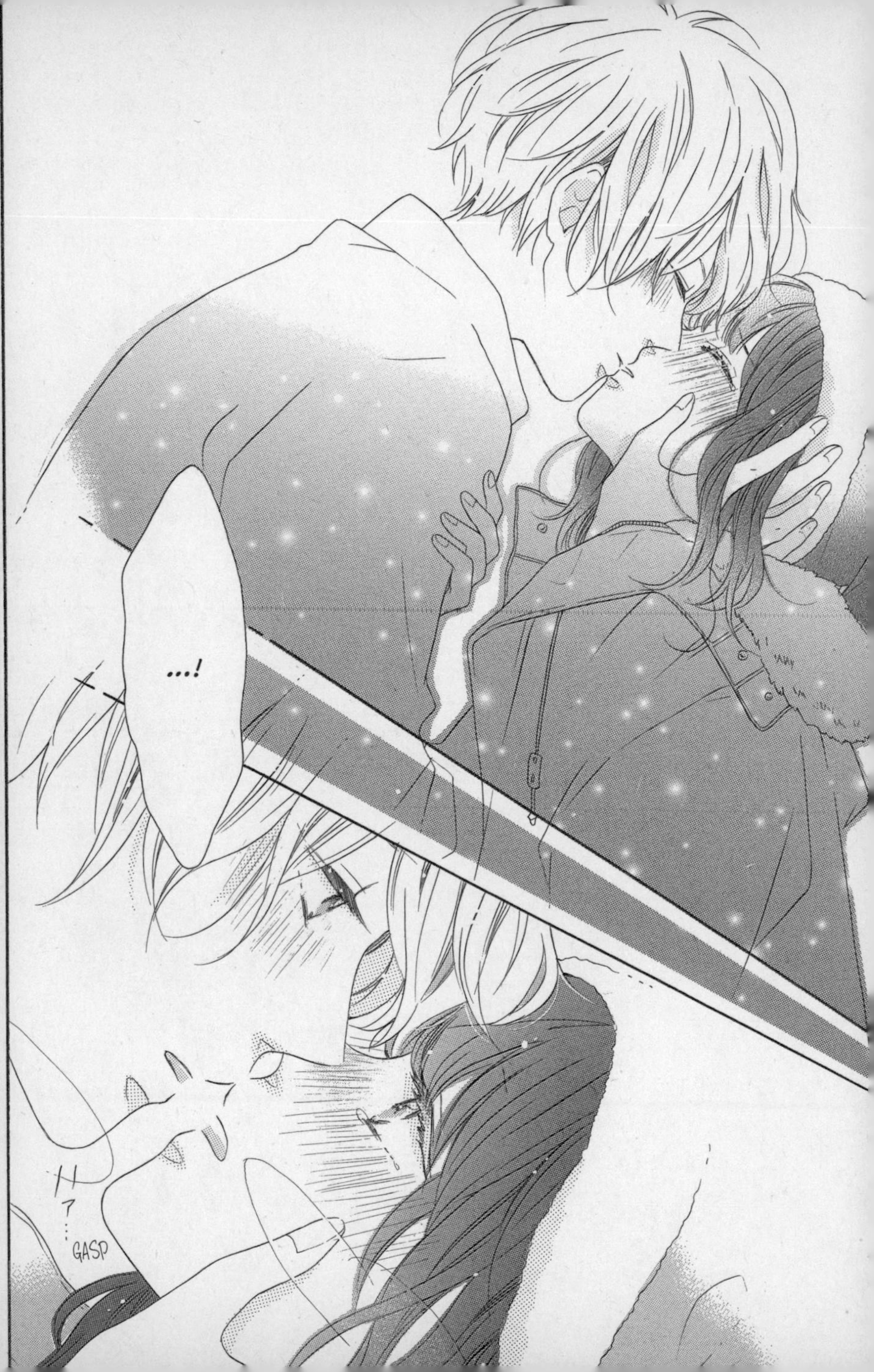
...!
ハァ…
GASP

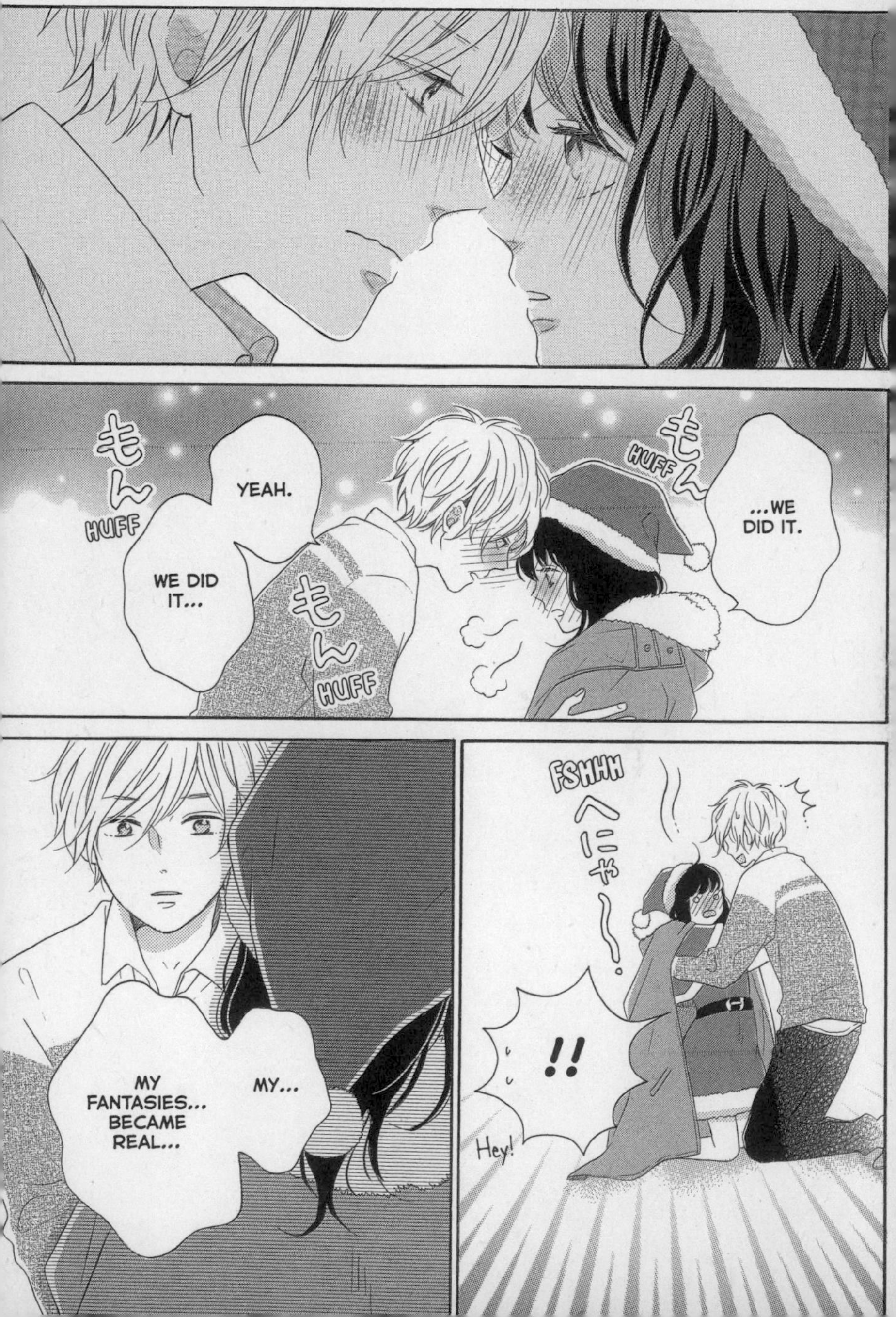
もん HUFF
...WE DID IT.
もん HUFF
YEAH.
WE DID IT...
もん HUFF
FSHHH へにゃ～～
!!
Hey!
MY...
MY FANTASIES... BECAME REAL...

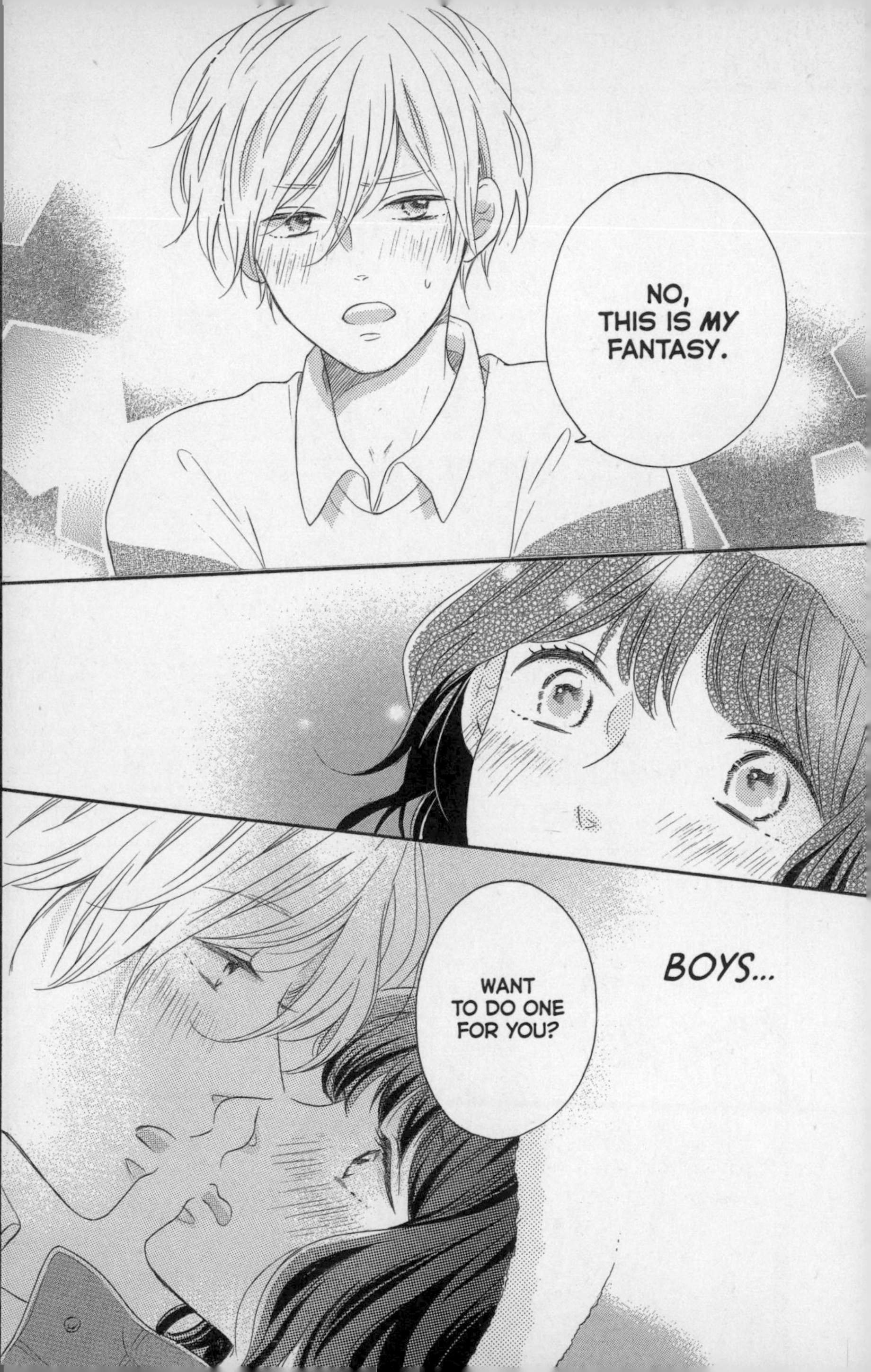
NO, THIS IS *MY* FANTASY.
*BOYS...*
WANT TO DO ONE FOR YOU?

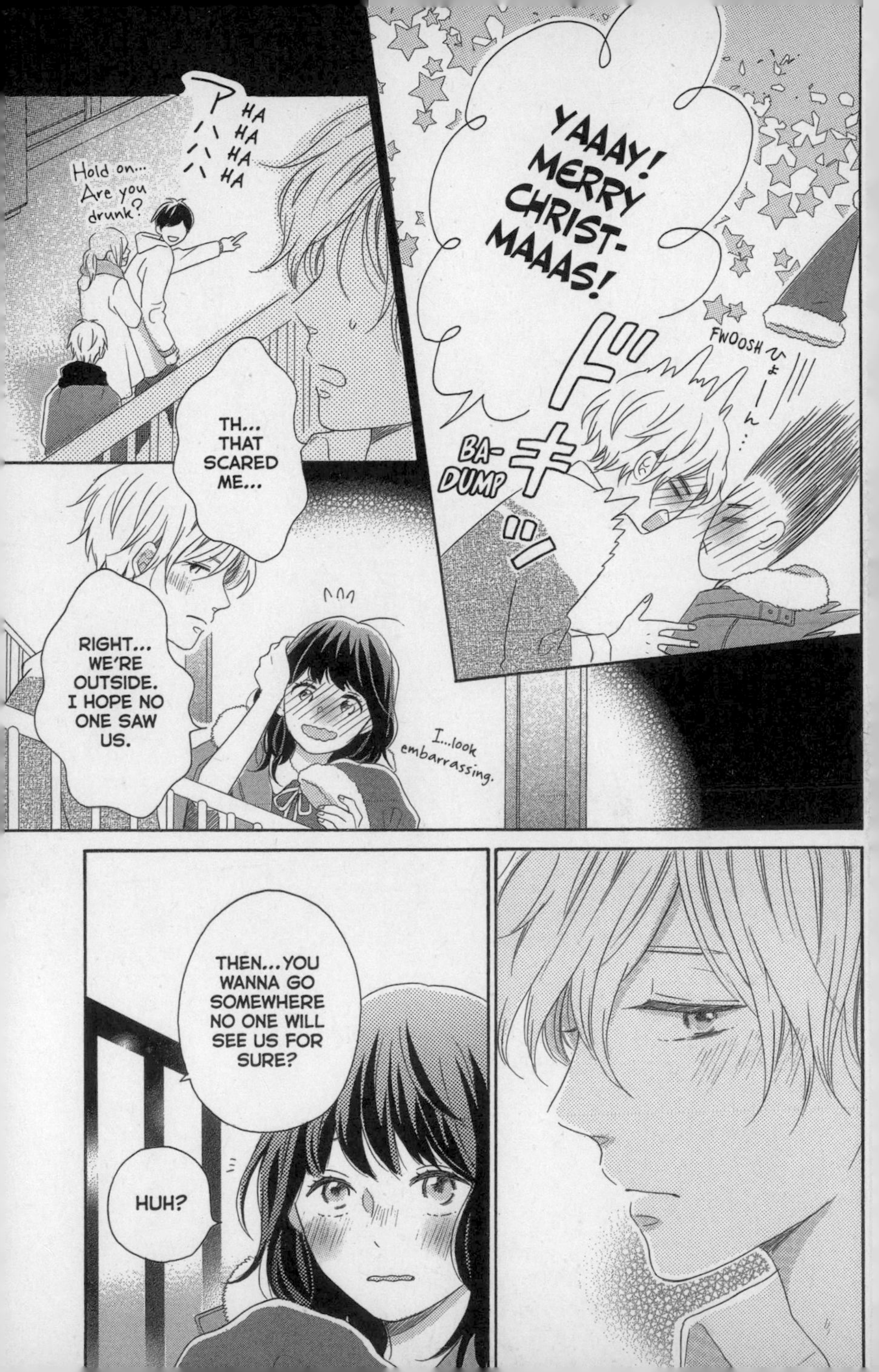
YAAAY! MERRY CHRIST-MAAAS!
FWOOSH
BA-DUMP
HA HA HA HA
Hold on... Are you drunk?
TH... THAT SCARED ME...
RIGHT... WE'RE OUTSIDE. I HOPE NO ONE SAW US.
I...look embarrassing.
THEN... YOU WANNA GO SOMEWHERE NO ONE WILL SEE US FOR SURE?
HUH?

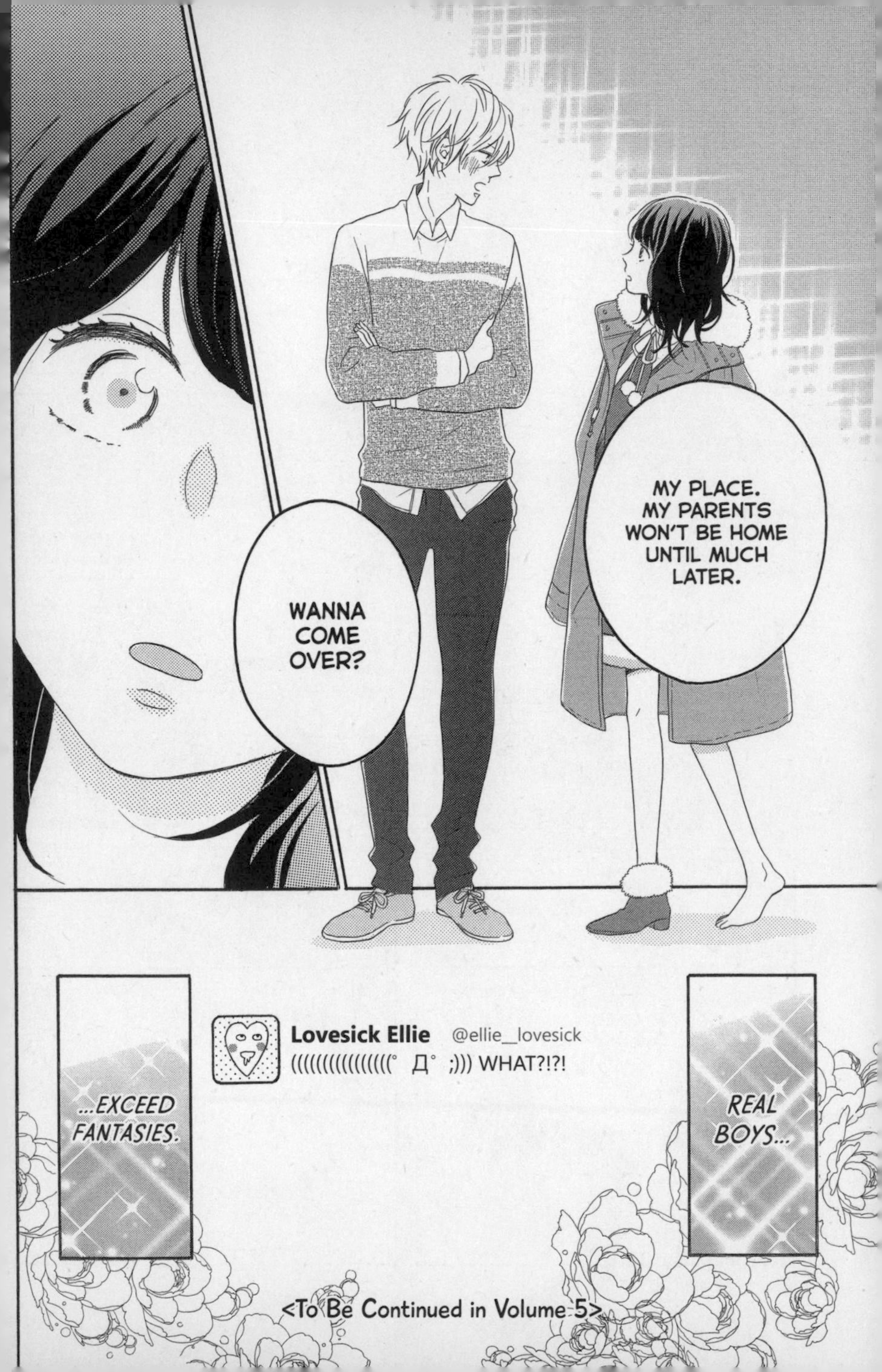
MY PLACE. MY PARENTS WON'T BE HOME UNTIL MUCH LATER.
WANNA COME OVER?
REAL BOYS...
Lovesick Ellie @ellie__lovesick
((((((((((((((((° Д° ;))) WHAT?!?!
...EXCEED FANTASIES.
<To Be Continued in Volume 5>

# ★ BONUS ★

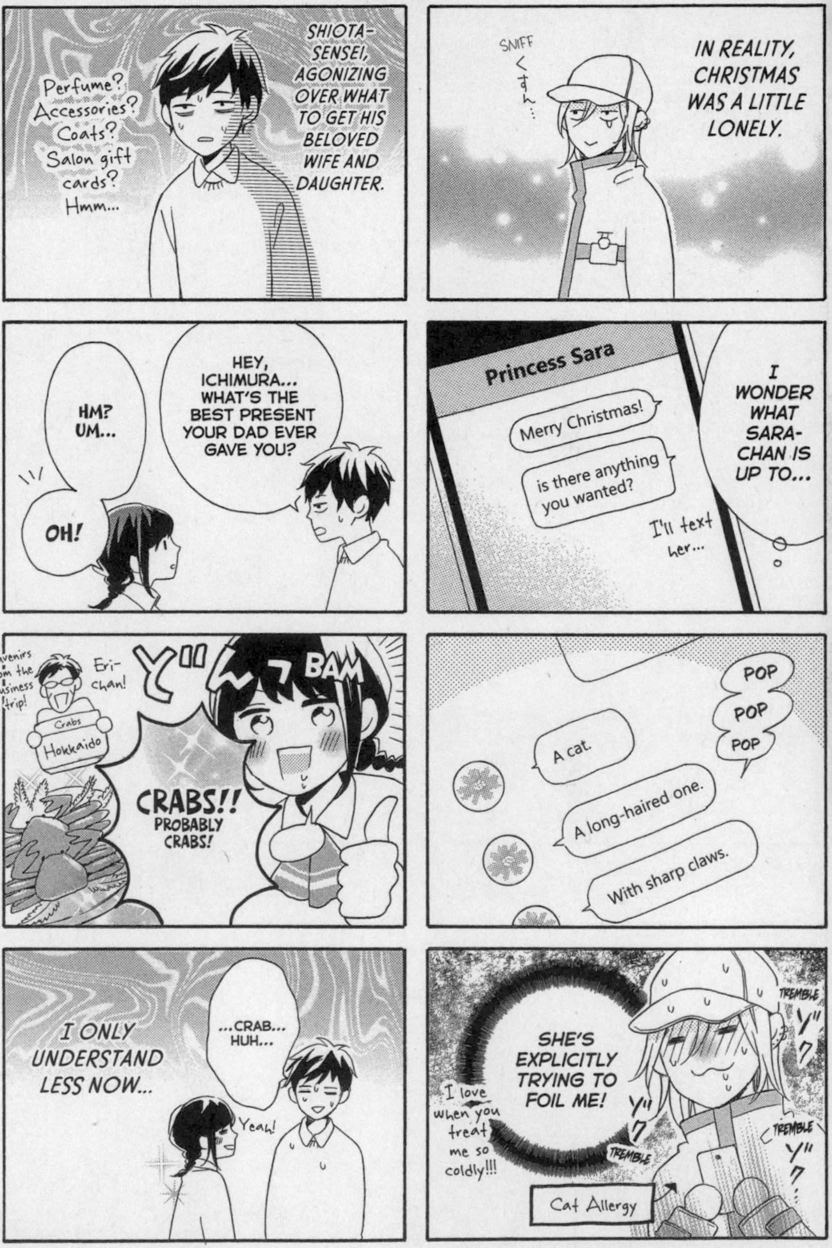

IN REALITY, CHRISTMAS WAS A LITTLE LONELY.
SNIFF
くすん…
I WONDER WHAT SARA-CHAN IS UP TO...
Princess Sara
Merry Christmas!
is there anything you wanted?
I'll text her...
POP
POP
POP
A cat.
A long-haired one.
With sharp claws.
SHE'S EXPLICITLY TRYING TO FOIL ME!
TREMBLE
ゾ"ク
TREMBLE
ゾ"ク
TREMBLE
ゾ"ク
I love when you treat me so coldly!!!
Cat Allergy
SHIOTA-SENSEI, AGONIZING OVER WHAT TO GET HIS BELOVED WIFE AND DAUGHTER.
Perfume? Accessories? Coats? Salon gift cards? Hmm...
HEY, ICHIMURA... WHAT'S THE BEST PRESENT YOUR DAD EVER GAVE YOU?
HM? UM...
OH!
BAM
CRABS!!
PROBABLY CRABS!
Souvenirs from the business trip!
Eri-chan!
Crabs
Hokkaido
...CRAB... HUH...
Yeah!
I ONLY UNDERSTAND LESS NOW...

# Lovesick Ellie

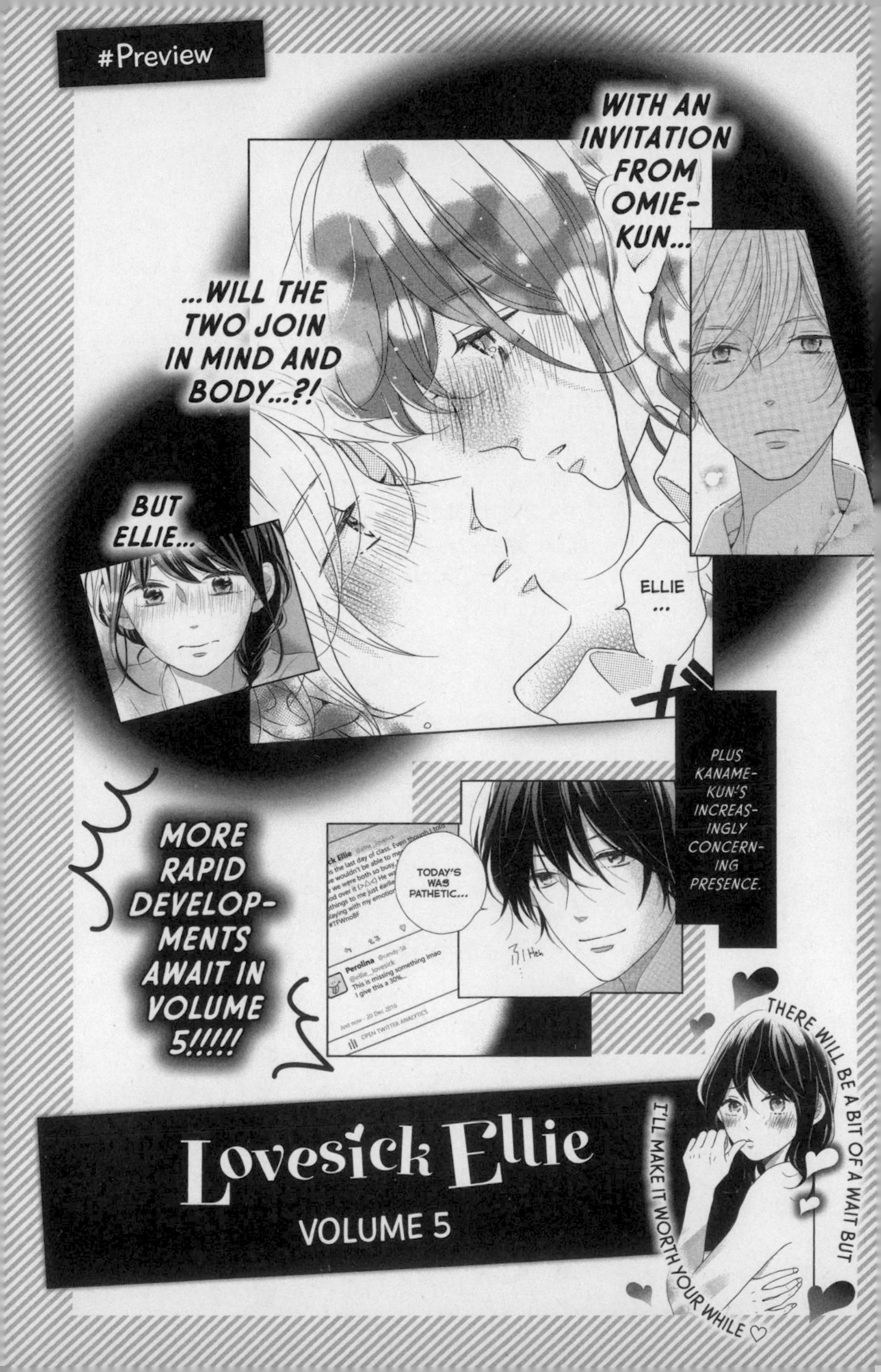
#Preview
WITH AN INVITATION FROM OMIE-KUN...
...WILL THE TWO JOIN IN MIND AND BODY...?!
ELLIE ...
BUT ELLIE...
PLUS KANAME-KUN'S INCREASINGLY CONCERNING PRESENCE.
TODAY'S WAS PATHETIC...
Heh
Perolina @candy-58
@ellie_lovesick
This is missing something lmao I give this a 30%...
Just now · 20 Dec 2016
OPEN TWITTER ANALYTICS
MORE RAPID DEVELOPMENTS AWAIT IN VOLUME 5!!!!!
THERE WILL BE A BIT OF A WAIT BUT I'LL MAKE IT WORTH YOUR WHILE ♡
Lovesick Ellie
VOLUME 5

# Lovesick Ellie

@Translation_Notes

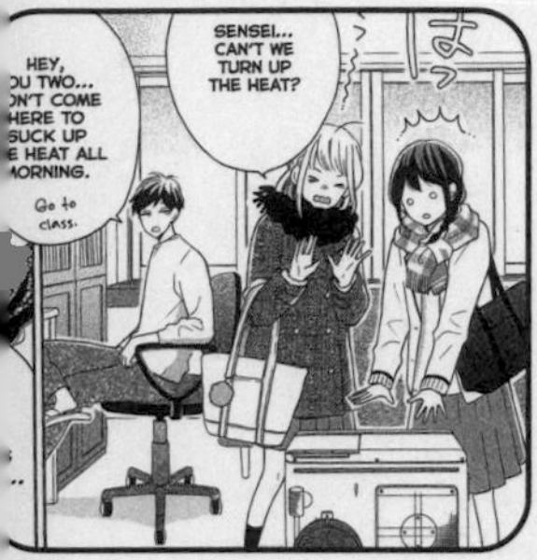
SENSEI... CAN'T WE TURN UP THE HEAT?
HEY, OU TWO... N'T COME HERE TO SUCK UP E HEAT ALL ORNING.
Go to class.

## **Portable heater** @page 10

Many schools in Japan do not have central air or heating, so portable heaters are used. This means it can be freezing cold in the hallways, or in the morning, when the school has recently opened for students. Usually in the morning, the staff rooms are the warmest place, until the classroom warms up. Sometimes you'll see a kettle resting on top of these heaters to be used for tea.

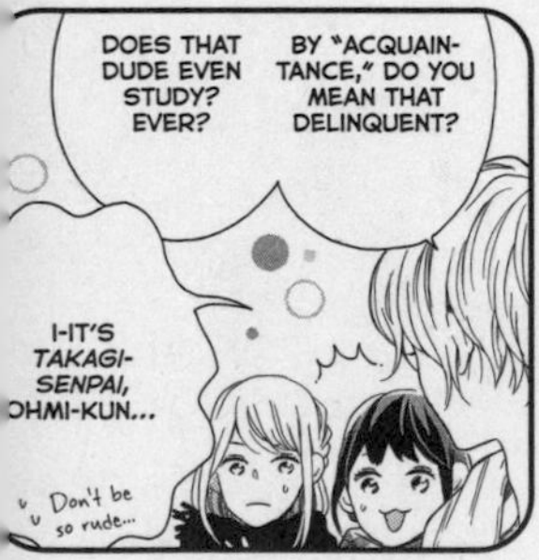
BY "ACQUAINTANCE," DO YOU MEAN THAT DELINQUENT?
DOES THAT DUDE EVEN STUDY? EVER?
I-IT'S *TAKAGI-SENPAI,* OHMI-KUN...
Don't be so rude...

## **Senpai** @page 13

Senpai is a suffix used to denote an upperclassman.

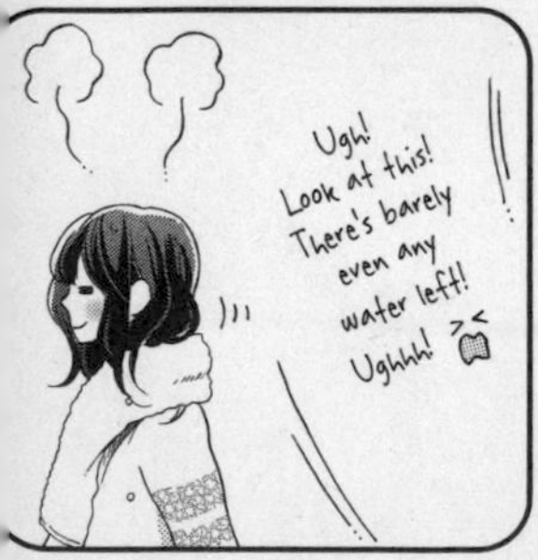
Ugh! Look at this! There's barely even any water left! Ughhh!

## **"There's barely even any water left!"** @page 48

In Japanese homes, bathwater is shared between family members. Before taking a bath, family members clean themselves outside of the bath with buckets or a shower nozzle, so the bathwater to soak in is clean. Unfortunately, the youngest in the family usually is the last in line to soak in the bath.

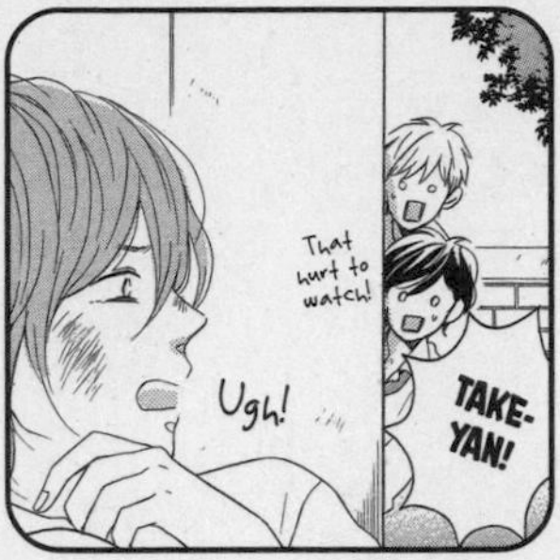
TAKE-YAN!
That hurt to watch!
Ugh!

**-yan** @page 68

-yan is another suffix to create a nickname.

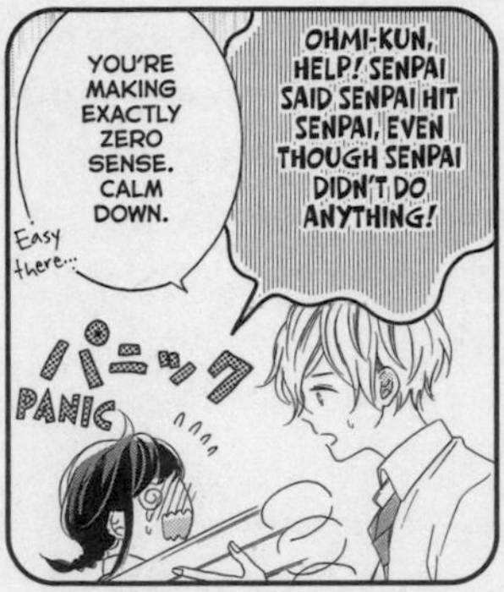
OHMI-KUN, HELP! SENPAI SAID SENPAI HIT SENPAI, EVEN THOUGH SENPAI DIDN'T DO ANYTHING!
YOU'RE MAKING EXACTLY ZERO SENSE. CALM DOWN.
Easy there...
PANIC

**"Senpai said Senpai hit Senpai [...]"** @page 71

Like how sensei is used without having to say the name of the teacher, the word senpai can be used to denote any upperclassman and be used in this general sense. Unfortunately, in Ellie's panic, she does not differentiate between which senpai did what.

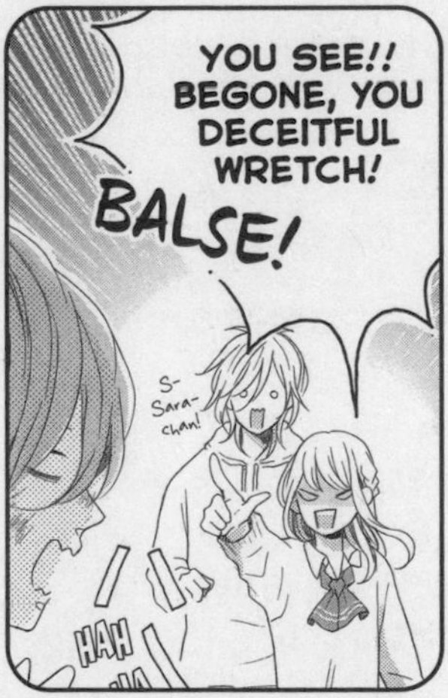
YOU SEE!! BEGONE, YOU DECEITFUL WRETCH!
BALSE!
S-Sara-chan!
HAH

**Balse** @page 76

"Balse" is the incantation used to destroy the castle at the end of Ghibli's Castle in the Sky. It has since become a prominent and beloved meme on 2ch and Twitter.

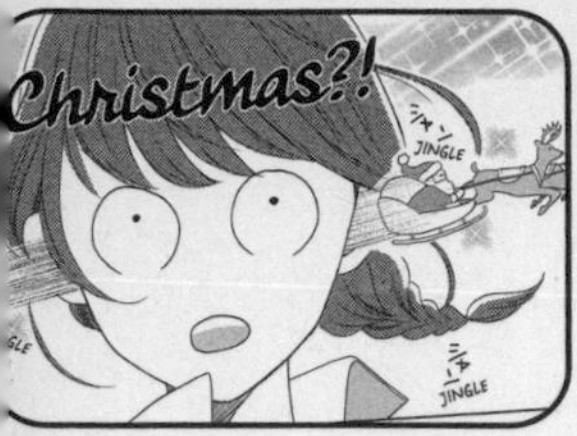
Christmas?!
JINGLE
JINGLE

**Christmas** @page 82

Unlike in most other parts of the world, Christmas in Japan is primarily a romantic affair. Christmas Eve is typically spent with one's significant other.

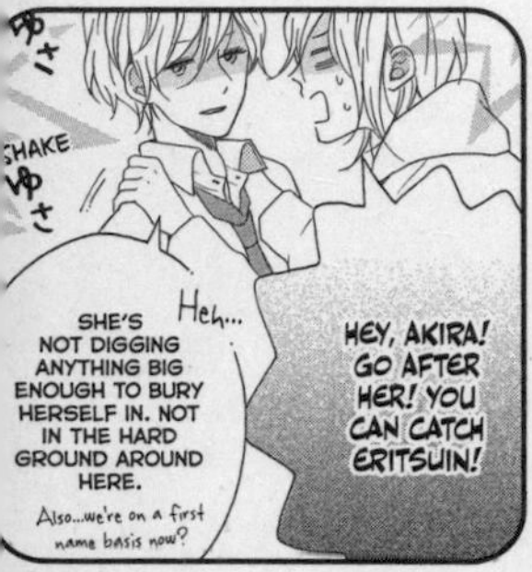
SHAKE
Heh...
HEY, AKIRA! GO AFTER HER! YOU CAN CATCH ERITSUIN!
SHE'S NOT DIGGING ANYTHING BIG ENOUGH TO BURY HERSELF IN. NOT IN THE HARD GROUND AROUND HERE.
Also...we're on a first name basis now?

**First-name basis** @page 90

When Takagi-senpai calls Ohmi-kun his first name of "Akira," this confuses Ohmi-kun as he does not necessarily think they are that close of friends. Switching from last name to first name is a significant step in a relationship—platonic and romantic.

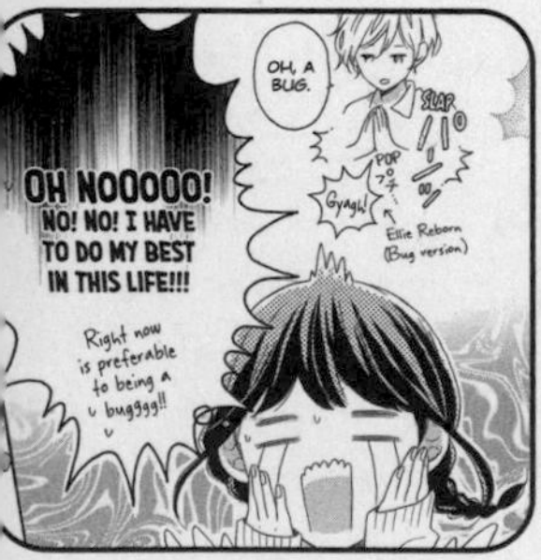
OH, A BUG.
SLAP
POP
Gyagh!
Ellie Reborn (Bug version)
OH NOOOOO! NO! NO! I HAVE TO DO MY BEST IN THIS LIFE!!!
Right now is preferable to being a bugggg!!

**Reincarnation** @page 129-130

In Buddhism, reincarnation does not necessarily mean someone will be reborn as a human being. There are several levels, one of which includes being reborn as a bug.

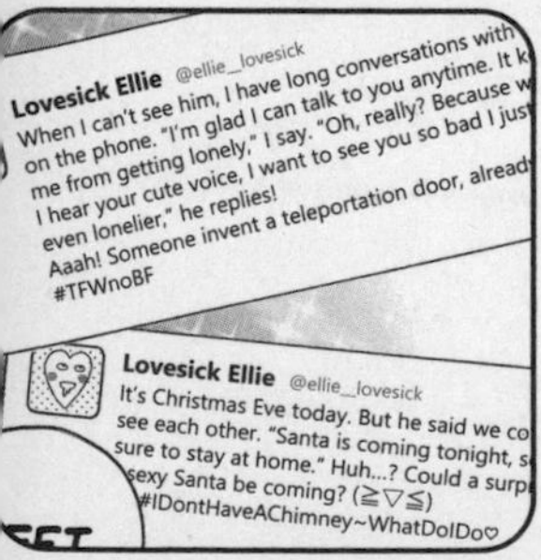
Lovesick Ellie @ellie_lovesick
When I can't see him, I have long conversations with
on the phone. "I'm glad I can talk to you anytime. It
me from getting lonely," I say. "Oh, really? Because
I hear your cute voice, I want to see you so bad I
even lonelier," he replies!
Aaah! Someone invent a teleportation door,
#TFWnoBF
Lovesick Ellie @ellie_lovesick
It's Christmas Eve today. But he said we
see each other. "Santa is coming tonight,
sure to stay at home." Huh...? Could a
sexy Santa be coming? (≧▽≦)
#IDontHaveAChimney~WhatDoIDo♡

**Teleportation door** @page 136

In the original Japanese, the popular Japanese character, Doraemon's "Dokodemo Door" or "Anywhere Door" is specifically referenced.

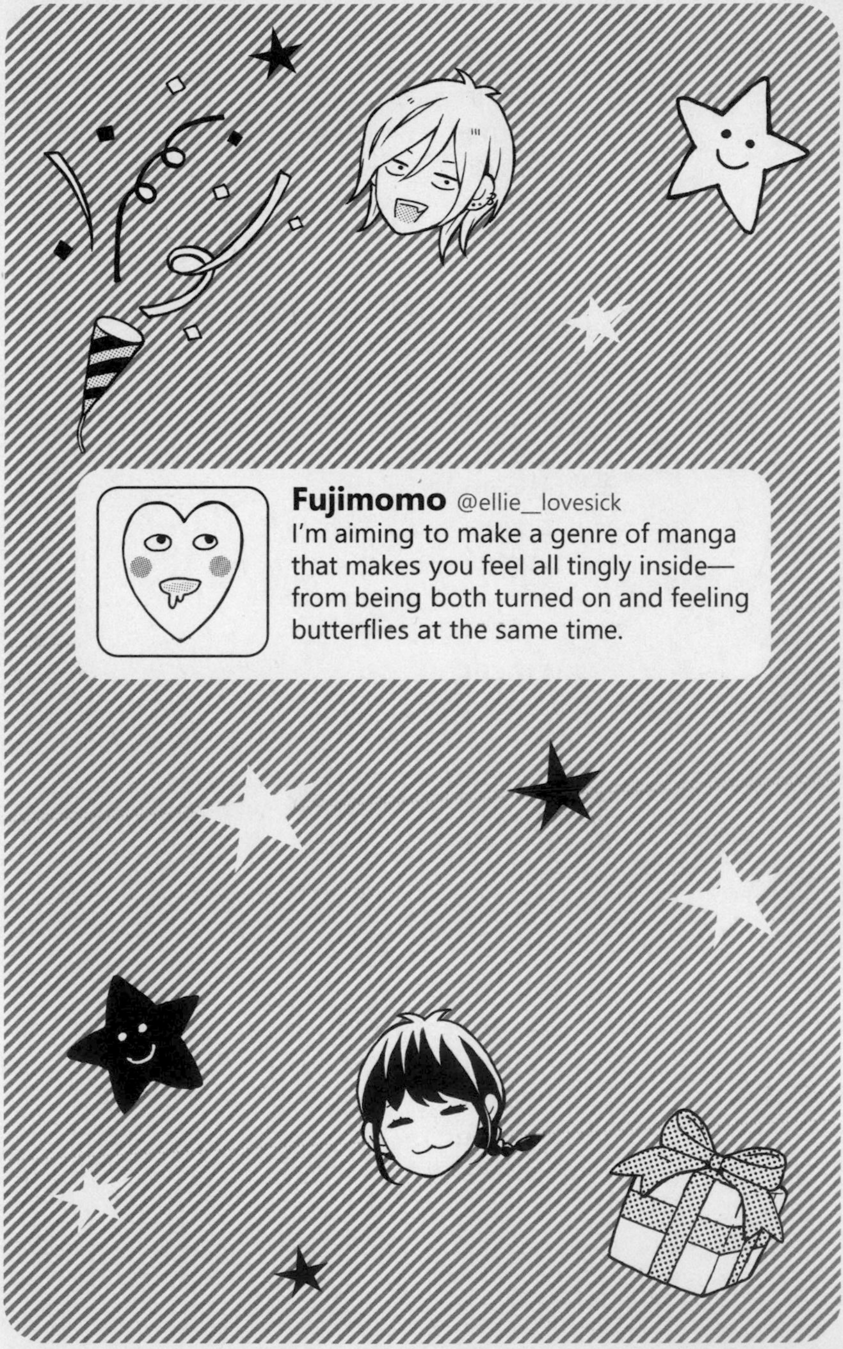
**Fujimomo** @ellie__lovesick
I'm aiming to make a genre of manga that makes you feel all tingly inside—from being both turned on and feeling butterflies at the same time.

Knight of the Ice ©Yayoi Ogawa

Yayoi Ogawa

# SKATING THRILLS AND ICY CHILLS WITH THIS NEW TINGLY ROMANCE SERIES!

A rom-com on ice, perfect for fans of *Princess Jellyfish* and *Wotakoi*. Kokoro is the talk of the figure-skating world, winning trophies and hearts. But little do they know... he's actually a huge nerd! From the beloved creator of *You're My Pet* (*Tramps Like Us*).

Chitose is a serious young woman, working for the health magazine *SASSO*. Or at least, she would be, if she wasn't constantly getting distracted by her childhood friend, international figure skating star Kokoro Kijinami! In the public eye and on the ice, Kokoro is a gallant, flawless knight, but behind his glittery costumes and breathtaking spins lies a secret: He's actually a hopelessly romantic otaku, who can only land his quad jumps when Chitose is on hand to recite a spell from his favorite magical girl anime!

# A SMART, NEW ROMANTIC COMEDY FOR FANS OF *SHORTCAKE CAKE* AND *TERRACE HOUSE*!

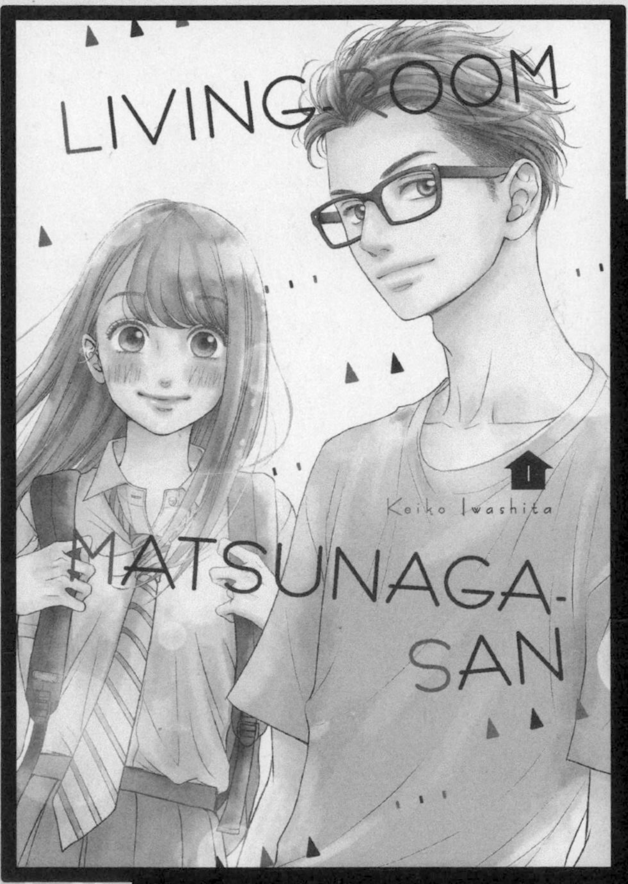
LIVING-ROOM
1
Keiko Iwashita
MATSUNAGA-SAN

A romance manga starring high school girl Meeko, who learns to live on her own in a boarding house whose living room is home to the odd (but handsome) Matsunaga-san. She begins to adjust to her new life away from her parents, but Meeko soon learns that no matter how far away from home she is, she's still a young girl at heart — especially when she finds herself falling for Matsunaga-san.

# PERFECT WORLD

### Rie Aruga

A TOUCHING
NEW SERIES
ABOUT LOVE AND
COPING WITH
DISABILITY

An office party reunites Tsugumi with her high school crush Itsuki. He's realized his dream of becoming an architect, but along the way, he experienced a spinal injury that put him in a wheelchair. Now Tsugumi's rekindled feelings will butt up against prejudices she never considered — and Itsuki will have to decide if he's ready to let someone into his heart...

"Depicts with great delicacy and courage the difficulties some with disabilities experience getting involved in romantic relationships... Rie Aruga refuses to romanticize, pushing her heroine to face the reality of disability. She invites her readers to the same tasks of empathy, knowledge and recognition."
—Slate.fr

"An important entry [in manga romance]... The emotional core of both plot and characters indicates thoughtfulness... [Aruga's] research is readily apparent in the text and artwork, making this feel like a real story."
—Anime News Network

# Something's Wrong With Us

### NATSUMI ANDO

**The dark, psychological sexy shojo series readers have been waiting for!**

**A spine-chilling and steamy romance between a Japanese sweets maker and the man who framed her mother for murder!**

Following in her mother's footsteps, Nao became a traditional Japanese sweets maker, and with unparalleled artistry and a bright attitude, she gets an offer to work at a world-class confectionary company. But when she meets the young, handsome owner, she recognizes his cold stare...

KC/
KODANSHA
COMICS

A Kodansha Trade Paperback Original

*Lovesick Ellie 4* copyright © 2017 Fujimomo
English translation copyright © 2022 Fujimomo

Published in the United States by
Kodansha USA Publishing, LLC, New York.

Publication rights for this English edition arranged through
Kodansha Ltd., Tokyo.

First published in Japan in 2017 by Kodansha Ltd., Tokyo
as *Koiwazurai no Ellie,* volume 4.

ISBN 978-1-64651-320-8

Printed in the United States of America.

9 8 7 6 5 4 3 2 1

Translation: Ursula Ku
Lettering: Allen Berry
Additional Lettering and Layout: Lys Blakeslee
Editing: Sarah Tilson, Maggie Le
Kodansha USA Publishing edition cover design by Matthew Akuginow

Publisher: Kiichiro Sugawara

Director of Publishing Services: Ben Applegate
Director of Publishing Operations: Dave Barrett
Associate Director of Publishing Operations: Stephen Pakula
Publishing Services Managing Editors: Alanna Ruse, Madison Salters
Production Managers: Emi Lotto, Angela Zurlo

KODANSHA.US

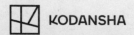